3303034462

of related interest

The Complete Guide to Asperger's Syndrome
Tony Attwood
ISBN 978 1 84310 495 7 (hardback)
ISBN 978 1 84310 669 2 (paperback)
eISBN 9781 84642 559 2

Autism Spectrum Disorders Through the Life Span
Digby Tantam
ISBN 978 1 84310 993 8 (hardback)
ISBN 978 1 84905 344 0 (paperback)
eISBN 978 0 85700 511 3

An A–Z of Genetic Factors in Autism
A Handbook for Professionals
Kenneth J. Aitken
ISBN 978 1 84310 976 1
eISBN 978 0 85700 490 1

The Autism Spectrum in the 21st Century
Exploring Psychology, Biology and Practice
Ilona Roth
With Chris Barson, Rosa Hoekstra,
Greg Pasco and Terry Whatson
ISBN 978 1 84905 087 6

The Imprinted Brain
How Genes Set the Balance Between Autism and Psychosis
Christopher Badcock
ISBN 978 1 84905 023 4
eISBN 978 1 84642 950 7

INFANTILE AUTISM

The Syndrome and Its Implications for a
Neural Theory of Behavior by
Bernard Rimland, Ph.D.

EDITED BY STEPHEN M. EDELSON, PH.D.

Forewords by Margaret L. Bauman, M.D.
and Temple Grandin, Ph.D.

Original Foreword by Leo Kanner, M.D.

Afterword by Sidney M. Baker, M.D.

Jessica Kingsley *Publishers*
London and Philadelphia

This edition published in 2015
by Jessica Kingsley Publishers
73 Collier Street
London N1 9BE, UK
and
400 Market Street, Suite 400
Philadelphia, PA 19106, USA

www.jkp.com

First published in 1964 by Appleton-Century-Crofts, Educational
Division, Meredith Publishing Company, New York.

Library of Congress Cataloging in Publication Data
A CIP catalog record for this book is available from the Library of Congress

British Library Cataloguing in Publication Data
A CIP catalogue record for this book is available from the British Library

ISBN 978 1 84905 789 9
eISBN 978 1 78450 057 3

Printed and bound in Great Britain

Disclaimer

Every effort has been made to ensure that the information contained in this book is correct, but it should not in any way be substituted for medical advice. Readers should always consult a qualified medical practitioner. Neither the authors nor the publisher takes responsibility for any consequences of any decision made as a result of the information contained in this book.

Dr. Rimland's original 1964 text has been reproduced verbatim in order to keep the historical significance of the entire book intact.

Contents

FOREWORD TO THE NEW EDITION

It has been 50 years since Dr. Bernard Rimland published his book titled *Infantile Autism: The Syndrome and Its Implications for a Neural Theory of Behavior*. A review of this book confirms beyond any reasonable doubt that Dr. Rimland was a man who was ahead of his time. In fact, it is startling how very close he was at the time to many of the concepts and hypotheses that we now consider innovative, based on modern basic science and clinical research.

Although the prevailing theory at the time related to parental causes for the disorder, Dr. Rimland spent a substantial part of this book providing observations as to why psychogenic factors were an unlikely cause of infantile autism and offering evidence for probable biologic mechanisms, most likely beginning before or close to the time of birth. Further, he hypothesized that both genetic and environmental components could be playing roles in the etiology of the disorder and suggested that autism could be the result of differing causes including prematurity, brain damage, and known genetic syndromes. Further, Dr. Rimland determined that there were many forms of autism and delineated 10–12 distinct subgroups based on his Diagnostic Check List for Behavior-Disturbed Children. Despite Dr. Rimland's observations, the concepts that ASD begins prenatally and that the disorder is heterogeneous in its causes, biology, and clinical presentation have only recently become accepted by the clinical and basic science research community.

With reference to the association of medical comorbidities in individuals with autism, Dr. Rimland alluded to the fact that many infants who became autistic as older children had serious feeding problems as newborns and had significant and prolonged episodes of crying and irritability. While gastrointestinal disorders were not specifically discussed, the idea that feeding problems were observed in early life in ASD raised the possibility that other organ systems outside of the brain might play an important associative role in disorder.

In his search for underlying neurobiological factors that could explain the signs and symptoms of autism, Dr. Rimland reviewed what was then known about the pathology of the brain in the disorder, which was relatively little at the time. However, he hypothesized that the reticular formation might be important due to its connectivity with multiple brain regions and because of its role in arousal, attention, and the sleep–wake cycle. Currently there is little pathological evidence to support this hypothesis. However, Dr. Rimland also hypothesized a role for the limbic system, most especially the hippocampus, which has been found to be abnormal in a number of post-mortem brain and imaging studies.

Clinically, Dr. Rimland highlighted the intelligence and special skills of many autistic individuals, specifically their exceptional memory. He discussed the possibility of pharmacological and "training" interventions, and described a number of sensory symptoms that have been associated with ASD. Finally, he suggested avenues for future research and provided us with his Diagnostic Check List, which many families have used over the years, the data from which make up a rich and extensive source of clinical information to this day.

In many ways, reading this book came as a shock. The fact that, as long ago as 50 years, Dr. Rimland highlighted so many of the clinical and biological concepts that have now become evident and confirmed based on more modern research, is astounding. Despite the relative lack of scientific support at the time, Dr. Rimland's careful observations, clinical instincts, and research-directed mind laid the groundwork for much of the scientific and clinical work which is at the forefront of our more modern approaches to the understanding of autism today. He was supportive of parents, families, and guardians, as well as those affected by the disorder. He was a strong advocate and leader, and was, without any doubt, a man ahead of his time. His passion and work over the years were amazingly insightful and paved the way for future generations of clinicians and investigators. This book is an unparalleled testament to his long and productive career, to his determination to solve the puzzle of autism, and to a brilliant and inquisitive mind. Please enjoy this book. It is a testament to this man's exceptional journey to find answers to one of the most complex medical disorders of our time. Even though he is no longer with us, Dr. Rimland still has much to teach us.

Margaret L. Bauman, M.D., Child Neurologist, Integrated Center for Child Development and Associate Professor of Pathology, Department of Anatomy and Neurobiology, Boston University School of Medicine

FOREWORD TO THE NEW EDITION

When I was a young child, some of my doctors were looking for a psychological cause of my problems caused by autism. When I was three, I had no speech and all the symptoms of classic autism. Fortunately, a neurologist recommended that I go to a speech therapy class that used many Applied Behavior Analysis (ABA) methods. Throughout elementary school, my psychiatrist kept attempting to find my "psychic injury." In the 1960s, most doctors still believed that there was a psychological basis to my symptoms. The psychiatrist started changing his opinion when he observed that my sister, who was only a year and a half younger, was developing normally. From this he concluded that my autistic symptoms were not caused by "bad mothering."

I first read *Infantile Autism* when I was in my 20s while studying for my master's degree in animal science. I was relieved to find out from this book that autism was a biological disorder and not a psychological problem. There were also some explanations for my sensory sensitivities and a craving for deep pressure. The next step was making a copy of Rimland's checklist and having my mother fill it out. The results of that checklist are in my first book, *Emergence: Labeled Autistic*. Dr. Rimland wrote the foreword and said this was the first book to explain autism from the inside.

Dr. Rimland is to be commended for presenting the first evidence that autism was a biological condition. When his book was published, he was a lone visionary. When a pioneer first presents his thesis, it will be attacked. When it is finally accepted, people will say it was obvious. At about the same time I read Rimland's book, I bought a poster titled, "On Creativity." This poster is still hanging on my wall by my desk. The poster states, "The unfortunate thing about being ahead of your time is that when people finally realize you are right, they'll say it was obvious all along. You have two choices in life: you can dissolve into the mainstream, or you can be distinct..." by Alan Ashley-Pitt.

While writing this foreword, I looked up Alan Ashley-Pitt and discovered that he was a name made up by a greeting card company that went out of business years ago. This made me wonder, did somebody on the autism spectrum who was creative and distinct write this quote? I could not find him on the Internet. Thank you, whoever you are, for giving me your quote that will continue to inspire me. Dr. Rimland was both creative and distinct, and he was a single voice when his book was first published.

Temple Grandin, Ph.D., Assistant Professor of
Animal Science, Colorado State University

INTRODUCTION TO THE NEW EDITION
Stephen M. Edelson

This year marks the 50th anniversary of one of the most important contributions to the field of autism. Although some areas of scientific knowledge form slowly, as researchers first establish a solid foundation and then gradually build toward a valid and replicable "truth," many areas of science take an abrupt turn when one individual makes a major discovery (which sometimes happens by accident) or takes a "step back" and critically reviews ideas that have received widespread acceptance. *Infantile Autism* is a prime example of how one person can redirect an entire field and, consequently, improve the lives of countless individuals.

Bernard Rimland's 1964 book, *Infantile Autism: The Syndrome and Its Implications for a Neural Theory of Behavior,* single-handedly transformed the way professionals, especially psychologists and psychiatrists, approached autism, moving the field from a psychodynamic, parent-blaming viewpoint to a physiological, science-oriented perspective. Soon after its publication, *Infantile Autism* was awarded the Century Psychology Series Award for its significant contribution to the field of psychology.

BACKGROUND

Soon after their son Mark was born, Dr. Rimland and his wife realized that he was not responding and acting like other infants. After consulting with several pediatricians, they were at their wits' end—just like many other parents then and now. Fortunately, Dr. Rimland's wife remembered reading a psychology textbook that described a child who acted differently from others. They searched through a pile of boxes, found the book, located the story, and realized immediately that their son had autism. This was the first time that Dr. Rimland saw the word "autism," even though he had completed advanced degrees in psychology just a few years earlier.

Like most parents, Dr. Rimland wanted to learn as much as possible to help his son. Having recently completed a doctoral degree in experimental psychology, he delved into the scientific literature and quickly learned that there was general consensus that autism was caused by parents, especially the mother. Basically, it was purported that the child's parents were much more concerned with their own lives than with providing physical and emotional support to their children. As many of you know, Bruno Bettelheim first introduced this theory, and healthcare professionals worldwide, including

Dr. Kanner, accepted Bettelheim's assertion even though there was no solid evidence to support such a claim. (Note: I am not referring to Bettelheim as a doctor since it was later learned that he never received a doctoral degree.)

Dr. Rimland and his wife were incensed at such a ridiculous allegation by the professional community, and Dr. Rimland set out on a five-year journey to figure out, as best he could, the underlying cause of autism. Since they lived in a small house, Dr. Rimland converted his side porch into an office so he could organize his materials and focus on writing a critical review of the current approach to autism. At that time he worked full-time for the US Navy as a civilian researcher, and so he spent evenings and weekends working on the book.

During his business travels for the Navy, Dr. Rimland spent his evenings searching for articles at local university libraries. In one instance, he convinced the head librarian at Tulane University to lock him inside their medical library overnight so he could find and read articles. In later years, Dr. Rimland recalled eating the stale food from the library's coin-operated vending machines throughout the night.

If Dr. Rimland found an article written in another language, he would locate translators through the Navy's network and hire them to translate the articles. The numerous drafts of the book were typed by hand and copies were mimeographed to share with others for feedback.

Although Dr. Rimland's initial plan was to write a review article for a journal, the manuscript grew so thick that his wife suggested that he consider writing a book instead. He stared at the stack for a few moments and soon realized that he had taken on a much bigger project than he had anticipated. Most of *Infantile Autism* was written in four years, and the last two sections, in which he proposed a theory on the underlying cause of autism, took one year to write.

During the writing of the book, Dr. Rimland had numerous correspondences with Dr. Leo Kanner, who later agreed to write the foreword to the book. A few years after the publication of *Infantile Autism*, Dr. Kanner is said to have apologized to parents at a conference for implying that they were responsible for their child's autism.

Once the manuscript was completed, Dr. Rimland submitted it to Appleton Century Crofts, the premier publisher of psychology books. *Infantile Autism* was reviewed and accepted for publication. In fact, the reviewers were so impressed with Dr. Rimland's thesis that the book was nominated for and awarded the Century Psychology Series Award for its significant contribution to the field of psychology.

GROUND-BREAKING PREMISES

Besides being critical of Bettelheim's parent-blaming theory, Dr. Rimland's book addressed other important issues related to autism, including diagnosis, genetics, cognition, and a possible neurological site of damage.

Psychogenesis vs. biology

In Chapter 3 of *Infantile Autism*, Dr. Rimland laid out the argument against a psychogenic cause for autism and clearly explained why autism was much more consistent with a biological cause. He pointed to many facts, some of which included: autism affects three or four boys to one girl; most siblings do not have autism; many of the symptoms of autism are similar to those of "organic brain damage"; and children with autism are usually different from birth.

Dr. Rimland's chapter was clear, concise, and logical; and many professionals were shocked to learn about the lack of research supporting a psychogenic view of autism. They quickly "jumped ship" and started to view autism as a biological disorder.

Diagnosis

Beginning in 1943, Dr. Kanner published descriptive papers in which he argued that autism was a disorder distinct from childhood schizophrenia. Dr. Rimland took a more straightforward approach in *Infantile Autism* by describing characteristics of child schizophrenia and comparing these symptoms with autism. For example, he noted that the two disorders had different patterns of onset, that language ability and physical responsiveness differed, and that hallucinations were a hallmark of schizophrenia but not of autism.

While writing *Infantile Autism*, Dr. Rimland felt that a checklist was needed to help parents determine whether or not their child might have autism. He wrote and included a suggested checklist in the Appendix titled "Diagnostic Check List for Behavior-Disturbed Children (Form E-1)." The checklist was developed primarily to diagnose Kanner's syndrome, or classical autism, even though many professionals in the field misunderstood his intentions and thought the checklist could diagnose all forms of autism.

To his surprise, many parents ripped Form E-1 from the book, completed the checklist, and mailed the pages to Dr. Rimland for his records, asking for suggestions on how best to help their children. In their letters, parents would sometimes mention additional symptoms that were not discussed in *Infantile Autism*. Dr. Rimland revised the checklist a few years later and called it Diagnostic Form E-2.

One final note: Besides diagnosing Kanner's syndrome, Dr. Rimland felt that the checklist could be used for subtyping since it was obvious that there were many forms of autism. The Autism Research Institute (ARI) recently analyzed the E-2 database, consisting of more than 40,000 cases, and found 10 to 12 distinct subgroups. We are now attempting to replicate these findings in an online survey (see AutismResearchSurvey.com).

Genetic component

In his book, Dr. Rimland also concluded that there was likely a genetic component, as evidenced by published reports on the higher prevalence of autism in identical twins than in fraternal twins. Basically, identical twins share the same genetic makeup, while fraternal twins overlap by about 50 percent. A few years later Dr. Rimland suggested that autism was likely caused by an interaction between genetics and the environment.

Cognition

In the chapter entitled "Autism as Cognitive Dysfunction," Dr. Rimland wrote: "…it is possible to trace its diversity of symptoms and manifestations to a single critical disability: *The child with early infantile autism is grossly impaired in a function basic to all cognition: the ability to relate new stimuli to remembered experience"* (page 106; italics in original). Basically, he argued, rather convincingly, that those on the autism spectrum have much difficulty relating what is currently happening in their surroundings to their past experience.

There are many components of memory, and researchers have found that episodic memory is dysfunctional in autism. In short, this type of memory refers to the storage and retrieval (i.e., recall) of autobiographical information—that is, experiences unique to the individual. Basically, this form of memory involves what a person has experienced in the past, such as what the person ate for lunch or where he or she purchased a specific item. Dr. Rimland's insight was, again, right on the mark!

Furthermore, the hippocampus in the brain is responsible for the creation of episodic memories, and anomalies of the hippocampus are among the earliest and most consistent neurological deficits documented in autism.

Underlying cause of autism

Dr. Rimland dedicated several chapters of his book to hypothesizing an underlying cause of autism. He suggested that a particular area of the brainstem, called the reticular formation, could be the primary site of dysfunction. The reticular formation is responsible for filtering incoming stimuli, regulating arousal and attention as well as the sleep–wake cycle, and much more. Autopsies of the brainstem have not supported Dr. Rimland's hypothesis.

When I first met Dr. Rimland in 1979, I asked him about his current thoughts on the reticular formation. He mentioned that, at that point in time, it made logical sense. He did not seem disappointed that his theory did not pan out since he was trained as a psychologist rather than a neurologist. However, he was clearly excited that researchers from some of the major universities were just beginning to study the neurology of autism.

Dr. Rimland was too specific in hypothesizing that autism stemmed from defects in a specific area in the brain. Current research indicates that many areas of the brain are affected. I should mention that researchers have found some abnormalities in the brainstem in autism. In addition, Dr. Woody McGinnis, Dr. Audya Tappan, and I have published a couple of papers in which we speculate that the nucleus tractus solitarius, a small structure in the brainstem and part of the blood–brain barrier, may be the site in which environmental toxins enter the brain. The most recent paper can be viewed at: www.AutismNTS.com.

DR. RIMLAND'S LEGACY

My first introduction to autism was a film documentary, titled *The Invisible Wall*, which I watched in an undergraduate child development course. A year later, I began studying autism with Ivar Lovaas. After reading *Infantile Autism*, I agreed with Rimland that understanding the physiology of those with autism was crucial to figuring out how best to help them. After many discussions about behavior-related issues with Lovaas, which sometimes led to friendly arguments, he introduced me to Bernard Rimland. Instantly, we began a long relationship, first as student and mentor and eventually as close colleagues.

I certainly was not the only person influenced by *Infantile Autism* as well as Rimland's other writings. The contributions to this reprinted book are a clear testimony to how Rimland's work has inspired generations of researchers.

Rimland's contributions during his almost 50 years in the field of autism are immeasurable. He was the founder of the Autism Society of America (formerly known as the National Society for Autistic Children) and the Autism Research Institute (formerly known as the Institute for Child Behavior Research). He served as head consultant for the movie *Rain Man*, pioneered the use of restricted diets and nutritional supplements, and actively supported the use of Applied Behavior Analysis (often referred to as ABA) as well as biomedical and sensory interventions. A few years prior to his passing in 2006, he started an initiative to understand and support adults on the autism spectrum.

I would like to thank the many contributors to this book for submitting updated information on many of the topics raised in *Infantile Autism*. We have learned a great deal in the past 50 years, but unfortunately we are still struggling with many of the basic issues including the underlying causes of autism, the most effective interventions, and even the basic question, "What is autism?"

In a way, one could say that Rimland drew the outline of the future for autism, and subsequent researchers have been coloring in the white spaces. He also made it clear that it was fine for us, actually encouraged us, to color outside the lines.

If you read *Infantile Autism* many years ago or this is your first time, you will be amazed at how many brilliant hypotheses and ideas Rimland put forth in his book. *Infantile Autism* is a true masterpiece, and it will continue to inspire researchers, practitioners, those on the autism spectrum, and family members for many more years. Rimland passed away in late 2006, but his spirit is still with us.

Foreword

There is a German proverb which, translated, says: He who builds on the roadside has many masters. Many times have I come to learn how true this is, and many times have I experienced the benefits of constructive criticism. However, there are passers-by who, after a fleeting glimpse, are ready to make categorical pronouncements about a new structure viewed from a distance. This happened when, about 20 years ago, I published a small number of observations which impressed me because of their phenomenologic uniqueness. I considered it my duty to report what I saw and to correlate, as much as possible, the described syndrome with ascertainable facts regarding constitutional and environmental data. It seemed to me that you have to know the "what" before deciding on the "why." Even at that, I ventured the opinion that we deal here with an innate phenomenon of a peculiar disability to form affective contacts.

For several years, there were no repercussions. Then came, in Europe as well as in this country, a series of case studies confirming the original observations. But then came also two parallel developments which tended to confuse the issue. The concept of "early infantile autism" (I could not think of a better name) was diluted by some to deprive it of its specificity, so that the term was used as a pseudodiagnostic wastebasket for a variety of unrelated conditions, and a nothing-but psychodynamic etiology was decreed by some as the only valid explanation, so that further curiosity was stifled or even scorned.

Dr. Rimland, who has communicated with me since 1959, has given much study and thought to the perplexities connected with early infantile autism. He has carefully and critically scanned the literature which, by now, has assumed the proportions of a fair-sized library. Adhering to the clinical criteria which I have set forth (and for this I am grateful to him), he has evolved a theory, or a logically cohesive chain of theories, which lends itself to respectfully sober scrutiny. If some of it is based on speculation, it is the kind of courageous speculation which, with its broad orientation, invites the sympathetic appraisal of a skillfully planned construct.

Dr. Rimland is building on the roadside. He will have many masters. It is hoped that the passers-by will stop and tarry long enough to become sufficiently acquainted with the edifice and then (and only then) make further contributions to the understanding of the puzzling clinical syndrome of early infantile autism.

Leo Kanner, M.D., Professor Emeritus of Child Psychiatry and
Honorary Consultant, The Johns Hopkins University and Hospital
Baltimore, November 24, 1963

Preface

This is a working paper. If it isn't, I don't know when it stopped being one.

This monograph got its start as a minor attempt to learn what was known about an exceedingly rare behavior disorder in children called early infantile autism. If the reader is surprised to find, from the title or the table of contents, that this monograph travels from infantile autism to a theory of behavior, he is no more surprised than the writer.

A wise man once observed that if you study an object of nature intently enough, if you focus upon it long enough all your powers of concentration and attention, there comes a point at which the macrocosm behind the object is suddenly revealed—in somewhat the way in which the vista beyond a keyhole is magnified if one purposefully advances his eye toward it. Unfortunately, the wise man neglected to reveal how one may assess the validity of his newly achieved view. My own response to the problem of evaluation was to record my findings in a mimeographed book which I named *Kanner's Syndrome of Apparent Autism* and mailed to a number of researchers who I hoped to interest in my work. My research on autism had overflowed from psychology into such fields as genetics, neurology, neurophysiology, and biochemistry, and I was well aware that it needed much more critical appraisal than I could give it.

The book's reception far exceeded my modest expectations. Especially gratifying was the selection of the book to receive the first Century Psychology Series Award.

During the past year the book has been extensively revised and supplemented. But it is still a working paper for me, and, it is my hope, for the reader.

The friends and colleagues who have helped me in this adventure are innumerable. There are too many to name, and I do not wish to engage in the odious comparisons which would be entailed by the attempt to single out those who warrant special mention.

I have thanked my partners personally, and I hope that they share with me the warm glow of seeing our work advance, and the gratifying realization that it has been our mutual privilege to be able to contribute.

The one partner whom I cannot bear to leave unnamed is my gentle wife Gloria, whose constant helpfulness, patience, and understanding throughout this trying endeavor I must acknowledge with wonder and gratitude.

B.R.

General Introduction

Two decades have passed since Kanner (1943) published his classic paper describing the paradoxical and bewildering disturbance of behavior in children which he called "early infantile autism." The presence of the disturbance in early infancy, the strange pattern of motor and language behavior which is reproduced with incredible accuracy in case after case, the occurrence in the same child of behavior typical of both genius and idiocy, and the complete absence of any evidence of physical or neurological defect have led many investigators to consider early infantile autism the most baffling of the behavior disorders. The virtually complete absence of any form of mental disorder in the families and relatives of the stricken children has served to intensify the puzzling nature of the disease. Nor has the problem been simplified by the fact that these children, almost without exception, come from homes of highly intellectual parents, none of whose other children are afflicted.

Despite the voluminous literature that has developed, the origin of this disease is as much a mystery today as it was 20 years ago. There is no known cause, and no known cure. Recovery, in those few cases where it has occurred, has apparently been spontaneous. The mystery of autism deepens when we consider that among the few who have recovered are some who had been afflicted so severely that they functioned at the idiot or imbecile level in pre-school years. Some of those who have recovered have retained in adulthood vestiges of the remarkable mental powers which they showed in childhood and which have proven so baffling to investigators of the disease. One recovered autistic child, for example, has become a mathematician, having completed his undergraduate training in mathematics at one of the nation's foremost universities in three years. Another is a meteorologist and composer. Chances for recovery are slight, however, and the great majority of the victims of infantile autism live out their years in empty hopelessness at home or in institutions.

The amount of attention devoted to early infantile autism has been far out of proportion to its small absolute numerical incidence. This is so partly because of the paradoxical aspects of the disease, partly because of the provocative nearness of the unusual cognitive ability of the children, and partly because their verbal and social behavior is so strikingly unique. The extreme rarity of the disease is attested to by the fact that Kanner himself, who is reported to have seen over 20,000 disturbed children in his more than 30 years of psychiatric practice, had by 1958 seen fewer than 150 cases of early infantile autism (Kanner, 1958a). This figure includes children brought to him for diagnosis from all parts of the world.

No consistent or cohesive theory has heretofore been advanced to account for early infantile autism. In the course of years, however, a number of papers have been published, some addressed to the problem of infantile autism and some not, which taken together converge toward what is to the present writer a cohesive—and perhaps even compelling—theory of the nature and origin of the disease. It is the primary purpose of this monograph to present this theory and suggest a program of research which will facilitate its evaluation.

Subordinate purposes are to present a complete and comprehensive view of present knowledge about early infantile autism, and to present for consideration several implications of the theory which relate to the possible neural bases for intelligence and personality in both normal persons and certain abnormal conditions such as *idiot savant* and schizophrenia.

The brain mechanisms postulated in this paper are admittedly very tentative and speculative. However, whether or not these specific hypotheses are in time confirmed, the writer is firm in his belief that Sarason and Gladwin were correct when they wrote of early infantile autism, "The importance of these cases to the development of a science of psychology would seem to be vastly beyond what their relatively rare occurrence in the general population would suggest" (1958, p. 345).

Part I

THE CONTROVERSIES AND THEIR RESOLUTION

A Critical Analysis of the Literature

Introduction to Part I

The four chapters which constitute Part I will each treat one of the four major controversies which attend the problem of early infantile autism.

Chapter 1 is addressed to the root problem: *Is infantile autism a clearly defined clinical and diagnostic entity?* Because much of the controversy on all other aspects of infantile autism can be traced to a misunderstanding of this point, Chapter 1 will be largely devoted to a detailed description of the disease. There can be no substitute for reading Kanner's lucid case histories (1943), but the descriptive data presented in Chapter 1 should prove useful in reducing the frequent overuse of the diagnosis. Several factors which have contributed to the confusion surrounding infantile autism are pointed out in the concluding section of Chapter 1.

Chapter 2 is concerned with a problem of far more significance than has heretofore been recognized: *How accurate are the assertions of Kanner and others that autistic children are almost invariably the offspring of highly educated and intelligent parents?*

Chapter 3 is concerned with the question of etiology: *Is autism an organic defect or is the family environment wholly or partly responsible?*

Chapter 4 discusses the question: *Is infantile autism merely a variation of childhood schizophrenia?*

It is the writer's belief that the evidence now at hand is sufficient to render unnecessary any continuation of controversy on these points.

These chapters are based primarily on what is believed to be a substantially comprehensive review of the American and European literature. The several known papers not available at the time of this writing are so noted in the bibliography.

INTRODUCTION TO CHAPTER 1
Stephen M. Edelson

The symptoms of autism that Rimland described 50 years ago are still considered core symptoms of the syndrome today. They include feeding difficulties, repetitive behaviors, insistence on sameness, suspected deafness, splinter skills, and unique expressive speech.

In *Infantile Autism* as well as the film documentary *The Invisible Wall*, Rimland mentions that there are different types of individuals with autism. In other words, not everyone with autism exhibits the same symptoms and behaviors, and the severity of these symptoms and behaviors varies considerably among those given the same diagnosis of autism. For this reason, we now use the term *autism spectrum disorder*—a term Rimland felt was appropriate.

Over the years, we have learned much more about the symptoms and behaviors associated with autism, including seizures and sleep disturbances. Although Kanner's initial paper published in 1943, titled "Autistic disturbances of affective contact," mentioned several medically related issues, such as eating and gastrointestinal problems, there was little discussion of such problems until the mid-1990s. At that time, Rimland, along with colleagues Sidney Baker and Jon Pangborn, spearheaded an effort to bring needed attention to gastrointestinal problems such as chronic diarrhea and constipation, and immune problems such as inflammation. More recently, researchers have also documented impairments in metabolism (e.g., problems in methylation, detoxification, and mitochondrial function).

Although autism is accepted as a spectrum disorder, Rimland often considered two related traits, difficulties in social interaction and impairments in communication, to be defining features of every case of autism. In other words, if someone had excellent social and communication skills, he or she was unlikely to be diagnosed with autism. Rimland always felt strongly that more objective measures were needed to diagnose autism, such as biomarkers.

Citing Kanner on page 40, Rimland wrote, "The prognosis of early infantile autism has not been influenced by any form of therapy." However, Rimland did comment on "...advice frequently given to the parents that the child be provided more stimulation" (page 41). Interestingly, within a short time after the publication of *Infantile Autism*, Rimland visited Ivar Lovaas at his autism clinic at UCLA. Witnessing the results that Lovaas was achieving,

Rimland quickly realized that autism was treatable. He soon founded the National Society for Autistic Children (currently the Autism Society of America) to inform parents throughout the country about the benefits of behavioral therapy. Much research published after *Infantile Autism* has clearly demonstrated the importance of early educational intervention in relation to prognosis. In many of his writing and lectures, Rimland also argued that other physiologically based forms of early intervention, such as biomedical and sensory interventions, were important with respect to a child's prognosis.

REFERENCE

Kanner, L. (1943). Autistic disturbances of affective contact. *Nervous Child*, 2, 217–250.

CHAPTER 1

The Syndrome of Early Infantile Autism

Background, Course, Diagnosis, and Prognosis

In 1943 Leo Kanner, then director of the Child Psychiatry Clinic at Johns Hopkins Hospital and author of the definitive textbook in child psychiatry, published his first description of a rare and remarkable behavior disorder in children. His paper, titled *Autistic Disturbances of Affective Contact*, was based on the striking similarities he had perceived in the case histories and behavior of 11 children brought to the clinic over a period of years. A year later he followed his initial detailed report with a brief paper in which he named the new syndrome "early infantile autism." Kanner applied this title because the children had been unusual "from the beginning of life," and because their aloof, withdrawn, "autistic" personalities caused them always to appear to be living in a private, inaccessible dream-world; isolated, seemingly by choice, from contact with others. (See Bruch [1959] for an interesting glimpse into Kanner's clinic at the time the diagnosis was formulated.)

A. BACKGROUND

Kanner's contribution in delineating the syndrome of infantile autism has made it possible to identify, in retrospect, a number of cases reported in the literature by earlier writers. Recently Vaillant (1962) has called attention to a very early textbook by John Haslam, written in 1809, which describes a five-year-old boy, identifiable as autistic, who had been admitted to Bethlehem asylum in 1799.

Witmer (1920) described a severely afflicted three-year-old boy who appeared in many ways to resemble the autistic cases of Kanner. At age seven, Witmer's case seemed destined to recover.

In 1921 Meyer and Richards (reported by Darr & Worden, 1951) described a young girl who is now clearly recognizable as a case of infantile autism. Darr and Warden's paper, written 28 years after the original case description, represents one of the few follow-up reports available.

Despert (1938) has presented several brief descriptions of children who had psychoses of "insidious onset." Certain of these cases, in contrast with her cases of "acute onset," are generally regarded as autistic.

Another early case of a girl afflicted with autism was reported in considerable detail by C. Bradley, in 1943, the same year in which Kanner's now classic report was published.

B. COURSE AND SYMPTOMS OF THE DISEASE

Because of its rarity, little is known about the conditions under which infantile autism occurs. By far the largest group of cases has been that reported by Kanner and his colleagues at the Johns Hopkins Hospital clinic. Much of the available information comes from the reports of Kanner's first 100 cases (Kanner, 1954a; Kanner & Lesser, 1958). The present writer's survey of the available literature supports the data provided on the first 100 cases.

Infantile autism occurs primarily in first-born males. The sex ratio is about three or four boys to one girl (Kanner, 1954a; Keeler, 1957; Anthony, 1958). Eighty of the first 100 cases were boys, 20 were girls. Fifteen of the 100 had no siblings, 43 were first-born, 23 second-, 13 third-, and six were fourth- or fifth-born.

Pregnancy and birth. Complications of pregnancy are reported to be no more common than usual in births producing autistic children (Kanner, 1954a; Kanner & Lesser, 1958). Keeler (1957), however, reports that many of the mothers of his cases (number not specified) had experienced bleeding in the first trimester of pregnancy; and that others had a history of miscarriage and stillbirths. One of the ten cases seen by van Krevelen (1963) had a history of maternal bleeding in the first trimester, and another was afflicted with rubella in the fifth month.

Twelve of Kanner's first 100 cases had been born prematurely. (The base rate for prematurity among whites in the United States is about 7%.) Keeler also notes an elevated incidence of prematurity in autistic children, and observes that for most a lack of movement was reported before birth.

The first two years. The child is usually exceptionally healthy and attractive, quite often precocious and alert in appearance. Very little that is unusual is noticed in the first months, except perhaps that feeding may be a problem. Some autistic infants are reported to have been apathetic and unresponsive in the first few months, while others have been given to implacable crying. Typically, it is not until about the fourth month that even a person experienced with babies may first notice anything unusual. The first awareness of any problem is often the observation that the child fails to make the usual anticipatory movements prior to being picked up. He also fails to make the usual adjustments of his body to adapt to the person carrying or holding him. Head-banging is common, both in the crib and while being held; the latter behavior causing considerable discomfort and chagrin to the adult holding him. Case histories of very young autistic infants have been supplied by Plenter (1955), Lazure (1959), Eveloff (1960), and Lewis and Van Ferney (1960).

Between the fourth and eighteenth months several disturbing symptoms will have begun to appear. These include prolonged rocking and head-banging in the crib, apathy and disinterest in the surroundings, unusual fear of strangers, obsessive interest in certain toys or mechanical appliances, highly repetitive and ritualistic play, insistence on being left alone and that the physical environment remain unchanged, and very unusual language behavior. Speech, of a very unusual sort, may have started early. Because speech is of special importance in early infantile autism, it will be discussed separately below, in conjunction with separate discussions of other behaviors of special interest.

By the time the child is 18 months to two years old the parents will have become quite concerned, especially if another child has been born which acquaints them with the much different normal pattern of development. One of the most disturbing of the symptoms is what has been called "autistic aloneness." The child may sit for hours staring into space, motionless, as if deep in thought. The autistic child looks highly intelligent and always appears to be mentally occupied during these periods of self-imposed isolation. Sometimes a fleeting, pensive smile will cross his face. The child's attention cannot be attracted by calling his name or speaking. No sign of attention is given.

Even more disturbing is the child's utter lack of interest in people. Most autistic children act is if other people did not exist (e.g., Chapman, 1957; G. Arnold, 1960; Loomis, 1960), but a few appear to have an active aversion to others (e.g., Plenter, 1955). Coupled with the disinterest in persons is frequently an active interest in inanimate objects.

Specific problems and behaviors. Professional help is often sought after the child has reached the second birthday. Not only has the child's development become of concern, he has become exceedingly difficult to live with.

Toilet training is ordinarily difficult to establish, though sometimes it can take place early. It is not uncommon for toilet training to start early, then be completely absent for several more years.

Feeding problems are almost the rule. Some children have ravenous appetites; others eat very little. Almost all have odd eating habits and preferences, however. Some children will take only milk. An autistic girl reported by Rattner and Chapman (1959) subsisted entirely on milk for her first six years. Others will never touch milk. One child went for several days without taking liquid until it was discovered he would drink only from a transparent container. Witmer's case would *not* drink from a transparent container, nor would he drink water. Other children have been reported utterly to refuse to drink liquids which were not at a certain precise temperature. Absolute refusal to use the hands is also sometimes reported, which means spoon feeding. Creak (1952) reports an autistic child who loved chocolate, but would eat it only if cut into squares; round chocolate was not acceptable. Certain autistic children are exceedingly neat and clean in their habits, becoming upset at untidiness. One such child began eating with a spoon with perfect precision at nine months. One girl would eat only sandwiches she made herself, starting at three years of age.

Repetitive behavior and fetishlike preoccupation with mechanical objects such as vacuum cleaners, stoves, light switches, and faucets is a common symptom. Any attempt to divert the child from this type of pursuit is met by an intense and violent temper tantrum: "...when he was lifted from the couch, put upon his feet and made to walk, he burst into a paroxysm of rage. His eyes became bloodshot; even his gums bled" (Witmer, 1920, p. 100). One child who loved to bounce in a "jump chair" wore out three reinforced canvas chair covers and broke the chair's steel frame before he became too large for it at age three. At age four this child became obsessed with water heaters and would look at one for hours, find pictures of water heaters in magazines, and carried one (actually a defunct flashlight cell) with him at all times, for several months.

Insistence on the preservation of sameness in the environment is one of the two most widely accepted diagnostic signs, the self-imposed isolation—"autistic aloneness"—being the other. Cases of extreme emotional reactions—violent tantrums or disconsolate weeping—are also commonly reported where no semblance of an external cause can be identified. In other cases a cause, often merely an accidental displacement of a piece of furniture, can be found (Kanner, 1951). A refusal to change clothes, especially pajamas, is often reported. Bedtime rituals are often long and elaborate.

Suspected deafness. Once the parents have begun to realize that their child's behavior is not normal, they almost without exception consider the possibility of a hearing defect. The parents have often been unable to attract the child's attention by speaking to him or calling his name. The child is often described as being "in a shell," or as "so completely wrapped up in his thoughts you can't talk to him." An unusual noise will sometimes evoke a reaction, while at other times even loud and unexpected noises will have little or no effect (e.g., Goldfarb, 1956; Anthony, 1958).

The child's ability to repeat tunes and to say some of the things he has heard belie the possibility of a hearing defect.

Differentiation from mental deficiency

Mental retardation is the next suspicion, but again certain contradictory observations are regarded as not supporting this classification.

Appearance. Kanner emphasizes that the children simply do not look retarded. He has frequently commented on the "strikingly intelligent physiognomies" of autistic children. Others have also noted that the dull, vacuous expression of the feeble-minded is not found in autistic children. Instead they appear always to be concentrating on something else. (Pictures of autistic children appear in the papers by van Krevelen [1952], Bakwin [1954], and Plenter [1955]. Oppenheim's case [1961], probably autistic; and the twins described by Kallman et al., [1940], possibly autistic, are also pictured.)

Early skilled performance. Another reason for not considering the children feeble-minded is the outstanding performance they display in many areas ordinarily considered closed to the mentally deficient. Early use of language, and early, or at least undelayed, motor ability is common. Some cases have been reported of delayed walking with sudden onset of good performance, as though the child could have walked earlier but did not. Other signs which help differentiate the autistic child from most of the mentally deficient are their excellent memories and musical abilities. The spatial abilities of autistic children are also frequently reported as being unusually good.

Memory. Coupled with the elaborate insistence that no change take place in the environment is, in many autistic children, a truly phenomenal ability to recall the exact state of the environment. Kanner describes autistic children who screamed in implacable fury when one block was experimentally turned in a jumble of blocks and toys left on the floor during the child's absence. Each block had to be returned to its exact place before the child was satisfied.

> Once blocks, beads or sticks have been put together by the child in a certain way, they are often regrouped later in exactly the same way, even though there was no definite design. The child's memory is phenomenal in this respect. After the lapse of several days, a multitude of blocks could be rearranged, most astonishingly...in precisely the same unorganized pattern, with the same color of each block turned up, with each picture or letter on the upper surface of each block facing the same direction as before. The absence of a block, or the presence of a supernumerary block was noticed immediately... (1951, p. 24)

Extraordinary memory seems almost the rule with these children. One child was able to reproduce an aria in a foreign language after hearing it only once. Another child was able to repeat the questions and answers of a Protestant catechism and name the Presidents at the age of two. According to Kanner and Lesser:

> The astounding vocabularies of the speaking children, the unusual memory for events, the excellent rote memory for poems and names, and the precise recollection of complex patterns and sequences, bespeak good intelligence in the sense in which this word is commonly used. Binet or similar testing can rarely be carried out because of limited accessibility, but the children perform surprisingly well on the Seguin Formboard. (1958, p. 720)

Spatial ability. The high level of spatial ability of the child with infantile autism is reflected in his good performance on the Seguin Formboard, and on jig-saw puzzle tasks. It has been noted by a number of writers that autistic children can sometimes assemble jig-saw puzzles as readily when the picture is facing down as when it is visible. May (1958) reported his young twin autistic sons to have engineered a ladder by pulling bureau drawers part way out to use as steps. The child's previously mentioned insistence upon sameness in the physical environment, including the arrangement of randomly scattered blocks and toys, indicates an unusual degree of spatial memory.

Motor and manual ability. Most writers regard the children as quite agile and graceful. Benda (1952, p. 501) states, "The autistic child is, surprisingly often, a beautiful child who impresses by his fast and graceful movements..." Waal's case (1955) at two and a half was as agile and dexterous as a four-year-old. The boy described by Loomis (1960) walked at eight months and was "really a high trapeze artist" at two. Rank and MacNaughton's case (1950) was "quick and light" with excellent motor coordination. While refusal to use the hands is a fairly common symptom, the children who do use their hands are remarkably dexterous. Creak (1952) and Rothenberg (1960) have each reported cases of three-year-old autistic boys who could balance a dime on edge. Other children have been very skilled at spinning and twirling jar lids and other round objects from an early age. One boy who was obsessed with balls was able, at 14 months, to catch a ball with either one or both hands. He could throw a ball across a room to within an inch or two of the hand of the adult playing catch with him. A 12-year-old boy, taught the numbers on a typewriter, could type the series to 1000 without error at an estimated 60 word-per-minute rate.

The child will sometimes induce an adult to act as his "hands" by leading the adult to the object desired or task to be performed and somehow communicating his wants (Rank & MacNaughton, 1950; Sherwin, 1953).

Musical ability. Astonishing musical ability is found in these children quite frequently, in some cases accompanied by perfect pitch (Kanner, 1943, etc.; Scheerer, Rothmann, & Goldstein, 1945; van Krevelen, 1952a; Sherwin, 1953; Keeler, 1958; May, 1958; see also Michaux et al., 1957). One of Kanner's earliest autistic cases, a member of the small minority who may be considered recovered, has become a composer in adulthood. A case reported recently by Anastasi and Levee (1960) as an adult *idiot savant* musician of great skill, gives every indication of having been an autistic child.

One of the three musically talented children reported by Sherwin (1953) was able to reproduce the notes of the scale "with extraordinary accuracy" at 14 months. At 17 months he spontaneously repeated in full an aria from *Don Giovanni*. Between his 18th and 36th months this child sang "a remarkable repertoire of music, consisting of symphonies by Mozart and Haydn, songs by Schubert and Brahms, selections from Carmen, a Tschiakowsky Piano Concerto and diversified well-known songs" (p. 825).

Special abilities in autism and idiot savant performance

Despite these signs of what Kanner calls "good cognitive potential," many autistic children do eventually become institutionalized as mentally deficient. It may be these children who figure in the stories which are heard now and then of psychologists being startled to find above-average test performance on certain tasks by mute and uncomprehending individuals who have shown no other sign of intelligence (Eisenberg, 1956; Kanner, 1949).

The possibility that some *idiot savants* may actually be cases of early infantile autism has been discussed by several writers (e.g., Scheerer, Rothmann & Goldstein [1945], Rosen [1953], Sarason & Gladwin [1958], van Krevelen [1958], Goldstein [1959], and Anastasi & Levee [1960]). The occurrence of isolated areas of extraordinary mental ability in individuals showing a low order of ability in all other areas does fit the picture of autism very well. *Idiot savants* have been noted with special abilities in calculation, music, art, mechanics, mental calendar manipulation, and memory. This list applies very well to the autistic child's often-reported special interests and abilities. It is interesting to conjecture that the silent, unreachable autistic child may indeed be "lost in thought"—reliving an experience in minute detail, hearing music long since forgotten or perhaps never heard by others, or playing games with numbers or objects manipulatable only in the recesses of his brain.

Of exceptional interest are the not uncommon reports of autistic children who become quite adept at reading aloud, but who have no apparent comprehension of what the words mean (Kanner, 1952; Benda, 1960). Other autistic children write but do not speak (G. Arnold, 1960; Oppenheim, 1961). The Oppenheim case, unlike that of Arnold, appeared to be able to communicate through writing. It is possible that Oppenheim's is not a true case of infantile autism.

The speech of autistic children. One of the most striking characteristics of early infantile autism is the baffling use of language by those autistic children who use speech. Because of his early speech, the child is frequently regarded as being highly precocious or "a budding genius." Words are learned with great rapidity in these cases, and sometimes the child is suddenly found to be using complete sentences at one year of age, even before the component words have been used singly. The language acquisition of one autistic child between his seventh and twelfth month was reported as follows: "mamma," "dada," "bear," "spoon," "hungry," "done," "ball," and "C'mon, let's play ball."

The speech is generally of a peculiar non-communicative kind, however, and is ordinarily produced in an empty high-pitched, parrot-like monotone. Whispering is very common, little or no expression is used, and, as it generally turns out, the speech is elicited only as specific responses to certain stimuli, and not as a means of communication. Naming of objects, for example, is common, but asking or answering questions is rare or absent. Desires are communicated by leading an adult by the hand to what is wanted. "No!" is often indicated by emphatically grunting and waving the arms.

Kanner has written extensively on the speech of autistic children (1946 and 1951, especially). He describes their speech in terms of "affirmation by repetition," "pronominal reversal," "extreme literalness," "metaphorical usage," "part-whole confusion," and "delayed echolalia."

The words *I* and *yes* are strikingly and consistently absent, often until the sixth or seventh year in the speaking autistic children. The boy discussed by Nesnidalova and Fiala (1961) did not use *I* until his tenth year. *You* is used for *I* (*pronominal reversal*), and *Yes* is indicated by repeating the question (*affirmation by repetition*). "Do you want some milk?" thus means, "I want some milk," or, "Yes, I want some milk."

An example of *literalness* is found in the boy whose father tried to encourage the use of the word *Yes* by carrying the child on his shoulders as a reward for saying it. The boy learned to say *Yes*, but only as an indication that he wanted his father to carry him, the original literal meaning to the child. To another boy *down* meant the *floor*. One boy was upset because his father spoke of hanging a picture *on* the wall, rather than *near* the wall.

Metaphorical use of language is illustrated by the boy who used the sentence, "Don't throw the dog off the balcony" to indicate "No." His mother had long before used this sentence to dissuade him from dropping a toy dog from a railroad station balcony. Another boy, at seven, used "He knocked me down" to indicate a blow, pat, spank, or bump, deliberate or accidental, caused by an adult or child of either sex.

Part–whole confusion is seen in the expression, "Do you want some catsup, Honey?" as used by one three-year-old autistic boy to ask for dinner, his favorite food being meat seasoned with catsup. The expression "bumped-the-head" was used by this child as a request for comforting, even though it was a hand or knee he offered for therapy.

Delayed echolalia is another common speech symptom. The child will simply repeat a phrase or sentence, often out of context and with no apparent purpose. "It's all dark outside," was reiterated constantly by an autistic child, day and night. Many autistic children repeat radio and television commercials endlessly (G. Arnold, 1960; van Krevelen, 1960). Arnold's case also reproduced video commercials in writing, with perfect spelling, at four.

Only about half of all autistic children are able to use speech. The others are either completely mute or may speak only once or twice in a lifetime. Kanner describes two cases in which a sentence has been used at ages four or five, in situations perceived by the children as emergencies, but never before or after (1949). One "emergency" was a prune skin stuck in the child's mouth, which elicited a panicky "Take it out!" Rothenberg's laconic case "Jonny" had said only "I can't" and "Go to hell" by age ten. The case reported by Anastasi and Levee did not learn to speak until age five.

C. PROGNOSIS

The prognosis for early infantile autism is closely linked to the speaking ability of the child. In a follow-up study of 63 autistic children it was found that 32 had useful, communicative speech at the age of five (Eisenberg, 1956; Kanner & Lesser, 1958). Sixteen of the 32 "speaking" children were able to achieve "fair" to "good" social adjustment, while only one of 31 "nonspeaking" children reached even the "fair" level. All three of those whose outcome was "good," as well as 16 of those 46 classified "poor," came from the "speaking" group. The median follow-up age was 15. Thirty-four of the 63 children had been institutionalized.

The particularly interesting case of an *idiot savant* which was reported recently by Anastasi and Levee (1960) merits consideration from the standpoint of prognosis. The data provided indicate strongly that the case was of an adult who had been, or still was, afflicted with early infantile autism. (Very little has been published relating to true cases of autism grown to maturity. The Eisenberg study [1956], Kanner's brief mention of several of his early cases [with Lesser, 1958], the Darr & Worden follow-up study [1951], and the case discussed by Bruch [1959] constitute the literature known to the present writer.)

The Anastasi–Levee case was able to live a protected life in the home of his well-to-do parents. He had been taught to read between his seventh and twentieth year and appeared to have a photographic mind which enabled him to quote long passages verbatim after a single reading. His ability to play the piano was great enough to attract professional musicians to his home to perform with him, despite his demanding and unreasonable personality. Kanner's cases (Eisenberg & Kanner, 1956) and the Darr and Worden case also demonstrated the striking lack of social intelligence and empathy characterizing the Anastasi and Levee case.

Anastasi and Levee report their case to have a dark, heavy beard, but undeveloped genitalia. This physical defect, minor problems among Kanner's children such as one with strabismus and another with clubfoot, a harelip condition reported by Putnam (1948), and the skin disorders described by Plenter (1955) and Benda (1960) are among the few defects noted by the writer in his survey of the literature.

The prognosis of early infantile autism has not been influenced by any form of therapy (Kanner & Lesser, 1958). Kanner has in fact commented that the children who received the most intensive psychiatric care have shown poorer records of recovery than those provided little or no professional treatment (1954b). He has observed, however, that the children raised in warm and affectionate surroundings tend to do somewhat better than those less fortunate. Several other writers have commented that autistic children tend to do best in a rigid, minimally stimulating environment (e.g., Mahler, 1952; May & May, 1959; Lovatt, 1962). This finding is in opposition to the advice frequently given to the parents that the child be provided more stimulation.

D. THE DIAGNOSIS OF AUTISM

It would appear, from the above presentation of symptomatology, that infantile autism is a distinctive and easily diagnosed disease of early childhood. Not brought out in the discussion, but facilitative of correct diagnosis is the fact that, to a marked extent, a large number of the symptoms described will appear in the same child. Thus, Kanner and Lesser state, "...taken in aggregate, the historical and behavioral features present so striking a picture that one should encounter little difficulty in making the diagnosis" (1958, p. 727). Van Krevelen (1952a), after noting that he had become skeptical about the existence of autism because no cases had appeared in the European literature for nearly a decade following Kanner's identification of the syndrome, wrote that when an autistic child was finally brought to him she was "as much like those described by Kanner as one raindrop is like another."

It might seem safe to infer, from the foregoing discussion, that there would be little controversy about the existence of infantile autism as a clinical entity, and little confusion as to its diagnosis. Nothing could be further from the truth.

Despite the distinctiveness of the syndrome, the reactions to Kanner's work range from applause for his achievement, through blanket and indiscriminate application of the label *autistic* to all manner of childhood behavior disorder, to utter denial that there is such a thing as infantile autism. Consider the contrasting opinions of Benda (1952) and Bender (1959). The former praises Kanner's contribution by stating that "the establishment of 'early infantile autism' as a specific condition of infancy must be considered a fundamental contribution to child psychiatry" (p. 500), while the latter argues that "...Kanner's syndrome of early infantile autism...is not a clinical or etiological entity" (p. 85).

It should be understood that early infantile autism is a very rare disorder. In 1958 Kanner wrote that he had seen fewer than 150 cases in 19 years—less than eight patients per year, despite the fact that his clinic served as "a sort of diagnostic clearing house" and that the patients "recruit themselves from all over the North American Continent and include some patients referred from other countries, one coming from as far as South Africa" (1958a, p. 110). Recently (in 1962), Kanner told the present writer that only about one child in ten brought to him after being diagnosed as "autistic" by others are true cases of infantile autism.

Van Krevelen, considered the European authority on autism, has seen only ten cases in the decade following publication of his first paper, although many of his colleagues have sent him children tentatively diagnosed as "autistic." Harbauer (cited by Spiel, 1961) found only one true case of infantile autism in 36,500 clinical cases.

Despite the rarity and distinctiveness of early infantile autism, there have appeared in the literature during the past few years a number of papers presenting analyses of large groups of children reported as having "infantile autism." Schain and Yannet (1960) have presented an excellent statistical description of 50 institutionalized children incorrectly identified as having "infantile autism." Knobloch and Grant (1961) identified 40 children as having "early infantile autism" from a group of 1000 referred because of "suspected deviation in development." Sarvis and Garcia (1961) report having seen 80 children with "autism," on the assumption that Kanner has sanctioned a permissive "broadening" of the term autism. (Kanner's most explicit statements on the specificity of the syndrome [1958a, 1958b] unfortunately have appeared only in European journals.)

In addition to these large groups, there have appeared in the literature, in the United States and abroad, innumerable articles on single cases and small numbers of children incorrectly described as autistic. It is often difficult to tell from the information given if the diagnosis is accurate. Indeed, it may be that some of the cases the present writer cites in this book to illustrate the phenomena of autism may in fact be instances where only some of the symptoms are shared with infantile autism, although an attempt to guard against this sort of error has been made. Most of the children erroneously classed as autistic are cases of childhood schizophrenia. A separate chapter has been devoted to the differential diagnosis of childhood schizophrenia from autism.

There appear to be three major reasons for controversy concerning the existence of autism and the confusion of autism with childhood schizophrenia: (1) the extreme rarity of autism, which appears to have precluded many writers from ever having seen a bona fide case; (2) the widespread belief in the psychogenic origin of childhood behavior disorders, which is not readily compatible with the existence of so specific a syndrome as Kanner has described; and (3) the generally inadequate state of psychiatric nosology. We will defer our discussion of points (1) and (2) and confine our attention for the present to the last mentioned point.

The problem of differentially diagnosing infantile autism has been brought into sharp focus by the recent publication of the previously mentioned article by Schain and Yannet. The thoroughness and explicitness of their paper has permitted identification of the problem. Unlike many previous writers on the topic, Schain and Yannet clearly and specifically state the criteria they have used in classifying their cases as autistic. There were three: (1) severe personality disorder characterized by extreme self-preoccupation and unrelatedness to people; (2) evidence indicating onset during first two years of life; and (3) lack of the severe motor retardation characteristic of most forms of gross mental defectiveness.

Schain and Yannet present data on their cases which differ markedly from those reported for classical cases of autism by Kanner and others. Twenty-one (42%) of the 50 children who fit the above criteria had a history of seizures. Kanner had reported only one case of grand mal in his first 100 cases of autism. In contrast to Kanner's finding that abnormal EEG recordings were no more common in his group than in the general age population, Schain and Yannet reported abnormality in five of the 11 cases for whom EEGs were available. Unlike Kanner's finding that the parents of his children differed dramatically from the mean in intelligence and educational level, Schain and Yannet reported very little difference from average in these measures. And some among Schain and Yannet's groups of 50 children, unlike cases described by Kanner and others, showed gross somatic problems such as arrested macrocephalus, cerebral hemorrhage, and blindness.

In commenting on their findings, Schain and Yannet observe:

> Such diagnoses as organic or chronic brain syndrome, congenital cerebral maldevelopment, epilepsy with mental retardation, and possibly others might be affixed to our cases by other observers... In reply, we can only emphasize that we have attempted to rigorously follow the criteria set forth above, in which the common denominator, as described by Kanner, involved "the children's inability to relate themselves in the ordinary way to people and situations from almost the beginning of life." (p. 564)

Earlier in their paper Schain and Yannet had noted, "...it should be emphasized that if the criteria as listed above were fulfilled, the presence of other conditions as diagnosed from the past history or by physical examination did not result in the exclusion of the child from this group" (p. 561).

These statements not only reveal the reason for Schain and Yannet's contradictory findings, but also permit us to isolate the cause of much of the confusion and controversy which has been the lot of early infantile autism: Kanner's criteria have almost universally been taken as being *necessary* and *sufficient* for diagnosis, rather than merely as a statement of minimum requirements. All autistic children must fit these criteria, but not all children who fit these criteria are autistic.

There is little to indicate that any child in Schain and Yannet's group, while diagnosed as autistic, showed the unique signs of Kanner's syndrome. No mention is made of pronominal reversal; of the expressionless, parrot-like voice; of obsessive interest in music or mechanical objects; of repetitive behavior and insistence on sameness, or of remarkable memory. Schain and Yannet state specifically that some of their children had a dull, retarded appearance in contrast to the "intelligent physiognomy" remarked on by Kanner, Benda, and others. It is clearly possible to meet Kanner's "two cardinal symptoms" of "extreme self-isolation, present in the first years of life, and obsessive insistence on the preservation of sameness" (Eisenberg, 1956, p. 607), without in fact being autistic.

Paradoxically, Kanner himself has contributed to the inordinate misapplication of the diagnosis of autism by stressing the "aloneness" and "preservation of sameness" aspects of the syndrome without indicating that these are necessary but not sufficient for establishing the diagnosis.

In a paper in which he deplored "the dilution of the concept of early infantile autism," and stated "the diagnosis has been made much too prodigiously" (1958a), he also said, "Because some autistic-like symptoms are found in innately retarded and in brain-injured children, the differential diagnosis, which admittedly does on occasion present difficulties, must depend on the clear evidence of the essential features of extreme aloneness and the desire for the maintenance of sameness" (p. 110).

More recently, Kanner has noted that the diagnosis is made "too quickly and erroneously," but he again stressed only aloneness and the preservation of sameness as the "salient components without whose presence the diagnosis should not be made" (1961, p. 1).

Since Kanner has in the past been careful to discuss the importance of the "symptom combination," it seems highly probable that in stressing aloneness and sameness he intended to be remedial rather than definitive. "There is, of course, no denying that overlapping symptomatology creates problems in trying to distinguish between different illnesses which have a number of features in common. But the problem is definitely not solved by the decree that the sharing of symptoms makes the diseases identical or that, because of the partial resemblance, a differentiation is unnecessary" (Kanner, 1958b, p. 142).

A solution to the problem of the diagnosis of autism is suggested by the "Check List of Symptoms of Autism of Early Life" provided by Polan and Spencer (1959). These writers give the case histories of five children (two being twins) who would probably all be classified as autistic, using Schain and Yannet's criteria. On applying their 30-point check list, developed from a review of the literature, to the five cases, the four bona fide cases of autism obtained scores of 24, 27, 20, and 20 (twins). The fifth case, while bearing a superficial resemblance to the others, had only five points checked.

The utility of the check list approach is illustrated by Vaillant (1962), who set a commendable example by using the Polan and Spencer check list in arriving at his conclusion that the five-year-old boy whose case history was published by Haslam in 1809 was autistic. Even using the limited information in Haslam's report (e.g., wept only briefly on separation from mother, whistled tunes very correctly) Vaillant was able to check 17 of the 30 points.

The Polan and Spencer approach has much to recommend it. A modified version of this type of instrument, prepared by the present writer, is provided in the Appendix.

A number of problems in the application of the check list remain to be solved. One problem relates to the need for different norms for the non-speaking children, where diagnosis is especially difficult. Another relates to the acceptability of evidence of organic pathology in cases of autism. Must a positive EEG finding or a history of encephalitis preclude a diagnosis of autism? The writer suggests that rigorous procedures for handling these and other problems be developed after a substantial amount of normative data becomes available.

INTRODUCTION TO CHAPTER 2

Stephen M. Edelson

Prior to the publication of *Infantile Autism*, much of the discussion about autism, starting in the 1940s after Kanner's first paper was published and continuing with Bruno Bettelheim's rantings, centered on the idea that parents' personality traits were the underlying cause of their children's autism.

When Rimland began to read the published literature on autism in the late 1950s, he was shocked to learn that most, if not all, professionals blamed mothers and fathers for causing autism in their children. These professionals even used the term "refrigerator mothers" to describe the cold and unaffectionate mothers they believed were responsible for autism. This idea was widely accepted by the professional community based solely on clinical opinion, without any supporting science.

Today, the notion that cold and unloving parents are the underlying cause of autism is considered archaic. There is research indicating that parents may experience stress (Davis & Carter, 2008), and this type of emotion is often attributed to the stress of raising a child on the spectrum. That is, they are viewed as an effect of raising a child with autism, not as a cause of the condition.

REFERENCES

Bettelheim, B. (1967). *The Empty Fortress: Infantile Autism and the Birth of the Self.* New York: The Free Press.

Davis, N.O., & Carter, A.S. (2008). Parenting stress in mothers and fathers of toddlers with autism spectrum disorders: Associations with child characteristics. *Journal of Autism and Developmental Disorders, 38*(7), 1278–1291.

CHAPTER 2

The Parents
of Autistic Children

The symptomatology alone of early infantile autism makes it an extraordinarily baffling disease. Yet investigators of the disease are confronted with an equally imposing challenge when they consider the family histories of the afflicted children. This chapter will review these findings, first reported by Kanner in 1943, and the controversy which has arisen over their credibility. Both the corroborating observations of numerous other investigators and logical inconsistencies in the objections to Kanner's findings will be shown to preclude the need for continued controversy.

In anticipation of a question which inevitably arises at this point, we may note that the weight of the presently available evidence (to be reviewed in Chapter 3) does not favor "environmental" causation of the disease. The theoretical significance of these findings will be presented in subsequent chapters.

Intellectual, educational and occupational status. In his original article Kanner provided the following description of the parents of his first 11 cases:

> Four fathers are psychiatrists, one is a brilliant lawyer, one a chemist and law school graduate employed in the Government Patent Office, one a plant pathologist, one a professor of forestry, one an advertising copy writer who has a degree in law and has studied in three universities, one is a mining engineer and one a successful business man.
>
> Nine of eleven mothers are college graduates. Of the two who have only high school education, one was a secretary in a pathology laboratory, and the other ran a theatrical booking office in New York City before marriage. Among the others, there was a freelance writer, a physician, a psychologist, a graduate nurse, and Frederick's mother was successively a purchasing agent, the director of secretarial studies in a girl's school, and a teacher of history.

Among the grandparents and collateral there are many physicians, scientists, writers, journalists and students of art. All but three of the families are represented either in *Who's Who in America* or in *American Men of Science*, or in both. (1943, p. 2)

In 1949, in reporting his findings based on 55 autistic children, Kanner observed that his "search for unsophisticated parents of autistic children had remained unsuccessful to date," and by 1954 he had gathered the following statistics on the first 100 sets of parents:

Fathers: Ninety-six were high school graduates (two of the non-graduates were immigrants). Eighty-seven entered college, 74 graduated college, 38 did postgraduate work. Thirty-one were business men, 12 engineers, 11 physicians (including five psychiatrists), 10 lawyers, 8 tradesmen, 5 chemists, 5 military officers, 4 writers, 3 Ph.D.s in science, 2 Ph.D.s in humanities, 2 teachers, 2 rabbis, and one each: psychologist, dentist, publisher, professor of forestry, and photographer.

Mothers: Ninety-two high school graduates, 70 of whom entered college; 49 graduated; 11 did postgraduate work. Seventeen were secretaries, 16 teachers, 6 business women, 6 librarians, 4 artists, 4 social workers, 3 writers, 3 nurses, 3 telephone operators, 2 psychologists; and one each: physician, lawyer, chemist, Ph.D. in humanities, physiotherapist and laboratory technician.

Ethnic origin. Kanner reported his patients to come largely of Jewish or Anglo-Saxon families, "no fewer than" 27 of his first 100 cases being Jewish (1954a). This is not necessarily suggestive of a racially based genetic linkage, since a random sample of persons in the professional level group in which autism tends to occur might well consist of 27 percent Jews. Fifty percent of employed male Jews occupy the professional, managerial and executive type positions which compose only 20 percent of urban occupations (McClelland, Baldwin, Bronfenbrenner, & Strodtbeck, 1958, p. 262). However, other children's diseases involving mental disorder, Tay-Sachs and phenylketonuria for example, are race-linked (tending to be found in Jews and Scandinavians, respectively), so the possibility of race linkage for autism must be considered. There has been little mention of racial background in the literature on autism. Putnam's case (1948) was of Italian origin and that of Stern (1952) was Jewish. Cappon (1953), and Cappon and Andrews (1957), have emphasized the disproportionate frequency of Jewish autistic children in their sample. Bruch (1959) has seen Negro twins with autism, and Arnold's case (1960) was Negro.

Personality. The parents are described as cold, bookish, formal, introverted, disdainful of frivolity, humorless, detached, and highly—even excessively— rational and objective. "Unemotional objectivity" is frequently reported to be an ideal important to the parents.

> Nevertheless, aside from the indisputably high level of intelligence, the vast majority of the parents of autistic children have features in common which it would be impossible to disregard...
>
> Most of the parents declare outright that they are not comfortable in the company of people; they prefer reading, writing, painting, making music, or just "thinking." Those who speak of themselves as sociable tend to qualify this by explaining that they have no use for ordinary chatter. They are, on the whole, polite and dignified people who are impressed by seriousness and disdainful of anything that smacks of frivolity. (Kanner 1949, p. 421)[1]

The rate of mental illness among the parents and blood relatives of Kanner's first 100 autistic cases was strikingly low, being only 13 out of 973 parents, grandparents, aunts, and uncles (Kanner, 1954a; Kanner & Lesser, 1958). This is in the order of one-third the rate in the general population.

Family life. There were virtually no divorces or separations in Kanner's group of parents. In his 1949 discussion Kanner made the following observations on the marital lives of his first 55 sets of parents:

> They describe themselves and their marital partners as undemonstrative... On the other hand, there are no major animosities. There has been only one separation or divorce of any of the 55 couples. The parents treat each other with faultless respect, talk things over calmly and earnestly, and give to outsiders the impression of mutual loyalty. So far as can be ascertained, there are no extramarital sex relations. One father, ready after much persuasion to yield to the temptations of an amateur actress, suddenly found himself sexually impotent; he went home, told his wife about it, and it was she who, without rancor, asked me for suggestions in a long-distance telephone call. (p. 421)[2]

The view that early infantile autism is wholly or partially "environmentally" determined may be traced in part to observations made by Kanner and others regarding the parents' attitudes toward and treatment of the child:

> Most of the patients were exposed from the beginning to parental coldness, obsessiveness, and a mechanical type of attention to material

---

1   Reprinted with permission of the *Amer. J. Orthopsychiat.* and the author.
2   Reprinted with permission of the *Amer. J. Orthopsychiat.* and the author.

needs only... Their withdrawal seems to be an act of turning away from such a situation to seek comfort in solitude. (Kanner, 1949, p. 425)[3]

The relationship to the child is an interesting one. Paradoxically, despite the "mechanical type of attention": "They (the mothers) were anxious to do a good job, and this meant mechanized service of the kind which is rendered by an overconscientious gasoline station attendant" (Kanner, 1949, p. 424). Pediatricians' instructions were carried out "to the letter."

Kanner has sometimes written of the "refrigerator" type of parent and recently a national magazine reported his view that children with early infantile autism were "the offspring of highly organized, professional parents, cold and rational," who "just happened to defrost long enough to produce a child" (*Time*, July 25, 1960).

But the children were not really unwanted: "It can be said only of several of the children that they were rejected in the sense in which this term is commonly understood. The majority of the children were not unwanted; the pregnancy as such was not unwelcome" (Kanner, 1949, p. 424). The parents had "not even a fleeting thought of abortion" (1954a, p. 383).

Because many writers cite the foregoing data as evidence for psychogenic etiology of the disease, it should be pointed out that unless one is *already* committed to the view that the parental behavior and personalities were not influenced by their own biochemical or neurological natures, one cannot attribute the child's behavior to psycho-social rather than hereditary factors. The evidence supports both views equally well. Often overlooked is the fundamental precept of scientific thought that "correlation does not imply causation."

Bender is one of the writers who questions the accuracy of Kanner's observations:

> It is not clear what he means by saying that there is evidence that autistic children have greater intellectual potentialities, unless he is referring to the family background of his colleagues, professors and intellectual sophisticates who have selected his services. (1959, p. 82)

Kanner has denied this assertion to the present writer, stating that his clientele had come "from the slums" and the "penthouses." Kanner's critics appear to have overlooked Kanner's comparison of the background data on the parents of autistic children with similar data on the parents of non-autistic children consulting him on the same basis:

---

3   Reprinted with permission of the *Amer. J. Orthopsychiat.* and the author.

A control study of the parents of private patients selected solely by virtue of being next in call number to each of the first 50 autistic cases revealed levels of educational attainment and professional status that were considerably lower. In the control group one does not find the dramatically evident detachment, obsessiveness, and coldness that is almost a universal feature of parents of autistic children. (Eisenberg & Kanner, 1956, p. 561)[4]

Actually, the criticism that Kanner's observations about the parents are the product of sampling bias is logically untenable, in addition to being contrary to the evidence. In order for Kanner to have identified one group of parents as unique he must have seen a wide range of types of parents, to permit a contrast. It does not seem likely that Kanner would be so naive that he would single out a group which was actually typical of his clientele. And if there were nonintellectual parents of autistic children, why did they bring only their non-autistic children to Kanner, leaving it only for the highly intellectual parents to bring their autistic children? Kanner has written that he has never met an unintelligent parent of an autistic child. Early infantile autism is far too profound a behavior disturbance to believe that a parent must be highly intellectual to realize his child is ill. Only one-third of autistic children ever reach a "minimal social adjustment."

Undoubtedly there are marked differences in the socio-economic levels of families utilizing the facilities of various child guidance clinics. Suppose Kanner's clinic were indeed to have had a disproportionate number of children from the "sophisticated, intellectual strata" Bender says came to see Kanner. This could account for the fact that Kanner saw a disproportionate number of children with early infantile autism, but it in no way disproves Kanner's assertion that such children come from intellectual families. If true, it would *support* Kanner's qualifications for making the assertion, and disqualify the opinions of those with a less elite clientele.

An interesting corollary to this last point suggests why it is that certain writers have tended to deny the existence of autism, or have equated it with schizophrenia and have denied Kanner's assertions with regard to the parents: due to locational factors or the availability of other facilities, their own clientele has not consisted of a large enough proportion of professional parents for them to have seen many true cases of early infantile autism.

Several writers have commented that the parents of the children reported by Peck, Rabinovitch, and Cramer (1949) differ markedly from the parents Kanner describes. The reason is simple: Peck, Rabinovitch, and Cramer were dealing (as they claimed) with schizophrenic children, not autistic,

---

4   Reprinted with permission of the *Amer. J. Orthopsychiat.* and the author.

as is also evident from the case history material they supply. The problem here is that Kanner's critics have failed to differentiate between childhood schizophrenia and autism, a matter to which the whole of Chapter 4 will be devoted.

Attempting to explain Kanner's observations about the parents by reference to *selective referrals* also involves logical inconsistencies. For one thing, Kanner had referred to the striking preponderance of intellectual forebears in 1943, in presenting his first 11 cases and *before* acquiring a reputation as an expert on autism. Further, very few parents, regardless of intellectuality, are acquainted with the differential expertise of child psychiatrists. It is the family physician or other professional worker who must make the referral. Such a process could hardly begin to account for Kanner's findings.

It has been pointed out that there are many reasons for believing that selective sampling could not account for the level of intellectual and educational endowment observed in these parents. But even if one were to disregard these reasons and attribute the observations to some inexplicable tendency for brighter than average and better educated people to present their autistic children for diagnosis, he would be unable to explain the *extremely high intellectual level* observed in the parents.

The data provided for Kanner's group of parents greatly exceed the educational and occupational levels reported for even the parents of Terman's (1925) highly gifted children who represented the *upper 1 percent* of California's school population. Indeed, in many respects, Kanner's group of parents exceeds the later achievement of Terman's gifted group itself (Terman & Oden, 1947, 1959). Where are the autistic children of the remaining 99 percent of the population?

Parental intelligence. Keeler (1957), who has done as yet unpublished objective research on this problem, reports that his "most detailed appraisal" indicates the parents "...truly do have high IQs...too high to be tested with presently available IQ tests." Kanner states that parents of autistic children are "indisputably intelligent" and "function in society with such distinction that they are often at the top of scientific, artistic, or commercial enterprises" (1954a). He has commented on the "large proportion of parents and grandparents who have appeared in *Who's Who* and have attained considerable distinction in scientific, artistic and literary fields" (1958; with Lesser). Goldstein's (1959) statement that the parents are "especially gifted," the Darr and Worden (1951) father who was an "exceptionally clever engineer" and mother who was "very intelligent," the "highly intelligent" physician discussed by Polan and Spencer (1959), and the engineer of "considerable competence" having a "very superior IQ" described by Ward and Hoddinott (1962) present cases in point. So also does Despert's (1951) "brilliant" minister. The use of adjectives like "indisputably," "especially," "exceptionally," "highly," and "very" to modify words like "intelligent," "gifted," and "clever" suggests we are dealing with unusual people. When it is further considered that these combinations were applied to professions such as "engineer," "physician," and "minister," the conclusion seems inescapable that we are not simply dealing with a random sample of parents astute enough to realize their child is ill, or articulate enough to describe the symptoms. The parents form a unique group.

Parental personality. Further, it is not just intellectuality which distinguishes Kanner's parent group. As Keeler (1957) points out "one does not see the same incidence of the highly intellectual, obsessive, cold, detached parents" among non-autistic children.

Another trait, which might be called "single-minded dedication to purpose," referred to as "conscientiousness" in the Darr and Worden case, is frequently reported among parents of autistic children. It is called "obsessiveness" by the somewhat psychogenically oriented Kanner and the more highly psychogenically oriented Eisenberg. It is amply demonstrated in the numerous case histories of autistic parents and grandparents reported by Kanner and Eisenberg in their various singly and jointly authored papers. Typical cases are of the man who continued to write his book while trapped in a wrecked train tilted 30 degrees from the vertical, and the prominent surgeon who spent practically all his waking hours studying the medical literature and the medical records of the people on whom he was to operate. When one of his sons turned out to be autistic, parental neglect was held to be responsible (Eisenberg, 1957).

A number of non-genetic explanations have been advanced for the unusual parental personalities. Two writers (Bruch, 1959; Gellner, 1959) have observed that the findings with regard to the parents may be, at least in part, a function of the ability of the more intellectual parents to describe the symptoms. This may be a factor, but it would not begin to account for the uniqueness and consistency of the findings. Goldstein (1959), who disagrees with Kanner on the nature of autism, makes a related point when he says that the parents tend to be especially gifted persons, who, because of their own high intelligence, may become overly interested in the intellectual capacities of the infant with a concomitant reduction in the "immediate relationship" between mother and infant. He does not believe this accounts for the disease, however.

Many writers, Eisenberg and Kanner (1956) among them, have observed that the non-intellectual aspects of the parents' personalities may be aggravated by the non-responsiveness of the child. It has also been recognized that the parents, perceiving that the psychiatrist regards them as having caused autism in the child, appear more cold and hostile to the psychiatrist than they otherwise would. But why do these reasons apply only to the parents of children with infantile autism?

The pre-1943 cases of autism. Perhaps the strongest support for Kanner's position comes from the highly confirmatory data accompanying the cases not known to him which preceded his original paper in 1943.

The five-year-old boy described by Haslam in 1809 appears to have been autistic, although he had had a severe case of measles which may or may not have resulted in the autism. On applying the Polan and Spencer Check List to Haslam's data, Vaillant (1962) was able to find 17 points of similarity with Kanner's cases. Some of the information given seems highly indicative of autism, such as lack of affect, ability to reproduce music accurately, and, especially, use of third rather than first person in speech. In view of the very low ratio of intellectual to manual workers in 1809 as compared to today, it seems of particular significance that the boy's mother was not only a historian, but "a careful historian."

Little information is provided about the background of Witmer's case (1920), probably one of infantile autism. What information is available (there being reference to a nurse, a vacation at the seashore, and a gardener) would support at least the idea of high socio-economic status.

The case reported by Meyer and Richards in 1921 was followed up and reported in detail by Darr and Worden in 1951 (see also Kanner's discussion following the case presentation). The case is clearly one of a girl afflicted with infantile autism. The description of the parents, written in 1921, confirms Kanner strikingly, almost word for word. The father was "an exceptionally clever engineer" and the mother was "conscientious" and "very intelligent." Both parents were "extremely active" in organizational work. Thus Kanner has antedated support in terms of parental intelligence, personality (if "conscientiousness" can be equated with the more psychogenically oriented terms like "compulsive'" and "obsessive") and with regard to high drive or activity level.

Despert has made a distinction between childhood psychoses of "acute" and "insidious" onset which is commonly regarded as at least approximating the distinction between childhood schizophrenia and infantile autism. The former is characterized by a period of normal behavior prior to affliction, while Kanner specifies autism as starting "at the beginning of life." The correspondence between autism and "psychoses of insidious onset" will not be perfect, as should be evident from Chapter 1, but it is instructive to consider Despert's findings.

In 1938, prior to Kanner's delineation of autism and its concomitant parental personality pattern, Despert presented several case histories relating to age and acuteness of onset. Of two cases of acute onset (probably schizophrenia), one set of parents were said to be in good economic condition, and one father was a newspaper manager. In one of the two cases of insidious onset, the psychosis did not start until nine years of age, which precludes a diagnosis of autism. This boy's father was a retail milk dealer.

The other case (case HL) of insidious onset, however, seems very much like one of autism. The patient was described as walking and talking before he was two; he knew many difficult words early; never seemed to be interested in conveying a thought, but mainly in learning to spell; was restless and asocial as early as 18 months; showed almost complete withdrawal; had an obsessive preoccupation with figures; and spoke in the third person. This was the only child in the group whose psychosis started early, who showed the autistic language symptoms and any form of *idiot savant* behavior and who was apparently not hallucinative. His father was a Ph.D., a professor of chemistry.

In 1947 Despert described another group of "schizophrenic" children, classified into "acute" and "insidious" onset. Although this paper was published several years after Kanner first described autism, her paper does not mention Kanner and it seems safe to assume that her report was not influenced by Kanner's prior work. The following data were provided on the parents:

Insidious onset: Case 1. Father successful business man, mother compulsive; Case 4. Father brilliant writer and public speaker, mother cold and unemotional; Case 5. Both parents brilliant; Case 7. No mention of the intellectual status, father described as immature, mother as insecure.

Acute onset: Case 2. Father is airplane pilot, mother tense; Case 3. Nothing about father, mother moody; Case 6. Both parents limited intelligence and of constricted interests.

All four of the children with insidious onset were interested in music, incidentally. Case 1 had "an extraordinary knowledge of recorded music," Cases 4 and 5 were each considered "a musical genius," and Case 7 knew "an extensive repertoire of popular and classical music."

A case of autism was described by C. Bradley (1943) which appeared at the same time as Kanner's initial description of autism. Bradley's paper did not refer to Kanner, and no reference to this case appears in Kanner's works until the third edition of Kanner's textbook, Child Psychiatry (1957). Bradley's case presentation supported Kanner's observations to the letter when he described the father of his case, a draftsman with training in architecture, as an "intelligent and educated man," with an "objective" viewpoint, whose "integrity (was) beyond question," and who had kept a detailed diary about his daughter for many years. The mother was a librarian. The child was raised in excellent surroundings, and there were neither family problems nor a history of mental disorders.

Bradley's mention of the father's detailed diary is especially interesting. Kanner has noted that autistic children are frequently accompanied by a detailed case history, and that this was true of no other type of child disorder. Kanner has called these histories a "veritable boon" in studying the cases (1949). The parents of his first case had prepared a 33-page typewritten history. Van Krevelen's first case was also accompanied by a detailed case history written by an intelligent, perfectionistic father, and van Krevelen regarded this as a remarkably rare occurrence. Eisenberg has been "repeatedly impressed with the almost uncanny objectiveness and obsessive accuracy of parents of autistic children" (1956, p. 607).

Parental descriptions post-1943. The cases of autism described in the literature after Kanner's first paper, like those which appeared earlier, are virtually unanimous in their support of Kanner's findings with regard to the high intelligence and cold, reserved, and efficient personalities of the parents.

Scheerer, Rothmann, and Goldstein's case "L." (1947), an *idiot savant* described as resembling Kanner's cases, was reported to have had intellectual progenitors for several generations, much like many of the cases described in Kanner's various works. One grandfather was "erudite," the other "a person of culture." An uncle is said to have a great gift for manipulating numbers. "L.'s" father, described as a businessman, "is also very quick in calculation." The mother, like the mother in the Darr–Worden case, was "a former school teacher of considerable intelligence." She, again like the Darr–Worden mother and the mother described by Bruch (1959), devoted much of her time to trying to educate the child.

Like Scheerer, Rothmann, and Goldstein's case "L.," Hans, described by Waal (1955), was a first-born male from a gifted family. A grandfather was described as very gifted. Hans' father was a freelance writer and his mother, again like "L.'s," a former school teacher.

Despert's case (1951) also resembles the Darr and Worden case in that both parents fit Kanner's description perfectly. In the case Despert described with Sherwin (1958) the mother was a "successful business woman," and "an active, aggressive woman" but the father was a "passive, good-natured business man." Keeler's (1957) highly intelligent electrical engineer father remarked that the child had received a "double dose" from both parents. The case report by Anastasi and Levee (1960) refers to a home of very high socio-economic level and to the parents as college graduates. The father was a "well-to-do-manufacturer." Jacques May, the father of autistic twins whose book *A Physician Looks at Psychiatry* has been referred to earlier, is a world-renowned medical ecologist and writer. An autistic boy referred to by Anthony (1958) was the son of a statistician. The "quiet and serious lawyer" and the "compulsive, highly intelligent" physician, described by Polan and Spencer (1959) both perfectly fit the prototype of the parent of the autistic child.

The father of the case described by Eveloff (1960) had gone to college and was the son of a physician. Lewis and Van Ferney (1960) described the father of an autistic child who was a rigid and meticulous college graduate.

Of unusual interest is the case described by G. Arnold (1960), a first-born male Negro. The father is a plater by day, attends music school three nights a week, and plays in a band on weekends. The mother is a high school graduate and "appears intelligent." (Census figures show that only some 20% of Negroes are high school graduates, a figure roughly comparable to the 14% college graduates among whites.)

Also of unusual interest is the apparently classical case of autism described by Oppenheim (1961).[5] The boy, her son, is a handsome first-born child, who at first appeared to be precocious and musically gifted. The parents describe themselves as reserved. The father is a self-employed accountant and the mother, judging from the article, has literary talent. The trait variously described as "conscientiousness," "single-mindedness," or "obsessiveness" appears here not only in the unusual persistence of the parents to find help for their son, but also in the mother's statement that she makes twice-a-week 320-mile round trips to the Purdue University clinic with her son and has been doing this for some 18 months.

Cunningham and Dixon (1961) described as a case of infantile autism a boy whose father was a "busy professional man" and whose mother was

---

5 Oppenheim has written the present author that she is not sure of the actual diagnosis of her son. One mother of an autistic girl (and the wife of a physician, incidentally), who has told the writer that she knew nothing about autism until seeing the Oppenheim article in a national magazine, said, "The description was so much like R—I nearly flipped!"

"intelligent." The mother described the boy as responsive until the age of two, however, which is not typical in autism.

The twin girls described as "typical examples of early infantile autism" by Ward and Hoddinott (1962) have a mother whose IQ falls "in the bright, normal grouping, while the father falls in the very superior range." The father has a responsible position in television production and research and impresses as a man of "considerable competence."

A number of European writers have also described cases of autism which contain descriptions of the parents. We have already referred to the four-year-old girl van Krevelen (1952b) described as being as much like Kanner's cases as "one raindrop resembles another" and who had an "intelligent, perfectionist" father. The father did possess "sufficient warmth of personality" and the "warm, intelligent mother" was deeply concerned about the child. One of Stern and Schachter's cases (1953) was the son of highly educated parents. The other was the daughter of parents of apparently normal intelligence. Popella's Case 1 (1955) was the son in a miner's family, with no family background of mental illness. His Case 2 was the daughter of a "very reserved cool-headed, critical thinking" teacher in a technical institute, and a "cool, egoistic" mother. Plenter's case (1955) was the daughter of an extremely intelligent mother, reserved but friendly, and a very affable father who was not intellectually gifted but was highly talented in art and music. The father of Schachter's case (1958) was described as an intelligent man whose plans for college had been interrupted by the war. The mother had completed two years of college work in philosophy and literature. The marriage was described as happy and the parents were devoted to the children.

Rather surprising support for Kanner's findings on the parental personalities comes from Bettelheim (1959b), who, as a rather extreme representative of the psychogenic school of thought, would not ordinarily be expected to regard the childhood psychoses as being differentiable (Kanner, 1958a, 1958b). Bettelheim wrote that the majority of the 19 cases of autism he has seen are from highly intelligent families, but that some are not. Despite his agreement with our argument, it should be noted that Bettelheim's definition of autism, as demonstrated in his writings, is not entirely identical to that of Kanner and the present writer.

Additional data on a plurality of cases comes from van Krevelen (1963), who lists as the occupations of the ten European cases he has seen: elementary school teacher, constructional engineer, clerk, industrial lawyer, civil servant, horticulturist, government official, florist salesman, police sergeant. It should be noted that, because of lower social mobility in Europe than in the United States, there is probably a lower correlation between intellectuality and occupational level. Nevertheless, van Krevelen's data clearly support Kanner's.

Van Krevelen (1960) has also described a boy diagnosed as autistic by others whose father was "a captain of industry." Van Krevelen does not regard this case as being truly autistic because there was evidence of earlier encephalitis, including EEG abnormality (1960, 1963). Kanner (1949) has stated that none of his cases has had a history of any physical trauma or infection to which the disorder might be traced. The present writer is nevertheless not convinced that van Krevelen's insistence on an absence of organic evidence is optimal. Of the 28 of Kanner's first 100 cases for whom EEGs were available, there were three definitely abnormal and four equivocal records, in addition to 21 negative cases. This does not differ from the 10 to 20 percent rate of abnormality which may be expected in a clinically normal group of children. Similarly, one must expect that some autistic children, like some normal children, will have a history of one or more high fevers or other suspect incidents. It is probably best to leave this question open at the present time. This and similar problems can be better attacked when an adequate body of quantitative data on a symptom and background check list becomes available for statistical analysis of symptom clustering.

Exceptions and questionable cases. It is of interest, however, that the few exceptions in the literature to the picture Kanner has painted of the parents have occurred where there are definite reasons to suspect fairly overt postnatal brain damage. Chapman (1957) and Bruch (1959) present cases where the parents were described as non-intellectual, and Bakwin (1954) presents a case where the father was merely described as a salesman. In all three cases the autistic children were identical twins placed under oxygen in infancy. We will return to this point later.

Haslam's case (Vaillant, 1962) whose mother was a historian; the Putnam case (1948), whose father was a successful businessman; Popella's case (1955), whose father was a teacher; and the Anastasi and Levee case (1960), whose parents were well-to-do college graduates, had all suffered severe infections early in life. The girl described by Sutton and Read (1958) as "bordering" on autism, and whose father was a physician, had an abnormal amino acid metabolism. The May twins (1958), whose father is a physician and medical ecologist, had also been placed under oxygen soon after birth. These cases are examples of known organic factors coupled with parental intelligence. One can but wonder in these six instances about the roles these factors might have played in the genesis of the child's disorder. Was the parental intelligence related to cause or was it incidental?

While the number of source publications to be covered is too large to permit a confident claim for comprehensiveness, it is the writer's belief that the great majority of the cases published in the American–European literature bearing descriptions of the parents of autistic children have been included in this chapter. Such coverage was attempted, and no case has been intentionally omitted.

Despite the presence of the few borderline cases in the preceding paragraphs in which the diagnosis and cause are blurred, the evidence overwhelmingly supports Kanner's unprecedented early report that the parents of autistic children form a unique and highly homogeneous group in terms of intellect and personality.

PARENT OCCUPATIONS

Stephen M. Edelson

In Chapter 2, titled "The Parents of Autistic Children," Rimland reviewed Leo Kanner's descriptive writings about parents as well as writings by other investigators. At the end of the chapter, Rimland concluded, "...the parents of autistic children form a unique and highly homogeneous group in terms of intellect and personality."

Although there has been only a limited amount of research on the intellect and personality traits of parents of children on the spectrum, research has indicated a higher rate of college education than in the general population (Van Meter et al., 2010) and an overrepresentation of engineers among fathers (Baron-Cohen et al., 1997). In addition, parents often experience more stress than the general population (Ornstein Davis & Carter, 2008); however, this is often attributed to the challenges of raising a child on the spectrum.

Dr. Rimland believed that there was a genetic component to autism. Many studies indicate that parents of children on the spectrum may have similar but not as pronounced autistic traits in several domains.

Cognition. Briskman, Frith, and Happe (2001) found that some parents of children on the spectrum exhibited a preference for nonsocial events and processed information in a manner similar to their children.

Language. Landa et al. (1992) found that parents of children with autism differed from other parents in their use of pragmatics (use of social language). Similar to individuals on the spectrum, these parents exhibited differences in three areas: disinhibited social communication, awkward/ inadequate expression, and odd verbal interaction.

Sensory. Mothers of children on the spectrum had atypical reactions to sensory stimuli (Uljarevic, Prior, & Leekam, 2014).

Social cognition. Similar to many people with autism, parents of children on the spectrum used different strategies than the general population for recognizing faces (Adolphs et al., 2008; Dawson et al., 2005), implying an impairment in social cognition.

Given the heterogeneity of the autism spectrum, it would not be appropriate to generalize these findings to all parents with children on the spectrum.

REFERENCES

Adolphs, R., Spezio, M.L., Parlier, M., & Piven, J. (2008). Distinct face-processing strategies in parents of autistic children. *Current Biology,* 18(14), 1090–1093.

Baron-Cohen, S., Wheelwright, S., Stott, C., Bolton, P., & Goodyer, I. (1997). Is there a link between engineering and autism? *Autism,* 1(1), 101–109.

Briskman, J., Frith, U., & Happe, F. (2001). Exploring the cognitive phenotype of autism: Weak "central coherence" in parents and siblings of children with autism: II. Real-life skills and preferences. *Journal of Child Psychology and Psychiatry,* 42(3), 309–316.

Dawson, G., Webb, S.J., Wijsman, E., Schellenberg, G., et al. (2005). Neurocognitive and electrophysiological evidence of altered face processing in parents of children with autism: Implications for a model of abnormal development of social brain circuitry in autism. *Developmental and Psychopathology,* 17(3), 679–697.

Landa, R., Piven, J., Wzorek, M.M., Gayle, J.O., Chase, G.A., & Folstein, S.E. (1992). Social language use in parents of autistic individuals. *Psychological Medicine,* 22(1), 245–254.

Ornstein Davis, N., & Carter, A.S. (2008). Parenting stress in mothers and fathers of toddlers with autism spectrum disorders: Associations with child characteristics. *Journal of Autism and Developmental Disorders,* 38, 1278–1291.

Uljarevic, M., Prior, M.R., & Leekam, S.R. (2014). First evidence of sensory atypicality in mothers of children with Autism Spectrum Disorder (ASD). *Molecular Autism,* 5(1), 26.

Van Meter, K.C., Christiansen, L.E., Delwiche, L.D., Azari, R., Carpenter, T.E., & Hertz-Picciotto, I. (2010). Geographic distribution of autism in California: A retrospective birth cohort analysis. *Autism Research,* 3(1), 19–29.

INTRODUCTION TO CHAPTER 3
Stephen M. Edelson

One could easily argue that Chapter 3 was the backbone of *Infantile Autism* as well as the beginning of the revelation for many that autism had an organic rather than a psychological etiology.

One major contribution from this chapter is Rimland's meta-analysis of previously published twin studies exploring the role of genetics in autism. Based on his calculations, Rimland was one of the first, if not the first, to conclude that there is a genetic contribution to autism. His conclusion was based on the high incidence of autism in monozygotic (identical) twins and a relatively low incidence in dizygotic (fraternal) twins.

In the decades since the publication of the book, thousands of published research studies in the areas of genetics, neurology, and biochemistry have documented numerous physiological impairments in those on the autism spectrum. In addition, comorbid medical problems, such as gastrointestinal, immune, and metabolic problems, have been well documented (see Amaral, Geschwind, & Dawson, 2011). However, the nature of the relationship between these medical problems and autism remains to be elucidated.

REFERENCE
Amaral, D., Geschwind, D., & Dawson, G. (eds, 2011). Autism Spectrum Disorders. New York: Oxford University Press.

CHAPTER 3

The Etiology of
Infantile Autism

*The Problem of Biological versus
Psychological Causation*

In the previous chapter we have presented what appears to the present writer to be incontestable support for Kanner's finding of unusual personality–intelligence configurations in the parents of children with early infantile autism. Many who have written on the problem of autism regard this finding as evidence for psychogenic etiology of the disease. This appears to be a plausible hypothesis and so should be subjected to critical evaluation to determine if it merits acceptance. Unfortunately, plausibility rather than consistency with evidence seems to be the criterion for many of the writers on early infantile autism. Consequently the hypothesis has been accepted without evaluation, and the literature on autism contains many papers in which it is asserted rather than suggested that psychogenic factors play a major part in the etiology of the disease. Indeed, a substantial proportion of these papers carry no indication that biological factors may play even a minor part in the disease.

This chapter will be devoted to a detailed consideration of the problem of the etiology of infantile autism. The present writer disagrees with Eisenberg and Kanner's assertion that "Arguments that counterpose 'hereditary' versus 'environmental' as antithetical terms are fundamentally in error. Operationally defined, they are interpenetrating concepts" (1956, p. 563). That heredity and environment are "interpenetrating" cannot be denied. But the conclusion that their interpenetration precludes analysis does not follow. Complex problems require that we *increase*, not diminish our analytical efforts, if we are to have hope of solving the problems confronting us (Burt, 1958; Cattell, 1960).

There are several reasons for drawing close attention to the consideration of etiology in infantile autism. These are, in order of increasing generality:

1. The welfare of individual autistic children and their families hinges closely upon the problem of specific etiology, as van Krevelen has amply demonstrated (e.g., 1958, 1960). If the disease is psychogenic, the causative factors need to be identified. On the other hand, if autism is determined solely by organic factors, there is no need for the parents of these children to suffer the shame, guilt, inconvenience, financial expense, and marital discord which so often accompany the assumption of psychogenic etiology. (For examples of this, see May, 1958 and Peck, Rabinovitch, & Cramer, 1949. Oppenheim, 1961 and Stuart, 1960 are also germane.)

2. So long as the practitioners who actually deal with autistic children feel satisfied that the disease is largely or entirely psychogenic, biologically trained research workers will feel disinclined to concentrate their efforts on the problem. It should be added at this point, in all frankness, that while the purpose of the review which follows was to investigate the specific etiology of early infantile autism, the issue is a broad one and a good deal of the material covered relates closely to the problem of causation of childhood behavioral disorders in general. The results of this work were surprising to the present writer and discordant with his previous beliefs. They may also be so to the reader. It is largely because of the large discrepancy between research findings and the remainder of the published literature that such detailed consideration is given the problem of etiology in this chapter.

Failing to find any adequate formulations of many of the inexplicit assumptions on both sides of the issue, the writer has attempted to articulate these, in his belief that a good part of the unique function of the psychologist is to try to articulate what seems ineffable.[1] No doubt much of this formulation will be challenged, and additional points will need to be added to those listed. We can do no better on this issue than to refer to Bacon's assertion that truth is more likely to emerge from error than from confusion.

3. There is yet another reason, one of considerable theoretical importance to psychology and psychiatry, for giving careful and reasoned attention to the etiology of early infantile autism. Sufficient evidence pointing toward a very unique and specific personality–intellectual configuration in

---

1 There are certain arguments, however, which defy our attempt to reformulate them in any testable way: "I believe that the child who shows autistic behavior has been traumatized in the early months of life since he symbolizes to the mother so definitely the hated sibling" (Ribble, in discussion of Despert, 1951, p. 350).

the parents of children having early infantile autism has been adduced to permit little doubt of the accuracy of Kanner's original observations on this point. If it should turn out that early infantile autism is biologically—not psychologically—determined, then the only logical way of accounting for the parents' unusual personalities and intelligence is biologically. This would mean that basic personality structure may, in at least some cases, be far more closely tied to the biological makeup of the individual than has heretofore been realized. Unless autism can be shown to be largely psychogenic in origin, or the evidence presented by Kanner and others concerning the parents can be disqualified, the conventional view that heredity must invariably act only in general and unspecific ways as a determinant of human behavior must be reconsidered.

This point appears to have escaped most writers in the field. Kanner, while he has not emphasized the implications of his finding, does refer to "the astounding fact" that his "search for autistic children of unsophisticated parents" had remained unsuccessful (1949, p. 421) and the "remarkable" absence of mental disorders in the children's parents and relatives.

Fuller and Thompson (1960) explain in their book *Behavior Genetics* that they hold Eysenck's work on the introvert–extrovert factor to be of great importance because "Here is a clear-cut case of a basic variable of temperament, relating to both personality and learning ability, that is strongly dependent on genetic factors. More work along these lines will undoubtedly be of great value" (p. 241). Because the study of infantile autism may lead to even more striking findings, it seems essential that close and thorough examination of the etiology of infantile autism be undertaken.

A. THE ARGUMENTS FOR PSYCHOGENESIS OF INFANTILE AUTISM

The case for psychogenesis of autism would appear to rest on the following arguments and assumptions:

1. No consistent physical or neurological abnormalities have been found in autistic children which could account for their condition.

2. Many autistic children have been raised by parents apparently deficient in emotional responsiveness, which could have pathogenic effects on the child.

3. Certain children raised in hospitals or orphanages where maternal contact was sparse have been reported to show an undue frequency of emotional difficulties.

4. The behaviors of the child—his indifference or aggressiveness, his refusal to speak (or "elective mutism"), his apparent withdrawal from the outside world—are interpreted as signs of "punishment" or "retaliation" against the parents.

5. Certain incidents in the life of the autistic child appear to be pathogenic and permit the disorder to be traced to them.

6. Psychotherapy or otherwise placing the child in a kind and understanding environment has beneficial effects.

7. The high incidence of first-born and only children suggests that parental attitudes may be causative.

Let us consider these points in turn:

1. *The absence of signs of organic impairment.* While the presence of physical symptoms is ordinarily regarded as conclusive proof of organicity, as in mongolism or phenylketonuria, the absence of such symptoms cannot be considered indicative of functional determination. This is so because "Neurological science thus far has been quite unable to furnish an adequate description of the neural processes involved in even the very simplest forms of mental activity" (Sperry, 1952, p. 292). Eisenberg and Kanner have said of autism, "...neurologic investigations of the integrity of central function remain as yet in their clinical infancy and a negative result with current methods cannot be regarded as a conclusive demonstration of the lack of central nervous system pathology" (1956, p. 560).

There are numerous cases in the literature where even gross brain disease which eventually caused the death of the child had escaped intensive repeated neurological examination and was found only post-mortem (e.g., Ross, 1959). Helier's disease and phenylketonuria were both considered "functional" childhood psychoses until their organicity was determined (Benda, 1960; Kanner, 1949). Nevertheless writers such as Despert (1947) and Bettelheim (1959b) have written that the possibility of organic damage in the cases they cite was "ruled out" by physical and neurological examination. May (1958) and van Krevelen (1960) have cited cases in which the possibility of organic damage was ruled out without even examining the children.

2. *Parental personalities.* Eisenberg and Kanner are among the many writers who subscribe to the notion that parental behavior is a factor in producing autism in the child, although, unlike many others, they are careful to qualify their position:

It is difficult to escape the conclusion that this emotional configuration in the home plays a dynamic role in the genesis of autism. But it seems to us equally clear that this factor, while important in the development of the syndrome, is not sufficient in itself to result in its appearance. There appears to be some way in which the children are different from the beginning of their extrauterine existence. (1956, p. 563)[2]

Kanner and Eisenberg do not specify *why* it is hard to escape the conclusion. They cite no supporting evidence. Plausible as the hypothesis may seem, there is no reason for accepting it in favor of competing hypotheses. This is a clear case of subscription to the fallacies that *post hoc ergo propter hoc*, and that "correlation implies causation."

How can one say that both the child's and the parent's behavior are not related consequences of the same genetic factors? The high incidence of the detached, over-objective personality in the children's parents is consistent with *both* the psychogenic and the biogenic views and thus cannot justifiably be used to support even the middle-ground position that hereditary *and* psychogenic factors contribute to early infantile autism. Granted, it may be *possible* that psychological factors contribute, but it has not yet been demonstrated that they do, to even a minor extent; nor has it been demonstrated that any familial environment, no matter how favorable, would have prevented the emergence of the disease.

There appears to be an implicit assumption that the uniqueness of the parental personalities constitutes evidence only for the "environmental" side of the controversy. It is apparently assumed that the parental personalities are *too specific* to be biologically determined, and must therefore themselves be environmentally determined and not capable of being transmitted genetically. Aside from the fact that this point of view begs the question of how personality is acquired, it appears to carry with it the unwarranted further assumption that the biological point of view must presuppose an impossibly complex "preprogrammed" nervous system to account for the parents' highly consistent and predictable personalities.

Actually, the biological view of autism need invoke no such complex mechanism. A very simply heritable mechanism can be postulated which could account for the parental behavior; and, were this mechanism to be impaired, for the autistic child's behavior as well. A mechanism very like the one to be proposed has already been suggested by other writers in a context which will be shown in Part III of this monograph to bear an interesting relationship to the problem of early infantile autism.

---

2   Reprinted with permission of *Amer. J. Orthopsychiat.* and the authors.

Perhaps it is in relation to the "parental personalities" that reference should be made to the recent work on "affectional systems" in monkeys (e.g., Harlow & Harlow, 1962a, 1962b). These points appear to be most relevant: The behavior of infant monkeys is relatively independent of the personality (or response repertoire) of the mother. Infant monkeys raised by cruel, rejecting, unsympathetic, and indifferent mothers reacted not by "autistic" withdrawal but by persistent and vigorous attempts to obtain the mother's attention. Even infant monkeys brutally beaten by mothers attempting to discourage contact showed no signs of maladjustment. Infant monkeys raised only with inanimate cloth-covered "mother surrogate" effigies showed no signs of maladjustment until adulthood, when their sexual functioning was found to be severely impaired.

The only way in which any of Harlow's infant monkeys could be treated to cause them to simulate "autistic" withdrawal was through total social deprivation for extended periods. But even 20 minutes a day of contact with other infant monkeys seemed sufficient to produce normal development.

With regard to the problem of absence of maternal contact, as differentiated from the nature of those with whom the subject is in contact, there is ample evidence at the human infant level.

3. *Maternal deprivation and hospitalism.* The works of Goldfarb, Spitz, Ribble, Bowlby, and others on the syndrome of "hospitalism" or "maternal deprivation" are frequently cited as analogous evidence that early infantile autism is psychogenic. The analogy with autism is a poor one, since the symptoms which characterize these infants do not resemble autism, as noted by Eisenberg and Kanner (1956), Keeler (1957), and others, and do not begin to approach autism in severity. Additionally, the special circumstances relating to the sampling and physical environment of these maternally deprived infants make them a poor basis on which to construct a psychogenic theory.

In 1951 Bowlby wrote that there was "no room for doubt...the prolonged deprivation of the young child of maternal care may have grave and far-reaching effects on his character..." (p. 46).

Despite Bowlby's assurance on the matter, psychologists have been very skeptical and critical of the hypothesis. The hospitalism studies have been subjected to criticisms of the gravest nature. Pinneau (1955), who earlier pointed out severe deficiencies in the work of Ribble in this area, has also called attention to what appear to be disqualifying errors in the work of Spitz and Fischer. Pinneau notes, to cite one example, that of the 59-point drop in the Development Quotient Spitz reported for his "maternally deprived" group of infants, 55 points were lost *prior* to the time at which most of the children were separated from their mothers! Stevenson (1957) has observed that the screened-off cribs Spitz has described may have resulted in the infants being deprived of adequate physical sensory stimulation, rather than of maternal affection.

With regard to Fischer's study of hospitalism, Pinneau noted that Fischer selected for study, at a home for unwed mothers, those infants with IQs under 90. Then, after observing their behavior in much the same way as is done in arriving at IQ scores for infants, she concluded that their poor performance was due to "hospitalism"!

Pasamanick and Knobloch have recently noted that the maternal deprivation hypothesis may turn out to be simply another instance of misdirection by the "*post hoc ergo propter hoc*" fallacy:

> Further, since a large number of children exhibit no significant difficulties after hospitalization, we must consider the possibility that it may be largely those children having some brain injury, with a consequent lowering of thresholds to stress, who are affected by hospitalization during infancy. (1961, p. 87)

They also note that a number of the hospitalized children included in Goldfarb's study were grossly defective or brain-damaged and suggest that this was why the children remained hospitalized rather than being placed in foster homes. This could readily account for the so-called "symptoms of hospitalism."

Faced with a rising tide of evidence disconfirming the maternal deprivation hypothesis from both his own subsequent work and the reports of other investigators, *Bowlby reversed his stand*. In 1956 he concluded that some of the workers who drew attention to the dangers of deprivation, including himself, had tended to "overstate their case." "In particular, statements implying that children who experience institutionalization... early in life commonly develop psychopathic or affectionless characters are incorrect" (Bowlby, Ainsworth, Boston, & Rosenbluth, 1956, p. 242). He noted that "only a small minority develop those very severe disabilities of personality which first drew attention to the pathogenic nature of the experiences" (p. 240).

Inasmuch as a small minority of any group of infants will show personality disorders, especially if they had been selected because of adverse circumstances surrounding pregnancy or birth, it does not seem that the proponents of the psychogenic view may look to the maternal deprivation hypothesis for support.

Actually, our attention to the maternal deprivation studies results not from their actual relevance to the problem of etiology of autism, but only from their having frequently been cited as analogous evidence favoring psychogenesis of autism. In actuality, the case history materials supplied by Kanner and others show very little reason for believing the children were neglected. Kanner observes that very few of the children were at least overtly rejected (1949). The mothers "were anxious to do a good job," and they performed like "overconscientious gasoline station attendants." The mother of Donald T, Kanner's first case of autism, for instance, tried to help her son by spending "all her time developing ways of keeping him at play with her" (1943, p. 217). The verbal behavior of the children is also suggestive of a good deal of contact with adults.

Bowlby's original statement that there was "no room for doubt" about the adverse effects of maternal deprivation is very similar to a statement made with equal assurance more than half a century before by the noted Langdon Down (Down, 1887, p. 89)—except that Down was sure that the *opposite* conclusion was correct—maternal emotionality causes idiocy!

4. *Child's behavior as suggestive of etiology.* Many writers consider the child's hostility or indifference to his parents as evidence that the parents are guilty of causing the disease. Noting that many autistic children were exposed to parental "coldness, obsessiveness, and a mechanical type of attention," Kanner observed that the children's "withdrawal seems to be an act of turning away from such a situation" (1949, p. 425). Elsewhere Kanner uses the term "retaliation." Others also have written in this vein.

It would seem more reasonable to regard the child's actions as *symptoms*, not as indications of etiology. In the case of the adult who insists that he is being persecuted by the Communists, the F.B.I., or by little green men from Mars, one does not take his statements at face value but only as an indication that he is ill. Unless there is reason for believing otherwise, it seems best also to regard the autistic child's symptoms solely as symptoms, even if "...the patient acts as if his mother is the source of his psychotic fears, and he attributes the potentiality of the same responses onto other humans" (Weiland & Rudnik, 1961, p. 552).

Does "elective mutism" really represent the child's *refusal* to speak? One cannot conclude this unless one is willing also to conclude that adult aphasics who are virtually mute until an emergency arises (Brain, 1960, p. 180) also had "elected" their disability.

Is the fact that many autistic children ignore humans and are interested solely in objects indicative only of some sort of "willful" rejection of mankind, or can this result from organic pathology? Nielsen (1951, p. 185ff.) describes a fully conscious patient who, after occipital lobe damage, was apparently blind with respect to "animate" objects, including the surgeon's fingers, a doll, and her own artificial teeth, but had no trouble in perceiving non-living objects. Another patient could perceive *only* animate objects after occipital and temporal lobe damage. Autos and mountains were not recognized, but flowers and an animal grazing near the autos were readily identified.

Nor does it seem to be widely appreciated that brain pathology can influence affection as well as cognition. Those who believe that an autistic child's behavior represents withdrawal from his parents should also believe, it would seem, that the sweet disposition and loving nature that is almost universal among mongoloid children stems from the pleasure the parents of these children must experience on viewing their offsprings' malady.

5. *Pathogenic incidents.* Many discussions of etiology of autism refer to certain specific events which are said to be traumatic to the child and thus causative of his disorder. The birth of a sibling, a stay in the hospital, the absence of one or both parents are examples of the incidents cited.

That such incidents can produce disorder has not been demonstrated. Many infants and children suffer exceedingly traumatic lives with no evidence of autism or other disorder, while some autistic children have backgrounds free of at least obvious pathogenic incidents.

Renaud and Estess (1961) have published a study of the "pathogenic incidents of childhood" as derived from intensive interviews with 100 above-average young men (military officers). Renaud and Estess discovered, to their considerable surprise, that there was just as much material of a supposedly "pathogenic" sort in the childhoods of these men as would have been expected in a clinically abnormal group. The implications of this finding are clear.

Stevenson (1957) explored the literature relevant to the proposition that personality is "plastic" in infancy and came to the conclusion that "If the experiences of childhood importantly influence the later personality, we should expect to find some correlation between such experiences and the later occurrence of mental disorders. In fact, no such correlations have ever been shown" (p. 153).

6. *Psychotherapy.* Indirect support for the psychogenic hypothesis is often inferred by writers who point to the improvement wrought through psychotherapy or by other means of modifying the child's social environment. As Kuten and Kuten (1958) point out, such evidence for psychogenesis typically comes from writers who cite only very small numbers of cases. Control groups are not used.

Kanner has discussed the results of psychotherapy for the first 42 of his cases with infantile autism, and has observed that: "29 did not get anywhere," including some who had "what is regarded as good psychotherapy." On the other hand, the 13 who recovered sufficiently to go to school "are children who have not had anything that is regarded as good psychotherapy or as psychotherapy at all..." (1954b, p. 471).

It might be argued that Kanner's group is too small to provide conclusive evidence that psychotherapy is ineffective in infantile autism, but, taken in aggregate, the evidence relating to the efficacy of psychotherapy in childhood (or adulthood, for that matter) is generally quite negative and thus lends no support for the psychogenic hypothesis (Astin, 1961; Eysenck, 1961; Hood-Williams, 1960; Levitt, 1957, 1960).

It should be noted that the force of this argument does not rest on the adequacy of the studies of the utility of psychotherapy, since it is not asserted here that the efficacy of psychotherapy has been disproven, but only that it is unproven.

In the absence of evidence that psychotherapy produces improvement in excess of base rate, writers who cite improvement in individual case studies as evidence that autism was psychogenically induced are taking an untenable position. This untenability is underlined by the further point that even if psychotherapy *could* be proven to be effective, it could not be taken as indicative of psychogenic causation any more than the efficacy of oxygen in heart failure proves that the heart failure was caused by a lack of oxygen.

7. *Birth order.* The high frequency of the first-born with autism is sometimes taken as evidence of psychogenicity. There are two obvious objections to this line of reasoning. First, there are many children with autism who have both younger and older normal siblings. Second, a high frequency of first-borns is also consistent with organic causation, since there are many physical disorders associated with primogeniture, especially in male infants. Pyloric stenosis, a digestive system disorder which becomes evident shortly after birth, has long been known to occur primarily in first-born male infants.

Among specific conditions having "mental" involvement, mongolism and anencephaly are reported to be disproportionately represented among the first-born (MacMahon & Sowa, 1961; Stott, 1960) as is epilepsy (Colver & Kerridge, 1962).

Studies which have attempted to relate birth order to parental behaviors and attitudes have far more often produced negative than positive results (Lasko, 1954). In view of these considerations, one can hardly argue that birth order data support psychogenesis in autism.

I have discussed the various factors that I have been able to identify or isolate as having been offered as evidence that early infantile autism is psychogenic in origin. In no case can it be argued that the psychogenic aspect of the factor is more potent than the biological aspect, nor, in fact, that the psychogenic factor can be shown to have *any* potency at all in the causation of infantile autism. We are not saying that psychogenesis is an imaginary influence; we are merely saying that there appears to be no evidence that it is anything but imaginary.

It may appear that the case for the psychogenic hypothesis has been understated. Yet the present writer is only one of many who have made a search for evidence and come to the conclusion that evidence is lacking. Stevenson (1957) has observed that:

> The literature of psychiatry abounds in articles asserting causal connections between the early experiences of life (especially training practices) and the later personality. The far fewer articles reporting objective studies of such relationships fail to support the assertions made. (p. 152)

In addition to his own well-documented review, Stevenson cites three previous review articles. More recently, Hebb (1958b) and O'Connor and Franks (1961) have come to similar conclusions after reviewing the relevant research.

B. THE CASE FOR BIOLOGICAL CAUSATION

Unlike the hypothesis that autism is psychogenically determined, there are a number of points of information which support the hypothesis that autism may result from a rare recessive trait, or be otherwise determined by biological factors. Kanner, in his various publications (especially with Eisenberg, 1956), has cited the first five points listed below as evidence against the psychogenic view. The remaining points have been identified by the present writer or others who have concerned themselves with this problem.

1. Some clearly autistic children are born of parents who do not fit the autistic parent personality pattern.

2. Parents who do fit the description of the supposedly pathogenic parent almost invariably have normal, non-autistic children.

3. With very few exceptions, the siblings of autistic children are normal.

4. Autistic children are behaviorally unusual "from the moment of birth."

5. There is a consistent ratio of three or four boys to one girl.

6. Virtually all cases of twins reported in the literature have been identical, with both twins afflicted.

7. Autism can occur or be closely simulated in children with known organic brain damage.

8. The symptomatology is highly unique and specific.

9. There is an absence of gradations of infantile autism which would create "blends" from normal to severely afflicted.

1. *Parents who do not fit the pattern.* "Some 10 percent" of parents of autistic children are warm and friendly and do not fit the personality stereotype reported so commonly for these parents (Eisenberg & Kanner, 1956). This point is also made in Eisenberg's article on the fathers of autistic children (1957). Keeler (1957) reports autism in a child adopted by warm and loving foster parents within ten days after birth. No mention of the natural parents was made. The parents of van Krevelen's case are specifically described as warm and affectionate, as are those mentioned by Chapman (1957), Schachter (1958), and others. The father described by van Krevelen does fit the "intelligent-driving personality" stereotype, however. While the physician and lawyer described by Polan and Spencer fit Kanner's pattern of intelligence and seriousness, the mothers did not. One was a "warm and gentle person" and the other was an "intelligent and efficient individual of normal emotional spontaneity." There are numerous other examples in the literature.

2. *"Autistic-type parents" with only normal children.* Many parents who do fit the personality stereotype exactly, and therefore might be expected to have autistic children if the psychogenic theory were correct, instead have perfectly normal children, as noted by Kanner and others (see especially Kanner, 1957), and as very probably can be verified from the reader's own experience.

The experiment conducted by Dennis (1941) on the development of infants under conditions of "minimum social stimulation" seems relevant to this point. Dennis raised fraternal twins from the end of their first month to the end of the fourteenth month by attending strictly to their material needs only. He gave no encouragement or approval of any sort. Despite this systematic attempt to serve the child in what must undoubtedly be a more detached and indifferent manner than Kanner's parents could have achieved inadvertently, Dennis concluded from his experiment that if the child's well-being was assured, his behavioral development would take its normal course.

Dennis' experimental treatment of children is certainly not to be recommended as routine. No one would willfully run the risk of injuring the child's sense of security, or any other aspect of his personality, even though the available research suggests that adverse effects, if there are any, may be too small to be detected by presently available methods. One is cautious even with a gun one has good reason to believe is not loaded. But Dennis' work certainly does suggest that the case for psychogenically induced adverse effect has been greatly overstated.

3. *Siblings are normal.* Kanner and a number of others have noted that many normal children are raised as siblings to an autistic child. It is a rarity to have more than one autistic child in a family, except in the case of twins. Of 131 siblings to Kanner's first 100 autistic children, only three could be regarded as probably autistic. Seven others showed evidence of emotional disturbance (Kanner & Lesser, 1958). This is a small proportion, especially when it is considered that these siblings were probably under closer scrutiny than normal and under severe stress as well (Creak & Ini, 1960). Rattner and Chapman (1959) have reported an autistic child in the middle of a series of 11 normal children. Polan and Spencer (1959) reported two normal siblings for each of the three cases of autism they described. Phillips (1957) reports all siblings of his cases to be normal. Both siblings of van Krevelen's (1952) case were normal, as were also both siblings of the girl described by Popella (1955) and by Sutton and Read (1958). Similar instances are plentiful.

Murphy and Preston presented a paper titled *Three Autistic Brothers* to the American Orthopsychiatric Association in 1954. While this paper has not appeared in print, Dr. Murphy was kind enough to supply the present writer with a copy for the purposes of this report. There are a number of similarities between the cases described by Murphy and Preston and the classical cases of early infantile autism described by Kanner, but it does not seem to the present writer that the brothers were in fact true cases of infantile autism. Murphy and Preston appear to have followed the practice of using the term "autistic" descriptively rather than diagnostically. They state that "The parents applied for psychiatric help because the middle boy was adjusting poorly in school. All three of the boys, aged 5, 10, and 14, were subsequently found to be autistic" (p. 1). Age of onset and certain other differences, in addition to the obvious accessibility of the brothers, make it appear unlikely that these brothers were actually afflicted with infantile autism. (These may be cases of Asperger's syndrome. See Spiel, 1961; van Krevelen, 1962; van Krevelen & Kuipers, 1962.)

4. *Autistic children unusual from the "moment of birth."* Kanner has often referred to autism as "inborn" and "innate." Even the psychogenically oriented writers do not appear to question this point. It is difficult to understand why pathology severe enough to be recognized so early is not considered

severe enough to cause later behavior disorder without the compounding of it with psychogenic factors which have yet to be demonstrated to be other than fictional.

5. *The high sex ratio.* That males are less viable than females from conception to old age is common knowledge. The attrition of males before birth is even greater than after. Males are susceptible not only to a great variety of sex-linked hereditary diseases, but also to later acquired infections and other adverse somatic conditions. Thus the occurrence of autism in three or four times as many boys as girls is consistent with the known greater vulnerability of males to organic damage. It would be hard to find a convincing psychogenically oriented explanation for this ratio, especially since boys tend to be more often welcome in our culture than girls, and especially so as first children.

6. *Twins with autism.* One of the strongest lines of evidence against psychogenic etiology of autism has come to light only in recent years. Keeler (1957, 1958) seems to have been the first to call attention to the incidence of autism in identical twins. He did not tabulate the cases of such twins known to him, but in a later personal communication to the writer (1960) Keeler referred to a set of identical twins in addition to the blind twins he had mentioned in 1958. Keeler pointed out that there were no known cases where only one of monozygotic twins was afflicted, nor where both of dizygotic twins exhibited autism. His 1957 paper refers to a set of fraternal twins where only one child was afflicted.

Kallman, Barrera, and Metzger (1940) also reported blind identical twins. These twin boys, congenitally blind with microphthalmia, showed motility patterns "strikingly similar" to those displayed by the blind children Keeler (1958) described as manifesting the syndrome of infantile autism. The verbal behavior of the twins described by Kallman et al. would also warrant their being considered as possibly autistic. They could, for example, repeat anything said to them, but showed little comprehension of the meaning. This is very typical of autism.

Chapman (1957), in reporting a case of identical autistic twin girls, also raised the issue of twinness, and called attention to the cases of identical twin boys reported earlier by Sherwin (1953) and Bakwin (1954).

Polan and Spencer (1959) reported still another set of identical twin boys. They referred to this set as the fifth known to them.

The present writer, who had independently become impressed with the frequency with which twins with autism were being reported, has attempted to tabulate all cases of probable autism in the literature involving multiple births. The list follows:

1. Kallman et al. (1940) identical twin boys.

2. Sherwin (1953) reported identical twin boys.

3. Bakwin (1954), another case of identical twin boys.

4. Eisenberg and Kanner (1956) described a set of twin boys, one of whom died in infancy before it could be discovered whether he was autistic like his brother. No reference to zygosity.

5. Keeler's (1957) fraternals, only one being autistic.

6. Chapman's (1957) identical twin girls.

7. Lehman, Haber, and Lesser (1957) reported identical twin boys.

8. Keeler's (1958) blind twins. Presumably, from Keeler's report, these are boys.

9. Polan and Spencer's (1959) identical boys.

10. Bruch (1959) referred to twin Negro boys with autism. In personal communication to the writer (1961), she identified these as identical twins.

11 & 12. Chapman (1960) reported knowledge of two additional sets of identical twins.

13. Keeler (1960, personal communication) one other set of identical autistic twins. Sex not stated.

14. Ward and Hoddinott (1962) described a set of concordant fraternal twin girls who were "typical examples of early infantile autism."

This compilation raises the number of known multiple births involving at least one case of autism to 14. Known cases involving twins reported to be monozygotic is thus raised from five (Polan and Spencer) to a new total of 11 (excluding sets numbered 4, 5 and 14). Each of these sets is concordant (i.e., both twins similar with regard to affliction–non-affliction). Kallman's set, reported prior to Kanner's delineation of autism, is the only one not so classified by the original author.

The identical autistic twin sons described by May (1958) in his book, *A Physician Looks at Psychiatry*, have been included in the above list.

Kanner has made no specific mention of twins in his group, with the exception of set 4, above, referred to incidentally in illustrating a point concerning the twin's parents. No mention was made of this or other multiple births in either Kanner's 1954a listing nor Kanner and Lesser's 1958 detailed listing of the birth conditions and order of the first 100 cases, nor in the listing of the mental status of his autistic patients' siblings.

(Correspondence has determined that the twins referred to by Eisenberg and Kanner were contained in separate sacs. Although dichorionic twins are usually fraternal, zygosity cannot be stated with certainty in this case.) In general, only one of three twin births is monozygotic, so one would expect to find 22 cases of dizygotic twins for each 11 monozygotic cases reported. Even allowing for errors in establishing zygosity, this appears to represent a strong overloading of monozygotic twins with autism, as opposed to dizygotic. Additionally, since only about one birth in 285 is of monozygotic twins (Allen & Kallman, 1955), there would also appear to be an overloading of such twins in the absolute total number of cases of reported autism. Including the fewer than 150 cases Kanner has reported (1958b), there are probably no more than about 200 bona-fide cases of autism referred to in the literature, not nearly enough to support finding 11 twin cases, let alone 11 monozygotic twin cases, on a chance-only basis.

Luxenburger (cited by Rosanoff, Handy, & Plesset, 1937) has demonstrated that one may expect to find a disproportionately high incidence of monozygotic and concordant twins in twin studies based on search of the literature. The degree of overloading reported by Luxenburger (which was considerably greater than that reported by Rosanoff et al.) would not begin to account for the high incidence of twins with autism reported above. Autism seems especially likely to be reported, even in single births, not only because its manifestations are so striking, but because the parents frequently take the child from clinic to clinic in the hope of finding someone who understands the disease (May, 1958; Rothenberg, 1960). Additionally, the early age of onset of autism, before irrevocable separation of twins is likely to take place, as well as an increased understanding of the importance of twin data to etiological research, make it appear unlikely that Luxenburger-type bias is an overriding or even important variable in the present instance.

The finding of at least 11 sets of monozygotic twins, all concordant, seems highly significant in terms of the biological etiology of the disease. Kety (1959) has remarked that Chapman's (1957) reference to three sets of identical autistic twins was suggestive. Ward and Hoddinott (1962), in describing their set of concordant fraternal twins, observe that for infantile autism "to appear in twins, particularly fraternal twins, is an event beyond statistical probability" (p. 191). That one of the two cases of reported fraternal twins is discordant (set number 5) serves only to enhance this finding. (The twin who died at five months in set 4, probably fraternal, was reported only as "more responsive" than his definitely autistic brother.)

The high susceptibility of twins to neurological defects does not adequately account for the high incidence of *identical* twins with autism.

While the ratio of *defective* monozygotic to dizygotic twins is lower than the one-to-one ratio found for non-defective twins (Rosanoff et al., 1937; Allen & Kallman, 1955), the preponderance of monozygotic twins with autism is nonetheless striking.

Kallman's data (1953; Kallman & Roth, 1956), widely accepted by the scientific community as providing the clearest evidence of the strong hereditary component in mental disorder (e.g., Knobloch & Pasamanick, 1961; Rosenthal, 1961; Meehl, 1962), show 9 percent of non-twin siblings to be schizophrenic when one sibling is affected, 15 percent of dizygotic twins to be concordant if one twin is schizophrenic, and 86 percent concordance if one of monozygotic twins is schizophrenic. When schizophrenia was diagnosed at an early age, between five and 11 years, only 71 percent of identical twins were concordant. Judged by these standards, the genetic element in autism would appear to be unusually strong.

It is of interest that in several cases of identical twins stricken with autism the degree of affliction, while invariably severe, is not quite identical (Sherwin, 1953; Lehman et al., 1957; Polan & Spencer, 1959). This suggests that while genetic factors may predispose toward autism post-conceptional factors could be operative (see Burt, 1958; and Price, cited by Rosenthal, 1961, for references on prenatal identical twin differences).

7. *Autism caused or simulated by known organic disease.* A line of evidence which suggests the organicity of early infantile autism stems from the many cases in which the symptomatology may be traceable to a post-encephalitic condition or other form of central nervous system injury. Some of these cases are those described by Anthony (1958), Rattner and Chapman (1959), Frankl (1943; see Sarason & Gladwin, 1958, p. 216), Ross (1959), Sutton and Read (1958), van Krevelen (1960), and possibly the cases of Anastasi and Levee (1960), Kallman et al. (1940), Popella (1955), Schachter (1958), and Vaillant (1962). The appearance of the syndrome in children given oxygen shortly after birth (Chapter 6) is also germane to this point.

These cases do not prove autism is *invariably* organic, but they at least indicate that the symptoms *can* be caused by organic agents. It is not believed that there is parallel evidence supporting the view that the symptoms of autism can be produced by socio-psychological factors.

8. *Uniqueness and specificity.* The high degree of interindividual similarity in the symptomatology of autism would seem to identify it as biological. As May (personal communication, 1959) has observed:

> I do not know any one of these children who did not have the rocking and banging of head...the particular interest in some machinery...

the typical speech patterns... This identity of symptomatology pleads strongly for a well-localized lesion...

Much experimental research in genetics has shown that what appears to be a complicated and varied syndrome can be traced back to a single initial fault in development (Roberts, 1959). It should be noted, however, that while a single abnormal gene may produce a remarkable variety of symptoms *within* an individual, the syndrome from individual to individual tends to be highly uniform, especially when it is a recessive gene that is at fault. In phenylketonuria, for example, there is a characteristic diversity of problems: motor involvement, seizures, eye and skin pigmentation effects, and skin sensitivity in addition to mental retardation. Yet each victim exhibits the *same* syndrome, because there is but a single recessive underlying defect.

That gene effects within the nervous system can be highly specific does not seem to be widely appreciated. C. E. Keeler (1940) has described an interesting study in which the exact locus of the inherited nerve lesion causing "waltzing" in guinea pigs was located. It was then possible to duplicate the inherited waltzing tendency by making carefully placed surgical lesions in normal animals. Keeler observed that "So steady is the hand of genetics and so accurate in repeating these operations that you may have a thousand identically operated specimens to study quite as readily as one" (p. 97).

Moorhead, Mellman, and Wenar (1961) have recently made a related finding in humans by tracing a family defect involving speech and mental retardation to a heritable chromosome translocation.

Thus intraindividual diversity of symptoms coupled with interindividual similarity appears to be not uncommon where specific organic defects are involved. If there are any environmentally produced behavior patterns which follow this model, they have escaped the attention of the present writer. That autism does fit this picture is not proof that autism is biological in origin, but it does add to the body of evidence for organic causation.

In connection with both this point and the previous one (i.e., phenocopying of autistic symptoms by organic disease), it may be of interest to note the many similarities in the symptoms of autism (Chapter 1) with those described for "brain-injured" children by Lewis, Strauss, and Lehtinen (1951); and by Strauss and Lehtinen in other publications. The similarities between autism and the symptomatology of brain injury should not permit the confusion of autism with the general brain-injured syndrome. The more general term "brain-injured" encompasses many cases whose lesions apparently include involvement of the brain areas in which profound but localized dysfunction, usually in genetically sensitive infants, may produce true early infantile autism.

Kanner has observed that some autistic-like symptoms are found in brain-injured (and innately retarded) children (1958b). However, the "brain-injured" in this sense will rarely show the composite of symptoms which defines autism. In Kanner's words, "The symptom combination in most instances warrants an unequivocal diagnostic formulation" (1951, p. 23).

9. *The absence of "blends."* If autism were a reaction to environmental factors we would expect it to exhibit not only the diversity of manifestations from case to case as a consequence of situational differences (above), but, in addition, the usual gradation in intensity, depending on the adverseness of the environment. Environmental adversity would ordinarily be assumed to follow a continuous, probably Gaussian distribution, rather than a dichotomous one. While there is variation in severity and in prognosis, the degree of variation does not account for the large void between autism and normal behavior. There have been few serious attempts to deny the existence of this void.

C. PSYCHOGENESIS AS AN INADEQUATE AND PERNICIOUS HYPOTHESIS

Perhaps it should be made explicit at this point that the writer does not presume to have shown that autism is biologically determined and that the psycho-social environment plays no part in its etiology. What the writer *does* assert is that a careful review of the evidence has revealed no support for the psychogenic point of view. The evidence is instead highly consistent with expectation based on organic pathology.

Our finding with regard to autism coincides with the more general view formulated by the participants of a recent conference on the causes of mental disorder (Milbank Memorial Fund, 1961):

> There seems to be no clearly demonstrated instance of either a cultural or social factor being known to be a predisposing factor in mental illness... The absence of clear-cut evidence does not show that the hypothesis is incorrect but only that it has not been demonstrated even once. (p. 379)

Neither Creak and Ini (1960) who intensively studied 100 sets of parents of psychotic children nor Peck, Rabinovitch, and Cramer (1949) who studied 50 sets of parents were able to find evidence of a psychogenic nature. What they did find was a good deal of suffering brought on by the child's behavior and a good deal of intense (and we might add unnecessary) feelings of guilt.

It is probably too early to suggest that psychogenesis as a *hypothesis* no longer be considered. ("Hypothesis" is used advisedly, because there appears to be too little evidence to support use of the term "theory.") No avenue for learning all that we can about the etiology of mental disorder should be unexplored. The detailed explication in this chapter of the arguments concerning the etiology of autism was in part intended to facilitate, and perhaps even to provoke, some long-overdue, rational, and articulate consideration of the problem, even at the expense of jointly provoking a measure of articulate and inarticulate wrath.

It is not questioned that distinction should be maintained between a disproven and an unproven hypothesis, but neither should there be a failure to distinguish between an unproven and an uninvestigated hypothesis. The psychogenic hypothesis is by no means uninvestigated.

Whatever may be the merit in being patient with psychogenesis as a hypothesis, there is much less in being patient with it as an assumed force-in-fact. The all too common practice of blatantly assuming that psychogenic etiology *can* exist or *does* exist in any individual case or in any given class of disorders is not only unwarranted but actively pernicious.

It is perhaps permissible for writers such as Weiland and Rudnik (1961) to "postulate" that "the expectation of murderous attack or of symbiotic engulfment by a psychotogenic mother results in a failure to progress beyond autism and in panicky attempts to escape from symbiosis into autism..." (p. 552), especially when they add (in a footnote), "We do not believe this has been demonstrated conclusively..." It is something else again when the implications of this view are translated into action, and psychogenic causation is assumed to be a reality rather than merely a hypothetical possibility.

Ross (1959) presents an interesting and instructive case history of an autistic girl whose mother had been held to be responsible for her child's plight because the mother's affection was considered "intellectualized and objectified." Only when the child died did the fact of extensive brain damage become evident. Intensive neurological examination had failed to reveal the difficulty before the child's death, which interrupted intensive psychotherapy. It was fortunate for the mother that the brain damage was of a sort that present-day techniques could disclose, else she would to this day be held responsible for her daughter's death.

Consider the case of "Jonny" (Rothenberg, 1960). After stating that Jonny, at 1½ pounds, was one of the smallest premature babies ever born in the United States to survive, and after noting that three and a half months spent in an incubator under high oxygen tension and heat lamps had turned the infant's hair orange and his skin chocolate brown, the author attributed his later severe behavior disturbance to lack of mothering while being incubated. "Cure" was said to be greatly facilitated by suddenly confronting Jonny with a model of the incubator—a personification of the mother who supplies only material needs and no nourishment of the ego. The possibility that organic brain damage might have resulted from such adverse physical conditions was apparently not seriously considered, yet it had been known for some time that a high concentration of oxygen is able to cause destruction of nerve tissue in infants.

Bettelheim (1959a) interpreted the psychosis of "Joey, the Mechanical Boy" as a reaction to his mother's hostility when the evidence was also quite consistent with hereditary determination, since the mother appeared to be severely mentally disturbed herself. (See also the reply by May to this article.) In this case, as in Rothenberg's, the appeal of the psychogenic concept appeared to preclude consideration of concealed organic defect. Somehow the adherents of the psychogenic hypothesis tend to overlook the possibility that the complex and little understood cerebrum could be structurally or chemically impaired.

In another case Bettelheim (1959b) found emotional isolation to have caused the psychosis of a girl who had been conceived, born, and raised by her Jewish parents in World War II in a small hole beneath a farm building in Poland. The hole was too cramped to permit an adult to stretch out. German soldiers were nearby (sometimes firing shots into the building) so that the mother had to smother the infant's cries. Not considered by Bettelheim was research showing the adverse effects on the offspring's emotionality of prenatal stress in the mother (e.g., Thompson, 1957), nor of sensory deprivation in the child.

It should not be thought, however, that workers in this field are universal in accepting environmental determination. Some writers have been frank in rejecting the psychogenic hypothesis. Keeler (1957), for example, has said, "I certainly do not adhere to the opinion put forth by some that infantile autism stems from a very specific type of pathological parent-child (especially mother-child) relationship." Anthony (1958) notes, "I do not think that traumata which sometimes seem to precipitate a psychosis in childhood are anything greater than normal developmental hazards (sibling birth, etc.). It is the predisposition that makes them vulnerable." Chapman (1960) also believes the role of the psycho-social environment has been overestimated: "...the degree of interpersonal pathology between parents and child rarely seems sufficient to explain the catastrophic interpersonal disorder of the child." Goldstein (1959), in his very illuminating discussion of autism, has pointed out clearly the gratuitousness of assuming psychogenesis as an etiologic factor in the disease.

In discussing the obvious prejudice against the hereditary viewpoint, Nolan Lewis (1954) points out, "It would seem that most of the prejudice against genetic inheritance stems from a feeling in the realm of wish fulfilment, based on the idea that acceptance of genetic factors would create an attitude of therapeutic hopelessness." Williams (1956) cites this point among others in his attempt to penetrate the prejudice against heredity. He notes that hopelessness is by no means justified by the evidence, and cites the ready correction of the effects of diabetes, phenylketonuria, and hypothyroidism as examples.

It should not be necessary to ask for recognition of the role played by genetic factors among persons trained in scientific thinking, but Williams has seen the need to do so:

> We therefore make a plea for an unprejudiced facing of the facts of heredity. We urge that such facts be accepted with as great readiness as any others. This plea seems necessary in view of the attitude which we have repeatedly noted, namely, that of willingness to arrive at "environmentalistic" conclusions on the basis of slender evidence while rejecting points of view which would emphasize the role of heredity, even though the weight of the evidence, viewed without prejudice, appears overwhelming. (p. 16)

When dark-haired and dark-eyed parents produce a dark-complexioned child, we all are quick to agree, "Mendel was right!" But when introverted parents produce a child who similarly shows little interest in socialization, the refrain inexplicably changes to "Aha, Freud was right!"

In arguing for more critical use of the diagnosis of autism, Kanner says:

> The misuse of the diagnosis of autism has played havoc with the comfort and finances of many parents of retarded children, who were made to feel that their attitudes and practices were primarily responsible for their offspring's problems, were made to submit themselves and the child to lengthy, expensive, and futile therapy, and were pauperized and miserable to the time the true state of affairs was brought to light. (1958a, p. 111)

Kanner's appeal for the protection of the parents of children misdiagnosed as autistic is certainly to be commended, but what of the parents of *accurately* diagnosed cases? In view of the present status of research on the efficacy of psychotherapy, and of the fact that the evidence for psychogenic etiology of autism is not, to use Kanner's term, "unequivocal" (1958a), it would seem that the parents of properly diagnosed autistic children might also be deferred from being made "pauperized and miserable," for the time being.

In a court of law it is impermissible to convict a person solely on evidence consistent with the hypothesis that he is guilty—the evidence must also be inconsistent with the hypothesis that he is innocent. This simple point of justice has been neglected, consistently, by those who deal with families having children afflicted with autism, and the damage and torment this practice has wrought upon parents whose lives and hopes have already been shattered by their child's illness is not easy to imagine nor pleasant to contemplate. To add a heavy burden of shame and guilt to the distress of people whose hopes, social life, finances, well-being, and feelings of worth have been all but destroyed seems heartless and inconsiderate in the extreme. Yet it is done, as May (1958), Oppenheim (1961), Stuart (1960), and van Krevelen (1960) amply illustrate.

In view of these pernicious implications and the absence of scientific evidence, the wide acceptance of the psychogenic view is difficult to understand. A partial explanation for the prevalence of this view may be found in Kanner's unguarded admission that he is perplexed by the fact that the great majority of the parents of autistic children have been able to rear non-autistic children, while other parents, who fit the parental typology perfectly, raised children who responded aggressively rather than by withdrawal: "...the existence of these exceptions is puzzling... It is not easy to account for this difference of reaction" (1949, p. 426). The same "puzzling" inconsistency is clearly present in other childhood mental disorders, such as mongolism, Tay-Sachs disease, and phenylketonuria, and is readily explained in terms of recessive inheritance.

Despert provides another example of a child psychiatrist who does not apply what she must certainly know of genetics to her thoughts on etiology:

> It is sometimes argued that these mothers had other children who were normal or relatively normal, but it must be remembered that a mother, biogenetically identical for all her children, may nevertheless psychogenetically differ widely from one child to the other. (1951, p. 345)[3]

"Biogenetically identical"—100 years after Mendel!

Perhaps we are painting too dark a picture. There are signs of a growing recognition that the failure to find support for psychogenesis may possibly lie in the inadequacy of the concept rather than in a lack of resourcefulness among its investigators. Despert, whose 1951 view was quoted immediately above and who in 1947 wrote of cases in which neurological disorders had been "ruled out" by examination, has written in 1958 that the possibility

---

3   Reprinted with permission of *Amer. J. Orthopsychiat.* and the author.

of finding constitutional factors in infantile autism was particularly strong (Despert & Sherwin, 1958). Ekstein, Bryant, and Friedman (1958) show a willingness to question "our prejudiced, one-sided consideration of etiological factors" (p. 653); and Bettelheim, for years a leader of the psychogenic school, was recently willing to "reserve judgment" about what causes autism, although he is still "pretty sure" that psychogenic factors "contribute" (1959b, p. 463).

Szurek, who started in 1946 "to test the hypothesis that the etiology of psychotic disorders of childhood are entirely psychogenic" (Boatman & Szurek, 1960, p. 389), takes a much weaker stand today in stating that certain "facts" "…seem to lend weight to the possibility that psychogenic factors are at least important" (p. 430). (The reader may wish to see these "facts.")

To the present writer these indications of a retreat from the psychogenic hypothesis, like Bowlby's previously cited disavowal of the maternal deprivation hypothesis, represent a timely and welcome willingness to let conviction be subordinated to evidence. The history of science proves this to be the first step toward progress.

A COMMENTARY ON CHAPTER 3

Robert K. Naviaux

The year 2014 marks the 50th anniversary of Dr. Rimland's historic book, *Infantile Autism*. This book stands today as a paradigm-shifting work of scholarship. In the 21 years that followed Leo Kanner's seminal description of 11 children with autism in 1943, a pernicious tide had been rising in America, the medical literature laying blame for the cause of autism on parental behavior. The technical literature described this as the "psychogenic" cause of autism, by which was meant that the "emotionally unresponsive" behavior of the mother was the direct cause of the disorder. The popular press rapidly coined the term "refrigerator moms" to describe this sad and false conclusion from mid-20th century medicine. This theory has now been thoroughly debunked, but not without producing emotional fallout and scientific ripple effects that are being felt to this day.

Dr. Rimland systematically evaluated the evidence for the psychogenic theory of autism in his book, and showed that it did not fit the facts. A major claim of proponents of the psychogenic theory was that since no brain or neuroanatomical abnormality had been identified in children with autism, the cause could not be "organic." To this day, progress in psychiatry has been hampered by the failure to accept the emerging view that every chronic brain disease is also a whole-body disease that can be understood and studied in terms of cellular chemistry, cell–cell communication, and metabolism. Dr. Rimland was an early advocate of this very modern idea. He understood that chemistry and metabolism represented the intersection of genes and environment, and, as such, could represent an organic basis of autism. He pointed out that several genetic brain disorders of childhood, including phenylketonuria (PKU), had no obvious neuroanatomical basis— no spot in the brain that was obviously misshapen or defective. The problem, then and now, is that the physicians, neurologists, and developmental psychologists who were best trained to care for children with autism and many other neurodevelopmental disorders of childhood were not well trained in chemistry and biochemistry, and naturally eschewed the role of chemistry and metabolism as the possible cause of neurologic disease.

The terms "psychogenic," "organic," "environmental," "biological," and "genetic" as used in 1964, and even in 2014, do not capture the important nuances of meaning that are needed to help the field of autism science to progress. Dr. Rimland cited 14 published twin studies to show the high concordance rates between identical twins with autism, and the much lower rates of concordance among fraternal twins and siblings. He also cited that among the 131 siblings of the first 100 children with autism reported by Leo Kanner, only three of 131 also had autism. The twin and sibling results were solid evidence for a strong multi-gene (not single-gene) component to autism. However, Dr. Rimland pointed out that shifting our conception of the cause of autism from a psychogenic theory to a biological theory was not without its own risks. He noted that some people would stop looking for treatments and prevention if autism was said to have a "biological" basis. Therapists and physicians might assume that because the disorder is biological (a term that meant "genetic" to most readers at the time) nothing can be done to improve the lives of affected children.

Once again, Dr. Rimland was ahead of his time. Although he could not have known it in 1964, many genetic diseases now have treatments that are not only life-saving, but can create the difference between a life of hardship, illness, and physical and mental disability, and a normal or near-normal life filled with all the joys of a happy childhood and productive adult life. Indeed, this fact lies at the foundation of the enormously successful universal expanded newborn screening programs now implemented throughout North America and Europe. In the US, 30–50 genetic and endocrine disorders are screened for at birth and within the first month. One of these is the great success story that led the way—PKU. In the 1950s a special diet was developed to treat children with PKU. In 1963, Massachusetts became the first state to screen newborn infants for PKU. Universal newborn screening for PKU in the US did not occur until shortly after 1996. However, now we know that when children with PKU are identified and treated in the first months of life, they go on to lead a virtually normal childhood and adult life. If PKU is not identified early, as was the case before 1963, all children with PKU were profoundly intellectually disabled, and a few even received a diagnosis of autism spectrum disorder (ASD).

What are the scientific ripple effects that resulted from the debunking of the psychogenic theory of autism? The ripples emerged from the polarizing effect of the psychogenic theory. A large effort was launched to examine the biological causes of autism. From the 1960s until now, this was taken largely to mean a search for the genetic or DNA basis of autism. Hundreds of millions of research dollars have been spent since the completion of the first draft of the Human Genome Project in 2001, to study the genetic basis of autism. Today we know from these comprehensive and exhaustive studies that over 20 classical Mendelian genetic diseases can increase the risk of ASD. We also know of more than 20 copy number variations in DNA that can increase the risk of ASD. However, no single one of these DNA mutations or variants accounts for more than 1–2 percent of all ASD.

These comprehensive genetic studies have also shown that not a single one of the "DNA causes" of autism actually produces autism in 100 percent of the children who have the mutated gene. For example, only about

35–60 percent of boys with Fragile X syndrome and 40 percent of those with Angelman syndrome have symptoms that qualify for a diagnosis of ASD. Practicing clinical geneticists face this biological fact daily. Single genes do not produce autism with deterministic certainty. And even when a single-gene mutation produces a recognized Mendelian syndrome, the severity of that disease is highly variable, even among siblings and other children with the same point mutation. This is prima facie evidence that even in the "genetic cases of autism," many additional genes and environmental factors must interact to produce the complex neurodevelopmental syndrome we call ASD. In addition, when all the single-gene forms are added up in the year 2014, they make up at most 10–20 percent of all of ASD. What is causing the remaining 80–90 percent?

If Dr. Rimland were alive today, he would be asking these same questions. Statistics from the US Centers for Disease Control have shown that when uniform DSM-IV diagnostic criteria are applied in three national surveys conducted in 2002, 2008, and 2010, the prevalence of autism spectrum disorders has risen from 1:150 in 2002, and 1:88 in 2008, to 1:68 in 2010. The data also reveal regional hot spots like New Jersey, where the prevalence of ASD in 2010 was 1:46 overall, and 1 in 28 in boys. Many epidemiologic studies have shown that environmental factors as varied as air pollution, maternal infection, and the use of drugs such as valproate during pregnancy can dramatically increase the risk of ASD in children, without changing DNA sequence, but possibly changing the epigenetic marking of DNA. Some geneticists dispute these data, citing changing cultural factors and uneven ascertainment and diagnostic criteria as the reasons for the apparent rise in the prevalence of ASD. However, the weight of the evidence suggests that the rise in autism is real, and has been increasing 10–15 percent per year since uniform DSM-IV diagnostic standards were adopted in 1994. Since genes cannot change this fast, it seems likely that changes in the chemistry of our environment, food chain, or other factors that are interacting with genes are responsible for the observed increase in the prevalence of ASD. The case for environmental factors affecting child health is made stronger by the observation that ASD is not the only disorder that has been rising in prevalence over the past 25 years. The prevalence of asthma, skin disorders, food allergies, thyroid disorders, and type I diabetes has also been increasing during this time, after showing no significant change in prevalence in the 25 years before 1990.

Later in his career, Dr. Rimland was a vocal advocate of nutritional and cofactor therapy to help treat ASD. In many ways, his efforts were analogous to the efforts that led to effective nutritional therapy of PKU and other genetic brain disorders of childhood that are currently part of universal newborn screening. The major difference was that Dr. Rimland did not have the tools available to him to fully characterize the metabolic features that underlie ASD, and to see the chemical changes that occur when effective treatments are found. He would be happy to see that great progress that has been made in just the past 5–10 years along these lines. Large technological leaps have been made in mass spectrometry that are allowing investigators to "see" deeper into the metabolism of autism than has ever been possible before.

A concept of metabolic primacy is emerging in neuroscience. It appears that even the formation of complex structures such as the synapses that connect neurons are controlled by metabolism. Ultimately, all the neurotransmitter systems such as glutamate, GABA, serotonin, dopamine, and acetylcholine are controlled by cell metabolism. We do not know yet where these advancements will lead. However, there is every reason to believe that Dr. Rimland's pioneering efforts will continue to point the way for the next 50 years, to a future filled with hope and new possibilities for early diagnosis and effective treatment for children with autism spectrum disorders.

INTRODUCTION TO CHAPTER 4
Stephen M. Edelson

Rimland dedicated much of Chapter 4 to comparing autism with childhood schizophrenia. Even far into the 1970s, there was confusion as to whether the two conditions overlapped or were distinct. In the 1960s and 1970s, the two diagnoses were sometimes considered interchangeable. In fact, the leading scientific journal on autism at the time, first edited by Leo Kanner, was initially titled the *Journal of Autism and Childhood Schizophrenia*. (Currently, it is called the *Journal of Autism and Developmental Disorders*.)

Although there are a few research findings suggesting a relationship between autism and schizophrenia—including several overlapping genes and neurological impairments (e.g., of the hippocampus and amygdala)—their developmental history, core symptoms, and prognosis are quite different.

REFERENCE
de Lacy, N., & King, B.H. (2013). Revisiting the relationship between autism and schizophrenia: Toward an integrated neurobiology. *Annual Review of Clinical Psychology, 9*, 555–587.

CHAPTER 4

The Differentiation of Early Infantile Autism from Childhood Schizophrenia

Most of the contemporary literature on early infantile autism is characterized by confusion of infantile autism with childhood schizophrenia. Kanner feels that the term schizophrenia covers many diagnostic entities, and while agreeing that autism might legitimately be classified as "one of the schizophrenias" (1949, 1954b) has been consistent in emphasizing the danger of letting autism be indiscriminately lumped with "schizophrenia": "It is almost impossible to see how the phenomenologically unduplicated autistic syndrome can be disregarded in favor of the bland subscription to the idea of an equality of all schizophrenias" (in Darr & Worden, 1951, p. 570). Kanner has pointed out that it has been largely the psychogenically oriented workers who have attempted to discard the concept of differential diagnoses: "The inevitable consequence of such an attitude would be a clinical hodgepodge which, if accepted, would be swallowed up as a mess of unrelated ingredients thrown together in one big pot" (1958b, p. 142).

Unlike their American counterparts, most European writers have taken the view that autism is a unique psychosis, in a class by itself or confounded with oligophrenia (Grewel et al., 1954; Plenter, 1955; Popella, 1955; Schachter, 1958; Stern, 1952; Stern & Schachter, 1953; and van Krevelen, 1952a, 1952b, 1953, 1954, 1955, 1958, 1960, 1962). On the other hand, Carboz (1955, cited by Fontes and Schneeberger-Ataide, 1958) believes autism to be a true form of childhood schizophrenia. Beaujard (1958) classifies autism with schizophrenia, but, like many others, is far from satisfied with the present status of nosology. The only East European article the present review disclosed was a Czech paper by Nesnidalova and Fiala (1961) who wrote, "We validated, through the study of our cases and the literature the authenticity of the differential diagnosis of Kanner's early infantile autism from childhood schizophrenia."

The present writer's view is that there is sufficient information at hand to demonstrate clearly that early infantile autism is *not* the same disease or cluster of diseases which has come to be called childhood schizophrenia, and that autism can and should be distinguished from it at all levels of discourse. Indeed, on reading many of the papers which describe schizophrenic children as autistic the writer is reminded of the story of the two men who were indistinguishable in appearance except that the tall thin one had a red beard and only one leg. Admittedly, while certain *individual* cases may occasionally be difficult or impossible to diagnose accurately, especially in the case of non-speaking children, the many differences appearing between the two diseases provide little excuse for confusing the two *classes* of disorder.

The problem of differentiating autism from schizophrenia is by no means a purely academic one. A failure to differentiate cannot help but impede progress toward solution of the problems both diseases present. For example, pooling autistic children, who almost never show any somatic problems, with schizophrenic children, who consistently do show such problems, will almost certainly becloud the findings from metabolic studies or other investigations of bodily function (e.g., Koegler, Colbert, & Eiduson, 1961). Similarly, a new drug or treatment which might work well for a small contingent of autistic children in a large group of schizophrenics might easily be judged ineffective on considering its effect on the entire group (e.g., Bender, Goldschmidt, & Sankar, 1962; Freedman, 1958a; Freedman, Ebin, & Wilson, 1962). This point may be well emphasized by noting Benda's (1960) practice of taking visiting psychiatrists to a ward where there are several patients with phenylpyruvic oligophrenia, letting them make the diagnosis of childhood schizophrenia, and "only then informing them that these are cases with positive phenylpyruvic acid in the urine" (p. 486). What a tragedy if phenylketonuria, now readily remediable, had been left undetected in the catch-all category "childhood schizophrenia." Our position is that early infantile autism can and should be differentiated from childhood schizophrenia now, even before a biochemical test like that for PKU has been developed.[1] Consider the evidence:

1. *Onset and course.* One of the basic requirements for a diagnosis of childhood schizophrenia is that the disordered behavior must follow an initial period of normal development. In distinction, early infantile autism is defined as being present "from the beginning of life." It is primarily because

---

1   Sankar, Cates, Broer, and Sankar have recently provided a biochemical procedure
     which discriminates between small groups of children they describe as autistic and as
     schizophrenic (in *Recent Advances in Biological Psychiatry*, Vol. 5, 1963, pp. 76–83).

of this distinction that autism has not been completely submerged into the category of schizophrenia.

It is not merely that the severe symptoms in childhood schizophrenia follow a period of normality. Instead, the child who later becomes schizophrenic is "almost uniformly" described by his mother as being the "best child she ever had." The pre-schizophrenic child is "easiest to care for, the most quickly trained, the cleanest, and, in short, nearly a perfect infant" (Hill, 1955, p. 111; see also Bowman & Sherman, cited by Mosse, 1958; Galvin, 1956; Stuart, 1960; and Wolman, 1957).

Kanner's point that the *course* of autism distinguishes it from childhood schizophrenia was emphasized by Anthony (1958), who points out with regard to the autistic child:

> We do not know, despite several follow-up studies, whether he ever develops the delusions and hallucinations characteristic of the adult schizophrenic, or whether he retains his early retardation and detachment unchanged. The Bender follow-up study would suggest the former, and the Kanner study the latter, which could imply that two different groups of children were involved. (p. 211)

2. *Health and appearance.* Autistic children have been described as almost invariably in excellent health, beautiful, and well formed, and usually of dark complexion (Benda, 1952, 1960; May, 1958; Kanner, 1949; Keeler, 1957). Kanner has made a special point of the unusually good general health of these children, the absence of any serious illness, the freedom from allergies, asthma, metabolic disturbances, and skin problems.

In sharp contrast, schizophrenic children are generally in poor health from birth. Respiratory, circulatory, metabolic, and digestive difficulties are so common (Bender, 1956; Keeler, 1957) that Fish (1957, 1959) has used these symptoms as a means of screening neonates for schizophrenia. Schizophrenic children are further described as having a thin, pale, translucent skin, blond hair and blue eyes, a receding chin, small face, and an almost fetus-like appearance. They are characterized by persistent tonic neck reflex, soft doughy muscle tone, choreoathetotic finger and hand movements, lax ligamenture, and other problems not reported for autistic children. In contrast to the often dark-complexioned autistic children, the schizophrenic children retain their light complexions even when of dark-complexioned races (Keeler, 1957). (Note that it is only the *somatic* characteristics of schizophrenic children which are present at birth. The behavioral abnormalities do not appear until later, as stated above.)

3. *Electroencephalography.* A number of studies (e.g., Kennard, 1949, 1953; Taterka & Katz, 1955) have reported that over 80 percent of schizophrenic children show abnormal EEG recordings. Of the 28 EEG studies reported by Kanner (Eisenberg & Kanner, 1956) on autistic children, 21 were negative, four equivocal, and only three definitely abnormal. With very few exceptions (e.g., Nesnidalova & Fiala, 1961; Popella, 1955; Schachter, 1958) cases presented by other writers confirm Kanner's finding that the EEG tends strongly to be normal in autistic children. The autistic girl described by Bradley (1943) was given four EEGs between her ninth and thirteenth years with no positive findings. Van Krevelen (1960, 1963) has, in fact, taken the position that positive EEG findings are preclusive of a diagnosis of autism.

Although the interpretation of EEG findings is often regarded with skepticism, perhaps a justifiable attitude in individual cases, the statistics cited above are based on the combined results of examinations given at many different places, at many different times, and by many different investigators. It would be hard to account for the observed differences between autistic and schizophrenic children in terms of any systematic bias. Further, the high incidence of positive EEG findings in schizophrenic children is consistent with the high level of somatic involvement reported in such children; and, as Bender (1961) points out, the immature type of EEG recording found is consistent with the maturational lag which she regards as of prime etiological significance in childhood schizophrenia.

4. *Physical responsiveness.* Autistic children typically do not adapt their bodies to their mothers or other adults when being carried or held. They are described as stiff and unresponsive. This is often the first sign that the child is autistic. In contrast to this sawhorse-like lack of accommodation in autistic children, schizophrenic children are noted for their strong tendency to "mold" to adults, like plastic or dough (Bender, 1956; Bruch, 1959).

It is largely this difference which has led Mahler (1952) to distinguish between what she refers to as the "autistic" and "symbiotic" psychoses of childhood. (On "symbiosis," see Despert & Sherwin, 1958; Goldstein, 1959.)

5. *Autistic aloneness.* The autistic child has been noted for failing to adjust to adults emotionally as well as posturally. His aloofness, his often complete indifference to the comings and goings of others, even his parents, has already been described. The term "autistic" was in fact applied to these children to reflect their apparent withdrawal from and seeming indifference to or rejection of the environment, including especially the social environment. Kanner used the term "disturbance of affective contact" in the title of his

first paper, and Ilg and Ames note that "This kind of child is characterized chiefly by his lack of warmth in human relations" (1955, p. 73). Note the sharp contrast between these descriptions and the characterization of the schizophrenic child:

> Contrary to the expectation that schizophrenic children will appear withdrawn in their social and human contacts, Bender emphasizes that their contact is pathologically invasive... The schizophrenic child, far from being cold, unresponsive or unappealing, immediately captures the empathy of the adult who often is seduced into a false evaluation of treatment possibilities. (Ekstein, Bryant, & Friedman, 1958, p. 596)

Although the "autistic" behavior of the autistic child helps us to distinguish his condition from childhood schizophrenia, heed should be paid to Goldstein's (1959) point that use of the term "autistic" begs the question of the nature of the child's illness by tacitly implying an analogy between the child's behavior and the "daydreaming" indulged in by the autistic adult. That some inaccessible adults apparently preoccupy themselves with pleasant phantasies provides no warrant for believing that a child who has never been accessible is similarly preoccupied.

6. *Preservation of sameness.* In addition to autistic aloneness, Kanner regards the insistence on the preservation of sameness as a cardinal symptom:

> It is remarkable to what extent the children will go to assure the preservation of sameness. The totality of an experience that comes to the child from the outside must be reiterated, often with all its constituent details, in complete photographic and phonographic identity. (1951, p. 23)

This is not at all common in schizophrenic children.

7. *Hallucinations.* Another distinguishing characteristic is the absence of hallucinations in the autistic child (Eisenberg, 1956). Schizophrenic children are reported to have many visual and auditory hallucinations, and in fact sometimes exhibit highly organized delusional systems (e.g., Bettelheim's "Joey, the Mechanical Boy," [1959a]; and Ekstein's "Space-Child," [1954]). The lack of reported hallucinations in autistic children has stimulated some imaginative writers to an admirably resourceful, but nevertheless gratuitous explanation—the negative hallucination, wherein the afflicted child pretends that nothing exists.

8. *Motor performance.* The excellent, and, in fact, often extraordinary, motor ability of autistic children, with regard to both gross body movements and finger dexterity has been described in Chapter 1. Schizophrenic children,

on the other hand, are much more often characterized by poor coordination, locomotion, and balance; and while twirling or spinning of small objects is common in both autism and schizophrenia, the autistic child's high degree of skill in these activities is not commonly reported in childhood schizophrenia.

Further, while bizarre or ritualistic hand movements and body rocking is reported in both conditions, autistic children do not typically exhibit such pathognomonic motor symptoms of childhood schizophrenia as body whirling and toe-walking (Bender & Helme, 1953; Lebowitz, Colbert, & Palmer, 1961; Goldfarb, 1961). (However, note that Kramer, Rabkin, & Spitzer, 1958, have challenged the use of whirling as a clinical test of childhood schizophrenia.)

9. *Language.* Not seen in childhood schizophrenia is perhaps the most striking and unique of all the symptoms of early infantile autism, the language pattern of affirmation by repetition, pronominal reversal (absence of the words "Yes" and "I"), delayed echolalia, metaphoric language, and part–whole confusion.

There can be no doubt of the accuracy of the observation by Kanner and others that the word "I" is not used by autistic children until about age seven, and then only sparingly. Weiland and Legg (1962) found no difference between "psychotic" children and a control group in the use of "I."[2] (However, Weiland's group was somewhat older than Kanner's, having a median age of 12.)

10. *Idiot savant performance.* The unusual memory, musical, and mechanical performances which fall in the realm of *idiot savant* phenomena, and which are routinely found in cases of infantile autism, have not, to the present writer's knowledge, been reported for childhood schizophrenia.

11. *Personal orientation.* While difficult to describe succinctly, a major difference between the autistic and schizophrenic child is found in his

---

2   The availability of quantitative methods of analysis makes research on speech and language highly desirable for purposes of differential diagnoses. Kanner's work on language in the autistic child has been cited in Chapter 1. More recently, Cunningham and Dixon (1961) and Pronovost (1961) have provided analyses of autistic speech, although the age of onset in the Cunningham and Dixon case raises the question of authenticity. A recent monograph by Bosch (1962), which has appeared too recently for incorporation of its content in the present work, is largely concerned with the speech of autistic children. Ekstein, Bryant, and Friedman (1958) cite several references to speech disturbances in childhood schizophrenia (see also Goldfarb, 1961), and G. Arnold (1960) also provides several references on this topic. The textbook by Luchsinger and Arnold which Arnold describes as presenting a survey of much of this material is being translated into English, according to a recent communication from Arnold.

orientation toward himself. This may be described by saying that the schizophrenic appears to be *dis*oriented, confused, and anxious, and often expresses deep concern about his relationship with his environment. He realizes he is confused. The autistic child is better described as *un*oriented, detached, appearing disinterested in the events occurring around him, and more aloof from and oblivious to the environment than in conflict with it. Again, the difference may be referred to as being characterized by frantic withdrawal and rejection for the schizophrenic, and by aloneness and non-participation for the autistic. Unlike the anxious schizophrenic, the autistic child gives the impression of independence and self-sufficiency. The schizophrenic child also tends to be more accessible than the autistic. Van Krevelen (1952a) has observed that autism lacks the element of dementia which characterizes schizophrenia. Comparative case histories are provided by Benda (1952, 1960), and by Despert and Sherwin (1958) which help illustrate these points. See also Cappon (1953) and Peck, Rabinovitch, and Cramer (1949).

12. *Conditionability.* A difference between autism and schizophrenia which has little immediate clinical use, but which appears to have considerable theoretical significance, lies in the facility with which conditioning can be accomplished. Mednick (1958) cites five studies which indicate that schizophrenics condition easily. In autism, however, one finds conditioning hard to establish and quick to extinguish (Anthony, 1958; Ferster & DeMyer, 1961).

13. *Twins.* As noted in Chapter 3, an unusual number of twins, especially monozygotic twins, has been reported with autism. Eleven of the 14 reported sets of autistic twins have apparently been monozygotic. The six reported studies of twins with schizophrenia, in contrast, show that schizophrenic twins follow the usual ratio of two or more dizygotic sets for each monozygotic set (Rosenthal, 1961a). This is also true for preadolescent schizophrenia (Kallman & Roth, 1956). Further, the apparent tendency we have described for autism to occur disproportionately often in twins is not found in schizophrenia (Rosenthal, 1961).

14. *Family background.* The extremely high educational and intellectual background and low divorce rate among parents of children with infantile autism has already been demonstrated. This is dramatically different from the familial background of childhood schizophrenia (Bender & Grugett, 1956; Creak & Ini, 1960; Kallman & Roth, 1956; Peck, Rabinovitch, & Cramer, 1949). Kallman and Roth classified 71 percent of the homes of their group of preadolescent schizophrenics as "inadequate."

15. *Familial mental disorder.* It has already been noted that the parents
and grandparents of autistic children show a strikingly low incidence of
mental illness. Out of 200 parents there was only one case of psychosis (a
postpartum depression). Siblings also tend to be in good mental health. The
often-quoted work of Kallman on the inheritance of schizophrenia reveals
a strong familial tendency which results in a much *higher* than average rate
of psychosis in the ancestors of schizophrenic children, not the much *lower*
rate found in the progenitors of the autistic group. Bender, in her papers
on childhood schizophrenia, has noted that some 40 percent of parents
were schizophrenic. In her paper with Grugett she states that *29 out of 30*
sets of parents manifested mental illness, usually schizophrenia.[3] Three of
the siblings were afflicted. This concordance rate among sibs agrees with
Kallman and Roth's estimate of about 8 percent, and not with Kanner's
(1954a) of only about 2 percent.

Writers who attempt to equate autism with schizophrenia find themselves
with a discomfiting absence of overt schizophrenia in the parents and families
of autistic children. A frequent response to this embarrassment is to explain
that the parents are really near-psychotics who are simply not disturbed
enough to hospitalize. Zilboorg's term, "ambulatory schizophrenia" has
sometimes been applied. This seems highly dubious. The hypothesis that
the parents of autistic children tend to be schizoid is at all plausible only
when one thinks solely in terms of one or two cases of withdrawn, intense
parents. If the parents as a group occupied a position near the schizoid
end of a scale of schizophrenic tendency, it would ordinarily be expected
that schizophrenia itself would occur in this group at a *higher* rate than
in the general population. The finding of an unusually *low* incidence of
schizophrenia in the several hundred parents of autistic children thus
renders as untenable the hypothesis that schizophrenia and autism are
somehow contiguous.

While we cannot elaborate on the implications at this point, it is of
considerable theoretical significance that even in those few cases in the
literature when there has been any family history of mental illness, it has
been a *depressive* condition and not a form of schizophrenia which has been
reported.

It is believed that the foregoing discussion has amply discredited the view
that early infantile autism is merely a variation of childhood schizophrenia.
In the writer's view it is clearly accurate and desirable to treat infantile

---

3   A statistical comparison of Kanner's figures on familial incidence of mental disorder
    with those of Bender shows there to be less than one chance in 10,000 that the two
    groups represent random samples from the same parent population.

autism and childhood schizophrenia as separate and quite unrelated disease entities. There will, of course, be some who will continue to apply the label "schizophrenic" to children with infantile autism. Psychiatric nosology is still a no-man's land where "Words mean what I want them to mean," to borrow Humpty-Dumpty's phrase. Such a refusal to consider the evidence and its implications will inevitably be a disservice to children afflicted with each disease.

Part II

A THEORY OF AUTISM

Its Nature and Cause

Introduction to Part II

The preceding chapters have constituted a review covering most of what is known about early infantile autism. The data are sparse but highly consistent. Objections could be raised to the conclusions which were reached in Part I, but unless the objections were based on a substantial body of new and differing evidence, it is the writer's opinion that the conclusions reached could be contested only with difficulty.

Part II, on the other hand, represents a less favorable balance between observation and interpretation. Part II is admittedly more speculative, and the phenomena under discussion are open to a wider variety of alternate interpretations. Despite this, it is believed that the theory of autism which follows is sufficiently plausible and parsimonious, and is sufficiently consistent with the evidence to warrant serious consideration.

The first two chapters of Part II are an attempt to formulate a simple but cohesive statement of the nature of the disability which produces the symptomatology of autism, and to link this disability with a specific brain mechanism. The third chapter in Part II is an attempt to relate the present theory of autism with pre-existing theory and data from related areas in biology. Part II is concluded with a chapter proposing research which will permit evaluation and extrapolation of the hypotheses set forth.

INTRODUCTION TO CHAPTER 5
Stephen M. Edelson

In the years since Bernard Rimland proposed a specific impairment in cognition, researchers have studied various components of cognitive processing in autism spectrum disorder, including attention, memory, and executive processing. One theory that has struck a chord in the field is the "weak central coherence" theory proposed by Francesca Happe and Uta Frith in 2006. According to this theory, those on the autism spectrum often have difficulty understanding context in a situation because of their inability to integrate information from a variety of sources in their environment.

Researchers have shown that several areas in the brain are impaired in autism, such as the frontal lobes, amygdala, and hippocampus. Abnormalities in these areas, as well as in their connections to other areas in the brain, may account for many of the documented cognitive processing problems (Goh & Peterson, 2012; Hill, 2006; Schmitz et al., 2006).

The update at the end of the chapter focuses primarily on memory, since Rimland's cognitive dysfunction hypothesis refers to an inability to retrieve information from long-term memory.

REFERENCES

Hill, E.L. (2004). Executive dysfunction in autism. *Trends in Cognitive Sciences*, 8(1), 26–32.

Goh, S., & Peterson, B.S. (2012). Imaging evidence for disturbances in multiple learning and memory systems in persons with autism spectrum disorders. *Developmental Medicine & Child Neurology*, 54(3), 208–213.

Happe, F., & Frith, U. (2006). The weak coherence account: Detailed-focused cognitive style in autism spectrum disorders. *Journal of Autism and Developmental Disorders*, 36(1), 5–25.

Schmitz, N., Rubia, K., Daly, E., Smith, A., Williams, S., & Murphy, D.G.M. (2006). Neural correlates of executive function in autism spectrum disorder. *Biological Psychiatry*, 59(1), 7–16.

CHAPTER 5

Autism as Cognitive Dysfunction

Baffling and paradoxical though early infantile autism has been considered to be, it is possible to trace its diversity of symptoms and manifestations to a single critical disability: *The child with early infantile autism is grossly impaired in a function basic to all cognition: the ability to relate new stimuli to remembered experience.* The vital connections between sensation and memory can be made only with difficulty. New sensation can be related only to sharply limited fragments of memory. The child is thus virtually divested of the means for deriving meaning from his experience. This impairment has two readily observable and interdependent consequences: (1) The child cannot understand relationships nor think in terms of concepts, symbols, analogies, or abstractions; and (2) He cannot integrate his sensations into a comprehensible whole—his perception of the world is vague and obscure.

A. THE CONCEPTUAL IMPAIRMENT

Part of the foregoing interpretation of the disease is not new. The idea that early infantile autism involves an inability to think conceptually was proposed by Scheerer, Rothmann, and Goldstein in 1945 and reasserted by Goldstein in 1959. As Sarason and Gladwin (1958) have pointed out, the monograph by Scheerer, Rothmann, and Goldstein has not received the attention it merits. The present writer had independently arrived at a formulation similar in many respects to that of Scheerer, Rothmann, and Goldstein from his own investigation of the problem before learning of their earlier paper.

Polan and Spencer (1959) also appeared to have had the conceptual disability in mind when they wrote:

The present authors suggest that the primary symptom of early infantile autism is a lack of integration pervading all behavior of the organism and manifesting itself in the distorted language, in the lack of social responsiveness, and in the lack of adaptability to environmental changes. (p. 11)

Let us consider Scheerer, Rothmann, and Goldstein's analysis of the condition of "L.," the *idiot savant* subject of their study:

L. suffers from an impairment of abstract attitude affecting his total behavior throughout. This expresses itself in the linguistic sphere by his "inability" to understand or use language in its symbolic and conceptual meaning; to grasp or to formulate properties of objects in the abstract (e.g., size, form, color); to comprehend or to evolve word definitions, similarities, differences, common denominators, logical analogies, opposites, metaphors; to conceive of the idea of causality, to raise the question "why" regarding real happenings, to deal with fictitious situations, to comprehend their rationale... The same impairment underlies his lack of social awareness and of curiosity in people... (p. 27)

Later in their paper Scheerer, Rothmann, and Goldstein note the "many parallels" between Kanner's autistic cases and their case L. (p. 57). (See also their case Q., p. 47.) They differ with Kanner's statement that the "fundamental disorder is the children's *inability to relate themselves* in the ordinary way to people and situations from the beginning of life," and with Kanner's interpretation that it is the "emotional resistance" of the child to change which accounts for the "inconsistent picture of mental ability, the obsessive repetitiousness, the shock reactions to loud noises and moving objects, and the 'truly phenomenal memory'..." (p. 57).

Scheerer, Rothmann, and Goldstein also take exception to Kanner's emphasis on the "affective" element in autism. They state:

...it is hard to see how an affective disturbance alone can account for what Kanner calls the "literalness" in these children, their inability to use "yes" as a *general* symbol of affirmation, detached from the specific situation in which it had been acquired; their inability to understand prepositions in the abstract sense. (Asked to put something down, the child puts it on the floor—understanding the word only in the originally acquired situational sense.) It is hard to follow Kanner when he makes the affect-anomaly responsible for "the absence of spontaneous sentence formation and the echolalia type of reproduction..." (p. 57)

These authors point out that excessively concrete thinking could readily account for what Kanner refers to as "pronominal reversal," the use of *you* for *I* ("*you* want some milk," when spoken by an autistic child, means "*I* want some milk"). They question whether the misuse of *you* for *I* is at all indicative of "affective disturbance," since the inability to comprehend the relational meanings of *you* and *I*, a symptom of impaired abstraction, would explain this phenomenon without reference to affect.

Scheerer, Rothmann, and Goldstein, and also Goldstein (1959), raise several other points which clearly and compellingly reject the hypothesis that autism is primarily an affective disturbance. For one thing, the fact that the children *willingly* memorized, while very young, lists of presidents, foreign lullabies, and nursery rhymes "with great facility" belies the need for sameness and aloneness and the rejection of human society that is an intrinsic part of the affective disturbance theory. Instead, it is noted, the children appear to have done all that they could with language—repeat it rather than understand it.

Many writers on early infantile autism have referred to it as basically a deficiency in "ego-development," regarding the inability to use "I" and the disinterest in others as evidence for an affective disorientation. There is indeed evidence for something akin to a "deficient ego" in the autistic child, but one need not refer to Freud to understand it. Scheerer, Rothmann, and Goldstein were clearly correct in emphasizing that the *I–You* problem appears to involve a difficulty in relational thinking, but the problem can be explained at an even more basic level by reference to the proposed general explanation of autism, which suggests a defective link between sensation and memory.

The development of the self-concept, the ability to perceive one's self as an entity, requires the exercise of an ability to abstract and accrete a certain essence from one's experiences. Each sensation and fragment of experience contributes to a person's perception of the world; and, in a normal individual, to his perception of himself as a unique object in that world. To an individual whose brain can deal only with isolated, unintegrated sensations, or at most with seemingly unrelated events, the building of an organized and unitary "ego" would seem to be impossible.

Consider the failure of the autistic child to understand the continuity of a story or motion picture, as described by Kanner (1943). The scenes or parts of the story are never comprehended as parts of a whole, but only as unrelated fragments. How can an individual with this level of conceptualization produce an integrated "ego" from his own experiences? Shown a picture of boys playing football, L. demonstrated the typically molecular perception of the world that characterizes autism by responding that they were "marching, shaking hands."

The failure of the child to develop an affectionate relationship with his family, a phenomenon attributed to a "pathologic parent–child relationship" by many writers can similarly be understood in terms of the child's inability to integrate and derive meaning from his experiences. The pleasant associations the normal child derives from contact with his mother, especially during feeding, are considered to play an important part in the development of affection. No association between "pleasure" and "mother"; no affection for mother. There may be some truth in the hypothesized diseased mother–child relationship, but the problem appears to lie in the relationship itself, which cannot take place in the child's impaired nervous system. Can maternal affection be said to exist for a child who lacks the capacity to interpret any form of stimulation?

Goldstein (1959) takes a somewhat different view—he attributes the child's failure to relate to others to the availability to the child of only primitive responses. This is consistent with his interpretation of autism as a response deficiency. As will be noted later, the problem can be traced to a still earlier point in the stimulus–response cycle.

The inability of autistic children to imitate others has been described by Ritvo and Provence (1953), Goldstein (1959), and others. Consider the role played by generalization in enabling one person to imitate another. First one must acquire the concept of similarity between one's self and the model. As already noted, establishing the concept of one's self requires a moderate amount of conceptual ability; establishing a useful analogy between one's self and another person—seemingly a basic requirement for imitation—demands a great deal more.

In contrast, the high level of form-perception demonstrated by autistic children (again described by Ritvo and Provence, as it has been by Kanner and others) does not require conceptualization. Fitting pieces into the form-board does not appear to demand much cognitive ability beyond mere sensation of the corresponding shapes. Perception, the linking of meaning to sensation, is not required, except insofar as the child must understand what his task is. Recall the autistic children who work jig-saw puzzles whether the picture faces up or down.

The children's often-noted amazingly retentive memories, which, like their form-board performances, have been cited as proof of good cognitive potential, represents another function which requires accurate sensation, but not conceptualization.

The conceptual failure to develop the idea of "self" appears to be accompanied in the autistic child by a comparable failure to develop any unified concept of other persons as such. People are treated like objects. One of Kanner's devices for diagnosing autism is to prick the child with a pin. If the child responds to the pin or the hand holding it, autism is indicated. If the child responds to the offending person, it is considered a non-autistic sign. This phenomenon, as well as the related phenomenon of the child's becoming angry at the *foot*, not the person, standing on his toy (1944) is consistent with the hypothesis that the child has failed to interrelate his experiences with other people so that the concept of "a person" is developed. Goldstein (1959), in his typically insightful manner, points out that it is only we *observers* who regard the foot on the toy as a mere instrument of the person. The autistic child cannot discern this relationship, so obvious to us, and modify his actions accordingly.

The child's "obsessive insistence on the preservation of sameness" and his often-reported intense fears can likewise be understood in terms of lack of comprehension. He does not understand the significance of any change, and so insists, often very emotionally, that the environment return to its original and presumably safer condition. Changes considered by us to be minor and irrelevant cannot be seen with as much understanding by the autistic child. We recognize, as the autistic child does not, which modifications of the environment alter its capacity to support our survival. Note the observation made in 1921 by an autistic girl's teacher (Darr & Worden, 1951): "An outstanding difficulty is that Jane is afraid of certain objects, e.g., the stove, and screams with terror at the sight of these things. Evidently she does not perceive them for what they really are" (p. 560).

The obsessive preoccupation with mechanical objects and household appliances almost universally reported for autistic children may readily be understood as a type of corollary to the resistance to change. Mechanical objects are highly consistent in their behavior and characteristics. They are interesting without being unpredictable. Light switches, faucets, vacuum cleaners, and jar lids are reliable enough to merit the child's confidence, and apparently challenging enough to maintain his interest.

Similar reasoning, based on the appeal of sameness and simplicity, may be used to explain the ritualistic repetitive behaviors, such as rocking and head-banging, which characterize the autistic child. The child can receive stimulation without excessive challenge to his cognition. In the case of repetitive behavior there may be a compounding factor of a blockage in the perceptual input, which might serve to distract a normal child and interrupt the behavior. This latter point will be discussed in greater detail later.

Kanner's own reports serve to support the conceptual impairment theory: "...autistic children show a peculiar type of obsessiveness that forces them to postulate imperiously a static, unchanged environment. Any modification meets with perplexity and major discomfort" (1951, p. 26). "Perplexity" does not fit well with the "affective disturbance" explanation espoused by Kanner elsewhere. Kanner's cases of the boy who was upset for many weeks by the broken cross-bar on a garage door, and the child who was disturbed because the Seguin Board star was not in the sky (1951) actually appear to be *cognitive* rather than affective in origin.

The experience reported by Eveloff (1960) is typical of many and illustrates well the cognitive disability: "She did not seem to comprehend that the records were needed to make the instrument function, even though she herself had put the records on many times before...she kept saying, 'Let's go find the record machine,' in a monotonous whine... I continued to explain to her what the situation was, over and over again. Eventually she began to show some sign of understanding..." (p. 74). Again quoting Eveloff: "Then gradually, after several weeks of repeating the same idea, she would come to have a useful, though stilted, verbal and intellectual grasp of that concept" (p. 74).

Closed-loop phenomena in autism. If we examine the autistic child's behavior analytically in an attempt to understand his thought pathology, one aspect of the problem emerges with particular significance: the remarkable identity between stimulus and response. This is most evident in the auditory sphere because it is easy to compare what is heard with what is said. The child's verbal responses are produced virtually unmodified by the experiences the child has had before, during, or since the moment of input. To make a mechanical analogy, it seems very much as though the material had entered the nervous system on a single track, proceeded to a point of storage without ever having been analyzed or supplemented, then later emerged from storage in virtually its original condition, on a parallel track, as an all-or-none response to some subsequent stimulus. There appear to be no switches or sidings along the track which would permit the input to be sorted, segregated, redistributed, or integrated with prior or subsequent input. If we may be permitted to change analogies, the autistic child's brain functions as though it were operated by a clerk rather than a chemist; raw material comes and goes, but the parcels are never opened and their contents are never mixed to form any useful compound.

These analogies do not represent an attempt at frivolity. They are instead a serious attempt to depict as clearly as possible a point of singular significance; the thought process of the autistic child as it can be inferred from his behavior.

The remarkable rote memory of the children, their extreme literalness, delayed echolalia, exceedingly accurate musical renditions, so-called concreteness of thought, and many other phenomena illustrate our point. G. Arnold's case (1960), who understood no language but who reproduced television commercials accurately by speaking and writing, may be recalled here. It might be said that *in early infantile autism stimuli are apprehended, but not comprehended.* This is so in the most literal sense of the words.

A striking illustration of the inability to integrate or relate remembered data meaningfully in an older child is provided by the following example: A case described by Scheerer, Rothmann, and Goldstein was asked: "Into what does the Mississippi River flow? A. Into the Gulf of Mexico. Q. Into what does the Rio Grande flow? A. Into the Gulf of Mexico. Q. What two rivers do you know that flow into the Gulf of Mexico? A. (He cannot answer)" (p. 46).

A similar example of inability to use stored information properly is seen in the autistic girl described by her mother (Kanner & Lesser, 1958): "She stops at all abstractions... She can count by rote. She can set the table for numbers of people if the names are given her or enumerated in any way, but she cannot set the table for three" (p. 714).[1]

Examples of this sort abound in the literature. Kanner's boy who always called his grandmother "55" because he once had heard her referred to as being 55 years old is a case in point (1946). Kanner's very first case, Donald (1943), who could not make the connection between his misconduct and his punishment may also be seen as a related problem.

One severely afflicted four-year-old autistic boy whose parent had slapped his hand lightly in an attempt to indicate non-verbally that the child's response to "close the door" was incorrect, learned instead to spank his own hand each time he was told to close the door. The connection had been made between the words "close the door" and the action of spanking the hand. Later, when the correct connection was made, the parents reported that the instruction was obeyed with obvious pleasure and enthusiasm, although there persisted for a year a vestigial spanking of one hand before the door knob was grasped. Some would call this a ritual. Van Krevelen (1952a) commented, with regard to his first case, that solid mental connections were made between a word and a concept, but in an odd and inappropriate way which caused him to wonder if the words were ever really understood.

The almost pathognomonic "*You–I*" reversal is clearly an example of what we refer to as closed-loop phenomena. A sentence such as "Do you want some milk?" enters the child's hearing apparatus, is stored without being disassembled or analyzed, and later emerges unchanged when an analogous stimulus situation arises.

The foregoing discussion has been concerned with the conceptual impairment in early infantile autism. While this impairment is clearly of prime

---

1   Consider the following explanation by Eisenberg and Kanner (1956) in the light of the foregoing example and the previously given data: "The vicissitudes of language development, often the most striking and challenging of the presenting phenomena, may be seen as the derivative of the basic disturbance in human relatedness" (p. 557).

importance, it is not in itself sufficient to account for all the phenomena. As Sarason and Gladwin (1958) ask with regard to the Scheerer, Rothmann, and Goldstein interpretation of autism as an impairment in abstract thinking, why are there signs of abnormality even before the child's ability to think abstractly is developed? In the following chapters we will turn our attention to this and to related problems which we wish to consider as part of a *perceptual impairment* in infantile autism. First, however, let us digress for a moment to consider a neural mechanism in the brain stem which has properties of considerable interest in the light of the foregoing discussion, and perhaps of even more interest in terms of discussion which is to ensue.

B. A HYPOTHESIZED RELATIONSHIP BETWEEN THE COGNITIVE DYSFUNCTION IN AUTISM AND THE RETICULAR FORMATION OF THE BRAIN STEM

The foregoing discussion would seem to imply that, in some very real way, memories, thoughts, and ideas are somehow locked into separate compartments of the autistic child's brain. They may be evoked by certain very specifically associated stimuli, but never in useful combination with other ideas, which themselves would appear to be similarly remembered only as isolated and unintegrated fragments of experience.

Where in the brain do incoming stimuli interact with previously stored experience to provide meaning to the former and exercise the *raison d'être* for the latter? In terms of our mechanical analogy, where can we find the sidings and switches whose absence, in fact or in effect, would produce the closed-loop, in-and-out-unchanged memory which characterizes so much of the behavior of the autistic child?

The academically correct and scientifically most defensible response to these questions is that nobody knows. And at least partly because the thought mechanisms involved and the questions themselves have not heretofore been formulated in this specific way, no one, to the present writer's knowledge, has addressed himself to this problem. But a good deal of relevant controversy and speculation has taken place in recent years concerning the functions of a small but highly complex network of nerve cells in the brain stem—the reticular formation.

In Chapter 6 we will consider some of the laboratory and clinical research on the functions of the reticular formation which have led several investigators to consider it as a possible site for the higher mental functions, despite its location in a phylogenetically ancient part of the brain. As will be demonstrated, certain research on these functions of the reticular formation tends to support our proposition that malfunction in this part of the brain may be the direct cause of the syndrome of infantile autism. For the present, we wish merely to point out that *anatomically* the reticular formation fits very well the requirements of the site of dysfunction in our mechanical model of autism.

The pivotal anatomical position of the reticular formation of the brain stem within the central nervous system may be understood by visualizing a slender arm with the fist enclosed in a rather large boxing glove. The cortex and its associated structures would roughly correspond to the glove, the brain stem and spinal cord to the flesh of the hand and arm, and the reticular formation to the bones of the hand and fingers. Like these bones, the reticular formation is actually composed of a series of identifiable but highly integrated substructures. But here the analogy ends.

Unlike the above depiction, the elements of the reticular formation are intertwined and interrelated to an extent which is quite beyond imagining. It has been referred to as a "thicket" of neurons, which are intermeshed not only with each other, but with all parts of the cortex. Clark has provided an excellent description of the reticular formation:

> ... It can be visualized as a sort of central core composed of scatterings of nerve cells entangled in an irregular and closely meshed network of nerve fibres, and extending up from the spinal cord through the brain stem to run into continuity with the intralaminar nuclei of the thalamus. As is now well known, the whole system is linked up indirectly with the cerebral cortex and by circuitous routes is capable of influencing and profoundly modifying cortical activity as a whole. Into the reticular formation stretching through the spinal cord and brain stem there stream numerous collaterals from the incoming sensory fibres of peripheral nerves, as well as a continuous succession of collaterals from many (perhaps all) of the ascending tracts of the specific sensory pathways. (1958, p. 10)

Like most who describe the reticular system, Clark has emphasized the ascending nerve tracts and consequently the effects of the reticular formation upon the cortex. It will be of importance to our discussion that the cortex may similarly exert descending influences on the reticular formation (Ellingson, 1956; Lindsley, 1958; Magoun, 1958a).

In terms of its anatomical location within the brain, in terms of its intricate neural structure, and in terms of its numerous neural connections to the sense organs and cortex, the reticular formation seems admirably well suited to supply the collaterals and interconnections within the normal brain whose functional absence in cases of autism could result in thought impairment of the type we have described.

The reticular formation has in fact been referred to by some writers as the "communications center," "central relay station," or "master switchboard" of the brain. While the concept of reticular function we wish to invoke is somewhat similar, it should be emphasized that such imaginative descriptions do not reflect the majority opinion concerning the role the reticular formation plays in mental functioning.

Ivanitskiy (1960) has discussed the problem of higher functions in his review of the world literature on the reticular formation. He emphasizes that its primary function is believed to consist in maintaining the tone of the cortex and of other parts of the brain at "the level optimum for the given moment." This is the widely accepted "arousal function," resulting from the so-called diffuse, non-specific effects of reticular stimulation. According to Ivanitskiy, "Attempts at creating a theory relegating the main role in carrying out the functions of consciousness to a non-specific system (theory of the centrencephalic system), has not been widely recognized by the majority of research workers" (p. 10).

Ivanitskiy admits, however, that "the idea of the diffuseness, 'nonspecificity' influences exerted by the reticular formation are being subjected to criticism on a progressively greater scale at the present time" (p. 7), and cites works by Olszewski, Brodal, Narikashvili, and Moruzzi as supplying evidence in support of the view that the reticular formation may serve purposes in addition to, or apart from, its maintenance and regulatory roles.

The role ascribed here to the reticular formation, that of providing a site for the linking of sensory input (real or symbolic) with the prior content of the brain, is admittedly highly speculative. It should be made clear that the general theory of autism offered in this paper is not contingent upon the correctness of this hypothesis. Nor is our theory of autism dependent upon the reticular formation as the actual site of the localized brain impairment which the theory does assume. Nevertheless, in the face of both supporting and contradictory evidence, we choose for the present to refer to the reticular formation as the site of the impairment. The advantages of being specific on this point appear to outweigh the risks entailed in being wrong.

And for reasons which will become clear later, we choose to emphasize the "linkage" function of the reticular formation even though Hebb (1955) has provided an alternative theory which could account for a cognitive failure as a consequence of a failure in the reticular formation's well-accepted arousal function. Hebb points out that sensory events have at least two functions: a cue function, required for guiding behavior, and the arousal function. He suggests that "we may assume that cortical synaptic function is facilitated by the diffuse bombardment of the arousal system" (p. 250).

An experiment by Fuster (1958) in which animal learning was facilitated by imposing an electrical current upon the reticular formation lends support to the idea that the reticular formation serves to enhance synaptic connecting, but provides no inkling as to whether the learning improvement results from facilitation of reticular or cortical synaptic functions. If it does turn out to be the reticular formation which is impaired in autism, Hebb's suggestion would appear less tenable, because autistic children learn very well, at least insofar as purely rote memory is concerned.

In a more recent paper (1959) Hebb does appear to attribute higher functions to the reticular formation. He notes that gross damage to the cortex (i.e., removal of one hemisphere) has been found to have no observable effect on intelligence, while even minor damage to the brain stem has more severe consequences.

Fessard (1954) had made this same point in reply to the attack made by Bremer upon Fessard's postulation of the reticular system as the basic mechanism of "nervous integration and conscious experience." Fessard, in defending the "bold hypothesis" that a subcortical center could perform such high functions, made his point concerning the differential effects of cortical and brain stem damage in conjunction with a discussion highly relevant to the "linkage" theory of reticular function proposed in this chapter:

> ...we are pretty sure that only some parts of brain are involved in any instantaneous conscious experience, and that unless we believe the possibility of an integration outside our world of matter and energy— which I do not—we have to conceive of a way through which such parts can communicate and rapidly interact, in spite of their often being supported by structures that lie wide apart. Now, however cautious one may be as regards the interpretation and generalizations to be given to experiments and clinical observations that show the minor role played by transcortical connections, one cannot deny or overlook the striking contrast between the tolerance of the cortex to mutilation and the existence of regions in the brain stem that are highly critical regarding consciousness. Consequently, I maintain that the first hypothesis deserves a serious examination, and should not be rejected too quickly under the pretext that it could not easily fit with our present views on the fundamentals of central nervous activity. (pp. 247–248)

Fessard went on to explain that his "first hypothesis" included the thalamic and sub-thalamic reticular systems as well as the reticular formation itself.

Penfield appears to have been the first to suggest that subcortical (centrencephalic) structures may serve higher functions than does the cortex, in 1936. Recently he has referred to the reticular formation as a possible locus (Penfield & Roberts, 1959).

Brain (1958), in an excellent review of related problems, refers to studies by Gastaut and by Jasper, Ricci, and Doane which support Penfield's contention by finding discriminative functions of the reticular formation. Clark (1958), in his discussion of the reticular formation, suggests "a mechanism of this sort" might be involved in inventive thinking and imagination.

Although a number of writers have followed Penfield in attributing consciousness and other higher mental functions to the brain stem (Brain, 1958; Clark, 1958; Fessard, 1954; French, 1957; Hebb, 1959, for example) there have been few attempts to specify the nature of these functions. As may be seen in his foregoing quotation, Fessard's idea is related to that proposed here. Penfield has referred to the centrencephalic system as being "responsible for the integration of the function of the hemispheres" (Penfield & Roberts, 1959, p. 21) and as being "forever busy with the organization of the present" (p. 233). French (1957) suggests that the reticular formation may contribute to "the focussing of attention, introspection, and doubtless all forms of reasoning" (p. 60).

If our hypothesis be correct that early infantile autism is due to a reticular lesion, a great deal of welcome light could be shed on the problem of higher brain function. This is one reason why we choose to be as specific and explicit as the circumstances permit.

Let us now give consideration to less hypothetical functions of the reticular formation and see what bearing they have on the problem of autism. We will presently return to the possibility that the reticular formation serves some very high functions.

COGNITIVE DYSFUNCTION

Impairment in Memory

Stephen M. Edelson

Bernard Rimland was clearly ahead of his time when he proposed a "cognitive" theory, not just with respect to autism, but with respect to psychology in general. At that time, behavioral psychology dominated the field in terms of explaining behavior. In those days, hypothesizing about a person's internal thought processes was frowned upon since the mind was considered a "black box." Behaviorists argued that professionals should not even speculate on thought processes since these unobservable phenomena could not be measured objectively.

While Rimland was a pioneer, he was not alone in discussing cognitive processes. Other prominent psychologists also began writing about cognition, including Posner and Rossman (1965), Neisser (1967), and Atkinson and Shiffrin (1968).

In "Autism as Cognitive Dysfunction," Chapter 5, Rimland proposed a cognitive impairment that he felt was central to autism. He continued to believe in this strongly for the rest of his career. In sum, he wrote:

> *The child with early infantile autism is grossly impaired in a function basic to all cognition: the ability to relate new stimuli to remembered experience.* (page 106; italics in original)

Based on his observations and a careful reading of the literature, Rimland argued quite concisely that those on the autism spectrum have difficulty understanding the world around them because they have an impairment in making associations (or "relationships") between memories from their past and their current situation. This, of course, would lead to much confusion about cause-and-effect relationships within their environment, and, consequently, impede their understanding of their surroundings. For example, a child with autism might occasionally touch a hot stove because he or she does not remember the burning sensation that resulted from touching the stove at an earlier time.

Rimland's cognitive theory was and still is consistent with many of the findings on cognition in autism. In the 1960s and 1970s, researchers speculated that the memory of those on the autism spectrum was similar to those with amnesia, implying an inability to recall past events. In time, more rigorous research showed that those on the autism spectrum have an impaired *episodic* or *autobiographical* memory, meaning that they are impaired in retrieving information from memory that is related to their personal experience (Gaigg, Dermot, & Gardiner, 2014; Tulving, 1983).

Soon after the publication of *Infantile Autism*, other researchers, especially those in the United Kingdom, began to study various aspects of cognition in autism. They included pioneers Beate Hermelin, Neil O'Connor, and Uta Frith.

Storage and retrieval of memories are important components in processing information. There are several ways to conceptualize information processing. In this update, I will rely on a traditional approach, briefly summarizing some of the major findings in each of the four areas below:

Attention ➤ Sensory memory ➤ Short-term and working memory ➤ Long-term memory

Attention. I remember a conference call in the late 1980s in which Rimland, Ivar Lovaas, and I spent several hours discussing various topics related to autism. When we discussed learning, the three of us agreed that attention was one of the core deficits in autism.

Actually, there is quite a bit of research on attention impairments in autism. One of the earliest findings pertains to a phenomenon termed "stimulus over-selectivity." First studied by Lovaas and colleagues in 1971 (and discussed in a review article in 1979), stimulus over-selectivity refers to a form of tunnel vision in which individuals focus on or attend to only one aspect of a stimulus, whether relevant or not, and ignore other parts. For example, if shown a fork, an individual with autism may attend to only the color and ignore the shape. As a result, it would be difficult to learn to discriminate a fork from a spoon.

Another problem in autism is an impaired ability to shift attention from one stimulus to another (Courchesne et al., 1994). When asked to change their focus of attention, individuals with autism continue to perseverate on the current stimulus, and only gradually refocus their attention to another stimulus. For example, if a child is playing with a toy and a parent walks into the room and begins to talk, the child will likely continue to attend to the toy for a little while longer and then gradually shift his or her attention to the parent's voice. As a result, the child may miss the first sentence or two, and have difficulty understanding what was said.

A third problem, which relates to social skills, is joint attention (see Bruinsma, Koegel, & Koegel, 2004 for a review). This form of attention occurs when two or more individuals attend to the same object. For example, it is typical for a child to look at an object a parent is looking at, or at least look in the same direction. Numerous studies show that joint attention is impaired in autism, and assessment of a young child's joint attention is often used to help screen for autism at an early age.

Sensory memory. This form of memory, sometimes referred to as "short-term sensory store," is actually a physical form of memory built into our sensory system. In vision, the image is stored in "iconic" memory and lasts, on average, for half a second. In hearing, sound is stored in "echoic" memory for three to four seconds and possibly longer due to the context of the auditory stimulus. In touch, a sensation is stored in "haptic" memory and lasts, on average, for two seconds.

Because it is difficult to assess the duration of these various processes, it is not clear whether or not those on the autism spectrum have a physical impairment in one or more of their senses. However, given that many individuals on the spectrum are hypersensitive or hyposensitive to stimuli, research is needed to understand the reason for their discomfort, and even pain, so we can treat them properly and improve their quality of life.

Short-term and working memory. Short-term memory involves the temporary storage of a limited amount of information for a relatively short duration. The research on short-term memory in individuals with autism is mixed, possibly due to the heterogeneity of the population.

In contrast, spatial working memory appears to be impaired in autism (Steele et al., 2007); however, some studies have not documented any impairment in working memory in this population (Ozonoff & Strayer, 2001). This form of memory involves holding and manipulating information in the mind. Working memory is a critical component of executive functioning, which includes planning, organizing, strategizing, and decision making.

Long-term memory. As mentioned earlier, research shows that episodic or autobiographical memory is impaired in many individuals with autism. In other words, many individuals on the spectrum have difficulty relating past experience with the present. Episodic memory is one of the many components of long-term memory.

There are other interesting findings regarding memory in autism. For example, research shows that individuals with autism have more accurate memories for non-social stimuli than for social stimuli (Boucher, Mayes, & Bigham, 2012). Consistent with these findings, researchers have documented impairments in face perception, affecting recognition of familiar faces (Klin et al., 1999).

Although cognition in autism has been studied for many years, researchers' findings are typically not considered and applied when developing educational curricula. Awareness of such basic cognitive processing deficits, such as memory, will likely aid in the creation of more efficient teaching strategies.

REFERENCES

Atkinson, R.C., & Shiffrin, R.M. (1968). Human memory: A proposed system and its control processes. In K.W. Spence & J.T. Spence (eds) *The Psychology of Learning and Motivation (Volume 2)*. New York: Academic Press.

Boucher, J., Mayes, A., & Bigham, S. (2012). Memory in autism spectrum disorder. *Psychological Bulletin*, 138(3), 458–496.

Bruinsma, Y., Koegel, R., & Koegel, L. (2004). Joint attention and children with autism: A review of the literature. *Mental Retardation and Development Disabilities*, 10(3), 169–175.

Courchesne, R., Townsend, J., Akshoomoff, N.A., Saitoh, O., et al. (1994). Impairment in shifting attention in autistic and cerebella patients. *Behavioral Neuroscience*, 108(5), 848–865.

Gaigg, S.B., Dermot, M.B., & Gardiner, J.M. (2014). Episodic but not semantic order memory difficulties in autism spectrum disorder: Evidence from the Historical Figures Task. *Memory*, 22(6), 669–678.

Klin, A., Sparrow, S.S., de Bildt, A., Cicchetti, D.V., Cohen, D.J., & Volkmar, F.R. (1999). A normed study of face recognition in autism and related disorders. *Journal of Autism and Developmental Disorders*, 29(6), 499–509.

Lovaas, O.I., Koegel R.L., & Schreibman L. (1979). Stimulus overselectivity in autism: A review of research. *Psychological Bulletin*, 86(6), 1236–1254.

Lovaas, O.I., Schreibman, L., Koegel, R., & Rehm, R. (1971). Selective responding by autistic children to multiple sensory input. *Journal of Abnormal Psychology*, 77(3), 211–222.

Neisser, U. (1967). *Cognitive Psychology*. Englewood Cliffs, NJ: Prentice-Hall.

Ozonoff, S., & Strayer, D.L. (2001). Further evidence of intact working memory in autism. *Journal of Autism and Developmental Disorders*, 31(3), 257–263.

Posner, M.I., & Rossman, E. (1965). Effect of size and location of informational transforms upon short-term retention. *Journal of Experimental Psychology*, 70(5), 496–505.

Steele, S.D., Minshew, N.J., Luna, B., & Sweeney, J.A. (2007). Spatial working memory deficits in autism. *Journal of Autism and Developmental Disorders*, 37(4), 605–612.

Tulving, E. (1983). *Elements of Episodic Memory*. New York: Oxford University Press.

INTRODUCTION TO CHAPTER 6
Stephen M. Edelson

Although Rimland stated that his ideas were "speculative," he made a logical case that the underlying neurological deficit in autism may involve the reticular formation. Since the publication of *Infantile Autism*, a considerable number of studies have examined the brain structure of those on the autism spectrum. One of the true pioneers in this area is Margaret Bauman, who wrote one of the forewords to this edition of the book. Later in this book, Martha Herbert discusses what is currently known about the role of the reticular formation in autism, in addition to providing an overall perspective on current neurological research (see update to Chapter 11 on page 272–277).

In this chapter, Rimland also discussed the role of arousal and its relationship to autism. Arousal was a popular topic of investigation during the 1960s. More recently, researchers have revisited arousal levels in autism, and they are finding impairments in both the sympathetic system (which increases arousal) and the parasympathetic system (which decreases arousal) (Ming et al., 2005, 2011).

Rimland also discussed several topics pertaining to the sensory system, including receptor preference, pain perception, and sensory sensitivities. He believed that we must understand sensory impairments in autism in order to properly treat the hyposensitivities and hypersensitivities that are common in this condition. Lucy J. Miller, Matthew Goodwin, and Jillian Sullivan have contributed an update on sensory research for this book (page 149–155).

Early on, Rimland believed that drugs might play a useful role in the treatment of autism, and he devoted a section in his book to psychopharmacology. Paul Hardy, a long-time friend and colleague of Rimland, provides an update on this area of treatment (page 146–148). Note: Over the years, Rimland realized that most drugs had serious side effects. As a result, he came to feel strongly that these drugs generally were not worth trying, given the frequently mediocre benefits.

After receiving many reports from parents worldwide about the helpfulness of certain vitamins and minerals, Rimland began studying the efficacy of these nutrients, viewing each reported case as an independent case study. After extensive evaluation, he found that vitamin B_6 improved general well-being in almost half of those with autism (Rimland, 1973; Rimland,

Callaway, & Dreyfus, 1978). Jon Pangborn, also a long-time friend and colleague of Rimland, offers an update here on vitamin B_6 (page 156–158). Rimland also discussed the possible role of hyperoxia soon after birth. Although studies have not shown a relationship between autism and hyperoxia, research has shown that complications are more likely during pregnancy, delivery, and the neonatal period in those with autism as compared with unaffected siblings and the general population (Deykin & MacMahon, 1980; Gardener, Spiegelman, & Buka, 2009).

REFERENCES

Deykin, E.Y., & MacMahon, B. (1980). Pregnancy, delivery, and neonatal complications among autistic children. *American Journal of Diseases of Children*, 134(9), 860–864.

Gardener, H., Spiegelman, D., & Buka, S.L. (2009). Prenatal risk factors for autism: Comprehensive meta-analysis. *British Journal of Psychiatry*, 195, 7–14.

Ming, X., Julu, P.O., Brimacombe, M., Connor, S., & Daniels, M.L. (2005). Reduced cardiac parasympathetic activity in children with autism. *Brain Development*, 27(7), 509–516.

Ming, X., Bain, J.M., Smith, D., Brimacombe, M., Gold von-Simson, G., & Axelrod, F.B. (2011). Assessing autonomic dysfunction symptoms in children: A pilot study. *Journal of Child Neurology*, 26(4), 420–427.

Rimland, B. (1973). High dosage levels of certain vitamins in the treatment of children with severe mental disorders. In D. Hawkins & L. Pauling (eds) *Orthomolecular Psychiatry*. New York: W.H. Freeman.

Rimland, B., Callaway, E., & Dreyfus, P. (1978). The effects of high doses of vitamin B6 on autistic children: A double-blind crossover study. *American Journal of Psychiatry*, 135, 472–475.

CHAPTER 6

The Specific Biology
of Infantile Autism

Sensory Phenomena, Psychopharmacology,
Autopsy Reports, and Hyperoxia as
Related to the Reticular Formation

In the preceding chapter the proposition was advanced that early infantile autism could be understood in terms of an impairment in the ability to relate the current objects of sensation with what had previously been stored in memory. The resulting behavior pathology was said to be divisible into two major components, the conceptual and the perceptual. The brain stem reticular formation was suggested as a possible site of the organic impairment which resulted in these cognitive problems. It was noted that suggesting the reticular system as a site for the conceptual impairment was highly speculative, and that only in the past few years had any support appeared in the literature for the idea that high mental functions could be based in the brain stem.

The perceptual phenomena, however, may be postulated to a brain stem locus with considerably greater confidence. In this chapter we will first discuss the perceptual phenomena which characterize autism in terms of present knowledge of the reticular system. We will then discuss other aspects of the specific biology of infantile autism as they may be related to reticular dysfunction.

A. THE RETICULAR FORMATION AND PERCEPTION
It is well established from electroencephalographic investigations that sensory stimulation evokes impulses from the reticular formation. Further, the reticular formation has been shown to play a vital role in the original

evocation of attention and in the maintenance of alertness, as well as in modulating the sensory activities of the receptor organs. Among many excellent papers describing those functions are those by Brain, 1958; French, 1957; Lindsley, 1958; Magoun, 1958a, 1958b, 1961; and Scheibel and Scheibel, 1960.

The perceptual capacities of autistic children have long presented one of the most puzzling aspects of the disease. We have subdivided the perceptual impairment into several categories, each of which will be considered separately in terms of relevant research on the reticular formation.

The veil of autism and the arousal function

The autistic child often appears to be surrounded by a mysterious veil which effectively isolates him from all external stimulation. Kanner has used the term "encapsulated." Parents of autistic children refer to this impairment in many ways: "I can't reach him," "My child seems to be in a shell all the time," "It's as though he can't see us or hear us, or won't." The very term "autistic," it was noted earlier, refers to this phenomenon. The child appears to be off in some distant dream-world.

Kanner described his first case as manifesting:

...an abstraction of mind which made him perfectly oblivious to everything about him. He appears to be always thinking and thinking, and to get his attention almost requires one to break down a mental barrier between his inner consciousness and the outside world. (1943, p. 218)

This problem was described again by Kanner in 1944: "...when spoken to, he went on with what he was doing as if nothing had been said. Yet one never had the feeling that he was willingly disobedient or contrary. He was obviously so remote that the remarks did not reach him" (p. 212).

Suspicion of deafness is very often the earliest interpretation placed on the inaccessibility of the autistic child by his parents. At least seven of Kanner's first 11 cases were thought deaf or hard-of-hearing. But even deafness would not explain the parents' inability to communicate with him or even attract his attention visually. Just as puzzling is the contradictory evidence which relates to the excellence of the child's hearing and vision—sometimes. The highly superior musical performance common in autistic children belies a hearing defect, and the child's disheartening ability to detect, and react catastrophically to, minute changes in the visual environment which have escaped his parents' notice (Kanner, 1951) certainly does not speak for any visual impairment in the usual sense.

The Darr and Worden case (1951) had an "...inability to cooperate... due to...an inattention associated with preoccupation of some sort." Lehman et al. (1957) state: "Of our nine children, only four...evidenced noteworthy awareness of things around them." Bergman and Escalona (1949), van Krevelen (1952a), Popella (1955), Goldfarb (1956), Anthony (1958), and Eveloff (1960) are among the many writers who have described children who could not be reached by sight or sound, who were not aware of even loud or unusual noises.

It is during the times that the children are especially deeply entranced that they take on the "vacuous distant stare" which Eveloff refers to as providing the wistful and pensive appearance that is "perhaps the most striking physical symptom in these children." Popella described an autistic child who looks at you as "though you were made of glass." These observations will be referred to again when we discuss "long eye"—the stare of a person too long subjected to a barren sensory environment.

Rothenberg includes in her description of "Jonny" a similar observation:

> Jonny seemed to lack sensation, seemed not to feel pain. You could strike him—or he might punch himself black and blue—but he wouldn't cry out. If you tickled him he didn't laugh; if you called his name he didn't respond; if there was a sound in the room he didn't hear it; and if you got within his range of vision, his ill-focused eyes didn't look at you but somewhere above or beyond you. (1960, p. 62)

Anthony's observations have led him to write (1958) that the autistic child lives in the "world of the young infant set in the twilight of consciousness." In one of the few attempts to perform systematic experimental work on autistic children, Anthony observed that they showed "no startle response at any time," nor did they show, with experience, any preparatory set.

What could account for such paradoxical phenomena? Is indeed the child rejecting his parents and the world because he senses a subtle hostility toward him, as the psychogenicists suggest? Is it really "retaliation" against the personalities of his "cold and detached" parents?

Perhaps not. It is well established that the reticular formation must be functioning to achieve and maintain a state of alertness. Persons suffering injury to the reticular formation become comatose (Daly & Love, 1958; French, 1957; Lindsley, 1958). French says such persons are "as shut off from communication as a vegetable." Laboratory animals with reticular formation lesions cannot be activated, even by intense stimulation (Ellingson, 1956).

What would be the behavior of a child whose reticular formation were badly impaired?

Is this the secret of the veil of autism?

Receptor preferences and the problems of recognition and meaning

Next in importance to the perceptual inaccessibility of the autistic child are the implications of his preference for the proximal senses, touch, taste, and smell over the distal senses, vision and hearing. Goldfarb (1956) has presented an extended discussion of receptor preferences. See also the discussions by Bergman and Escalona (1949), Ritvo and Provence (1953), and Bettelheim (1959b). One child severely afflicted with autism appeared to be functionally blind in many respects. Until the age of three, pictures carried no meaning whatever for him, nor could his attention be directed to any object in the environment outside of his arm's length. Polan and Spencer (1959) report another autistic child who could not seem to perceive pictures. They also report a set of twins who did not focus their eyes.

One of Goldfarb's cases was a boy, presumably autistic, who very willingly ate ice cream when it was placed in his mouth, but made no effort to obtain it when it was offered to him. Many other writers have made reference to the liking autistic children have for sweets. Anthony (1958) and Ferster and DeMyer (1961, 1962) have used candy in their attempts to condition the children.

The girl described by Eveloff (1960) could not understand why she could not take in her hand the cane painted on a life-size dummy. Repeatedly rubbing her hand over the surface had little effect in showing her its two-dimensional character.

The difficulty autistic children have in their visual search behavior seems to represent another aspect of this fundamental impairment, the inability to cope with figure–ground relationships. Anthony (1958) and Kanner have both referred to this problem. Kanner's case (1951) looked only where an object had formerly been, even though it was very near and plainly visible. This is a striking phenomenon to observe. The children's relief and pleasure when they finally "see" the object they have been seeking is plainly evident. Children such as those described by Bruch (1959) and Kanner (in various publications) who walk "over" or "through" other persons could also be suffering from figure–ground perceptual disturbances.[1]

---

1 A psychogenic account: "For these children danger lies in the voice and in the visual glance, which, for them, can destroy and damage. Hence, to avoid such annihilation, he avoids or denies the stimuli" (Bruch, 1959, p. 24).

Mahler (1952) has described autistic children as having "a peculiar inability to discriminate between living and inanimate objects, even in a perceptual sense" (p. 291). Goldfarb's case, John, showed visual inattention to both human and nonhuman objects. He did not distinguish between people, and "even his mother was vaguely perceived."

Mahler's case, Lotta, was given to fingering objects "like blind people do." Bergman and Escalona (1949), and Ritvo and Provence (1953) describe similar cases.

In his discussion of the preferences for touching, tasting, and smelling objects, Goldfarb pointed out the similarity of this behavior with the actions of the Klüver-Bucy monkeys, whose temporal lobes and parts of the associated structures, especially the hippocampus, had been ablated. The mouthing, smelling, etc., behavior is generally considered to be due to visual agnosia, the inability to recognize objects visually with regard to meaning or function (Morgan & Stellar, 1950).

Thus it would seem that the preference of autistic children for the proximal and contact senses might be explained by their simply not being able to perceive—to attach meaning to the input from their distance receptors.[2] We again find autistic behavior understandable in terms of an impairment in the ability to attach memory to sensory input. We may recall here the remark made by the teacher of the girl described by Darr and Worden to the effect that the girl screamed in terror at the sight of objects, like a stove, because she did not seem to recognize them for what they were.

The autistic child's almost universal failure to adapt his body in anticipation of being picked up is, according to Kanner, usually the parent's first sign of the child's affliction. The most objectively demonstrable fact about perception, Sperry (1952) has pointed out, is that *an organism that has perceived a given object is prepared to respond with reference to it.* "This preparation-to-respond is absent in an organism that has failed to perceive" (p. 301).

Could impairment in the function of the reticular formation account for these various indications that perception is absent or nearly absent in autistic children?

One of the best-known responses of the reticular formation is the strong impulse evoked on the presentation of a new or unusual stimulus to the animal (Sharpless & Jasper, 1956). Subsequent presentations, even if louder or brighter, have a lesser effect. This implies perception, or something closely

---

2   The distance receptors are sometimes referred to as "mediate," in distinction from the "immediate" (un-mediated) contact or proximal receptors, which provide for direct experience of the stimulus object by the body. Sight and hearing depend instead on energy emanated by or reflected from the object.

akin to it. If sensation alone were involved, there would be little reason to expect differential reactions from the first to subsequent presentations.

As the process by which meaning is given to the object of attention, perception may be seen to require a brain mechanism similar to that specified in the previous chapter as required for conceptual thought: a means for deriving utility from a present idea or sensation by referring it to prior experience. Lindsley (1958) provides support for our suggestion that the reticular formation offers a means and a site where this integration may take place. Lindsley, after noting that barbiturate anesthesia blocks the reticular formation while leaving the specific sensory pathways open, observes that "the sensory messages thus apparently get to the cortex, but whatever is required for their integration is absent since the animal or human does not respond to these messages in any meaningful way. Hence without the reticular activating system it appears that discrimination is not possible..." (p. 55).

It would be difficult to find a better laboratory demonstration of van Krevelen's (1952a) description of his autistic patient: "blind while seeing, and deaf while hearing."

The perception of pain

A third category of perceptual phenomenon reported for some autistic children is their insensitivity to pain.

Rothenberg's description of Jonny, wherein an amazing deficiency to perceive pain is shown, has already been cited. He might even "punch himself black and blue" without crying out. Stern and Schachter (1953) have referred to a boy who has not the slightest perception of danger in fire or sharpness. Others have reported related findings, but this phenomenon does not appear to be as universal among autistic children as those previously discussed.

Goldfarb's (1958) discussion indicates pain insensitivity to be common among schizophrenic as well as autistic children. Bettelheim (1959b) has also referred to insensitivity to pain and cold in his interesting discussion of the possibility that so-called "feral children" may in fact be autistic.

Mahler (1952) provides an interesting example of pain insensitivity in her discussion of Lotta, the autistic girl referred to earlier. Her therapist had given Lotta a toy flashlight, which Lotta mouthed, as is common among autistic children. Later, upon seeing her mother use an automobile cigarette lighter, Lotta placed the lighter to her own mouth, as she had been doing with the flashlight. Although the lighter scorched Lotta's lips severely,

Lotta showed no pain reaction.[3] Mahler observed that this insensitivity to peripheral pain was especially interesting, since Lotta on another occasion showed keen sensitivity to visceral pain.

In discussing pain insensitivity in autistic children, Bruch (1959) has suggested that the children "possess a neural apparatus to perceive pain, but vary from the normal in their inner perception of pain…" (p. 24). She goes on to explain that pain insensitivity may be related to the "shortcomings of the environment in which the child grew up, where he was not helped to achieve awareness of distress or the techniques for the communication of pain" (p. 25).

While Bruch's attributing of inadequate pain perception to improper child rearing is not substantiated by any evidence, it is nonetheless interesting to compare her ideas with the observations made by Melzack (1961), who has extensively studied pain with laboratory and controlled clinical methods: "The amount and quality of pain we feel are also determined by our previous experiences and how well we remember them, by our ability to understand the cause of the pain and grasp its consequences" (p. 41). Here again we find a symptom of autism (deficient pain perception) to be related to the ability to link sensation with experience, a function we at least tentatively attribute to the reticular formation. While the problem of perceiving pain is obviously complex, it is of interest that Melzack says intractable pain may be relieved by severing certain nerve tracts stemming from the reticular formation. This operation has the effect of removing the suffering and its related components from the patient's perception, while the *sensations*

---

3   Readers familiar with Mahler's account may be somewhat surprised, as was the present writer, at Bettelheim's (1956, p. 509) version of it: "Within the benign and constructive setting of the treatment room, a little girl greatly enjoyed playing with a flashlight her analyst had given her. Driving home in the car with her mother from the analyst's office, the girl put the car's hot cigarette lighter to her mouth, causing severe scorching of her lips. The presence of the mother had changed a pleasurable experience into a destructive one." Bettelheim failed to mention Mahler's belief that the autism was *inherent* (Mahler's italics) and that Lotta had previously been mouthing the flashlight and was now imitating her mother's use of the lighter. Nor did he mention Lotta's insensitivity to pain, which was Mahler's primary purpose in relating the incident. Later (1959b), when concerned with pain insensitivity *per se* (rather than with devising support for the psychogenic view), Bettelheim presented Mahler's version quite accurately. Ironically enough, in this very same paper (1959b) Bettelheim rejected Reverend Singh's detailed *participant* account of finding wolf-children among living wolves on the grounds that "Hindsight is easy," and by noting that one's needs and beliefs can too easily distort his interpretation of events. Despite his reinterpretation of certain of the available evidence on feral children, Bettelheim's hypothesis that feral children may be autistic is quite plausible. His conclusion that the evidence suggests autism to be "due in large part, if not entirely" to "extreme emotional isolation" is not.

which formerly evoked pain continue to remain. Has this operation served to reduce the effect of previous experience on pain, the previous experience which Melzack says is so important in our appreciation of pain as noxious? Melzack's data appear to be consistent with our suggestions that: (a) autism involves an inability to relate sensation and experience; and (b) that the reticular formation may serve as the site of this integration.

Sensory sensitivity

In 1949 Bergman and Escalona described five cases of very young children who showed unusual sensitivity to sensory stimulation. They suggested that the children were very similar to those described by Kanner, but did not definitely claim that the children were in fact autistic. The accounts of early impressions given by these children do sound much like those made by autistic children in their marked interest in music and in that "unusual giftedness such as might be observed in the budding of a genius" was believed to be present. The unusual sensitivities seem unlikely to have been specific sense organ effects because several modalities were involved. Most writers on autism do accept the Bergman and Escalona cases, at least four of whom became psychotic, as autistic.

Apparently related sensitivities have been reported for older autistic children by others, e.g., May and May (1959). Phillips (1957) has proposed a related theory of autism which holds that certain excessively responsive infants may conflict with the environment in futile rage, then withdraw in defeat from further contact.

In terms of the present theory of autism, overreactions to sensory stimulation could readily be explained as a failure to learn response inhibition. Perception is selective. It consists in learning what to ignore, what is irrelevant, fully as much as it consists in learning what to focus attention upon. The child with so-called sensory sensitivities may be so badly impaired in his ability to suppress differentially the irrelevant stimuli in his perceptual field that he reacts to levels or types of stimulation which for normal children would be subliminal, or would at least be subconsciously ignored.

A recent paper by Bridger (1961) refers to studies in the Russian literature which pertain to infants like the Bergman and Escalona cases who have unusual sensory sensitivities and who tend either to become psychotic or highly gifted. Bridger's own work relates to sensory habituation and discrimination in neonates, which he discusses as possible reticular functions.

This problem of sensitivity may be what Jasper (1958a) had in mind when he wrote:

...the function of the reticular system in normal adaptive or integrative behavior may be more in the nature of preventing a general arousal to all stimuli, with control of selected responsiveness to significant stimuli. Indiscriminant arousal reactions to all stimuli could only result in chaotic behavior, as may be the case in certain mental disorders. (p. 321)

The severely disturbed autistic girl described by Plenter (1955), as having "no harmonic relationships between the several sense functions" appears to be one of many cases in point.

The effects of sensory deprivation

It has been postulated that autism is the result of a cognitive defect. The evidence presented thus far may understandably fail to be completely convincing to those familiar with the syndrome. The disease is widely considered to be a psychosis, not a form of deficiency. The child's inability to perceive his parents' affection for him, coupled with his own inability to integrate complex emotions, can explain only part of the reason the disease has been viewed as affective. There is evidence of psychosis even apart from the disturbed relations with parents and others. If autism is a form of amentia, why have psychiatrists so often tended to classify it with schizophrenia?

It is only in the past few years that an answer to this question has become available. Strangely enough, this answer is a byproduct of the Korean War.

The astonishing and disheartening success enjoyed by the Chinese Communists in "brainwashing" American and Canadian prisoners led to emergency investigations of the techniques used. As described by Hebb (1958b), these investigations showed that the human personality is extremely vulnerable to sensory deprivation—to being placed in an environment lacking or deficient in external sensory stimulation:

It is hardly necessary to say that the experiment, taken as a whole, was very unsettling to us... It is one thing to hear that the Chinese are brainwashing their prisoners on the other side of the world; it is another to find, in your own laboratory, that merely taking away the usual sights, sounds and bodily contacts from a healthy university student for a few days can shake him, right down to the base: can disturb his personal identity, so that he is aware of two bodies (one hallucinatory) and cannot say which is his own, or perceives his personal self as a vague and ill-defined something *separate from his body*, looking down at where it is lying on the bed; and can disturb his capacity for critical judgment, making him eager to listen to and believe any sort of preposterous nonsense. (p. 111)

In view of the importance of external stimulation to an adult, who already has an understanding of the world, how important must such stimulation be to a child? Bruner (1959) has discussed the especially far-reaching effects of early sensory deprivation. And what of the child whose sense organs are intact, but whose neural structure does not permit stimuli to register? There appears to be adequate reason for believing the perceptual abilities of autistic children to be so severely impaired that sensory deprivation psychosis must be considered a real possibility.

Among the traits considered characteristic of early infantile autism are apathy, detachment, and irritability. These are also typical of the sensorily deprived individual (Hebb, 1958b; Levine, 1960; Solomon, Leiderman, Mendelson, & Wexler, 1957).

The strange way in which the autistic child stares into space has been the subject of much comment. Kanner describes this look as "thoughtful," and the preoccupied appearance it gives the child is largely responsible for his application of the term "autistic." That the child's appearance is not "thoughtful" is suggested by van Krevelen (1958), who refers instead to a vacant, unfocussed staring into space, quite different in nature from the interpretation made by Kanner. Rank and MacNaughton (1950) describe a girl who, with eyes "unfocussed, looked through rather than at one" (p. 55; see also Rank, 1949). Compare this with "long-eye," which Levine refers to as a not uncommon experience among men who have been isolated in the polar regions for some time. These men "stare right at you but never see you and just sit and look into space and not talk" (p. 241). The men are further described as "detached from the external environment" and appearing "to respond only to an internal dream world."

Thus there is obviously a good deal of behavioral similarity between the victims of early infantile autism and the victims of sensory deprivation. It is particularly noteworthy that a number of experiments have shown that it is not lack of sensory stimulation *per se*, but lack of *meaningful* sensory stimulation which is so disturbing, since subjects provided varying but non-meaningful stimuli also became psychologically disturbed (Zubek, Pushkar, Sansom, & Cowing, 1961). Note also that it is important to distinguish between *sensory deprivation* and *social deprivation*, which is the concept that the "hospitalism" studies addressed themselves to. The former condition is far more severe and intense. Few subjects can tolerate more than a few hours of sensory deprivation. Solomon et al. cite a number of accounts by explorers, sailors cast adrift, etc., who survived social deprivation for many months.

Is there a locus in the brain which is thought to be most closely associated with the phenomenon of sensory deprivation? According to Zubek et al. (see also Heron, 1957; Scott, 1957) it is widely thought that the reticular formation is this site.

B. PSYCHOPHARMACOLOGY

The current state of confusion surrounding the diagnosis of infantile autism, particularly the confusion of autism with childhood schizophrenia, is nowhere more apparent, and nowhere more urgently in need of correction, than in the area of drug therapy. The psychopharmacological literature contains a number of papers in which trial use of drugs has been conducted on samples purporting to consist of or to include autistic children. It is possible to ascertain that the term *autistic* has been used too loosely in some cases and not as loosely in others. The present author is preparing for separate publication a paper dealing with this issue and certain other aspects of the psychopharmacological approach to infantile autism (Rimland, in press). For this reason, only those aspects of the problem most closely related to our present discussion will be presented here.

Lehman, Haber, and Lesser (1957) reported the use of reserpine in nine children described as severely autistic. The effects were mainly tranquilizing, and did not result in any of the children approaching normality. Two of the younger children, however, did show substantial improvement. It is interesting, in the light of previous discussion on sensory preferences, to find that the children, "none of whom evidenced noteworthy awareness of things around them," did prefer the sweetened medication used. Benda (1955) has reported favorable results using Rauwolfia root, a compound containing reserpine, on several autistic children.

Bein (1957) has observed that while the mode of action of reserpine is very uncertain, an important site of action is clearly the reticular formation. Killam (1957) and Bovet, Longo, and Silvestrini (1957) have made similar observations. Bein makes the interesting point that the action of reserpine seems restricted to the descending influences of the reticular system and refers to previous work by himself in which evidence is provided suggesting a high degree of specificity in the reticular system.

Sherwin, Flach, and Stokes (1958) have reported the use of triiodothyronine in two psychotic children. One of these appears to be autistic. Both cases showed improvement—smiles appeared, greater interest in the environment was shown, the children displayed affection and even used a few words.

The basis of triiodothyronine action is to improve the adrenaline balance. While Rothballer (1956) has shown the reticular formation to be extremely responsive to adrenaline, we cannot, of course, assume that it is this mechanism which accounts for the improvement observed in the cases under consideration.

Freedman (1958a, 1958b) and Kugelmass (1959) have reported that iproniazid is of some value for autistic children. Kugelmass has reported no details, but Freedman's group of 14 "autistic schizophrenic children" contained "several" of Kanner's type (1958a). It is not possible to tell from the data given what effects were observed in the cases of true autism, but it may be inferred that the improvement rate was about 50 percent. Freedman's single case of "early infantile autism" (1958b) did show improvement with iproniazid.

In terms of previous discussion, it is interesting to find that the children began "scanning their environment rather than being completely indifferent to it" and, "some responded to commands of direction for the first time in their lives." Thus we see notable improvement in the distal senses.

The site of action of iproniazid appears to be in the brain stem (Shore, 1958; Rowe, 1959) but Schallek (1960) did not observe it to have a direct effect upon the reticular formation (nor the cortex). Evidence was found to suggest the amygdala as a possible site.

Lehembre (1962) has reported excellent results in a case of autism treated with 1.2 mg/day of Triperidol. After several weeks tremors developed which were controlled with largactil and disipal. Use of the three drugs led to continued improvement.

Perhaps the most promising of the drugs tried with autism is deanol ("Deaner," by Riker Laboratories), a relatively new psychic-energizer which is specially recommended for children with learning and behavior problems.

Deanol (DMAE, the p-acetamidobenzoic salt of 2-dimethylamino-ethanol) is believed to act as a precursor of acetylcholine (Pfeiffer, Jenney, Gallagher, Smith, & Bevan, 1957). It occurs naturally in the mammalian brain and may be considered primarily nutritive rather than medicative. It is of very low toxicity, and has no significant side effects.

Among the studies in which deanol has been reported used for children's behavior disturbances is one by Tobias (1959) which included two autistic children. Since the table in which Tobias provided a breakdown of his cases included schizophrenia, emotional disturbance, retardation, and brain damage as separate categories, it seems safe to assume that the term "autistic" was not being used indiscriminately.

Both cases of autism reported by Tobias showed "Good" improvement. "Good" was the second of four categories—not quite as good as "Excellent," which required "Spectacular reversal" of symptoms and was achieved by only two children of 20.

Improvement bordering on spectacular was observed by the present writer in a four-year-old autistic child who unquestionably belonged to the Kanner category. After a short time on 150 mg/day of deanol, mutism disappeared and was replaced by slowly developing but still autistic speech. Continuous disconsolate weeping, broken earlier only by prolonged, violent, unexplainable, and uncontrollable temper tantrums, quickly gave way to a sunny and smiling disposition, and the parents reported that for the first time simple commands such as "Bring it here" or "Close the door" were understood and obeyed. Later, simple tasks such as opening the door for the family cat and placing milk bottles on the porch were performed with obvious pleasure.

Contrary to previously published information, the medication seemed to have an immediate, if short-lived, effect. (However, the present reported latency and duration of effects agree with the findings of Pfeiffer, Goldstein, Munoz, Murphree, & Jenney, 1963.) The child seemed to crave the drug, especially when the old unhappy disposition seemed about to return. His parents reported that he would lead them to the cupboard where the drug was kept when medication time arrived. He would pick up three pills with his amazingly nimble fingers in one smooth and flawless movement and devour the pills instantly despite their somewhat bitter taste. The parents observed that deanol had so dramatic and immediate an effect that even the child's two-year-old sister would suggest that her brother needed his pills when his disturbing behavior began.

As in some of the cases described by Tobias, experimental withholding of the drug quickly brought noticeably regressive behavior on the several occasions it was tried.

After two years the dosage was increased to 300 mg/day as a result of a change in the producer's recommendations. The increase brought a spurt of improvement for several weeks until the child suddenly refused further medication. The improvement was maintained even after six months with no medication. At age seven the picture was one of severe retardation rather than psychosis, and the words "I" and "Yes" were slowly appearing.

The effects of deanol seem to be primarily cognitive and only secondarily affective. This is indicated by its effects on normal subjects—an increase in alertness and in the ability to concentrate (Murphree, Jenney, & Pfeiffer, 1959) and by the findings reported by Geller (1960) in his carefully controlled study in which deanol was compared with a sedative and a placebo in three randomly assigned groups of 25 disturbed children each. The sedative and deanol were both helpful but in quite different ways. Geller suggested that the affective problem could be the result of the fatigue and frustration experienced by the disturbed child in trying to deal with his environment when he was not cognitively equipped to do so. (This is an interesting point. Imagine the child's reaction to the futility of living in an incomprehensible world run by what must appear to him to be demanding, ritualistic, arbitrary, and inconsistent psychotics—us!)

Good results on three cases of autism cannot form the basis for great optimism. As Williams (1956) has emphasized, however, good results on even one case can provide important insight into the basis for a pathological condition. Ebbinghaus's work on memory, using himself as sole subject, is still widely cited. Although scant, the data do suggest the possibility of a drug specific for autism.

Not all experience with deanol in autism has been favorable. Several trials with it have had to be discontinued because the children become hyperactive (personal communication to writer). This could possibly be a consequence of the child's requiring supplementation to his B-vitamin intake. Riker Laboratories indicates supplemental B_6 may be advisable, and some workers have suggested that deanol may also increase the B_1, B_{12}, and pantothetic acid demand. Despite the generally negative results reported for glutamic acid, its role in the production of acetylcholine may recommend it for use in autism, perhaps as an adjunct to deanol.

There are also vast interindividual differences in responsiveness to deanol (Pfeiffer et al., 1963). One laboratory study found doses 50 times as great as those producing a reaction in two-thirds the animals to have no effect on the remaining third[4] (Killam, Gangloff, Konigsmark, & Killam, 1959).

Of particular interest to us is the finding, by now well established, that the reticular formation is the primary site of action of deanol (Gangloff & Brown, 1959; Himwich, 1959; Kaneko, Hishikawa, Shimizu, Yasuhiko, Kageyama, & Fukui, 1960; Killam et al., 1959; Pfeiffer et al., 1957). Deanol is found concentrated in the reticular formations of animals having ingested it, and in live animals it markedly lowers the threshold at which reticular stimulation induces an EEG reaction. Facilitation of transmission through the reticular formation is an expected consequence of the use of deanol, since, as Ward (1958) has reported, reticular transmission seems unusually dependent upon the availability of acetylcholine.

---

4 Biochemical comparison of brains of rats responsive and non-responsive to deanol would appear to be of considerable practical and theoretical value.

C. AUTOPSY FINDINGS AND OTHER ATTEMPTS TO DETERMINE THE ORGANIC BASIS OF AUTISM

Despite the consistency of much available data with the hypothesis of reticular impairment, final and conclusive proof of the hypothesis awaits the results of post-mortem examinations of accurately diagnosed cases. So far as the writer has been able to determine, such data are not available. Kanner has informed the writer that one of his early cases died in a traffic accident, but no autopsy was performed.

There have, however, been several references to autopsy reports of children referred to as autistic. While it is probable that none of these would be regarded as pure cases of the Kanner type, let us consider them briefly.

Anthony (1958) has referred to an autopsy of an autistic child with sclerosing leucoencephalitis. No further information was provided.

Schain and Yannet (1960) report, as the sole autopsy report available to them, a child who showed dropping out of cells in the hippocampal formation. They observe that this is a typical finding in epilepsy and other cerebral disorders. It was noted in Chapter 1 that Schain and Yannet were overinclusive in their diagnosis. Half of their cases had had convulsions, for instance, while this was true of only one of Kanner's cases. We can therefore not depend on the classification of the autopsied case as one of true autism.

It is of interest, however, that the limbic system, of which the hippocampal formation is a part, is considered by Schain and Yannet to be a possible site of the autistic disorder. The limbic system, while not including the reticular formation, has extensive connections with it. MacLean (1955, 1958, and elsewhere) has developed a theory concerning the significance of the interaction between the limbic system and the cortex. His theory is intended to help explain the relationships between intellectual and emotional behavior, and thus has obvious implications for the problem of autism. While the site of the limbic–cortical interaction is not known, MacLean suggests the reticular formation as the most likely possibility.

The most relevant and well-reported autopsy report available to us has been presented by Ross (1959). While the paper is titled *An Autistic Child*, the case is obviously secondary in that the behavior disturbance did not start until just before the fourth birthday, after a severe infection. However, the behavioral symptoms are similar to those of true autism (inaccessibility, lack of response to affection, repetitive play and speech, phenomenal memory for details but poor comprehension, etc.), so consideration of the findings is indicated.

Post-mortem examination showed such extensive degeneration of several brain areas that it is impossible to specify with confidence damage to any one area as being of special significance. Ross does, however, call attention to the fact that the lesions observed in the reticular formation could readily account for the child's difficulties in attending and concentrating.

It is of particular interest in the Ross case that, like many cases of pure Kanner-type autism, numerous intensive physical and neurological examinations at several hospitals and clinics had failed to find any organic basis for the child's problems. This continued to be true to the time she finally succumbed at age 11 to the effects of her extensive brain lesions.

The symptoms had been attributed to overly "intellectualized and objectified" affection on the part of the mother. After extensive physical examinations at a large hospital center the consensus had been reached that the problem was "a product of an unsympathetic, non-understanding family situation rather than of organic neurological or physiological factors" (p. 4). This diagnosis persisted despite the sudden onset of the symptoms, after four years of normal behavior, subsequent to a severe illness; despite the obvious concern of the parents for the child; and despite the thriving "exuberant" younger sister of the patient, who lived in the same home environment. Psychotherapy was given three times a week until the time of the child's death.

Of interest at this point is the discovery of abnormal 5-hydroxytryptamine metabolism in a girl whose symptoms are suggestive of autism (Sutton & Read, 1958; see also Waisman's remarks on this case, in *Yearbook of Pediatrics* 1959–60). Schain and Yannet reported, however, that their own investigation of 5-hydroxytryptamine metabolism in cases they described as autistic did not suggest abnormality. In both of these reports the problem of diagnosis obscures the significance of the work.[5]

Another biochemical investigation in which problems of diagnosis may have obscured significant findings was the determination of blood ceruloplasmin level in a group of psychotic children, by Koegler, Colbert, and Eiduson (1961). Their comparison of the copper metabolism of 34 schizophrenic children with 13 control group children did not reveal a significant difference. An attempt to keep separate in the analysis the data from a subgroup of autistic children was defeated because the investigators were unable to make the required differentiation. It is hoped that the material supplied in Part I of this monograph for diagnosing autism and differentiating it from schizophrenia will be useful in future investigations of this type. (See also the Appendix.)

While standard electroencephalograms of autistic children typically do not indicate pathology, the use of stereotaxically implanted electrodes for the

---

5   For a recent biochemical test, see footnote 1 on page 94.

investigation of subcortical centers may be more fruitful. Schain and Yannet (citing Speigel, Wycis, Baird, & Szekely, 1957), refer to this technique as being well established. The present writer has seen no references to its use with autistic children.

D. HYPEROXIA AS A POSSIBLE CAUSATIVE FACTOR
The writer's study of the case histories of children with early infantile autism has revealed what appears to be an unusually high incidence of children administered medical oxygen soon after birth or in early infancy. It is particularly interesting that the use of oxygen was mentioned quite casually in each instance (except in the cases of the children blinded through over-oxygenation). This suggests oxygen may have been used in other cases but not reported.

One line of evidence linking autism to over-oxygenation comes from the case reports of closely simulated autism in children who have been blinded in infancy by retrolental fibroplasia. Retrolental fibroplasia has been shown to be a result of destruction by therapeutic oxygen of incompletely vascularized tissue in the premature retina. Patz (1957) has presented an excellent review of this work.

Green and Schecter (1957) and Keeler (1958) have presented the case histories of a group of children blinded with retrolental fibroplasia who show many unmistakable signs of early infantile autism. Head-banging, rocking, musical interest, and the typical language syndrome appear in the case histories. Keeler writes that there are differences from pure autism, but the similarity is certainly great and the differences are not evident in the case histories. The present writer has personal knowledge of similar cases and Bender (1959) refers to others. The behavioral symptoms have sometimes been attributed to the isolation resulting from blindness, or to isolation plus the rejection of the blind child by his parents. *Keeler, however, did not find the autistic syndrome in a control group of 18 children blinded at birth from other causes.* The possibility must then be considered that the oxygen may be causing damage, vascular or of another type, to the brain itself.

The second line of evidence concerns autistic non-blind children exposed to oxygen in early infancy. This point has not been raised before, to the present writer's knowledge. A case of identical twin boys, both having autism, was reported by Bakwin (1954). The use of oxygen was mentioned briefly in the medical history of the boys. The use of oxygen was again referred to briefly by May (1958) in *A Physician Looks at Psychiatry*, in which he describes his own handsome, musically gifted, but mute autistic identical twin boys. Oxygen was given to the boys, who did not require it, as an act of special consideration by the hospital because their father was a physician. More recently, Rothenberg (1960) has presented the case of an autistic boy who had been under oxygen in an incubator for an extended period. As noted earlier, the boy's symptoms were interpreted as resulting from feelings of rejection brought on by his stay in the incubator and the consequent absence of the mother.

Chapman (1957) has presented the case of premature identical twin girls, both of whom exhibited early infantile autism. While the use of oxygen was not mentioned in this case, the small size of the infants (1332 and 1928 grams) and their seven-week hospital stay suggest incubation. Chapman has indicated (personal communication) that he believes the twins were given oxygen.

Bruch (1959) reported having seen autistic Negro twin boys. On inquiry, she responded that the twins were identical and had spent one month under oxygen.

The occurrence of autism in the four sets of non-blind twins noted above is of interest for two reasons. The first is that, as noted by Keeler, Chapman, and Polan and Spencer, and discussed earlier by the present writer, autism tends to occur in identical twins.

The second reason for paying special attention to the occurrence of autism in the oxygenated twins is that, as noted by Kinsey, Jacobus, and Hemphill (1956), *oxygen damage resulting in severe retrolental fibroplasia occurs three times as often in children of multiple birth placed in oxygen as in children of single birth.* This difference between single and multiple births in vulnerability to oxygen damage cannot simply be attributed to differences in size or degree of prematurity, since Kinsey's samples of premature infants did not differ in these factors (N = 586 single births and 114 multiples).

The data presented above are quite consistent with the hypothesis that oxygen in excess of an infant's tolerance can in some cases produce or simulate infantile autism. The writer believes this hypothesis warrants serious consideration, even though it is known that no medical oxygen was given in the majority of cases of autism. Very possibly oxygen is not the agent of damage in these cases. On the other hand, *retrolental fibroplasia has been known to occur in children not exposed to medical oxygen,* as discussed by Patz (1957), Williams (1958), and Chisholm (1960). While the occurrence of retrolental fibroplasia in the absence of medically administered oxygen is rare, it is probably no rarer than is early infantile autism.

Newborn infants differ enormously in their response to oxygen and oxygen deprivation. Pennoyer, Graham, and Hartmann (1956) and Graham et al. (1957) have called attention to the remarkable variation between individual infants in blood-oxygen saturation at birth, the values found ranging between 10 percent and 90 percent. This group has also pointed out the large and puzzling differences which exist with regard to individual susceptibility of infants to anoxia. Some markedly anoxic infants show no ill effects, while healthier-appearing infants suffer impairment. Related research has been reported by Grossman and Greenberg (1957), who cite great differences in respiration rates in neonates—individual infants vary between 16 and 93 breaths per minute. Reflex vasodilation has also been reported to vary markedly between newborn infants, by Richmond and Lustman (1955). Kinsey's data also showed marked differences in susceptibility to hyperoxia; only a small percentage of infants developed retinal damage even at oxygen levels above 50 percent. Other infants suffered damage even at the 30 percent level. A dramatic example of differential susceptibility to oxygen damage is illustrated by the previously discussed Rothenberg case, where Jonny's three and one-half months in an incubator left him with no retinal damage. The retinas of other children have been destroyed by much less exposure to oxygen.

In view of the apparently great variations between infants in oxygen need and tolerance, it should not be surprising if certain infants could suffer central nervous system damage even at the supposedly safe 20 percent atmospheric level of oxygen, particularly if birth occurred while the most vulnerable parts of the brain were as yet unvascularized.

Keeler, and Green and Schecter did not consider oxygen damage a likely cause of the autism simulated in their cases of oxygen-blinded children. Nor do most writers who have considered the problem regard it as likely that an excess of oxygen can cause brain damage in the newborn (James, 1961; see also discussion following the James paper, by Pasamanick), although the possibility of oxygen damage has not been ruled out as Krause (1955) has emphasized.

Williams (1958), on the other hand, reviews much evidence to show that the incidence of severe mental deficiency associated with retrolental fibroplasia (10–40% in various studies) considerably exceeds the 4 to 10 percent rate found in prematurity in general (see also Blank, 1959). Gyllensten (1959a, 1959b, 1960) has recently begun experimental investigation of oxygen effects on the cortices of newborn mice, and has been able to demonstrate vascular damage. As of several years ago he had not investigated the possibility of subcortical damage (personal communication). Gyllensten's extensive bibliography on oxygen effects on the brain (1959b) should not be overlooked by those interested in this topic.

The present writer suggests that oxygen damage to the brain of the human newborn is rare, but that it does occur in certain predisposed individuals. Research on this problem is needed. Discovering the basis for the lowered threshold to oxygen damage in twins may provide clues to the genesis of autism, as well as to the genesis of frequent mental retardation in twins. I. C. Michaelson has found, through India ink injections, unusual fragility in the retinal capillaries of fetal twins (personal communication). Ashton (1957) suggests that the vascular damage may be secondary to oxygen-induced metabolic failures in the tissues surrounding the retinal vessels. Patz, in his series of publications on retrolental fibroplasia, discusses a number of possible mechanisms for oxygen damage (see especially Patz, 1953, 1957).

Benda (1952, 1955) and Benda and Melchior (1959) have referred in passing to autism as sometimes resulting from neonatal anoxia. Possibly Benda has seen autism in some oxygenated premature children, and, unlike the present writer, concluded it was the original disease and not the "cure" which caused the autism. For several reasons the present writer does not consider anoxia to be a likely cause: (1) Some of the cases of autism cited in this paper were given oxygen but were not seriously anoxic. May's twin boys, for example, were placed in an incubator only as an "act of consideration" for their physician father. (2) Anoxia has been the subject of both laboratory and follow-up studies, on a large scale, for many years. This, it would seem, would have afforded an ample opportunity for the link between anoxia and autism to become established. (3) The remarkably specific symptoms of autism argue for localized damage. The damage oxygen presents to newly developing blood vessels suggests oxygen might impair a late-developing center, essential to the higher function of the brain. Anoxia research so far suggests no very specific locus for anoxic damage (Masland, 1958), but it may be possible that an excess of oxygen could constrict some brain capillaries, and thus cause localized anoxia distally.

The writer knows of no evidence to suggest that the reticular formation may be especially vulnerable to oxygen damage in the newborn. Both the retina and the reticular formation do share a similarity in comprising a multitude of small associative nerve cells. Their sharing the Latin root *rete* (net) in their names may be no coincidence, though it is thought by some that the retinal "net" refers to its capillary rather than its neural structure. The neural complexity of the retina does appear to rival that of the reticular formation (see Estable, 1961).

Also, both the retina and the reticular formation are used in processing sensory data, clearly a postnatal function, which suggests that their ontogenetic development may be parallel. The writer's efforts in trying to learn if the retina and brain stem develop vascular systems at about the same time have not been successful to date, although he has learned of several Russian references that may be relevant to this point (e.g., Ata-Muradova, Volokhov, cited by Anokhin & Agafonov, 1961).

E. DISCUSSION

Much of the foregoing discussion has been used to demonstrate that a good deal of the available evidence implicates the reticular formation as a likely site of the brain dysfunction which causes early infantile autism. This was not so for our last topic, hyperoxia, where evidence relating to the reticular formation is absent.

Despite our emphasis on the reticular formation, it should by no means be thought that the evidence is entirely incriminating of the reticular formation. While it is, for instance, widely thought that the reticular formation plays a critical role in sensory deprivation phenomena, Zubek et al. present evidence favoring a temporal lobe site in sensory deprivation. Similarly Rosenzweig (1958) discusses, in a different context, certain phenomena in connection with temporal lobe lesions that may be seen to be related to the phenomena of autism.

More directly relevant to our hypothesis of reticular dysfunction in autism is the report by Sprague, Chambers, and Stellar (1961) in which experimental lesions in the non-reticular tracts of the brain stems of cats were found to simulate with remarkable accuracy the symptoms of children with early infantile autism. Animals with lateral lesions in the upper brain stem became highly inaccessible and indistractible; engaged in ceaseless stereotyped behavior; assumed blank, staring, masklike facial expressions; become mute and unaffectionate (including cats that had previously been friendly); did not seem to appreciate sensory stimuli, were unresponsive to pain, mouthed many kinds of objects, and were either anorexic or voracious. The authors thus have ample support in saying that the behavior of their operated cats bears "striking resemblance" to the behavior of autistic children. The possibility of explaining these results by suggesting that the reticular formation serves different functions in lower mammals than in man seems somewhat diminished by the work of Voronin (1961).

The exact relevance of the above findings to the theory of reticular function proposed in the present paper is not clear at this time. The lesions which produced the above symptoms were in the lateral lemniscal tracts, and gross damage to the reticular formation not involving these tracts did not duplicate the symptoms. On the other hand, the lesions did serve to deafferent at least the reticular formation of the rostral midbrain. It should also be noted that unilateral lesions affected only one side of the cat in the manner indicated—a condition never reported for infantile autism. In those few cases of children in whom a close simulation of autism appears to have been brought about by infection, it would seem that either both tracts must have been injured, or that there is elsewhere in the brain some single site at which injury can produce the same effects. Very likely biochemical dysfunctions, including the effects of damage to the vascular system, have different effects than do surgical lesions at the same site. The fact that the Sprague et al. cats were mature when the lesions were produced also raises problems in interpretation.

Despite the existence of evidence apparently inconsistent with our hypothesis that the reticular formation is the major site of dysfunction in autism, the balance of evidence, and the heuristic value of being explicit in our hypothesis, appear to warrant for the hypothesis our continued, though still tentative, support.

REFLECTIONS ON BERNARD RIMLAND AND THE 50TH ANNIVERSARY OF *INFANTILE AUTISM*

Paul Millard Hardy

In Chapter 6, Dr. Rimland continues to provide further evidence for his paradigm-shifting concept of autism as a biologic disorder, not a psychologically induced disorder. He presents the hypothesis that the reticular formation, and possibly the temporal lobes, within the brain may be the key location of the dysfunction in autism, especially sensory deprivation. During the next two decades, this hypothesis began to slowly shift the focus of the scientific community from psychodynamic issues of abnormal mothering, so entrenched in the medical community, to brain dysfunction.

I personally experienced an example of the intensity of this entrenchment, five years after the publication of *Infantile Autism* in 1964. I was a second-year medical student at the University of Rochester School of Medicine and the Department of Psychiatry was in a twitter: a revered professor from the University of Chicago was spending a few days as a visiting professor. His name was Bruno Bettelheim. His visit left an indelible mark as I had not seen members of the esteemed, psychodynamically oriented Department of Psychiatry exhibit such reverence to anyone. There was standing room only for his keynote lecture and it was discussed for months thereafter.

After meeting Bernie Rimland a decade later with all his humility and lack of pomposity, I looked back with a smile at how an academic Department of Psychiatry had worshiped an emperor in his new clothes. The experimental psychologist, who more importantly was a relentless parent, slowly began to move an academic mountain with his insight and passion.

Dr. Rimland's effort to place the locus of this etiology in the biology of brain function as opposed to maternal deprivation served as the stimulus for modern-day research into the neurobiology and psychology of autism for the next half-century. It would be 14 years before Michael Rutter and Eric Schopler's book, *Autism: A Reappraisal of Concepts and Treatment* (1978) was published, and, indeed, Dr. Rimland's work was referenced four times in the opening chapter, "Diagnosis and Definition."

Although Dr. Rimland's initial hypothesis about the reticular formation and the temporal lobes was proved incorrect based upon all the new scientific evidence over the past 25 years, Dr. Rimland acknowledged that this might be the case. What is significant, however, is that Dr. Rimland was the first investigator to vigorously argue that the abnormal biology was in the brain. It is most impressive that Dr. Rimland was able to digest and synthesize the scientific literature up to 1964 in such a cohesive fashion. His citations of such noted researchers as Penfield, Sperry, and Bowlby are awe-inspiring. Stephen Edelson's anecdote of the all-nighter in the Tulane University library highlights the intensity and diligence that Dr. Rimland put into his research.

Perhaps the most important and prophetic statement in Chapter 6, Section B, is the opening sentence under "Psychopharmacology":

> The current state of confusion surrounding the diagnosis of infantile autism, particularly the confusion of autism with childhood schizophrenia, is nowhere more apparent and, and, nowhere more urgently in need of correction, than in the area of drug therapy. (page 134)

Very similar thoughts would be articulated by Magda Campbell 14 years later in the chapter on psychopharmacology in Rutter and Schopler's 1978 publication:

> As the review of literature shows, psychopharmacology of autistic and schizophrenic children is still in a primitive state. Improved research design and methodology is urgently needed.

In 1978, I began my first job as a behavioral neurologist at the Eunice Kennedy Shriver Center which is affiliated with the Department of Neurology of the Massachusetts General Hospital in Boston. I worked at a state school for the developmentally disabled that housed over 1300 adolescents and adults. Approximately 850 individuals were on psychotropic medication, 95 percent of whom were on antipsychotic medications, which in those days were pharmacologic sledgehammers. In retrospect, many of these individuals were on the autism spectrum. Indeed, there was major confusion surrounding the diagnoses of autism and schizophrenia. Pharmacologic treatment was truly primitive. If you were autistic, or intellectually impaired, you were considered not to have the cognitive capacity to be anxious or depressed.

Unfortunately, on this 50th anniversary of the publication of *Infantile Autism: The Syndrome and Its Implications for a Neural Theory of Behavior,* little progress has been made in the pharmacology of autism. Currently, there are only two psychopharmacological agents approved for treating the behavioral symptoms of autism, neither one treating core features of autism. Both of these newer atypical antipsychotic major tranquilizers, risperidone and aripiprazole, can be of significant benefit for some individuals but often at a significant cost in terms of side effects, especially weight gain associated with the metabolic syndrome, and tardive dyskinesia.

During the last 15 years of Dr. Rimland's life, he conceived of and fostered the development of the novel idea concerning comorbid conditions embedded in autism. He suggested that these can be treated more specifically and effectively which, in turn, may reduce the degree of autistic behaviors, symptoms, and signs. In 1997, I was the typical card-carrying neuropsychopharmacologist with a prescription pad always at my side, trying various medications to help severe behaviors such as self-injury, aggression, and property destruction. Dr. Rimland began to foster a methodology whereby clinicians looked at the role of gastrointestinal disorders, metabolic disorders, occult infections, but most importantly nutritional disorders in helping children and adults on the autism spectrum. It is a path that has made all the difference. For his wisdom, I shall remain forever grateful.

REFERENCE

Rutter, M., & Schloper, E. (eds, 1978). *Autism: A Reappraisal of Concepts and Treatment.* New York: Plenum Press.

RIMLAND'S CONTRIBUTIONS

The Role of Sensory Processing Challenges in Autism Spectrum Disorders

Lucy Jane Miller, Matthew Goodwin, and Jillian C. Sullivan

Bernard Rimland published his ground-breaking book *Infantile Autism: The Syndrome and Its Implications for a Neural Theory of Behavior* in 1964, changing the world for individuals with autism spectrum disorders (ASD) forever.

In the foreword Leo Kanner essentially recanted his own previous suggestion that poor parenting contributed to the development of ASD, which Bruno Bettelheim had expanded, leading to the harmful psychogenic "Refrigerator Mother" theory of ASD (1967).

Rimland presented evidence suggesting that the underlying cause of ASD was "organic" or biologic and not due to "cold and detached" parents (Rimland, 1964, p. 96). Rimland reviewed literature of the time, citing Hebb, Penfield, and others, heralding the future of biologically based research into sensory processing differences that are now commonly recognized in ASD. A key component of Rimland's theory was that "autism could be understood... as an impairment in the ability to relate...objects of sensation with what had previous been stored in memory" (1964, p. 93). He divided the symptoms into two categories, conceptual and perceptual, positing that the reticular formation might be the brain site responsible.

Publishing about the same time, Jean Ayres delved deeply into Rimland's contention that the autism phenotype included a sensory component. Ayres cited many of the same neuroscientists as Rimland during her long-term, successful line of sensory-based research within the broader culture of occupational therapy. She expanded on Rimland's contention that individuals with ASD, as well as a wide range of other developmental difficulties, could make considerable functional advances after impairments in underlying sensory and motor systems were addressed.

Although the road to acceptance of Sensory Processing Disorder has been surprisingly controversial (Zimmer et. al., 2012), the recent publication of the DSM-5 includes sensory-based criteria in the classification of ASD, specifically "hyper- or hypo-sensitivity to sensation or unusual interests in sensory aspects of the environment" (American Psychiatric Association,

2013, p. 50). In addition, strong evidence now suggests that sensory and motor features underlie a wide range of psychopathologies including ADHD, dyslexia, personality and affective disorders, and schizophrenia. These symptoms often appear prior to the more differentiated or classic symptoms of mental health disorders (Levit-Binnun, Davidovitch, & Golland, 2013).

EVIDENCE FOR NEUROBIOLOGICAL DIFFERENCES IN ASD

Rimland's theories focused on deficits in the brain stem, the first relay station for transmitting sensory information higher in the brain, and highlighted the reticular formation as a possible source for autistic sensory symptoms (Bear, Connors, & Paradiso, 2007). Rimland's conjectures, based on a thorough review of the neuroscience literature, are partly supported by current research. For example, children with ASD have differences in this brain region compared to controls based on findings from a two-year MRI study of neural mechanisms (Akshoomoff et al., 2002). Jou et al. (2013) also validated differences in brainstem functioning, structure, and growth trajectories in ASD. Research published after Rimland's landmark book confirms that the locus of neural symptomatology includes the brainstem, but suggests that brain involvement is not limited to the brainstem.

The following neurological differences in ASD have also been implicated:

- **Neural circuitry level**—differences in *connectivity* in children with ASD, including enhanced functional connectivity between the "sensory gateway" thalamus and the cortex (Mizuno et al., 2006) and abnormal white matter connectivity (Marco et al., 2011).

- **Sensory processing level**—disturbances in ASD in neural systems involved in *unimodal and multi-sensory processing, temporal synchrony, and attentional processes.* (For reviews, see Bahrick & Todd, 2012; Marco et al., 2011.)

- **Cardiovascular and electrodermal autonomic level**—atypicalities after sensory challenges in ASD compared to non-ASD populations, implicate differences in *sympathetic and parasympathetic* nervous system functioning (Benevides & Lane, 2013; Goodwin et al., 2006; Schaaf et al., 2013; Schoen et al., 2008; Woodard et al., 2012).

- **Hypothalamic–pituitary–adrenal (HPA) axis**—dysregulation in ASD, with higher peak responses and longer recovery times reported (Spratt et al., 2012). Enhanced cortisol *responses to stress* in children with ASD, as well as depressed cortisol levels, may signal of chronic stress (Spratt et al., 2012; Corbett et al., 2009).

EVIDENCE FOR HYPER- AND HYPO-RESPONSIVE SENSORY PROCESSING PHENOTYPES IN ASD

Rimland reviewed written case accounts of children with autistic symptoms and sensory over-responsivity, leading to his conjecture that "certain excessively responsive infants may conflict with the environment in futile rage, then withdraw in defeat from further contact" (Phillips, 1957, as cited in Rimland, 1964; see page 131). Rimland noted that these unusual sensitivities resulted in children with ASD responding to levels of stimulation that typically developing children do not notice consciously. Although Rimland proposed a neural basis for the disorder that he knew was not yet confirmed, later findings validated many of his conclusions, suggesting that *over-reactive responses* to sensory stimuli are related to responses in primary sensory cortices, the amygdala, hippocampus, as well as sites that are more frontal and prefrontal (Green et al., 2013). At the *genetic level*, variation in the autism candidate gene GABRB3 appears to modulate tactile sensitivity, with single nucleotide polymorphisms (SNP) on the GABRB3 autism candidate gene being associated with different levels of tactile sensitivity in typically developing children (Tavassoli et al., 2012).

Rimland also noted that ASD may include sensory under-responsivity: "Jonny seemed to lack sensation... You could strike him...and he wouldn't cry out. If you tickled him he didn't laugh; if you called his name he didn't respond" (Rothenberg, 1960, cited in Rimland, 1964; see page 126). Rimland noted this might be related to "an impairment in the ability to attach meaning to sensory input" (page 128) and an inability "to link sensation with experience" (page 130). Confirming Rimland's observation, modern researchers have discussed issues of sensory under-responsivity in ASD, including difficulties extracting and generalizing regularities in the environment, poor predictive ability, difficulties in response inhibition, and a failure to adapt to sensory input (Markram et al., 2008; Qian & Lipkin, 2011).

Related to sensory under-responsivity, brain regions coding for positive social touch via C-afferent nerves in the skin have been shown to be less responsive in individuals with high numbers of autism-related traits (Voos, Pelphrey, & Kaiser, 2013), suggesting that individuals with autism may be over-responsive to certain sensory stimuli but under-reactive to rewarding positive social touch. Such *hypo-responsivity* can affect beneficial traits of regulation, attachment, and maturation in the developing brain (Feldman, 2012) and have significant deleterious effects on parent–infant synchrony—a biobehavioral model that impacts mutuality and engagement.

Rimland further noted the "autistic child's almost universal failure to adapt his body in anticipation of being picked up" (1964, p. 98; see page 128). Current researchers have validated this keen observation, suggesting that sensory and motor symptoms are early indicators of brain vulnerability. For example, Baranek (1999) conducted a retrospective video analysis of first-year birthday party tapes and demonstrated that sensory-motor symptoms were present as early as 9–12 months of age in children who later displayed autistic features.

Although the nature of the underlying mechanisms responsible for these sensory and peripheral biological differences is still a heated topic of research, evidence suggests that Rimland's early theories are meritorious. For instance, six subtypes of sensory processing function have been suggested by a recent nosology (Miller et al., 2007). Children with ASD almost always fall into one or more of these sensory subtypes, reflecting not only the almost universal nature of sensory processing differences in ASD, but also that a mixed pattern of sensory modulation, sensory discrimination, and sensory-based motor patterns often exist in ASD (Liss et al., 2006; Gal, Cermak, & Ben-Sasson, 2007). Physiologic investigation also suggests that children with ASD exhibit both over- and under-responsivity (Schoen, 2008). Regardless of which sensory pattern or subtype a child displays, these sensory difficulties negatively affect daily functioning and adaptive behavior (Lane et al., 2010).

SENSORY-BASED INTERVENTIONS

In this republication of *Infantile Autism*, a celebration of Dr. Rimland's lifetime achievements, a brief note about sensory-based therapies is warranted. These therapies are designed to ameliorate sensory processing differences in a wide range of children and adults, and have a particularly long history of use in ASD. Notably, according to one survey, sensory-based intervention usage is widespread, with over 60 percent of parents of children with ASD endorsing the treatment (Green et al., 2006). However, tremendous heterogeneity exists in what is defined as sensory-based intervention. Ayres (1972) developed and provided preliminary outcome data (Ayres, 1974) on sensory integration therapy. Ayres' Sensory Integration Treatment® is a clinic-based, child-directed intervention, with the goal of increasing the ability to respond appropriately to domain-specific and multi-sensory input. Improvements at the foundational neurological level are proposed to increase higher-level adaptive, cognitive, and social functioning abilities. A systematic review of studies of Ayres' intervention demonstrated in general that positive effects occur in children's individualized goals (Case-Smith, Weaver, & Fristad, 2014).

Another sensory-based intervention is single sensory modality treatment. These are *adult-directed* therapies, generally designed to influence a child's arousal through use of a specific sensory protocol, e.g., proprioception and touch with a special brush (Wilbarger & Wilbarger, 2001), weighted blankets, pressure and weighted vests, sitting on a therapy ball, and other similar techniques (Case-Smith et al., 2014). A review of existing research suggests that single-modality protocols are not generally effective compared with multi-modal or integrative therapies (Case-Smith et al., 2014).

Finally, a more recent sensory-based intervention has been proposed (Miller, 2014). Using a more global occupational therapy approach, the STAR model proposes an intensive (3–5 times a week) short-term (20–30 one-hour sessions) intervention based on fostering arousal regulation, interpersonal engagement, and self-esteem/confidence within a process of joyful and successful play rather than addressing more circumscribed sensory-based issues. The STAR model highlights parental involvement and coaching. The theory of change in the STAR model is parent education, with parents participating in the child's therapy sessions and approximately 20 percent of all sessions involving parent and therapist only (i.e., no child is present). By increasing social participation, self-regulation, and self-esteem, a global shift in quality of life not only for the affected individual but also for the individual's family is achieved with the ultimate marker of success the shared experience of *joie de vivre*.[1] The intervention is *process-based* rather than activity-based; cultivating parent–child interaction enhances acquisition of developmental goals but specific developmental skill acquisition is not a targeted outcome. Thus, the intervention moves away from "treating" developmental aspects of sensory processing and instead turns toward participation and relationships within a rich sensory milieu including natural settings such as playgrounds rather than focusing on clinic environments.

The STAR model moves the therapeutic model from: (1) sensation to participation; (2) development to relation; (3) child-centered to *family-centered*; (4) child improvement to parent empowerment; and (5) activity-oriented to process-based. Although early evidence of the effectiveness of this intervention model is promising (Miller et al., 2007), additional research is clearly needed.

In conclusion, Rimland's insights have made a lasting impression on the diagnosis and treatment of individuals with ASD. Rimland was aware that the theory of change in autism would continue to evolve. The new treatment model noted above suggests a need to re-evaluate arousal regulation and relationships in intervention outcomes in ASD.

Key to Rimland's empirical and philosophical contribution was the belief that the continued acquisition of new knowledge is a perpetual process. We support his thesis, which, when embodied without prejudicial clinging to one's own theories, we believe unshackles us all from dogma and gives light to truth.

---

1   Translation: Joy in life.

REFERENCES

Akshoomoff, N., Pierce, K., & Courchesne, E. (2002). The neurobiological basis of autism from a developmental perspective. *Development and Psychopathology,* 14(3), 613–634.

American Psychiatric Association (2013). *Diagnostic and Statistical Manual of Mental Disorders, Fifth Edition (DSM-5).* Washington, DC: American Psychiatric Association.

Ayres, A. (1972). *Sensory Integration and Learning Disabilities.* Los Angeles, CA: WPS.

Ayres, A.J. (1974). *The Development of Sensory Integrative Theory and Practice: A Collection of the Works of A. Jean Ayres.* Dubuque, IA: Kendall/Hunt Publishing Company.

Bahrick, L., & Todd, J. (2012). Multisensory processing in autism spectrum disorders: Intersensory processing disturbance as a basis for atypical development. In B.E. Stein (ed.) *The New Handbook of Multisensory Processes.* Cambridge, MA: MIT Press.

Baranek, G.T. (1999). Autism during infancy: A retrospective video analysis of sensory-motor and social behaviors at 9–12 months of age. *Journal of Autism and Developmental Disorders,* 29(3), 213–224.

Bear, M.F., Connors, B.W., & Paradiso, M.A. (2007). *Neuroscience: Exploring the Brain, Third Edition.* Baltimore, MD: Lippincott Williams & Wilkins.

Benevides, T.W., & Lane, S.J. (2013). A review of cardiac autonomic measures: Considerations for examination of physiological response in children with autism spectrum disorder. *Journal of Autism and Developmental Disorders,* October, 1–16.

Bettelheim, B. (1967). *Empty Fortress: Infantile Autism and the Birth of the Self.* New York: The Free Press.

Case-Smith, J., Weaver, L.L., & Fristad, M.A. (2014). A systematic review of sensory processing interventions for children with autism spectrum disorders. *Autism,* January.

Corbett, B.A., Schupp, C.W., Levine, S., & Mendoza, S. (2009). Comparing cortisol, stress, and sensory sensitivity in children with autism. *Autism Research,* 2(1), 39–49.

Cottingham, J., Stoothoff, R., Murdoch, D., & Kenny, A. (1641/1993). *The Philosophical Writings of Descartes.* Cambridge: University Press Cambridge.

Feldman, R. (2012). Parent–infant synchrony: A biobehavioral model of mutual influences in the formation of affiliative bonds. *Monographs of the Society for Research in Child Development,* 77(2), 42–51.

Gal, E., Cermak, S., & Ben-Sasson, A. (2007). Sensory processing disorders in children with autism: Nature, assessment, and intervention. In R.L. Gabriels & D.E. Hill (eds) *Growing Up With Autism: Working with School-Age Children and Adolescents.* New York: Guilford Press.

Goodwin, M.S., Groden, J., Velicer, W.F., Lipsitt, L.P., et al. (2006). Cardiovascular arousal in individuals with autism. *Focus on Autism and Other Developmental Disabilities,* 21, 100–123.

Green, S.A., Rudie, J.D., Colich, N.L., Wood, J.J., et al. (2013). Overreactive brain responses to sensory stimuli in youth with autism spectrum disorders. *Journal of the American Academy of Child & Adolescent Psychiatry,* 52(11), 1158–1172.

Green, V., Pituch, K.A., Itchon, J., Choi, A., O'Reilly, M., & Sigafoos, J. (2006). Internet survey of treatments used by parents of children with autism. *Research in Developmental Disabilities,* 27(1), 70–84.

Heidegger, M. (1927/2010). *Being and Time: A Revised Edition of the Stambaugh Translation.* New York: SUNY Press.

Jou, R.J., Frazier, T.W., Keshavan, M.S., Minshew, N.J., & Hardan, A.Y. (2013). A two-year longitudinal pilot MRI study of the brainstem in autism. *Behavioural Brain Research,* 251, 163–167.

Lane, A.E., Young, R.L., Baker, A.E., & Angley, M.T. (2010). Sensory processing subtypes in autism: Association with adaptive behavior. *Journal of Autism and Developmental Disorders*, 40(1), 112–122.

Levit-Binnun, N., Davidovitch, M., & Golland, Y. (2013). Sensory and motor secondary symptoms as indicators of brain vulnerability. *Journal of Neurodevelopmental Disorders*, 5(1), 26.

Liss, M., Saulnier, C., Fein, D., & Kinsbourne, M. (2006). Sensory and attention abnormalities in autistic spectrum disorders. *Autism*, 10(2), 155–172.

Marco, E.J., Hinkley, L.B., Hill, S.S., & Nagarajan, S.S. (2011). Sensory processing in autism: A review of neurophysiologic findings. *Pediatric Research*, 69, 48R–54R.

Markram, K., Rinaldi, T., La Mendola, D., Sandi, C., & Markram, H. (2008). Abnormal fear conditioning and amygdala processing in an animal model of autism. *Neuropsychopharmacology*, 33(4), 901–912.

Merleau-Ponty, M. (1996). *Phenomenology of Perception*. Delhi: Motilal Banarsidass Publishers.

Miller, L.J., Anzalone, M.E., Lane, S.J., Cermak, S.A., & Osten, E.T. (2007). Concept evolution in sensory integration: A proposed nosology for diagnosis. *American Journal of Occupational Therapy*, 61(2), 135–140.

Miller, L.J., Fuller, D.A., & Roetenberg, J. (2014). *Sensational Kids: Hope and Help for Children with Sensory Processing Disorder (SPD)*. New York: Penguin Group.

Mizuno, A., Villalobos, M.E., Davies, M.M., Dahl, B.C., & Müller, R.-A. (2006). Partially enhanced thalamocortical functional connectivity in autism. *Brain Research*, 1104(1), 160–174.

Qian, N., & Lipkin, R.M. (2011). A learning-style theory for understanding autistic behaviors. *Frontiers in Human Neuroscience*, 5, 77.

Rimland, B. (1964). *Infantile Autism: The Syndrome and Its Implications for a Neural Theory of Behavior*. New York: Appleton-Century-Crofts.

Schaaf, R.C., Benevides, T.W., Leiby, B.E., & Sendecki, J.A. (2013). Autonomic dysregulation during sensory stimulation in children with autism spectrum disorder. *Journal of Autism and Developmental Disorders*, August, 1–12.

Schoen, S.A., Miller, L.J., Brett-Green, B., & Hepburn, S.L. (2008). Psychophysiology of children with autism spectrum disorder. *Research in Autism Spectrum Disorders*, 2(3), 417–429.

Spratt, E.G., Nicholas, J.S., Brady, K.T., Carpenter, L.A., et al. (2012). Enhanced cortisol response to stress in children in autism. *Journal of Autism and Developmental Disorders*, 42(1), 75–81.

Tavassoli, T., Auyeung, B., Murphy, L.C., Baron-Cohen, S., & Chakrabarti, B. (2012). Variation in the autism candidate gene GABRB3 modulates tactile sensitivity in typically developing children. *Molecular Autism*, 3(1), 6.

Voos, A.C., Pelphrey, K.A., & Kaiser, M.D. (2013). Autistic traits are associated with diminished neural response to affective touch. *Social Cognitive and Affective Neuroscience*, 8(4), 378–386.

Wilbarger, P., & Wilbarger, J. (2001). *Sensory Defensiveness: A Comprehensive Treatment Approach*. Santa Barbara, CA: Avanti Educational Programs.

Woodard, C.R., Goodwin, M.S., Zelazo, P.R., Aube, D., et al. (2012). A comparison of autonomic, behavioral, and parent-report measures of sensory sensitivity in young children with autism. *Research in Autism Spectrum Disorders*, 6, 1234–1246.

Zimmer, M., Desch, L., Rosen, L.D., Bailey, M.L., et al. (2012). Sensory integration therapies for children with developmental and behavioral disorders. *Pediatrics*, 129(6), 1186–1189.

VITAMIN B$_6$

Jon B. Pangborn

The year 1964 began an era of enlightenment for those concerned with the stubbornly intractable condition of autism. Mostly, the credit for this goes to Dr. Bernard Rimland for authoring his book *Infantile Autism*, which stands even today as a landmark in published psychology. This book presents his research, thoughts, and conjectures about possible causes and treatments for the condition. Most importantly, he dispelled the then-accepted dogma that autism was the result of uncaring parents who were detached from their child's need for love and interaction, and he replaced this concept with possible organic factors that might result in brain dysfunction.

As investigations have proceeded through the years, some of Dr. Rimland's ideas have been left by the wayside, while others remain in focus with expanded emphasis. We now realize that autism encompasses a spectrum of behavioral and communication dysfunctions, and that it may include internal pathologies such as infections, gastrointestinal disorder, and chronic inflammation. Causative factors vary from inborn predispositions that include (rare) inherited genetic disorders and epigenetic or gene expression problems, to acquired insults from environmental toxicants. The latter are worsened by poor nutrition and inability of mom or infant to detoxify the damaging chemical junk that's now almost everywhere in our world. Most damaging are the many organochlorine and organophosphate toxicants that we use for purposes that range from growing food crops to making war.

Near and dear to Dr. Rimland's heart was the apparent need by many autistic individuals for B-vitamin supplementation, especially vitamin B$_6$, pyridoxine. This is only mentioned briefly in his book (page 137). But think what heresy it was (and may still be in some circles) to mention vitamins and autism in the same sentence! He didn't claim that B$_6$ cured anything, just that it might alleviate some of the undesirable features that are presented, such as hyperactivity. And he didn't believe that all with autistic features would benefit from B$_6$ supplementation, but he did maintain that a trial, for several weeks, should be provided to all with the disease.

In our bodies, vitamin B$_6$ or pyridoxine is chemically changed and has phosphate added ("phosphorylation") to form a coenzyme, pyridoxal phosphate. A coenzyme assists in the performance of chemical reactions that are part of our metabolism. Pyridoxal phosphate is required to support some important detoxifying processes (methylation, sulfation), and without sufficient pyridoxal phosphate, we can't make enough critically important cell and tissue detoxifiers (glutathione, taurine) from an essentially required nutrient, methionine. Furthermore, methylation chemistry is required for neurons and neuronal networks to perceive and respond appropriately to external news that is brought by messenger molecules. So, Dr. Rimland's brief mention of vitamin B_6 was prescient.

As investigations proceeded, an empirical finding occurred. Vitamin B_6 supplements work a whole lot better if some magnesium is given along with the vitamin. Decades went by before we understood the reason for this, and thanks to the research done at ARI's request by Dr. Rosemary Waring, we now know that magnesium assists sulfation chemistry that might otherwise be slowed down by too much pyridoxal phosphate.

What are some other B_6-assisted metabolic processes pertinent to autism?

- It's needed for insertion of antioxidant (hydrogen) into cell mitochondria via a process called the "malate shuttle."

- As pyridoxal phosphate, it's required to change glutamate or glutamic acid into GABA (gamma-aminobutyric acid), which may be needed to stop seizures.

- Without B_6, we can't form serotonin from dietary tryptophan, and inadequate serotonin results in inadequate melatonin. This leads to eating disorder and poor sleep. Sound familiar? In my experience, these will be problems for at least four out of ten untreated autistic children.

As with all essential nutrients, teamwork is the key to success. Supplementing just one B-vitamin is a bad idea, as is testing just one nutrient to prove or disprove benefit. Dr. Rimland told the story of a farmer explaining to a government agent how he put concreted fence posts into the ground to make them strong and permanent. Upon returning to Washington, the agent was told that the procedure had to be tested one step at a time to prove validity. So they dug a hole and put the post in. It fell over. Then they put sand in. The rain washed it away and the post fell over again. Then they tried gravel and the post stayed up until the next rain. Finally they poured in cement powder, but the wind blew it away and again the post fell over. The government had step-by-step proof that concrete cannot be used to secure a fence post.

Besides magnesium, pyridoxine supplements work well with zinc supplements because zinc activates the phosphorylation process that forms pyridoxal phosphate. Vitamin B_2, riboflavin (in coenzyme form) hastens formation of pyridoxal phosphate, and melatonin is reported to be the agent that signals cells when it's time to do the phosphorylation. For methylation chemistry to work well, vitamins B_{12} and folate also need to be functioning adequately.

What's the track record for vitamin B_6 supplementation (with magnesium) in autistic children, as reported to ARI by parents and caregivers? With over 7000 responses, 49 percent showed improvement in some presented behaviors or problems related to autism; 46 percent had no discernible change, and 4 percent had worsened in some way (rounded percentages, 2009 data). This is a better: worse ratio of about 12:1. No medication or drug is even half as successful per this ARI data. Admittedly, parent-provided observations are anecdotal, are from uncontrolled studies, and we don't know what other nutritional supplements were used during the B_6 trials. Still, the results are remarkable.

Vitamin B_6 is only a small part of the nutritional therapy arsenal for autism. You can request from ARI a copy of its latest Publication 34, "Parent Ratings of Behavioral Effects of Biomedical Interventions" to get a summary of all the responses. Besides B_6 and magnesium, some of the other heroes are: melatonin (66% improvement), essential fatty acids (59% improvement), and zinc supplements (54% improvement). Zinc assists the conversion of pyridoxine to pyridoxal phosphate.

For more information about nutritional therapy for autism, see Pangborn 2013.

REFERENCE

Pangborn, J.B. (2013). *Nutritional Supplement Use for Autism Spectrum Disorder.* Autism Research Institute.

INTRODUCTION TO CHAPTER 7
Stephen M. Edelson

Rimland devoted much of Chapter 7 to the topic of intelligence in autism, proposing a "brightness gone awry" hypothesis in which these children have an "inborn capacity for high intelligence." For many years, researchers evaluating the intelligence of individuals with autism agreed that, in the majority of cases, intelligence levels ranged from low to moderate. However, a critical review of the scientific literature, and especially the early work, uncovered a rather widespread lack of scientific integrity (Edelson, 2006). In addition, when intelligence testing for individuals with autism involves non-social stimuli, the resulting scores are much higher. Recently, the Centers for Disease Control and Prevention estimated that approximately half of those with autism have an average or above-average intelligence (CDC, 2014).

Rimland also hypothesized a possible impairment in the cerebral vascular system, and investigators have confirmed such a decrease in blood flow in the brains of children and adults with autism (George et al., 1992; Yang et al., 2011).

REFERENCES

Edelson, M.G. (2006). Are the majority of children with autism mentally retarded? A systematic evaluation of the data. *Focus on Autism and Other Developmental Disabilities*, 21(2), 66–83.

George, M.S., Costa, D.C., Kouris, K., Ring, H.A., & Ell, P.J. (1992). Cerebral blood flow abnormalities in adults with infantile autism. *Journal of Nervous and Mental Disease*, 180(7), 413–417.

Centers for Disease Control and Prevention (2014). Prevalence of autism spectrum disorder among children aged 8 years—Autism and developmental disabilities monitoring network, 11 sites, United States, 2010. *Morbidity and Mortality Weekly Report*, 63(2), March 28, 2014.

Yang, W.H., Jing, J., Xiu, L.J., Cheng, M.H., et al. (2011). Regional cerebral blood flow in children with autism spectrum disorders: A quantitative mTc-ECD brain SPECT study with statistical parametric mapping evaluation. *Chinese Medicine Journal*, 124(9), 1362–1366.

CHAPTER 7

The Theory

Integration and Support

In the foregoing chapters of Part II we have presented evidence indicating that early infantile autism is caused by an inability to associate stimuli in the foreground of consciousness with all but a limited fragment of the content of memory instilled by previous experience. We have suggested that the symptoms could be the consequence of an impairment in the function of the reticular formation of the brain stem, and have presented data from the neurophysiology laboratory and elsewhere in support of the hypothesis of reticular impairment. The prevailing feeling that autism is a form of psychosis rather than of mental retardation has been explained as an expected consequence of effective sensory deprivation (or, more exactly, of perceptual disability). A number of case studies were reported which led to the hypothesis that, at least in some instances, early infantile autism could be caused or very accurately simulated by an excess of oxygen given in early infancy. In view of known vast differences in infant reactivity to oxygen, it was suggested that even atmospheric oxygen tension might exceed the tolerance threshold for a small fraction of genetically predisposed infants, as it appears to in some cases of retrolental fibroplasia.

Still unanswered by the theory as thus far presented are some of the most puzzling and paradoxical aspects of the problem of early infantile autism. Why are only certain children afflicted with early infantile autism? Why predominantly first-born males? Why mainly children of highly educated and intellectual parents?

In this chapter we will propose and cite evidence to support the final postulate of the theory: Children stricken with early infantile autism as a primary disorder were genetically vulnerable to autism as a consequence of an inborn capacity for high intelligence. This postulate brings what is known about infantile autism into a consistent relationship with a considerable body of pre-existing theory and knowledge. Our major task for this chapter is to make explicit the relationship between this aspect of the present theory of autism and related theories in the neighboring fields of psychology and biology. Certain of the other phenomena of autism, less central to the theory, will be shown in Part III to be also consistent with it.

A. THE INHERITANCE OF INTELLIGENCE AND ITS BIOLOGICAL SUBSTRATE

The problem of assessing the relative effects of hereditary and environmental influences has a long history of controversy which we could not begin to treat adequately here. The issue is still hotly contested. Burt's (1958) statistical analysis of complex data based on intelligence scores made by early-separated twins and other groups have led him to attribute some 88 percent of variation in intelligence to hereditary factors and only 12 percent to non-hereditary influences. Cattell, Stice, and Kristy (1957), analyzing similar data but using a somewhat different method of analysis, attributed 92 percent and 8 percent of variance respectively to hereditary and environmental influences.

On the other hand, Pasamanick and Knobloch (1960; see also Knobloch & Pasamanick, 1961), basing their conclusions largely on the distribution of Development Quotients among preschool children, argue that "at conception individuals are quite alike in intellectual endowment except for the few quite rare hereditary neurologic defects" (p. 16).

Most of the evidence cited to support the environmental view concerns the IQ scores which occupy the lower half of the intelligence distribution. It indeed seems true that exogenous factors, whether prenatal injury such as Pasamanick and Knobloch emphasize or cultural impoverishment such as is reported in the canal boat and mountain hollow studies, may result in depressed IQ scores. A low IQ does not necessarily indicate a corresponding deficiency in intellectual potential.

As one progresses upward along the IQ scale, however, the environmental arguments become less cogent, and presumably the controversy would become less intense. Recently, for example, the news services carried the story of a two-and-a-half-year-old girl who has read some 60 books, many on scientific topics, and who discussed intelligently with reporters such topics as the merits of various types of rocket fuels. While her home environment was no doubt stimulating, it seems clear that very few children, even if intensively coached, could begin to match her achievement. Though rare, such cases lead us to believe that very high intelligence, whether or not it requires an unusually favorable environment to flourish, does require an uncommonly adaptive nervous system.[1] High intelligence demonstrably does tend to run in families, and we assume here that these qualities are largely of an inherited sort.

Lashley (1947) has emphasized that at birth individual brains "differ enormously in structure" and that much of this variation is hereditary. There may be many biotypes for high intelligence, just as there are for mental deficiency, but it does not seem improbable that children of the Kannerian type may have in common a specific genetic background which predisposes them to high intelligence, if nothing goes awry. Evidence supporting Kanner's assertion of "indisputably" high parental intelligence was provided in Chapter 2. It was pointed out that the educational and occupational levels reached by the parents of Kanner's first group of 100 autistic children greatly exceed the levels reported for the parents of Terman's highly gifted children who represented the upper 1 percent of California's school population, and in many respects Kanner's group of parents surpassed the later achievement of Terman's gifted group itself.

Thus far we have been using the term "intelligence" without definition. Goddard (1946) has made a survey of the various definitions of intelligence offered by psychologists interested in the problem. The first definition on Goddard's chronological list was offered by Ebbinghaus, in 1913: "Bringing together a multitude of independent concomitant impressions into a unity [sic] meaningful, or in any way purposive whole."

After reviewing the definitions provided during the 33 years since Ebbinghaus, Goddard suggested the following as conveying the essence of intelligence: "…the degree of availability of one's experiences for the solution of immediate problems and the anticipation of future ones" (p. 68).

These definitions of intelligence describe precisely what we have earlier specified to be lacking in autistic children—the capacity for achieving understanding by appropriately combining the elements of remembered experience. Being definitions of intelligence, they also describe precisely a function the forebears of autistic children must perform unusually well.

It may seem paradoxical that the parent's strong point should turn out to be the child's weak point. Could an inherited tendency to develop a brain highly efficient in integrating experience have backfired, so to speak, and resulted instead in a brain highly deficient in this ultimately important capacity? A little later in this chapter we shall show that this possibility is not as unlikely as it may initially appear to be. It has ample precedent in both experience and theory.

---

1   Burt (1961) has recently called attention to some of the brightest minds in history who were raised in extraordinarily poor environments. Despite their surroundings, their genius was usually evident in childhood.

First, however, let us consider a related aspect of the problem. Apart from parental intelligence and its heritability, is there additional reason to think of autistic children as having originally been predisposed toward unusual intelligence? For several reasons, each suggestive rather than compelling, our giving serious consideration to the hypothesis appears warranted.

One of the most puzzling characteristics of autistic children has been their intelligent appearance. Kanner has referred to their "strikingly intelligent physiognomies," and has often cited the intelligent appearance of the children as being of primary importance in discriminating infantile autism from mental deficiency. It would be easy to discount the importance of such a subjective notion as the appearance of being intelligent, but numerous other writers have also commented on the same point. (Photographs of autistic children were referenced on page 35.)

Some writers have, in fact, used the intelligent appearance of autistic children as proof that the children *are* highly intelligent, and assert (in the complete absence of both evidence and analogue, we might add) that their intelligence has become nonfunctional because of unfavorable parental attitudes. Van Krevelen has objected to this view (especially in his 1958 paper) and has pointed out that the tested IQs of the children should not be disregarded—tests of IQ are needed precisely because subjective estimates of intelligence can be very misleading. Van Krevelen's view, like the present writer's, is that autism is a rare and unique form of oligophrenia.

It is interesting that the intelligent appearance of autistic children should evoke so much comment, even from persons who realize how misleading such judgments can be. Kanner, it must be assumed, has acted advisedly in emphasizing the point of appearance. In addition to his classic textbook on child psychiatry, he is the author of a text on mental deficiency and his monograph on the judgment of facial expressions from photographs is cited in Woodworth's *Experimental Psychology* (p. 251).

It is the present writer's belief that the common types of impairment of brain which result in the dull appearance of most of the severely retarded do not occur in infantile autism. That the aberration in autism is of a highly localized sort was inferred earlier from the very unique and specific intra- and interindividual behavior syndrome. It may also be inferred from the specificity with which it is possible to state the nature of the basic cognitive impairment (i.e., inability to integrate past and present experience).

That autistic children have the basic capacity for being highly intelligent has often been concluded from their early speech. Such speech consists of naming, a "closed-loop" process which does not appear to tax their impaired function. It is of interest that the children do tend to be precocious in this way and in other ways which lead to the impression of "unusual giftedness" in early infancy mentioned by many writers. Such evidence of mental ability which is available prior to the impaired function's becoming conspicuous by its virtual absence does support the contention that, except for his unique impairment, the autistic child's brain tends to be unusually adaptive. One is reminded of the anencephalic child who behaves quite normally until about the fourth month, when the functions of his missing cortex would ordinarily have begun to appear.

Support for our position that autistic children were to have been endowed with unusually high intelligence comes also from a demographic comparison of autistic children with samples known to be highly gifted. Kanner's description of background variables consists of the following points, *each of which is also specifically true of Terman's group of highly gifted children*: (1) preponderance of first-born; (2) preponderance of boys; (3) considerably greater than chance proportion of Jewish children; (4) parents from professional and managerial occupations; (5) very low incidence of mental illness in family; (6) high frequency of eminent relatives; (7) attractive physical appearance. The only point of difference is that Terman's children tended to be larger than average, and Kanner has described his groups as tending to be slender. A size difference could easily be a side effect of affliction.

The probability of the profiles matching so closely on a chance-alone basis is quite small. While the similarity cannot be construed as proof of the hypothesis that autism is high intelligence gone awry at its outset, the similarity with the gifted group is certainly consistent with the hypothesis under discussion. Stated differently, the statistics on autistic children are almost exactly what would be expected of a random sample of highly gifted children.

Other gifted groups than Terman's have been found to have the same disproportionate frequency of first-borns, males, and Jews (e.g., Hollingworth, 1942; Roe, 1952; Bello, 1954). Hollingworth's group of 12 children with IQs exceeding 180 were the brightest that 23 years of search in New York City had produced.[2] Ten of the 12 were first-born, eight were boys, and 13 of the 24 parents were Jewish.

---

2   It should perhaps be pointed out that Hollingworth's IQs were obtained prior to 1937, when the Stanford–Binet was revised. The fact that the earlier version of the Stanford–Binet had a somewhat smaller standard deviation than the 1937 revision (Terman & Merrill, 1937) made little difference for the vast bulk of the children tested, who were near the mean. Differences in standard deviations are cumulative, however, and in terms of equal standard scores, a 1916 Stanford–Binet score of 180 is equivalent to a score of 202 on the more familiar 1937 revision.

Bello's survey of America's top young scientists produced figures strikingly similar to those for Kanner's group, both for the total sample of 87 outstanding scientists and for the top 20 in the group. For the top 20, Bello's percentages were 100 percent male, 90 percent first-born, 30 percent Jews. Kanner's figures were 80 percent, 58 percent, and 27 percent respectively. In the general US population, these figures are approximately 50 percent, 42 percent, and 3 percent.

Another line of approach to the question of whether autism represents a miscalculation of nature which resulted in extreme dullness rather than extreme brightness relates to the intelligence of siblings. Unfortunately there is very little data on this point.

Kanner's listing of the mental condition of the 131 siblings of his first 100 cases was concerned only with emotional disturbance (1954). (Only ten could be considered to any extent disturbed.) Popella (1955) refers to a sibling who was a very good student. The three brothers described as autistic by Murphy and Preston (1954) were referred to earlier in the present paper as probably not fully meeting the diagnosis of early infantile autism, although there were some distinct similarities to Kanner's cases. Whatever the relevance, their two-and-a-half-year-old sister was described as being a "smart and precocious little girl, with poise and charm far in advance of her years and with highly developed language ability." Also of possible relevance is the very similar case of Arthur P., whose sister's IQ was 160 (Tredgold & Soddy, 1956). Of the two brothers of Darr and Worden's case (1951) one was "brilliant" and one was "not too intelligent."

The present writer has personal knowledge of four siblings of autistic children. These are not presented as a representative sample. On the other hand, no case has been omitted. One adult half-brother has a Ph.D. degree in nuclear physics. Another is working toward a Ph.D. in mathematics. A brother of an autistic girl is in the gifted student program in a city which requires a minimum IQ of 148 for entrance to the program. The fourth case, the younger sister of an autistic child, has been described as extremely bright by several psychologists. All of the above cases are emotionally well adjusted, to the best of the present writer's knowledge.

It should be a relatively easy matter to obtain IQ scores or records of educational achievement for a considerably larger group of siblings of autistic children. It should not be necessary to specify that any such investigation need use accurately diagnosed cases. A distinction should be made between the siblings of "pure" cases, where no possibly precipitating conditions, such as infection or oxygen therapy, are known, and secondary cases where such factors could have been causative or contributory. One could guess that the mean would tend to be lower and the variance larger in the group composed of siblings of secondary cases.

B. THE PARADOXES OF INTELLIGENCE

We have considered several points of evidence supporting the "brightness gone awry" hypothesis of predisposition to early infantile autism. These were: parental and sibling intelligence, appearance, good performance in isolated areas and at early ages, and demographic similarity with gifted groups. The few cases of superior intellect in recovered cases of autism (Kanner, 1952; Kanner & Lesser, 1958) may also be cited as supporting evidence. Further support for the hypothesis may be drawn from two sources. Like the preceding discussion these points must be considered suggestive rather than compelling.

The first is that there is ample—although heretofore unappreciated—precedent for the following hypothesis: virtually every category in which an inordinately high percentage of giftedness is found is also characterized by an excess in the incidence of the severely mentally deficient:

1. *Familial tendency.* Galton observed in *Hereditary Genius* (1892) that families showing a prevalence of genius also exhibit an undue incidence of idiocy. Schain and Yannet (1960) make the related observation that retarded children of intelligent parents tend to be especially severely retarded.

2. *Birth order.* Every major study of genius from the pioneering works of Galton, Cattell, Ellis, and Terman to the more recent studies, such as those by Hollingworth, Roe, and Bello cited in the previous section has found the first-born to be greatly in evidence. Yet the first-born are also over-represented among the mentally retarded (Cowie & Slater, 1959; Malzberg, 1950; Penrose, 1949; Rosanoff, Plessett, & Handy, 1937).

3. *Ethnicity.* Jews, as noted earlier, appear far more often on lists of genius and intellectual eminence than their small percentage in the population would suggest. Yet Jews also greatly exceed their quotas in terms of incidence of severe mental deficiency (Fishberg, 1911; Malzberg, 1950; Benda, 1952).

4. *Sex.* Similarly, in examining the extremes of the distribution of intelligence, we find males to exceed females both among the highly gifted and highly defective. This paradox has a sizable literature, and in this it appears to be alone among those described here.

These and other paradoxes of intelligence are receiving extended examination in another paper by the present writer (in preparation). Our immediate interest in these phenomena concerns simply the fact of their existence. The fact that conditions which ordinarily predispose to high intelligence may also predispose to low intelligence does not lend direct support to the present theory of autism, but it does provide a precedent which should preclude an over-ready rejection of the hypothesis.

The data which we show here to be paradoxical have been reported in numerous investigations. They thus cannot be considered chance findings. Nor is it likely that high intelligence is an accidental deviation in an individual whose constitution predisposed him to be dull. The opposite is far more likely to be true. We must give serious consideration to the hypothesis that an infant's road to intelligence lies along a knife-edged path, and the higher the potential intelligence, the steeper and more precarious the slope.[3]

The actual biological mechanisms which account for the phenomena described are unknown, but principles and hypotheses have been proposed in a variety of contexts which may profitably be applied to the problem. There are several reasons for expecting that individuals destined to reach the higher states of development may be most vulnerable to damage by adverse environmental conditions:

1. Stockard (1931) has pointed out that prenatal noxious effects or deficiencies exert their greatest damage upon the *most rapidly developing organs*. Thus, an individual developing a highly differentiated nervous system may be more liable to neurological defect during development than the average. There is also evidence that specific nervous system vulnerability may be inheritable (Cowie & Slater, 1959).

2. Loeb (1945) observes that the process of evolutionary adaptation sometimes overshoots its mark and becomes maladaptive for individual organisms. Thus, thrombosis appears to be a maladaptive extrapolation of a still-evolving blood-clotting mechanism. Similarly, certain forms of cancer appear to be the uninhibited expression of an adaptive bodily response— the replacement of virus-destroyed cells. Could early infantile autism be analogously the pathological consequence of an uncontrolled adaptive process in nervous system development?

3. An "evolutionary theory of intelligence" articulated by Kuttner (1960) holds that the more intelligent the species of animal, the longer during the development of individuals within that species does the nervous system

---

3 Yacorzynski and Tucker (1960) suggested a similar hypothesis in pointing out an excess of high and low IQs in their groups of children born prematurely or precipitously. Graham and Ernhart (1961) have criticized the hypothesis. The present writer's pending paper on "the paradoxes of intelligence" will offer direct support for Yacorzynski and Tucker on both empirical and theoretical grounds.

remain plastic and adaptable. The nervous system of man, for example, continues to mature for a proportionately very great part of the life span. If this principle is applied to *interindividual* as well as to *interspecific* development rates (ontogeny recapitulating phylogeny), it might be expected that the nervous systems of children predisposed to be bright would be in a developing—and highly vulnerable—state for an unusually long time. In some cases, it might be expected, for too long a time.

4. It is well known that certain traits which are beneficial in heterozygous inheritance can be highly maladaptive in their homozygous form (Masland, Sarason, & Gladwin, 1958; Roberts, 1959). That is, a characteristic can be beneficial if inherited from one parent, while detrimental if inherited from both. One of the parents described by Keeler (1957) as highly intelligent referred to this hazard in remarking that the child had received a "double dose"—too much of a good thing.

Related examples are common in animal breeding. A pair of champion collies, each manifesting the narrow head much sought after in that breed, may produce a litter of defective pups, each having a maladaptively limited cranial capacity. Boxers bred too closely for the narrow hips desired in that breed sometimes produce a female whose pelvic dimensions are too small for her litter. And who has not encountered the fawning neurotic cocker which results from excessive inbreeding of that normally affectionate animal?

C. THE HYPOTHESIS OF OXYGEN INTOLERANCE AND THE CEREBRAL VASCULATURE

The peculiar differences in oxygen tolerance among infants have already been emphasized in connection with retrolental fibroplasia, and the occurrence of retrolental fibroplasia in infants not given oxygen was referred to as a possible example of the unusual susceptibility of part of the central nervous system to environmental oxygen in a few rare individuals.

Kallman, Barrera, and Metzger (1940, based on Roberts, 1937) make the following point in connection with the blind (microphthalmic) twin boys, possibly autistic, described earlier:

> ...the trait carrier during the critical stages of its development may for genetic reasons be abnormally sensitive to non-genetic influences, and...these influences, although entirely trivial in the case of normal persons, may be capable of modifying the development of the brain...

Consequently, small and normally unimportant variations in environmental stimuli may make all the differences between mental normality and various types of mental abnormality... (p. 35)

It is the *immature* vasculature in the retina which is ravaged by oxygen in retrolental fibroplasia. If a potentially very intelligent child, whose brain was continuing to develop at a rapid rate, were exposed to atmospheric oxygen (or, worse yet, to relatively high concentrations of medical oxygen) while the vasculature was still immature, damage to the vasculature of his brain could result. Morphological similarities between the retina and reticular formation have already been referred to. And since the retina and the reticular formation have related functions (the processing of environmental stimuli), a parallel in their developmental timetable may be inferred. In a genetically sensitive individual (as proposed by Kallman et al., above), even excessive crying and consequent hyperventilation might conceivably exceed the tolerance level for oxygen, with consequent damage to either the retina or the brain. We have proposed that damage to the brain is especially likely in individuals having a certain hereditary background.

Is there reason for regarding intelligence as being especially dependent upon the efficiency of cerebral circulation? Yes. Donaldson (1932) and Hindze (1926, cited by Tredgold & Soddy, 1956) report just such a relationship. And, so far as the present writer has been able to determine, there is no other known physiological substrate for non-pathological variation in human intelligence. The evidence on this point is sparse, but there does appear to be some support for it (Weidenrich, 1948; Podolsky, 1946).[4] Earlier theories which placed intelligence in the cortex have been consistently rejected, both by the studies correlating intelligence with cranial capacity or brain weight (Donaldson, 1932; Wechsler, 1952; Eccles, 1958), and by the failure to demonstrate that intelligence decrements consistently follow surgical removal of even major quantities of cortex (Hebb, 1959).

Since the human brain consumes one-fourth to one-half the total oxygen input of the body, it would not be surprising if, through sheer logistics, the efficiency of the cerebral vascular system imposed an upper limit on the functional effectiveness of the brain itself. Nor would it be surprising if the diameter and quantity of cerebral blood vessels turned out to be a heritable

---

4   The writer has recently encountered a suggestion, which he has been unable to verify at the time of this writing, that children afflicted with aortic coarctation may tend to be unusually bright. Aortic coarctation is a constriction of the aorta which shunts a large volume of blood toward the brain and upper body. (It is of special interest in view of our discussion of biological paradoxes that persons with this condition, most of whom are men, tend to have unusually handsome and well-developed upper bodies, and present the very picture of robust health. Few live past their 30s.)

correlate of individual differences in intelligence. Somehow structural traits, such as arteriole size or length of limb, seem to be more popularly acceptable as inherited than "functional" attributes like intelligence or athletic ability.

The hypothesis of oxygen damage to the cerebral vascular system is only one of a number of mechanisms which might be inferred. It may be significant to re-emphasize at this point, however, that twins have been shown to be highly susceptible to oxygen-produced vascular destruction—and that autism also appears to strike at twins.

It may also be significant that "pure" cases of early infantile autism are almost invariably beautifully formed, having no stigmata. This suggests that the crippling factor takes its effect *very late* in the development of the infant—perhaps at birth or shortly after. Patz (1957) has commented on the very sharp rise in blood oxygen saturation at birth. Mongoloidism is unlike early infantile autism in presenting many bodily stigmata. Even before the recent discoveries of chromosomal aberrations in mongoloids, the faulty bone structure in the fingers had indicated an early action on the part of this disease—probably before the 16th week following conception.

That certain infants may be susceptible to damage by something apparently as innocuous as atmospheric oxygen is not really unlikely. The literature of allergy is replete with cases of persons severely afflicted by environmental factors to which the rest of us are immune. Severe illness has been known to result in some persons from ingestion of the minute quantity of metal dissolved from an "insoluble" stainless steel vessel in which water has been stored. And persons experiencing unhappy reactions to strawberries are known to all of us. Even such common substances as wheat, corn, and eggs frequently evoke severe allergic reactions. Persons having *porphyria cutanea tarda* blister and ache at a single exposure to a sun ray.

The fact that autistic children are severely *impaired* but not completely *blocked* in their integration of ideas is not inconsistent with the hypothesis that a vital part of the brain may be receiving an insufficient supply of blood. Gross damage to nerve tissue itself does not appear to duplicate the syndrome of autism, even if the damage involves the brain stem (Daly & Love, 1958; French, 1952; St. Onge & Calvert, 1959). The fact that some few autistic children do recover may shed light on this problem, but the present writer is not acquainted with the capacity of the brain to permit new blood vessels to develop.

INTRODUCTION TO CHAPTER 8
James B. Adams

Dr. Rimland made an extremely bold statement in the first paragraph of this chapter, stating that "The major purpose of this chapter is to discuss certain steps needed to reduce or eliminate early infantile autism." He further states that "A secondary purpose is to broaden the scope...beyond the syndrome of autism...to progress on a broad front on the problems of mental abnormality." In other words, he suspected that many of the underlying causes of autism and treatments for it might well relate to other disorders—and he was right.

He focused his chapter on five areas: diagnosis, etiology, therapy, training, and "broader implications." Here we will briefly review each of them, and then discuss the larger picture.

DIAGNOSIS

Dr. Rimland correctly highlighted the great importance of the need for rigorous diagnostic methods, so that autism could be easily and properly diagnosed. In the last 50 years, there have been substantial advances in the development of new diagnostic tools, including the Autism Diagnostic Interview—Revised (ADI-R) and the Autism Diagnostic Observation Schedule (ADOS). However, these tools require substantial training, so they are used primarily for research and not usually for clinical diagnosis. Even today, 50 years later, diagnosis of autism is often difficult, especially for higher-functioning autism/Asperger's cases.

One important development in the diagnosis of autism is the need to define clinical subtypes. While writing *Infantile Autism,* Dr. Rimland worked on the development of the E-2 checklist, which was originally created for the diagnosis of autism, but is now being used by Dr. Edelson to search for sub-types of autism based on specific sets of clinical symptoms. Preliminary research results appear very promising.

ETIOLOGY

Dr. Rimland focused his discussion of etiology on medical, not psychological, causes of autism. He proposed to investigate possible medical factors, such as oxygen deprivation at birth, by determining their frequency in children with autism vs. the general population, and by determining the prevalence of autism in those who had an exposure to that medical factor. This proposed methodology is excellent, and has been used by many researchers to identify a number of risk factors for autism in the last 50 years.

Dr. Rimland also discussed the importance of medical tests, such as EEG testing, to assess brain function. In fact, EEG testing has proven to be extremely helpful in assessing seizures (present in up to 30% of adults with autism) and abnormal but sub-clinical EEG activity (present in 60–80% of individuals with autism). Similarly, related methods of evaluating brain function such as functional MRIs have improved our understanding of differences in brain function of people with autism.

CHEMOTHERAPY

Dr. Rimland discusses the need for controlled trials of chemical agents that may be effective for treating autism. He cites several interesting cases of the occurrence of speech in children with autism and aphasia under emergency situations, suggesting the importance of adrenaline or other neurotransmitters. In fact, a wide range of psychiatric medications have been used to treat children with autism, but unfortunately they have not generally led to improvement in core symptoms. Dr. Rimland and Edelson gathered survey data from over 27,000 families on the effectiveness of different medications, nutritional supplements, and special diets, and found that nutritional supplements and special diets were generally more likely to be effective and much less likely to have adverse effects. Based on this feedback from over 27,000 families, many of whom he talked to personally, Dr. Rimland eventually became opposed to the use of psychiatric drugs for treating children with autism, and instead focused on the use of nutritional supplements, diets, and behavioral interventions.

TRAINING

Dr. Rimland clearly stated his belief that autism was treatable with behavioral approaches, which was a radical idea at the time when autism was believed to be a lifelong, untreatable condition. He discusses several examples of training programs to increase basic skills and build self-reliance. These strong recommendations for training led to his later advocacy of Applied Behavioral Analysis by Lovaas and others, and Dr. Rimland was an early strong advocate for ABA, which is now one of the most common and most effective treatments for many children with autism.

BROADER IMPLICATIONS

In addition to the challenges of autism, Dr. Rimland pointed to the "unusual giftedness" of some individuals, which is still often overlooked. He believed that basic research into autism may lead to a better understanding of intellectual development, and that solving the puzzle of autism may lead to new methods to improve intellectual function. This hypothesis is intriguing; hopefully it will eventually turn out to be correct.

Dr. Rimland commented on the much greater rate of autism in males than females, which still holds today, and hypothesized that this was due to greater vulnerability of males during prenatal and early postnatal periods. This hypothesis, including greater vulnerability to toxic chemicals and toxic metals, and possible protective effects of estrogen, is still actively being investigated today. Consistent with Dr. Rimland's argument, Dr. Simon Baron-Cohen and his colleagues have documented an association between autism, maleness, and fetal exposure to maternal testosterone.

Dr. Rimland also commented on the high rate of co-occurrence of autism and cognitive disability in twins, especially monozygotic twins, which share both genetic and environmental factors, and research on twins and genetics has been a major focus of autism research for the last several decades, and continues to be of great interest today.

He also commented on birth order as an important factor to consider, and in fact some recent research has shown birth order to be important. However, whereas Dr. Rimland thought first-borns might have greater variation in ability (at both high and low ends of the spectrum), some recent research suggests that autism symptoms and intellectual impairments are greater among second-born than first-born. The reasons for this remain unclear, however, and more research is still needed after 50 years.

Finally, Dr. Rimland discusses at length the hypothesis that prenatal complications, and not parenting style, are likely of great importance. In fact, over the last 50 years, many prentatal factors such as infections and chemical exposures, have proven to be important risk factors, and taking folic acid during the first 1–2 months after conception has been shown to reduce the risk of autism by approximately 40 percent or more. Dr. Rimland discussed the possible role of the prenatal environment as a contributor to the child's autism. He also felt that the higher rate of males to females was an important clue to understand the etiology of autism.

Overall, this chapter represents many pioneering ideas of Dr. Rimland, and most of them have been important research areas in the last 50 years, and continue to be important today. His emphasis on prenatal risk factors, genetics, and environment were important, as well as the emphasis on behavioral and medical interventions. He would often say that "Autism is treatable," and this pioneering idea is slowly replacing the older notion of autism as a lifelong, incurable disorder.

CHAPTER 8

Ideas for Research

The major purpose of this chapter is to discuss certain steps needed to reduce or eliminate early infantile autism as a source of mental disability. A secondary purpose is to broaden the scope of the present concepts beyond the syndrome of autism. Despite its rarity and uniqueness, infantile autism appears to share certain common etiological ground with other forms of mental incapacity. This chapter will also undertake to specify some of these relationships and to demonstrate how progress in research on early infantile autism may contribute to progress on a broad front on the problems of mental abnormality.

A. DIAGNOSIS

Research on the problem of infantile autism is greatly impeded by the lack of a means for making rapid and accurate diagnoses of individual cases of autism. The most promising immediately feasible approach to diagnosis appears to be a check list of symptoms such as the one advocated by Polan and Spencer.

Perhaps better than Polan and Spencer's simple list would be a comprehensive form covering many aspects of behavior, appearance, familial background, medical history, etc., which could be scored initially with both an "autism" and a "childhood schizophrenia" key. Applying this check list to standardization groups of carefully diagnosed cases would enable differential cutting scores to be established which would greatly enhance the probability of accurate diagnosis for both conditions.

Judging from Polan and Spencer's tentative results, true cases of early infantile autism would score in the high 20s on a 30-item check list, while misdiagnosed cases might score 10 or lower. Using such a list on a large sample of mentally ill children would presumably yield a bimodal score distribution, with the few cases of true autism easily distinguished at one end of the scale. Later, keys could be developed to facilitate the fractionation of childhood schizophrenia into more meaningful subcategories. Once such diagnosis is placed on a sound scientific basis, etiologically and therapeutically oriented research on electroencephalographic, biochemical, genetic, paranatal environmental, and other factors could be expected to make steady and rapid progress.

The writer's proposed experimental instrument for the diagnosis of autism is presented in the Appendix.

B. ETIOLOGY

The hypothesis that an excess of oxygen given in infancy can precipitate autism in certain cases is open to research from several directions. If the diagnostic check list suggested above were available it should be easy to identify, in institutions and elsewhere, a sizable group of accurately diagnosed autistic children. The incidence of those having received medical oxygen in infancy could then be compared with the incidence in an appropriately selected control group.

Another approach entails following up children given extended oxygen treatment in early infancy to determine if autism or simulated autism appears inordinately often. Cases could be obtained from hospital records and from the many studies conducted during the 1950s on oxygen tolerance and retrolental fibroplasia. Patz (1957) and Gyllensten (1959b) cite many references to such studies. Several of the studies cited by Patz and Gyllensten or listed independently in Chapter 6 have, in fact, involved follow-ups of such children. Krause (1955), for example, refers to 36 severely retarded children among the group he studied. It would be of interest to find whether any of these simulate the autistic syndrome.

Differential mental testing of children blind with retrolental fibroplasia has so far yielded little information directly related to the hypothesis that oxygen given in infancy can affect mental performance in the highly specific ways posited by the present theory (Axelrod, 1959; Cohen, 1960), although some indication that these children might be deficient in ability to generalize has been noted by Cohen (personal communication, 1960). The very large individual differences among infants in tolerance and response to oxygen level makes definitive research on this problem difficult.

Campbell (1940) has noted that the similarity in the vasculature of the retina and the brain should lead to a search for brain disease analogous to conditions affecting the retina. Krause reported no visible brain damage had been found in the few cases of post-mortem examination of oxygen-injured children known to him, but he suggested that this failure was likely to be a result of present-day technical inadequacies. Benda (personal communication, 1961) is continuing his own investigation of this problem. The development of sensitive techniques for discovering brain vascular damage, such as that reported by Courville (1958), presents an encouraging indication of much-needed progress in this area.

Animal research on oxygen-induced early brain damage appears to be another potentially valuable approach. Gyllensten, as noted earlier, has found oxygen damage to the brains of infant rats, but has concentrated his efforts on the cortex. The present writer knows of no research on oxygen damage to the brain stem. Problems encountered while conducting oxygen experimentation on young animals have been discussed in several of the papers by Patz.

Animal learning studies, in addition to histological examination of oxygen-injured animals, would be of great interest. The present theory of autism would suggest that form discrimination and learning set problems would be especially likely to reveal the deficiencies predicted.[1]

Although electroencephalographic studies of autistic children have generally proven negative, EEG comparisons of autistic and normal children involving reactions known to reflect reticular function would be of special interest (i.e., arousal, habituation, etc.). Drug studies (particularly of deanol) using EEG methods would also seem desirable. The use of subcortical electrodes (page 139–140) represents another approach of apparent value.

C. THERAPY AND TRAINING
Chemotherapy

As noted in Chapter 6, controlled research on the therapeutic value of deanol in a sample of accurately diagnosed cases of autism seems indicated. Because of its effects as a cerebral vasodilator, nicotinic acid may prove useful in autism, if the present theory is accurate in anticipating vascular insufficiency. In a later chapter a hypothesis will be advanced which indicates LSD-25 might also be worth trying in the treatment of infantile autism.

French (1959) cites several studies indicating that both oxygen and carbon dioxide have marked effects on the reticular formation. These agents should be considered for possible use in chemotherapy for autism. The sensitivity of the reticular formation to adrenaline (Rothballer, 1956), and the fact of the sudden appearance of rudimentary speech in autism under emergency conditions (Kanner, 1949; Rothenberg, 1960) suggest that adrenaline be added to the list of agents which should be investigated for possible therapeutic use.

---

1   In view of the evidence cited earlier that intelligence (in humans, at least) may be a function of the cerebral blood sufficiency, and of Ashton's (1957) hypothesis that the budding of capillaries may be stimulated by a deficiency in oxygen in the surrounding tissue (in the retina, at least), it might be worthwhile to see if slightly *lowering* the oxygen level for newborn animals might not in some cases result in an *increase* in intelligence. The relevance to Yacorzynski and Tucker's findings of unexpectedly high intelligence in certain formerly anoxic humans (page 167) is obvious. Surgical simulation of aortal coarctation (page 169) in newborn animals may also be of interest, but it is possible that cerebral circulation may be less a limiting condition in animals than in humans.

The occasional appearance of speech in autistic children, which has given rise to the notion of "voluntary" mutism, has also been observed in aphasics in times of stress. Hughlings Jackson has observed that even mute or inarticulate aphasics sometimes become capable of swearing eloquently when angered (Brain, 1960). Does a rise in adrenaline level account for this? Perhaps also a function of variations in blood chemistry are the fluctuations in responsiveness observed in brain-injured animals; e.g., the Klüver-Bucy monkeys (Klüver, in Jeffress, 1951) and the brain stem-injured cats reported by Sprague, Chambers, and Stellar (1961). These few cases are important because they suggest that significant chemotherapy may be possible even in severe cases of overt tissue damage.

Training

While no form of psychiatric treatment has been known to alter the course of autism, it may still be possible to train autistic children to make optimum use of the resources available to them. May and May (1959) have described the approach used at their residential center for autistic children (see also Lovatt, 1962), and Oppenheim (1961) has presented the highly encouraging results of a training program formulated for her child by Kephart. (Presumably the techniques she employed are those described by Strauss and Kephart, 1955.) Although the writer does not agree with Rothenberg's interpretation of autism, her methods of promoting self-reliance in her patient appear to have merit.

The little which is known about the training of autistic children is highly consistent with the specific formulation we have made in Chapter 5 concerning the nature of the autistic impairment. To the extent that our analysis adds to the understanding of autism, it may be helpful in the development of specially adapted training methods.

In discussing the training of autistic children, Goldstein (1959) has emphasized what he refers to as "concrete and situational determination." According to Goldstein, "...these children 'learn' only by doing; through specific movement and activities they can be brought into contact with a desired task" (p. 549). This is what Oppenheim had to do when she manipulated her child's fingers so he could learn to handle toys other than the rubber ball he played with unceasingly. This is also what the mother reported by Ritvo and Provence (1953) resorted to when she found that her 20-month-old autistic child could not learn to play pat-a-cake by imitation.

Thus, the process of training autistic children appears to rest on the realization that stimulus patterns (including, apparently, proprioceptive patterns) "go in and out (the nervous system) unchanged," to use a phrase employed in Chapter 5. One might also infer that since *meaning* cannot serve its usual role in guiding the learning of autistic children, it may be necessary to rely on the use of lavish praise and other forms of overt reward to provide direction as well as incentive to the child's efforts. Discovering ways of making optimum use of the autistic child's limited ability to learn, and especially discovering ways of increasing the child's ability to generalize what he has learned, would appear to offer challenging problems for future research.

Schopler, in a recent and as yet unpublished paper, has independently suggested the reticular formation as the site of impairment in infantile autism. Based on his own work using tactile stimulation as an approach to therapy in autism (Schopler, 1962; see also Waal, 1955), and on Hebb's suggestion that reticular arousal is prerequisite to learning (page 115–116), Schopler makes the interesting proposal that therapeutic reticular arousal may be provided in autistic children through tactile stimulation, as a substitute for the distal receptor stimulation which seems particularly defective in autism. This is a resourceful idea that merits further investigation.

D. BROADER IMPLICATIONS OF RESEARCH ON AUTISM

Inasmuch as infantile autism is clearly a source of unhappiness to children afflicted, to their families, and to the community at large, there can be no doubt that research on infantile autism is necessary and important in itself. If our hypothesis that children stricken with autism have also often been predisposed to unusual giftedness is correct, research leading to the prevention and perhaps cure of autism becomes all the more imperative.

While research directed toward the control of early infantile autism is thus important on its own account, there are yet other reasons for making autism the object of the most intensive kind of scientific attack. One of these reasons is that the extraordinary specificity and consistency of the symptoms of autism give rise to new hypotheses concerning the mode of function of the normal brain. These hypotheses, which are consistent with a wide variety of disparate psychological phenomena, will be discussed in the concluding chapters of this monograph. A second reason resides in the fact that while autism itself is an exceedingly rare disease, it is one of the few separate diseases which can be isolated for study in the massive conglomeration of conditions which contribute to mental retardation.

As we noted earlier in our discussion of the "paradoxes of high and low intelligence" (page 166–168), autism tends strongly to occur under conditions which also predispose toward other forms of mental retardation. But, unlike most other forms of retardation, autism tends strongly to occur without complicating health problems or physical symptoms. The generally favorable family background of autistic children helps rule out the possibility of difficult-to-cope-with familial deficiency. Thus, the study of autism may shed much-needed light on some of the biological bases of intelligence and on conditions predisposing to exogenous retardation. It is possible that autism may be used as a fine-edged tool—an opening wedge—in the general scientific attack on the problems of abnormal mentality. The remainder of this chapter will be devoted to exploration of some of these ideas.

One of the most prominent of the similarities in the incidence of autism and other mental disorders, including mental deficiency and childhood schizophrenia, is the high incidence of disorder among males. Since many of these disorders are present at birth, and indeed appear to be highly related to the markedly lower viability of males in the pre- and early postnatal period, psychogenic explanations would seem to be quite inadequate.[2]

It seems clear that research is needed on sex-linked biological factors which also relate to nervous system function. For instance, the calcium metabolism, critical in neural function, is far less apt to malfunction in females (Stockard, 1931). Another lead is suggested by Sackler et al. (1952), who point out that during its development in the uterus, the female infant is surrounded by a hormonal environment much more likely to be compatible with its own than is the male. With reference to this problem, Sackler et al. call attention to the thyroid problems that have frequently been reported among mothers of schizophrenic children. As we have noted earlier, other writers refer to schizophrenic infants as immature, both homeostatically and in terms of appearance. It would appear that studies are badly needed in which frequent endocrinal assays are made during infancy, the findings to be correlated with later mental development in the children. Especially are such studies needed among mothers presenting a high risk of producing abnormal children.

The significant work of Nolting (cited by MacMahon & Sowa, 1961) showing a relationship between maternal vitamin C blood level in pregnancy and mental abnormality in her child is of special interest because of the importance of vitamin C in capillary system vitality (see also Kubala &

---

2   The idea that the high incidence of mental retardation in males is a function of a generally greater vulnerability in males to adverse conditions during pregnancy and birth, and that this vulnerability is reflected in more extreme degree by the high mortality among male fetuses and infants, was expressed by Rosanoff et al. in 1937. This anticipated by almost 20 years the "continuum of reproductive casualty" espoused more recently by Benjamin Pasamanick and his colleagues. But Rosanoff et al. themselves appear to have been similarly anticipated by nearly two decades, by Eardley Holland (cited by Gellner, 1959).

Katz, 1960). Studies are also needed in which sex-linked biochemicals are systematically varied in laboratory animals, to be studied in their differential effects on the intellectual functions of male and female offspring.

The relatively frequent occurrence of both autism and mental deficiency in twins, especially monozygotic twins, represents another starting point for research. What are the physiological and biochemical differences between twins and single births? Do single-born autistic children tend to deviate from normal in any of these same ways? Michaelson's previously mentioned finding that twins tend to show excess permeability of the retinal blood vessels is the only finding in this area known to the present writer.

The biological consequences of being first-born represents another rich area for research. The readiness with which psychogenic explanations may be generated to explain the successes and failures of the first-born or only child has probably served to suppress research on this problem. Freud, for example, explained his own eminence in terms of the attention he was given as the first-born of eight children. Others, during a recent revival of interest in personality as related to birth order, have explained *negative* traits (low rate of first-borns among fighter pilots, high rates of alcoholism and reading disability, etc.) on the grounds that the first-born become dependent as a result of excessive attention. The remarkably consistent failure of researchers to verify this type of hypothesis (i.e., hypotheses relating parental attitudes and practices to child behavior) has already been discussed in Chapter 3. These failures do not, of course, rule out the possibility of purely experiential explanations, but should increase our skepticism with regard to them.

A second reason for looking for a physiological basis for the unusual findings with regard to birth order, rather than stopping, as most workers have, with "psychodynamic" explanations, is that many of the psychological concomitants of birth order show relevance to birth order only at the extremes of their distribution, rather than being expressed in some degree at all levels. The bulk of research on birth order and intelligence, for example, reports no consistent differences in the *mean* IQs of children differing in sibling rank (Schoonover, 1959). Yet the findings are incontrovertible that the first-born are highly overrepresented at both tips of the distribution of mental competence, as we noted in Chapter 7. One does not generally expect this kind of a distribution from an accretion of experiences, but "all-or-none" findings are not unexpected where physiological mechanisms predominate.

A third reason for attending more closely to the physiological aspects of birth order is that a number of physical afflictions are known to be related to birth order. Rh incompatibility is perhaps the most widely known of these. Pyloric stenosis is very similar to autism in that it affects primarily first-borns, males, and shows a race-linkage. (Negro children are especially vulnerable.) Other conditions showing a high incidence among the first-born are mongolism, anencephaly, hydrocephaly, epilepsy, and cleft palate (MacMahon & Sowa, 1961; Stott, 1960).

In so far as the writer has been able to determine, very little is known regarding the biology of primogeniture, other than the markedly longer labor common in first-births. Animal research on this problem would seem highly desirable. Existing data could be examined, for example, to determine if there is more variability in the maze-learning scores of first-litter versus later-born rats. Litter size could be investigated simultaneously. Data such as that gathered in Terman's studies could be analyzed to find if gifted children (who were predominantly first-born) tended to have less often been preceded by miscarried or stillborn siblings than matched controls. (The mothers of Terman's gifted group did tend to have very few stillbirths, but their relatively high socio-economic status could easily have accounted for this.)

The present writer has for some time sought, with little success, specifically presented biological hypotheses which might account for the incontestable findings relating excess variability in mental competence to birth order, other than the obvious hypotheses relating to blood type and birth injury. The several hypotheses which follow are offered in an attempt to fill this void.[3]

---

3 Another hypothesis regarding birth order stems from the research of O.S. Heyns and his collaborators at the University of the Witwatersrand, South Africa. Heyns has been experimenting with the use of intermittent decompression of the maternal abdomen during the last two months of pregnancy and during the early part of labor. The woman is daily placed in an apparatus which permits creation of a partial vacuum about her midsection for about one-half hour, thus temporarily lowering the intra-amniotic pressure. (For a photograph see *Newsweek*, Dec. 7, 1959, p. 66.) Examination of the placenta after delivery usually shows marked improvement of the vasculature. In a study on a group of European and Bantu women (Heyns, Samson, & Graham, 1962), very favorable effects were seen in the infants, and multiparous mothers reported these children to be "advanced" over their earlier ones. Mr. A. O. H. Roberts, of the South African National Institute of Personnel Research, who called this work to my attention, informs me that the beneficial effect has recently been noted as especially favoring the first-born. The researchers hypothesize that the decompression is particularly effective in improving placental circulation for the primaparous mother, whose abdominal muscles tend to be especially firm. These findings, considered in conjunction with the present writer's suggestion (page 175–176) that mild hypoxia may in some cases be beneficial in stimulating the development of the cerebral vasculature, help provide a solution for the paradoxical findings on the intelligence of the first-born. (To the previously cited reports relating cerebral blood sufficiency to intelligence [page 169], may be added the recent work of C. Kennedy [cited by Sankar, Cates, Broer, & Sankar, 1963], who has reportedly shown differences in cerebral blood flow in retarded and normal children.)

1. Whereas sleep and rest may often be easily scheduled during a mother's first pregnancy, in later pregnancies the demands of child-rearing are such that sleeping late of a morning and taking an afternoon nap may become rare luxuries. Masland (1961) has noted research showing that physical activity of the mother is related to outcome of pregnancy. If rest patterns were of importance, the "curious" finding Masland mentions relating to the pregnancy outcomes of working mothers might have a ready explanation.

2. Similarly, while the mother is ordinarily exposed to relatively few colds and infections, especially of the types which afflict children, during her first pregnancy, her subsequent pregnancies usually occur during a period in which she is exposed to all manner of child-borne plagues and diseases.

3. A third hypothesis relating to birth order is of psychosomatic origin. The activities of a normal child provide the endocrine system of his mother with a good deal of exercise. The emotions of the parent of a young child vary widely, each day bringing its quota of love, joy, anger, and it would seem not uncommonly, fear (for the child's welfare), and wrath. The biochemical environment of any sibling-in-waiting would accordingly be quite different than it was for the first child. Maternal emotionality during pregnancy does bear a relationship to the later behavior of the offspring, presumably through the blood endocrine levels (Ader & Belfer, 1962; Masland, 1961; Thompson, 1957).

The above hypotheses are in accord, it would seem, with West's (1960) report that both the first-born and the latter-born of large families are overrepresented in his sample of 813 scientists, and with the suggestion referred to by Bello (1954) that when top-level scientists are not first-born, there is a rather long interval between their birth and the birth of the next younger sibling. The factors we have hypothesized above would seem less influential if there were siblings old enough to share the mother's tasks during pregnancy, or if there were no very young siblings in the home during the period of pregnancy.

Another problem of interest relates to the joint occurrence of primogeniture and maleness. For instance, in the case of autism, are both boys and girls equally likely to be first-born? What is the relationship between sex and birth order in other forms of mental disorder?

It appears to have escaped the attention of the many workers who have studied birth order in adult schizophrenia and found no relationship that there *is* a birth order effect in childhood schizophrenia, as may be seen in the data of Bender (1955) and Kallman and Roth (1956) just as there is in infantile autism. (Kallman & Roth report that there is no etiologic significance to be attached to their birth-order statistics on preadolescent schizophrenia, but by this they appear to be referring to psychogenic effects, since they do not include only children in their tabulation. When onlies are included as first-born, the birth order effect appears.)

Of the several paradoxes of high and low intelligence discussed in Chapter 7 as being related to the etiology of early infantile autism, study of racial background seems least likely to be productive. This is so partly because biological racial differences have already been studied so thoroughly in the past, with little results. Even here, however, there are recent findings which suggest a direction for further research. Pasamanick and Knobloch (1960) have found, for instance, that Negro infants are some three times more likely to experience prematurity than whites.[4]

In the writer's view, one of the most important of the areas of research to which the study of autism leads relates to the study of the brain mechanisms for processing information. Psychology has too long permitted these mechanisms to be overshadowed by the heavy concentration of attention which has been focused upon the specific *content* of experience. New findings which have recently come to light make it clear that those of us who wish to understand behavior must cease regarding the brain as "just so much porridge" and instead focus attention upon the brain's mechanisms for employing the informational input available to it.

Some of the research which leads to this conclusion has been reported by Pasamanick and his colleagues in various publications. In one study, for instance (Pasamanick, Rogers, & Lilienfeld, 1956), the birth records of a group of nearly 500 behavior-disturbed school children, who had in general not been considered neurologically abnormal, were compared with the birth records of a control group of closely matched classmates who did not manifest school behavior problems. Despite the presumably learned basis of the behavior problems, it was found that complications of pregnancy were markedly more common in the births of the behavior-disturbed group than in the control group. A diversity of other behavioral

---

4   It might be noted parenthetically that this finding provides an important "truce zone" in the nature–nurture controversy—the nature side appears to be supported in its contention that observed differences between races in test scores are biological in origin and not solely reflections of cultural bias in the tests or consequences of cultural poverty among the testers; while the nurture side may take comfort in the real possibility that the IQ differences observed may merely imply racial differences in vulnerability to a preventable health problem, rather than being immutable genetically determined differences in intelligence *per se.*

abnormalities, such as reading disability, speech problems, and tics also have been traced to the same apparent source (Pasamanick & Knobloch, 1960).[5]

Closely related work has been reported by Stott, who has found such problems as temperament impairment (1959) and juvenile delinquency (1962) to be related to otherwise undetected pre- and paranatal injury to the child. Stott refers to the work of several German investigators who find "drive" and a trait called "forthcomingness" to be impaired in children with a history of prenatal complications, and calls attention to the similarity in behavior abnormality found in rats and mice subjected to prenatal maternal stress. Both Pasamanick and Stott regard the so-called "maternal-deprivation" syndromes, which were discussed in Chapter 3, as being the consequence of prenatal stress rather than of affectional insufficiency.

There is thus a good deal of support for the idea that important, apparently basic, personality disturbances can be traced to the prenatal environment of the child. Indeed, the present writer regards this research, which has shifted the burden of guilt from purely speculative *parental* influences to proven *prenatal* factors, as representing one of the truly important scientific contributions in recent history. As Stott has put it, "It can no longer be lightly assumed, therefore, that proneness to behavior disturbance is a result of postnatal conditioning, and the possibility of congenital factors even among children of normal mentation, must be considered" (1962, p. 782).

The fact that personality variables such as emotional expression, restraint, and drive level may be so readily impaired by adverse prenatal conditions suggests that these traits may be highly dependent upon brain mechanisms which relate to the *accessibility* to the individual of his prior experience, rather than being traceable to the *content* of his experience as had previously been supposed. The present writer's study of the specific cognitive impairment in infantile autism has led to hypotheses concerning the brain mechanisms which may be related to these traits. These will be discussed in the following chapters, in conjunction with their implications for the phenomena of autism itself.

---

5   A recent study by Osterkamp and Sands (1962) has in fact disclosed a significantly greater incidence of birth and pregnancy difficulties in the mothers of schizophrenic children than neurotic children. The mothers of the schizophrenic children also attempted breast feeding significantly more often than mothers of neurotic children (27 out of 41 as opposed to 17 out of 40) but "The results were interpreted in terms of the mothers' unconscious negative feelings toward the infants" (p. 366).

THE FETAL STEROID THEORY OF AUTISM

Simon Baron-Cohen, Bonnie Auyeung,
and Michael Lombardo

Autism is more common in males than females (Baron-Cohen et al., 2011). To understand this increased male risk for autism, we tested if fetal steroid hormones play a role in the etiology of autism and autistic traits, because fetal steroids are relevant, along with the sex chromosomes, to sexual differentiation of the brain (Geschwind & Galaburda, 1985). We instigated and extended the Cambridge Child Development Project, testing how normative variation in amniotic fluid levels of FT correlated with later brain and behavioural development postnatally. This longitudinal study began in 1999 (Baron-Cohen, Lutchmaya, & Knickmeyer, 2004). Women were selected who underwent amniocentesis for clinical reasons. Their otherwise typically developing children have been tested postnatally at five time points (one, two, four, eight, and 12 years old). We have completed 21 experiments, summarized in Figure 1.

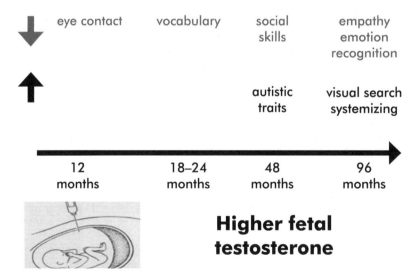

Figure 1: The Cambridge Child Development Project

Grey: Traits that were positively correlated with fetal testosterone (FT).
Black: Traits that were negatively correlated with FT.

185

SUMMARY OF PAST STUDIES

1. Eye-contact is reduced in children with an autism spectrum condition (ASC) (Swettenham et al., 1998). In typical 12-month-old children, amount of eye contact inversely correlates with FT levels (Lutchmaya, Baron-Cohen, & Raggatt, 2002a).

2. Language is often delayed in children with ASC (American Psychiatric Association, 2000). In typical children at 18 and 24 months, rate of vocabulary development is inversely correlated with FT levels (Lutchmaya, Baron-Cohen, & Raggatt, 2002b).

3. Social relationships is a key area of difficulty in autism (American Psychiatric Association, 2000). In typical four-year-olds quality of social relationships inversely correlated with FT levels (Knickmeyer et al., 2005).

4. Theory of Mind (ToM) is a key cognitive deficit in autism (Klin, 2000). In typical children frequency of intentional propositions are inversely correlated with FT levels (Knickmeyer et al., 2006).

5. On the 'Reading the Mind in the Eyes' Test (Baron-Cohen et al., 2001) of advanced ToM, people with autism score below average (Baron-Cohen, Wheelwright, & Hill, 2001). In typical children, ToM performance inversely correlates with FT levels (Chapman et al., 2006).

6. Girls with autism show reduced gender-typical play (Knickmeyer, Wheelwright, & Baron-Cohen, 2007). In typical children FT levels predict sexually differentiated play behaviour (Auyeung et al., 2009a).

7. On the child version of the Empathy Quotient (EQ-C), children with autism score below average (Auyeung et al., 2009b). In typical children EQ-C score inversely correlates with FT levels (Chapman et al., 2006).

8. On the Embedded Figures Test (EFT) of attention to detail, children with autism score above average (Jolliffe & Baron-Cohen, 1997). In typical children scores on the EFT positively correlated with FT levels (Auyeung et al., 2012).

9. On the child version of the Systemizing Quotient (SQ-C), people with autism score above average (Auyeung et al., 2009b). In typical children SQ-C scores are positively correlated with FT levels (Auyeung et al., 2006).

10. Using volumetric-based morphometry (VBM), volume of right temporo-parietal junction (RTPJ) and a cluster in the amygdala are positively correlated with FT, while the volume of the planum temporale/parietal operculum (PT/PO) and posterior lateral orbitofrontal cortex (plOFC) are negatively correlated with FT (Lombardo et al., 2012a). These areas are associated with ToM, language, empathy, and fear processing, and

are atypical in autism in structure and/or function (Lombardo et al., 2012b).

11. Many studies report atypical corpus callosum (CC) in autism (Piven et al., 1997; Keary et al., 2009). FT is positively correlated with more rightward asymmetry of the isthmus sub-region of the CC (Chura et al., 2010).

12. People with autism find emotional faces less rewarding (Volkow et al., 2009; Bijttebier et al., 2009; Delmonte et al., 2012). FT predicts increased sensitivity to happy faces in the caudate, putamen, and nucleus accumbens, structures sensitive to reward and manipulations of testosterone later in life (Lombardo et al., 2012b).

13. On the Quantitative Checklist for Autism in Toddlers (Q-CHAT) (Allison et al., 2008), a dimensional measure of autistic traits at 18 months of age, children with autism score high. Q-CHAT scores are positively predicted by FT levels (Auyeung et al., 2010).

14. On the Childhood Autism Spectrum Test (CAST) (Scott et al., 2002), a measure of autistic traits on which children with autism score high, FT levels are positively associated with CAST score (Auyeung et al., 2009b).

15. On the child version of the Autism Spectrum Quotient (AQ-Child) (Auyeung et al., 2008) that also measures autistic traits, and on which children with autism score high, FT levels are positively correlated with AQ (Auyeung et al., 2009b).

16. Single nucleotide polymorphisms (SNPs) in the genes related to the sex steroid pathway (CYP19A1, CYP17A1, CYP11B1, HSD11B1, HSD17B4, HSD17B2) are nominally associated with autistic traits and/or a diagnosis of Asperger's syndrome (AS) (Chakrabarti et al., 2009). CYP19A1 codes for aromatase, the enzyme that catalyzes the conversion of testosterone to estradiol. Testosterone is converted to estrogen in the fetal brain through aromatase, and exerts its effects through estrogen receptors. SNPs in the estrogen receptor genes (ESR1 and ESR2) are associated with higher AQ scores in the general population, as well as with a diagnosis of AS (Chakrabarti et al., 2009).

17. Both adult males and females with autism have elevated serum androstenedione relative to controls (Ruta et al., 2011).

18. Women with autism and their mothers have elevated rates of polycystic ovary syndrome (PCOS), acne, dysmenorrhea, hirsutism, and tomboyism, all associated with hyper-androgenism (Ingudomnukul et al., 2007).

19. Elevated levels of luteinizing hormone and free androgen index are found in women with autism (Schwarz et al., 2010).

20. People with autism, and their first-degree relatives, have a lower 2D:4D ratio (Manning et al., 2001), a marker of exposure to the ratio of FT to fetal estradiol (FE) (Lutchmaya et al., 2004; Zheng & Cohn, 2011).

21. The Statens Serum Institute (SSI) in Copenhagen curates the Historic Birth Cohort (HBC) containing 100,000 amniotic samples dating back to 1981. The HBC is linked to the Danish Psychiatric Central Register (DPCR), a central database of every psychiatric diagnosis in Denmark. We focused on a population of N = 19,677 amniotic fluid samples from singleton births between 1993 and 1999. We tested levels of Δ4 sex steroids and cortisol. N = 128 males who were later diagnosed on the autism spectrum. We analyzed the autism spectrum as one group, rather than sub-grouping. Compared with typical control males (N = 217) who did not differ on gestational age at amniocentesis, APGAR score, or maternal and paternal age, all fetal steroids are elevated in the amniotic fluid of fetuses who went on to later develop autism, compared with those who went on to be typically developing (Baron Cohen, et al., 2014).

We found elevated fetal steroids (see Figure 2) in males who went on to develop autism. This is one of the earliest developmental hormonal/non-genetic biomarkers for autism. In particular, we found the whole Δ4 sex steroid pathway (progesterone, 17α-hydroxyprogesterone, androstenedione, and testosterone) and cortisol were elevated in the amniotic fluid of males who went on to develop autism. This was found across all subgroups on the autistic spectrum (Baron Cohen et al., 2014).

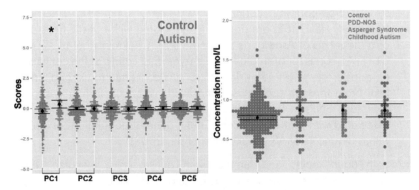

Figure 2: Group differences in amniotic fluid hormone concentration levels

Left panel: Mean PCA scores for each component. The autism group shows elevation on the first PC (principal component), a 'steroidogenic' factor.
Right panel: Mean hormone concentrations after the data is reconstructed from the first PC scores and loadings. All three autism spectrum subgroups show this elevation, and all five steroid hormones loaded equally onto PC1.

REFERENCES

Allison, C., Baron-Cohen, S., Wheelwright, S., Charman.T., et al. (2008). The Q-CHAT (Quantitative Checklist for Autism in Toddlers): A normally distributed quantitative measure of autistic traits at 18–24 months of age: Preliminary report. *Journal of Autism and Developmental Disorders*, 38(8), 1414–1425.

American Psychiatric Association (2000). *Diagnostic and Statistical Manual of Mental Disorders, Fourth Edition (Text Revision) (DSM-IV)*. Washington, DC: American Psychiatric Association.

Auyeung, B., Knickmeyer, R., Ashwin, E., Taylor, K., & Baron-Cohen, S. (2012). Effects of fetal testosterone on visuospatial ability. *Archives of Sexual Behavior*, 41(3), 571–581.

Auyeung, B., Baron-Cohen, S., Chapman, E., Knickmeyer, R., Taylor, K., & Hackett, G. (2006). Foetal testosterone and the child systemizing quotient. *European Journal of Endocrinology*, 155, S123–S130.

Auyeung, B., Baron-Cohen, S., Ashwin, E., Knickmeyer, R., et al. (2009a). Fetal testosterone predicts sexually differentiated childhood behavior in girls and in boys. *Psychological Science*, 20(2), 144–148.

Auyeung, B., Baron-Cohen, S., Wheelwright, S., Samarawickrema, N., & Atkinson, M. (2009b). The Children's Empathy Quotient (EQ-C) and Systemizing Quotient (SQ-C): Sex differences in typical development and in autism spectrum conditions. *Journal of Autism and Developmental Disorders*, 39(11), 1509–1521.

Auyeung, B., Baron-Cohen, S., Ashwin, E., Knickmeyer, R., Taylor, K., & Hackett, G. (2009b). Fetal testosterone and autistic traits. *British Journal of Psychology*, 100(1), 1–22.

Auyeung, B., Baron-Cohen, S., Wheelwright, S., & Allison, C. (2008). The Autism Spectrum Quotient: Children's Version (AQ-Child). *Journal of Autism and Developmental Disorders*, 38(7), 1230–1240.

Auyeung, B., Taylor, K., Hackett, G., & Baron-Cohen, S. (2010). Foetal testosterone and autistic traits in 18- to 24-month-old children. *Molecular Autism*, 1(1), 11.

Baron-Cohen, S., Lutchmaya, S., & Knickmeyer, R. (2004). *Prenatal Testosterone in Mind: Amniotic Fluid Studies*. Cambridge, MA: MIT/Bradford Books.

Baron Cohen, S., Auyeung, B., Nørgaard-Pederson, B., Hougaard, D.M., et al. (2014). Elevated fetal steroidogenic activity in autism. *Molecular Psychiatry*, June.

Baron-Cohen, S., Lombardo, M.V., Auyeung, B., Ashwin, E., Chakrabarti, B., & Knickmeyer, R. (2011). Why are autism spectrum conditions more prevalent in males? *PLOS Biology*, 9, e1001081.

Baron-Cohen, S., Wheelwright, S., & Hill, J. (2001). The "Reading the Mind in the Eyes" test revised version: A study with normal adults, and adults with Asperger syndrome or high-functioning autism. *Journal of Child Psychology and Psychiatry*, 42(2), 241–252.

Baron-Cohen, S., Wheelwright, S., Spong, A., Scahill, L., & Lawson, J. (2001). Are intuitive physics and intuitive psychology independent? A test with children with Asperger syndrome. *Journal of Developmental and Learning Disorders*, 5, 47–78.

Bijttebier, P., Beck, I., Claes, L., & Vandereycken, W. (2009). Gray's Reinforcement Sensitivity Theory as a framework for research on personality-psychopathology associations. *Clinical Psychology Review*, 29(5), 421–430.

Chakrabarti, B., Dudbridge, F., Kent, L., Wheelwright, S., et al. (2009). Genes related to sex steroids, neural growth, and social-emotional behavior are associated with autistic traits, empathy, and Asperger syndrome. *Autism Research*, 2(3), 157–177.

Chapman, E., Baron-Cohen, S., Auyeung, B., Knickmeyer, R., Taylor, K., & Hackett, G. (2006). Fetal testosterone and empathy: Evidence from the Empathy Quotient (EQ) and the "Reading the Mind in the Eyes" test. *Social Neuroscience*, 1(2), 135–148.

Chura, L.R., Lombardo, M.V., Ashwin, E., Auyeung, B., et al. (2010). Organizational effects of fetal testosterone on human corpus callosum size and asymmetry. *Psychoneuroendocrinology*, 35(1), 122–132.

Delmonte, S., Balsters, J.H., McGrath, J., Fitzgerald, J., et al. (2012). Social and monetary reward processing in autism spectrum disorders. *Molecular Autism*, 3(1), 7.

Geschwind, N., & Galaburda, A.M. (1985). Cerebral lateralization: Biological mechanisms, associations and pathology. III. A hypothesis and a program for research. *Archives of Neurology*, 42(7), 634–654.

Ingudomnukul, E., Baron-Cohen, S., Wheelwright, S., & Knickmeyer, R. (2007). Elevated rates of testosterone-related disorders in women with autism spectrum conditions. *Hormones and Behavior*, 51(5), 597–604.

Jolliffe, T., & Baron-Cohen, S. (1997). Are people with autism and Asperger syndrome faster than normal on the Embedded Figures Test? *Journal of Child Psychology and Psychiatry*, 38(5), 527–534.

Keary, C.J., Minshew, N.J., Bansal, R., Goradia, D., et al. (2009). Corpus callosum volume and neurocognition in autism. *Journal of Autism and Developmental Disorders*, 39(6), 834–841.

Klin, A. (2000). Attributing social meaning to ambiguous visual stimuli in higher-functioning autism and Asperger syndrome: The Social Attribution Task. *Journal of Child Psychology and Psychiatry*, 41(7), 831–846.

Knickmeyer, R., Baron-Cohen, S., Raggatt, P., & Taylor, K. (2005). Foetal testosterone, social relationships, and restricted interests in children. *Journal of Child Psychology and Psychiatry*, 46(2), 198–210.

Knickmeyer, R., Baron-Cohen, S., Raggatt, P., Taylor, K., & Hackett, G. (2006). Fetal testosterone and empathy. *Hormones and Behavior*, 49(3), 282–292.

Knickmeyer, R.C., Wheelwright, S., & Baron-Cohen, S.B. (2007). Sex-typical play: Masculinization/defeminization in girls with an autism spectrum condition. *Journal of Autism and Developmental Disorders*, 38(6), 1028–1035.

Lombardo, M.V., Ashwin, E., Auyeung, B., Chakrabarti, B., et al. (2012a). Fetal testosterone influences sexually dimorphic gray matter in the human brain. *Journal of Neuroscience*, 32(2), 674–680.

Lombardo, M.V., Ashwin, E., Auyeung, B., Chakrabarti, B., et al. (2012b). Fetal programming effects of testosterone on the reward system and behavioral approach tendencies in humans. *Biological Psychiatry*, 72(10), 839–847.

Lutchmaya, S., Baron-Cohen, S., & Raggatt, P. (2002a). Foetal testosterone and eye contact in 12-month-old infants. *Infant Behavior & Development*, 25, 327–335.

Lutchmaya, S., Baron-Cohen, S., & Raggatt, P. (2002b). Foetal testosterone and vocabulary size in 18- and 24-month-old infants. *Infant Behavior & Development*, 24, 418–424.

Lutchmaya, S., Baron-Cohen, S., Raggatt, P., Knickmeyer, R., & Manning, J.T. (2004). 2nd to 4th digit ratios, fetal testosterone and estradiol. *Early Human Development*, 77(1–2), 23–28.

Manning, J.T., Baron-Cohen, S., Wheelwright, S., & Sanders, G. (2001). The 2nd to 4th digit ratio and autism. *Developmental Medicine and Child Neurology*, 43(3), 160–164.

Piven, J., Bailey, J., Ranson, B.J., & Arndt, S. (1997). An MRI study of the corpus callosum in autism. *American Journal of Psychiatry*, 154(8), 1051–1056.

Ruta, L., Ingudomnukul, E., Taylor, K., Chakrabarti, B., & Baron-Cohen, S. (2011). Increased serum androstenedione in adults with autism spectrum conditions. *Psychoneuroendocrinology*, 36(8), 1154–1163.

Schwarz, E., Guest, P.C., Rahmoune, H., Wang, L., et al. (2010). Sex-specific serum biomarker patterns in adults with Asperger's syndrome. *Molecular Psychiatry*, 16(12), 1213–1220.

Scott, F., Baron-Cohen, S., Bolton, P., & Brayne, C. (2002). The CAST (Childhood Asperger Syndrome Test): Preliminary development of UK screen for mainstream primary-school children. *Autism*, 6(1), 9–31.

Swettenham, J., Baron-Cohen, S., Charman, T., Cox, A., et al. (1998). The frequency and distribution of spontaneous attention shifts between social and nonsocial stimuli in autistic, typically developing, and nonautistic developmentally delayed infants. *Journal of Child Psychology and Psychiatry*, 39(5), 747–753.

Volkow, N.D., Wang, G.J., Kollins, S.H., Wigal, T.L., et al. (2009). Evaluating dopamine reward pathway in ADHD: Clinical implications. *Journal of the American Medical Association*, 30(10), 1084–1091.

Zheng, Z., & Cohn, M.J. (2011). Developmental basis of sexually dimorphic digit ratios. *Proceedings of the National Academy of Sciences of the USA*, 108(39), 16289–16294.

WISDOM AND VISION
A Comment on Rimland's Concept of "Training" for Children with Autism
V. Mark Durand

Rimland's discussion of training as a possible intervention for autism (in just five short paragraphs) was prescient in many ways. For example, he wrote, "While no form of psychiatric treatment has been known to alter the course of treatment, it still may be possible to train autistic children to make optimum use of the resources available to them" (page 177). The idea that you could teach these children useful skills was revolutionary at the time, and foreshadowed a more optimistic view of this disorder. Previously, Kanner's autism was regarded as having a devastating prognosis, and was believed to be the result of poor early parenting ("refrigerator" mothers). Emerging behavioral concepts based on the principles of learning suggested to Rimland that these children could in fact acquire new skills, and if a child was not learning a skill it was the fault of the interventionist, and not the disorder.

Commenting again on training, Rimland noted, "One might also infer that since *meaning* cannot serve its usual role in guiding the learning of autistic children, it may be necessary to rely on the use of lavish praise and other forms of overt reward to provide direction as well as incentive to the child's efforts" (page 177). This intuitive view describes the developing concepts that would later be referred to as Applied Behavior Analysis (ABA). At around the same time that Rimland was writing his influential book, Charles Ferster was working with these children using the very overt rewards mentioned by Rimland. Although Ferster's view of the origins of autism is now generally discounted (he, too, believed that inadequate parenting—specifically insufficient reinforcement—was at the root of the development of autism), he provided a valuable perspective by showing that children with this disorder responded to simple behavioral procedures (Ferster & DeMyer, 1961). Ferster used basic, single-case experimental designs and patterned his work after the learning experiments of B. F. Skinner on pigeons and rats. He found that he could teach children with autism very simple actions, such as putting coins in their proper slots, by reinforcing them with food (Ferster, 1961).

Ivar Lovaas at UCLA took Ferster's approach further by demonstrating the clinical importance of these findings. He reasoned that if people with autism responded to reinforcers and punishers in the same way as everyone else, we should be able to use these techniques to help them communicate, to help them become more social, and to help them with their behavior problems (Lovaas & Smith, 1989). Although much refinement of this work has occurred over the ensuing decades, the basic premise—that people with autism can learn, and that they can be taught some of the skills they lack—remains central in the treatment of these individuals.

Another of Rimland's important early insights was revealed in a comment on "generalization" that became the focus of a great deal of subsequent research by applied behavior analysts: "Discovering ways of making optimum use of the autistic child's limited ability to learn, and especially discovering ways of increasing the child's ability to generalize what he has learned, would appear to offer challenging problems for future research" (page 178). Although we can only read between the lines, it's likely that his experience with his own son showed how challenging it was for this population to generalize skills to new people or settings. If you taught a child with autism to request a cookie in the kitchen, that skill would probably not be used by the same child in the dining room. It became clear that special techniques had to be discovered to ensure that these children used their new skills under all circumstances (Horner, Dunlap, & Koegel, 1988). Fortunately, there is now a great deal of evidence pointing to highly effective treatments based on more contemporary ABA techniques that incorporate developmental considerations. These include highly effective programs that teach social communicative skills (e.g., Kasari et al., 2012b; Schreibman & Ingersoll, 2011) as well as interventions to deal with problem behaviors (Durand, 2012).

What could not have been envisioned 50 years ago was the enormous progress that could be made with many children with autism if they were exposed to intensive intervention at a very early age. In an influential study, Lovaas and his colleagues at UCLA reported on their early intervention efforts with very young children with autism (Lovaas, 1987). They found that giving these children intensive behavioral treatment for their communication and social skills problems for 40 hours or more per week improved their intellectual and educational functioning. Targeting these skills in the early years is potentially important for helping the child develop more sophisticated social repertoires (Mundy & Neal, 2000; Poon et al., 2012a). A growing research base suggests that these skills can be facilitated among very young children with ASD (Lawton & Kasari, 2012; Wong & Kasari, 2012); preliminary follow-up data suggests variations of this approach might facilitate later development of language (Kasari et al., 2012a).

Although Rimland's writings did not foretell the revolution that would be brought about by early and intensive behavioral intervention, it is significant to note that recent research is showing how behavioral intervention may be one of the best treatments for the very thing that Rimland saw as causing the disorder (Durand, 2014); note that his was one of the first voices to suggest that the problems experienced by people with autism were due to dysfunctions in the young child's brain. Some exciting research suggests that intensive early behavioral intervention might "normalize" the functioning of the developing brain in these children, compared to children with autism who do not receive this treatment (Dawson et al., 2012; Voos et al., 2013). Clearly, there was a great deal of wisdom and vision in just those five paragraphs.

REFERENCES

Dawson, G., Jones, E.J.H., Merkle, K., Venema, K., et al. (2012). Early behavioral intervention is associated with normalized brain activity in young children with autism. *Journal of the American Academy of Child & Adolescent Psychiatry, 51*(11), 1150–1159.

Durand, V.M. (2012). Functional communication training: Treating challenging behavior. In P.A. Prelock & R. J. McCauley (eds) *Treatment of Autism Spectrum Disorders: Evidence-Based Intervention Strategies for Communication and Social Interactions*. Baltimore, MD: Paul H. Brookes.

Durand, V.M. (2014). *Autism Spectrum Disorder: A Clinical Guide for General Practitioners*. Washington, DC: American Psychiatric Association.

Ferster, C.B. (1961). Positive reinforcement and behavioral deficits of autistic children. *Child Development, 32,* 437–456.

Ferster, C.B., & DeMyer, M.K. (1961). The development of performances in autistic children in an automatically controlled environment. *Journal of Chronic Diseases, 13*(4), 312–345.

Horner, R.H., Dunlap, G.E., & Koegel, R.L. (eds, 1988). *Generalization and Maintenance: Life-Style Changes in Applied Settings*. Baltimore, MD: Paul H. Brookes.

Kasari, C., Gulsrud, A., Freeman, S., Paparella, T., & Hellemann, G. (2012a). Longitudinal follow-up of children with autism receiving targeted interventions on joint attention and play. *Journal of the American Academy of Child & Adolescent Psychiatry, 51*(5), 487–495.

Kasari, C., Rotheram-Fuller, E., Locke, J., & Gulsrud, A. (2012b). Making the connection: Randomized controlled trial of social skills at school for children with autism spectrum disorders. *Journal of Child Psychology and Psychiatry, 53*(4), 431–439.

Lawton, K., & Kasari, C. (2012). Teacher-implemented joint attention intervention: Pilot randomized controlled study for preschoolers with autism. *Journal of Consulting and Clinical Psychology, 80*(4), 687.

Lovaas, O.I. (1987). Behavioral treatment and normal educational and intellectual functioning in young autistic children. *Journal of Consulting and Clinical Psychology, 55*(1), 3–9.

Lovaas, O.I., & Smith, T. (1989). A comprehensive behavioral theory of autistic children: Paradigm for research and treatment. *Journal of Behavior Therapy and Experimental Psychiatry, 20*(1), 17–29.

Mundy, P., & Neal, A.R. (2000). Neural plasticity, joint attention, and a transactional social-orienting model of autism. In G. Laraine Masters (ed.) *International Review of Research in Mental Retardation (Vol. 23)*. London/San Diego, CA: Academic Press.

Poon, K., Watson, L., Baranek, G., & Poe, M.D. (2012). To what extent do joint attention, imitation, and object play behaviors in infancy predict later communication and intellectual functioning in ASD? *Journal of Autism and Developmental Disorders, 42*(6), 1064–1074.

Schreibman, L., & Ingersoll, B. (2011). Naturalistic approaches to early behavioral intervention. In D.G. Amaral, G. Dawson, & D. Geschwind (eds) *Autism Spectrum Disorders*. New York: Oxford University Press.

Voos, A.C., Pelphrey, K.A., Tirrell, J., Bolling, D.Z., et al. (2013). Neural mechanisms of improvements in social motivation after pivotal response treatment: Two case studies. *Journal of Autism and Developmental Disorders*, 43(1), 1–10.

Wong, C., & Kasari, C. (2012). Play and joint attention of children with autism in the preschool special education classroom. *Journal of Autism and Developmental Disorders*, 42(10), 1–10.

BERNARD RIMLAND'S *INFANTILE AUTISM*

Relevance to Modern Biomarkers of Autism

Richard E. Frye

This year marks the 50th anniversary of Dr. Bernard Rimland's seminal book, *Infantile Autism: The Syndrome and Its Implication for a Neural Theory of Behavior*. Dr. Rimland was the first to understand a basic idea about autism spectrum disorder (ASD) that is only recently becoming more apparent to scientists and medical doctors—that ASD is not purely a psychological disorder, but is rooted in the abnormal functioning of biological systems. He felt that objective science would lead the way to better understanding the causes of ASD. I think he would be pleased to see recent developments in the field that examine novel and important hypotheses, many of them funded by the institute that he founded.

A timely review outlines recent growth in the areas of science and medicine focusing on ASD (Rossignol & Frye, 2012a). Mostly within the last decade, novel areas of important physiological systems of the body are starting to be investigated, as compared to more traditional established areas of research such as genetics, theory of mind, and stress. These novel areas of research focus on the dysfunction of the immune system (Rossignol & Frye, 2012a, 2014) and the energy generation system called the mitochondria (Frye & Rossignol, 2011; Rossignol & Frye, 2012b), as well as the role of systems for controlling toxic radicals known as reactive oxygen and nitrogen species (Frye & James, 2014). The other important area of research that has expanded is the study of environmental toxicants which, combined with underlying genetic vulnerabilities, could cause these physiological disturbances that lead to neurodevelopmental disorders (Rossignol, Genuis, & Frye, 2014). There are very critical reasons why this deeper and more complete recognition of the abnormalities associated with ASD are important, including the fact that we can now understand how biological systems can be perturbed early in life to result in a change in the developmental trajectory of the brain to cause ASD. Indeed, we are starting to understand the complexity of the disorder and—perhaps most important—we are seeing how we might approach fixing these abnormalities in order to optimally treat individuals with ASD so they can have a healthy and productive life. This new understanding is also echoed by recent studies that demonstrate that there are both genetic and environmental components that come together to increase the risk of developing ASD (Hallmayer et al., 2011).

One of the areas that Dr. Rimland pioneered was an understanding of the medical symptoms associated with ASD. However, what we are learning is that the symptoms do not necessarily help us understand the underlying causes of ASD in an individual, and do not always predict the underlying medical and physiological abnormalities. Thus, in recent years the research has turned towards the development of biomarkers to help us predict the underlying medical and physiological abnormalities in a particular individual with ASD. Research has particularly focused on both traditional and novel measures of abnormal metabolic systems, comprising abnormalities in redox, folate, and mitochondrial metabolism, immune dysfunction and dysregulation, abnormalities in gastrointestinal function with particular concentration on the microbiome, abnormalities in brain activation and metabolism, and markers of toxicant exposure and detoxification metabolism. Abnormalities in many of the same biomarkers that are measured systemically in blood have also been found in the brain, suggesting that biomarkers based on peripheral blood testing may be reflective of the ongoing abnormal processes in the brain (Rossignol & Frye, 2014). Interestingly, biomarkers have evolved from indicating ongoing disease processes in children who have already developed ASD, to biomarkers that can be obtained at or before birth in order to predict the development of ASD. Of course, the exciting potential of these latter biomarkers is the ability to prevent the development of ASD by applying treatments before symptoms develop.

Recent reviews have outlined the high rate of abnormalities in traditional biomarkers of mitochondrial disease such as lactate, pyruvate, and alanine, (Rossignol & Frye, 2012b) as well as more novel biomarkers of mitochondrial disease such as particular patterns of abnormalities in acyl-carnitines (Frye, Melnyk, & MacFabe, 2013). Studies have varied widely in the prevalence of mitochondrial disease and dysfunction in children with ASD, potentially due to the particular tissue in which mitochondrial function is measured (Frye et al., 2013), and the realization that new types of mitochondrial disease exist and need to be discovered (Frye & Naviaux, 2011; Rose et al., 2014a, 2014b).

Abnormalities in redox metabolism and resulting elevations in oxidative stress have been uncovered in a significant number of children with ASD, and recent reviews have confirmed the consistency of specific biomarkers, including abnormalities in glutathione and cysteine (Frye & James, 2014; Frustaci et al., 2012) and oxidative damage to nuclear (Melnyk et al., 2012) and mitochondrial DNA (Napoli, Wong, & Giulivi, 2013), proteins (Rose et al., 2012), and lipids (Damodaran & Arumugam, 2011). In addition, the importance of abnormalities in redox-related pathways, including those involved in folate, methylation, and tetrahydrobiopterin metabolism, are beginning to be appreciated. Biomarkers of the methylation pathway, including methionine, S-Adenosyl methionine, and S-Adenosyl homocysteine are being revealed as abnormal (James et al., 2006). These abnormalities in the methylation pathway can have functional implications, resulting in changes in methylation of DNA (Melnyk et al., 2012), individual gene promoters (Lv et al., 2013), and histones (James et al., 2013), which can abnormally turn genetic and enzymatic pathways on and off. Abnormalities in the folate pathway such as the newly described folate receptor alpha autoantibodies appear to have clinical implications for treatment (Frye et al., 2013). Abnormalities in tetrahydrobiopterin, an important cofactor for neurotransmitter and nitric oxide production, have also been found in individuals with ASD, and a recent study suggests that biomarkers of nitric oxide metabolism may be used to best measure abnormal tetrahydrobiopterin metabolism in children with ASD (Vargas et al., 2005).

Studies have pointed to abnormalities in immune system function, with many studies outlining specific biomarkers that can be measured. Measurable biomarkers include autoantibodies to specific neural elements (Rossignol & Frye, 2012a; Gesundheit et al., 2013) as well as other important proteins that are essential for healthy metabolism (Frye et al., 2013), depression of IgG and IgM antibody production (Heuer et al., 2008), abnormalities in cytokine levels in the peripheral blood (Gesundheit et al., 2013), brain tissue (Vargas et al., 2005), and cerebrospinal fluid (Vargas et al., 2005), and activation of neuroimmune cells, particularly the microglia (Rossignol & Frye, 2014; Vargas et al., 2005). One compelling area of biomarker research is the discovery of maternal fetal brain antibodies that have the potential to prenatally predict the development of ASD during pregnancy so that treatments can be applied to prevent ASD from developing (Braunschweig & Van de Water, 2012).

Given the high rate of gastrointestinal problems in children with ASD, especially in children with more severe ASD (Adams et al., 2011), many studies have recently examined the role of the microbiome in ASD. Many studies have demonstrated that there is a shift in the colonization of species in the gastrointestinal tract in children with ASD (Finegold et al., 2010). Given the ability of gut bacteria to produce metabolites that can disrupt gut function and systemic and brain metabolism, it is believed that these alterations in the microbiota could play a significant role in the pathogenesis and symptoms associated with ASD (Cryan & O'Mahony, 2011). Most studies have used pyrosequencing (Finegold et al., 2010; De Angelis et al., 2013) and/or real time polymerase chain reaction (Wang et al., 2011) to measure species and microbiota diversity. Other studies have measured bacterial metabolites such as p-cresol (De Angelis et al., 2013) and short-chain fatty acids, particularly acetate, propionate, and butyrate (Wang et al., 2012).

Clearly there is a lot of work to be done in many diverse areas related to biological abnormalities associated with ASD, and many biomarkers are under development. This is a growing and important area of scientific investigation, as biomarkers can not only help us understand some of the underlying biological abnormalities associated with ASD, but can be used to subgroup children with ASD so that they are provided the most appropriate treatments in order to optimize their development and reduce their symptoms.

REFERENCES

Adams, J.B., Johansen, L.J., Powell, L.D., Quig, D., & Rubin, R.A. (2011). Gastrointestinal flora and gastrointestinal status in children with autism: Comparisons to typical children and correlation with autism severity. *BMC Gastroenterology*, 11, 22.

Braunschweig, D., & Van de Water, J. (2012). Maternal autoantibodies in autism. *Archives of Neurology*, 69(6), 693–699.

Cryan, J.F., & O'Mahony, S.M. (2011). The microbiome-gut-brain axis: From bowel to behavior. *Neurogastroenterology and Motility: The Official Journal of the European Gastrointestinal Motility Society*, 23(3), 187–192.

Damodaran, L.P., & Arumugam, G. (2011). Urinary oxidative stress markers in children with autism. *Redox Report: Communications in Free Radical Research*, 16(5), 216–222.

De Angelis, M., Piccolo, M., Vannini. L., Siragusa, S., et al. (2013). Fecal microbiota and metabolome of children with autism and pervasive developmental disorder not otherwise specified. *PLOS ONE*, 8(10), e76993.

Finegold, S.M., Dowd, S.E., Gontcharova, V., Liu, C., et al. (2010). Pyrosequencing study of fecal microflora of autistic and control children. *Anaerobe*, 16(4), 444–453.

Frustaci, A., Neri, M., Cesario, A., Adams, J.B., et al. (2012). Oxidative stress-related biomarkers in autism: Systematic review and meta-analyses. *Free Radical Biology & Medicine*, 52(10), 2128–2141.

Frye, R.E., DeLatorre, R., Taylor, H.B., Slattery, J., et al. (2013). Metabolic effects of sapropterin treatment in autism spectrum disorder: A preliminary study. *Translational Psychiatry*, 3, e237.

Frye, R.E., & James, S.J. (2014). Metabolic pathology of autism in relation to redox metabolism. *Biomarkers in Medicine*, 8(3), 321–330.

Frye, R.E., Melnyk, S., & MacFabe, D.F. (2013). Unique acyl-carnitine profiles are potential biomarkers for acquired mitochondrial disease in autism spectrum disorder. *Translational Psychiatry*, 3, e220.

Frye, R.E., & Naviaux, R.K. (2011). Autistic disorder with complex IV overactivity: A new mitochondrial syndrome. *Journal of Pediatric Neurology*, 9(4), 1–4.

Frye, R.E., & Rossignol, D.A. (2011). Mitochondrial dysfunction can connect the diverse medical symptoms associated with autism spectrum disorders. *Pediatric Research*, 69(5 Pt 2), 41R–47R.

Frye, R.E., Sequeira, J.M., Quadros, E.V., James, S.J., & Rossignol, D.A. (2013). Cerebral folate receptor autoantibodies in autism spectrum disorder. *Molecular Psychiatry*, 18(3), 369–381.

Gesundheit, B., Rosenzweig, J.P., Naor, D., Lerer, B., et al. (2013). Immunological and autoimmune considerations of autism spectrum disorders. *Journal of Autoimmunity*, 44, 1–7.

Hallmayer, J., Cleveland, S., Torres, A., Phillips, J., et al. (2011). Genetic heritability and shared environmental factors among twin pairs with autism. *Archives of General Psychiatry*, 68(11), 1095–1102.

Heuer, L., Ashwood, P., Schauer, J., Goines, P., et al. (2008). Reduced levels of immunoglobulin in children with autism correlates with behavioral symptoms. *Autism Research: Official Journal of the International Society for Autism Research*, 1(5), 275–283.

James, S.J., Melnyk, S., Jernigan, S., Cleves, M.A., et al. (2006). Metabolic endophenotype and related genotypes are associated with oxidative stress in children with autism. *American Journal of Medical Genetics. Part B, Neuropsychiatric Genetics: The Official Publication of the International Society Of Psychiatric Genetics*, 141B(8), 947–956.

James, S.J., Shpyleva, S., Melnyk, S., Pavliv, O., & Pogribny, I.P. (2013). Complex epigenetic regulation of engrailed-2 (EN-2) homeobox gene in the autism cerebellum. *Translational Psychiatry*, 3, e232.

Lv, J., Xin, Y., Zhou, W., & Qiu, Z. (2013). The epigenetic switches for neural development and psychiatric disorders. *Journal of Genetics and Genomics*, 40(7), 339–346.

Melnyk, S., Fuchs, G.J., Schulz, E., Lopez, M., et al. (2012). Metabolic imbalance associated with methylation dysregulation and oxidative damage in children with autism. *Journal of Autism and Developmental Disorders*, 42(3), 367–377.

Napoli, E., Wong, S., & Giulivi, C. (2013). Evidence of reactive oxygen species-mediated damage to mitochondrial DNA in children with typical autism. *Molecular Autism*, 4(1), 2.

Rose, S., Frye, R.E., Slattery, J., Wynne, R., et al. (2014a). Oxidative stress induces mitochondrial dysfunction in a subset of autistic lymphoblastoid cell lines. *Translational Psychiatry*, 4, e377.

Rose, S., Frye, R.E., Slattery, J., Wynne, R., et al. (2014b). Oxidative stress induces mitochondrial dysfunction in a subset of autism lymphoblastoid cell lines in a well-matched case control cohort. *PLOS ONE*, 9(1), e85436.

Rose, S., Melnyk, S., Pavliv, O., Bai, S., et al. (2012). Evidence of oxidative damage and inflammation associated with low glutathione redox status in the autism brain. *Translational Psychiatry*, 2, e134.

Rossignol, D.A., & Frye, R.E. (2012a). A review of research trends in physiological abnormalities in autism spectrum disorders: Immune dysregulation, inflammation, oxidative stress, mitochondrial dysfunction and environmental toxicant exposures. *Molecular Psychiatry*, 17(4), 389–401.

Rossignol, D.A., & Frye, R.E. (2012b). Mitochondrial dysfunction in autism spectrum disorders: A systematic review and meta-analysis. *Molecular Psychiatry*, 17(3), 290–314.

Rossignol, D.A., & Frye, R.E. (2014). Evidence linking oxidative stress, mitochondrial dysfunction, and inflammation in the brain of individuals with autism. *Frontiers in Physiology*, 5, 150.

Rossignol, D.A., Genuis, S.J., & Frye, R.E. (2014). Environmental toxicants and autism spectrum disorders: A systematic review. *Translational Psychiatry*, 4, e360.

Vargas, D.L., Nascimbene, C., Krishnan, C., Zimmerman, A.W., & Pardo, C.A. (2005). Neuroglial activation and neuroinflammation in the brain of patients with autism. *Annals of Neurology*, 57(1), 67–81.

Wang, L., Christophersen, C.T., Sorich, M.J., Gerber, J.P., Angley, M.T., Conlon, M.A. (2011). Low relative abundances of the mucolytic bacterium Akkermansia muciniphila and Bifidobacterium spp. in feces of children with autism. *Applied and Environmental Microbiology*, 77(18), 6718–6721.

Wang, L., Christophersen, C.T., Sorich, M.J., Gerber, J.P., Angley, M.T., & Conlon, M.A. (2012). Elevated fecal short chain fatty acid and ammonia concentrations in children with autism spectrum disorder. *Digestive Diseases and Sciences*, 57(8), 2096–2102.

Part III

SOME POSSIBLE IMPLICATIONS OF THE THEORY OF AUTISM FOR A THEORY OF BEHAVIOR

Introduction to Part III

"...in the present state of neurological inquiry (and more particularly the central problem of mind-brain relationships) there is a very real need for the formulation of new ideas to supplement the routine investigations of the microscope and calculating' machine." (Sir W. LeGros Clark, 1958, p. 12)

Part I of this paper was an attempt to marshall and reorganize what is known of early infantile autism. Speculation was kept to a minimum. Part II contained some speculation, but for the most part only that necessary for the development of the theory. Part III is frankly, admittedly, and perhaps even unabashedly more speculative than Parts I and II.

There has been much criticism in recent years of what has been disparagingly called "neurologizing," "physiologizing," or "neuromythology." One could hardly quarrel with Proust's observation that "mental activity is easy, if it doesn't have to conform to reality." But who is to draw the line which separates theory from speculation? And who can indict speculation rigorously, without himself becoming speculative in the process?

In partial placation of the tradition of "no speculation," the following three ground rules were devised and applied to the hypothesizing which follows: (1) Speculation should be identified as such. (2) Speculation should not run contrary to the data. (By "data" we specifically exclude the opinions of even the most estimable of experts; man's progress is clearly a chronicle of authority refuted.) (3) Speculation should be stated as explicitly as possible, to facilitate evaluation.

The hypotheses presented in Part III were in large part developed to account for certain well-documented and readily verified paradoxes contained in the literature on early infantile autism. Paradoxes are too often scorned and rejected—impatiently cast aside as being impertinently at odds with what we know. To afford paradoxes such ill-treatment is to perform the "blackest act of all," the act of not thinking. The paradox should be welcomed as perhaps the only visible outcropping of an underlying and unknown truth, despite its demands on our open-mindedness and imagination.

Part III is also an attempt to relate, in a manner consistent with the theory, certain of the data of early infantile autism with existing theories of personality and cognition. Subordinate purposes of Part III are to present alternative explanations for certain parts of the theory, and to elaborate points which would have been disruptive had they been detailed in the midst of the theory.

INTRODUCTION TO CHAPTER 9
Stephen M. Edelson

At the time Bernard Rimland wrote *Infantile Autism*, most professionals approached autism from a psychodynamic perspective, basing their views largely on Kanner's and Bettelheim's writings about the personalities of parents of children with autism. This is no longer an issue except in a very few countries, including France and Argentina.

Although Rimland speculated that parents may have "an unusual—perhaps an extreme—degree of intellectual control over emotions," there has been little research on this topic. However, there clearly are factors that impact parents' emotional well-being, such as the stress of raising a child with a developmental disability (Davis & Carter, 2008).

Rimland also noted that there appeared to be a low rate of mental illness in families with children on the autism spectrum, except for the possibility of manic depression. His speculation may be true for Kanner syndrome, since Rimland relied much on Kanner's writings. However, large-scale studies have shown a relationship between autism and other disabilities, including schizophrenia and bipolar disorder (Sullivan et al., 2012).

Rimland also wrote in detail about how autism and schizophrenia may be on different ends of the memory spectrum, suggesting that individuals with autism may have difficulty retrieving information from memory, while retrieval flows "*too freely*" in schizophrenia. This is an interesting hypothesis and needs further investigation.

REFERENCES

Davis, N.O., & Carter, A.S. (2008). Parenting stress in mothers and fathers of toddlers with autism spectrum disorders: Associations with child characteristics. *Journal of Autism and Developmental Disorders, 38*(7), 1278–1291.

Sullivan, P.F., Magnusson, C., Reichenberg, A., Boman, M., et al. (2012). Family history of schizophrenia and bipolar disorder as risk factors for autism. *Archives of General Psychiatry, 69*(11), 1099–1103.

CHAPTER 9

Some Implications of Early Infantile Autism for the Study of Personality

The theory as previously presented holds that primary cases of early infantile autism are those of children who have suffered an impairment in a brain mechanism which might have led to the introverted but highly intellectual personalities which characterized their forebears. The tasks of the present chapter are to specify neural mechanisms, consistent with the theory, which could result in the affective characteristics so frequently reported for the parents of autistic children; and to relate these postulated mechanisms to the larger body of existing personality research and theory.

A. EMOTION AND THE PARENTAL PERSONALITIES

Kanner's description of the parents of autistic children (presented in Chapter 2) included not only high intelligence, but very often an introverted, perfectionistic, hyperobjective personality. Other writers have consistently confirmed a high incidence of this type of personality among the parents of autistic children.

There are several factors which may explain at least part of this phenomenon. One is that the perceptions of child psychiatrists, like the perceptions of other persons, are in part determined by their existing needs and beliefs. Since many of these practitioners are deeply committed to the psychogenic point of view, they tend to see the parents as highly pernicious. As a consequence, the use of terms like "compulsive," "narcissistic," "rigid," etc., in their reports is not unexpected. Indeed, a disturbing amount of ill-concealed hostility toward the parents is evident in many persons who treat disturbed children (see May, 1958 and Oppenheim, 1961, for examples).[1]

A second factor derives from the first: The parents, realizing that they are regarded as responsible for the problem, react coldly, which tends to confirm the therapist's suspicions. A third factor is that the parents' behavior may in large part be a response to their being rebuffed and rejected by the child. This last point has been especially stressed by Kanner and a number of other writers (e.g., Rees, 1956; van Krevelen, 1960).

Although these and similar factors no doubt provide at least a partial explanation for the unique personalities displayed by the parents of autistic children, they do not in themselves seem entirely adequate. For one thing, they would tend to apply to the majority of parents of disturbed children and thus would not account for the uniqueness of the personalities of the parents of autistic children: "In the control group one does not find the dramatically evident detachment, obsessiveness, and coldness that is almost a universal feature of parents of autistic children" (Eisenberg & Kanner, 1956, p. 561). We will have to look further for an answer to the problem.

We may start by examining the hypothesis that the parents themselves are abnormal or maladjusted. Several points of evidence cited in Part I of this monograph tend to refute such a hypothesis: (a) the low incidence of mental illness in the parents, grandparents, etc.; (b) the low incidence of broken homes; (c) the low rate of abnormality among siblings of the autistic child; and (d) the high educational and professional attainments of the parents. In Part II we have cast further doubt on the "pathologic parent" theory by showing that the syndrome of autism is itself readily explainable as primarily a *cognitive*, not an affective problem. And immediately above we have noted that such factors as need-determined perception are likely to have contributed to the psychiatric reporting of abnormality in the parents. All in all, it would seem that our analysis of the problem posed by the parental personalities need not be confined to the area of abnormal psychology.

Being relieved of the burden of psychopathology, it becomes possible to propose a relatively simple explanatory concept: An unusual—perhaps an extreme—degree of intellectual control over the emotions. This concept subsumes the two general characteristics which in turn subsume most of the other descriptions applied to the parents: *objectivity* and *unemotionality*. If the

---

1   Luborsky (1962) has recently noted that child psychiatrists tend to identify with their child-patients and are hostile to the parents partly because of a felt need to "rescue" the child. The hostility to parents may also stem from the general resentment against persons in authority which Luborsky reports as common in the child psychiatrists known to him.

reader will review briefly the previously provided descriptions he will see the cogency of this interpretation.

Objectivity: Freed of a pathological bias, often-used adjectives like "compulsive" and "obsessive" become "non-impulsive." That is, the parents may tend to direct their efforts toward very specific goals, or to be relatively indistractible. This interpretation is highly consistent with many of Kanner's phrases such as "disdainful of frivolity" and "quiet and serious." It is also consistent with the high level of achievement the parents show. As Hollingworth (1942) emphasizes, intelligence alone does not guarantee achievement—only one highly gifted person in three achieves notably. "Perfectionistic," "humorless," and "rigid," when one realizes these terms have been applied by persons predisposed to find abnormality, may also be reinterpreted as suggesting a high degree of goal orientation. Eisenberg (1956) has remarked on the "almost uncanny objectiveness" of the parents, and van Krevelen (1960) has described them as "painstaking and accurate informers."

Unemotionality: Terms like "unemotional," "cold," "detached," "coolheaded," "reserved," "introverted," "inhibited," "formal," and "undemonstrative" have been repeatedly applied to the parents of children with early infantile autism. These terms too fit the hypothesis of extreme emotional control.

Kanner's description of the unperturbed father who was busily continuing to write his book when a rescue squad opened the wrecked train car in which he was a passenger illustrates this point well, as does his story about the surgeon-father who remained unruffled when Kanner deliberately tried to arouse him to anger by questioning his affection for his children. Most of Kanner's other cases also demonstrate emotional control, such as Charles' father who was "gentle, calm, and placid," and his mother who was a woman of "remarkable equanimity" (1944, p. 213). Cited earlier was the memorable mother who telephoned Kanner "without rancor" to discuss her husband's near seduction.

The often-used term "introverted" is perhaps best defined as indicating "not given to emotional spontaneity" (Nagle, 1960), which emphasizes its relationship to our hypothesis (see also Mann, cited by Carrigan, 1960).

Kanner's recent description of the parents in a national magazine includes both factors, objectivity and unemotionality: "All too often this child is the offspring of highly organized professional parents, cold and rational—the type Dr. Kanner describes as 'just happening to defrost enough to produce a child'" (*Time*, July 25, 1960, p. 78).

Viewed as the act of persons who place a premium on rationality, the advance preparation of a written case history, so often remarked upon as unusual, becomes less surprising. It does lead to more efficient use of time in the psychiatric interview.

There is considerable evidence which indicates that traits relating to emotional expressivity have a large genetically determined component (Cattell, 1950; Eysenck, 1956). Davenport (1940) provides data on the inheritance of uncontrollable violent temper as a Mendelian dominant and Gottesman (1960) reports introversion to have the highest coefficient of heritability of the traits he studied.

The physiological bases of emotional expression and control are still quite obscure, but there appears to be little doubt that descending impulses from higher centers in the cortex are essential to emotional control. And while their theories on the exact role played by the reticular formation in the maintenance of emotional control differ, Hebb (1955), M. Arnold (1960), and Bharucha-Reid (1960, 1961, 1962) agree on the importance of the reticular formation in performing this function. Hebb's theory that the reticular formation provides the motive power or driving force in facilitating cortical activity has already been discussed and will be referred to again. Hebb, basing his theory on Lindsley's (1951) activation theory of reticular function in emotion, emphasizes the disruptive role played by extreme activation of the reticular arousal system. In doing so he points out the often overlooked importance of emotional control by citing the wartime studies which show that in the emotional pressure of battle no more than 15 to 25 percent of men under attack even fire their rifles, let alone use them efficiently. He cites Tyhurst's studies of behavior in emergency and disaster in which a large proportion of individuals suffer confusion, paralyzing anxiety, and hysteria. By citing these studies, Hebb implicitly underlines the extent and significance of interindividual variation in emotional control.

In 1959, Hebb again emphasized this point: "It is no longer idle fantasy to raise, as a problem for consideration, the possible relation between the activity of the brain-stem reticular formation and the behavior of the front-line soldier who does not raise his rifle to hold off the enemy, or the man who is killed in traffic because paralysed by impending disaster" (pp. 269–270).

The views on emotion of Strauss and Kephart (1955) are also of interest. While they do not refer specifically to the reticular formation, they suggest that panic behavior may result from the slowness of conduction of small fiber connections between midbrain and cortex, which results in midbrain rather than cortical management of decision. Emotion is described as a phylogenetically old defense-preparatory response, antithetical to precise cortically-mediated reactions.

Arnold's theory ascribes to the reticular formation a role closely akin to the one preferred by the present writer. She suggests that the reticular formation performs in "a system mediating the appraisal of sense impressions" (Vol. 11, p. 152). Appraisal of sense impressions would specifically seem to involve the bringing of sensory input into conjunction with the content of memory.

A very similar concept was invoked in our earlier discussion of pain perception, where the painful stimulus was sensed, but the unpleasantness was greatly diminished by severing nerve tracts entering the reticular formation and thereby (theoretically) eliminating the effects of remembered experience. The ease with which an uncritical emotional outburst (sham rage) can be evoked in a decorticate animal is quite consistent with the point of view that emotional control may require or be facilitated by a high degree of availability to brain stem centers of the traces left by prior experience. Obviously the nature or content of these traces must be of great importance, and our concentration of attention on mechanisms rather than on the messages they convey should not be construed to indicate that experience is necessarily regarded as being of lesser importance.[2] Our focus of interest on the neural mechanisms results from the finding, discussed in Chapter 3, that there is no evidence that non-organic factors play a part in the etiology of early infantile autism. Our problem is therefore restricted to biological mechanisms, and especially those which may be heritable.

In terms of our present problem, we suggest that the specific personality configuration of the parents of autistic children may result largely from their ready availability of emotion-inhibiting remembered experience. In a person whose neural apparatus permits a high degree of efficiency in what Arnold calls "appraisal," might not stimuli tend to evoke a relatively low level of affective response, resulting in a less "emotive" (to use Nagle's concept) individual? Stimuli ordinarily evoking anger, as well as stimuli ordinarily

---

2   We refer here to *psycho-social experience* as opposed to what may be called *biological experience*. This distinction is an important one and we feel it has not been afforded sufficient attention. In the above context, being smiled at or fondled by a parent is an example of psycho-social experience while being exposed to high tension oxygen is an example of biological experience. The distinction was made earlier in considering the differential effects of sensory deprivation versus lack of social stimulation. That an environment may be adverse both psychologically and biologically (i.e., food deprivation may produce both hunger and malnutrition) does not alleviate the need for recognition that two factors may be involved. When this distinction is not made, the effects of the environment are typically and uncritically assumed to be psycho-social rather than biological in nature, as, for example, in the case of behavioral differences between identical twins.

evoking joy, love, and related affective responses may tend to be responded to critically and analytically, and therefore coldly and dispassionately.

It was precisely such a mechanism—facility of communication between percept and memory—which we suggested might account for the high intelligence reported for the parents of autistic children. Many definitions of intelligence revolve on this central concept, as we showed in the previous chapter (e.g., "the degree of availability of one's experiences," Goddard, 1946). According to Thurstone (1921, cited by Goddard, 1946) the first of three vital components of intelligence is the "capacity to inhibit instinctive adjustment."

We are emphasizing here that the same neural mechanism, present in highly efficient form in the parents and in highly inefficient form in the children, could account for a good deal of the personalities and intelligence of both.

In opposition to this view it might be argued that not all intelligent people are emotionally inexpressive, and not all emotionally expressive people are unintelligent. This is obviously quite true. Admittedly, we have discussed but one of many possible mechanisms which might influence or determine personality. Our argument must assume that, at least in some individuals, the neural mechanism we have described is a dominating influence.

B. DRIVE AND THE PARENTAL PERSONALITIES

Having been set to thinking about the above somewhat unusual assumption, the writer's interest was aroused upon coming across this statement by Kahn and Cohen (1934):

> ...the over- as well as the under-development of certain brain areas serves as a sort of background of certain plus and minus members of the species or, in other words, of certain superior and deficient types... We are of the opinion that there exist personality types which owe their existence, at least partially, to a special organization of the brainstem. (p. 748)

What is particularly interesting is that the foregoing quotation appeared in an article referred to by Scheerer, Rothmann, and Goldstein as having been in part based upon observation of case "L.," the *idiot savant* boy who was identified as being autistic both in their original paper (1945) and by Goldstein (1959).

Kahn and Cohen were primarily concerned with what they called "organic drivenness." By "organic" they meant to specify the trait was biologically (but not necessarily pathologically) based, and by "drivenness" they referred to its manifestation as extreme vigorousness. "Drivenness" may consist of pure motor activity as well as activity directed toward very specific goals.

While the relationships between the personality characteristics we have been discussing (and attributing also to "the special organization of the brainstem") and the characteristics described by Kahn and Cohen are not perfectly clear, they do appear to be related. Very many autistic children are markedly hyperactive, and it is of interest that Frankl's case (1942), whom Sarason and Gladwin (1958) identified as bearing many similarities to Kanner's cases, was specifically described as manifesting the "organic drivenness" syndrome.

Kahn and Cohen, who believed that the trait they described has a large hereditary component, observed that:

> The accomplishments of some of the organically driven patients may indeed be remarkable. Although they may often display a multitude of diversified interests they somehow possess great ability to integrate them. (p. 752)

Those familiar with Kanner's writings will recall numerous instances of persons who fit this description among the parents and relatives of autistic children. Kanner has often commented upon the unusual drive and achievement shown in the parents and blood relatives of his cases. In his original article on autism, he referred to the mother who was "successively a purchasing agent, the director of secretarial studies in a girls' school, and a teacher of history" (1943, p. 248). There are many similar examples.

Among the descriptions of persons who fit the Kahn and Cohen pattern of remarkable accomplishment, perhaps Kanner's description of the grandfather and relatives of one of his patients is the most memorable:

> One grandfather, whose recently published autobiography tells of a life of uncanny versatility, was at various times a medical missionary, professor of tropical medicine, dean of a large medical school, curator of an art museum, manganese mining engineer, novelist, painter who exhibited in Paris, the representative of a sewing machine firm and, if this also is an achievement, pretty much of a Don Juan. One of his sons is a much-read novelist, another the author of adventure and horror stories, and a third a radio news commentator. His daughter is a singer. Our patient's father, the second of the five children, is a plant pathologist, a very conscientious and reliable scientist. (1949, p. 423)[3]

---

3   With permission of *Amer. J. Orthopsychiat.* and the author.

Further examples of relatives with unusual "drive" are the maternal grandmother of Charles N. (1944), who was very "dynamic, forceful, hyperactive...has done writing and composing," and perhaps also the surgeon described earlier who was so completely and constantly immersed in his work that he was uncertain whether or not he could recognize his children on the street.

Despert (1951) described a father of an autistic child who fit both Kanner's description and Kahn and Cohen's—a "brilliant" minister, "a man of vigorous intellect" having "an insatiable drive for activity."

It may be then that the highly developed, highly complex emotional-intellectual system in the brain stem postulated for the parents of autistic children has a corresponding—and similarly situated, if we are to believe Kahn and Cohen (and Hebb)—motivational function.

That individual differences now attributable to variations in brain stem function may play an exceedingly important part in determining human personality is a position advocated for many years by Duffy. Recently (1957) she pointed out that the concepts of drive and emotion could be more readily understood by referring to differences in the degree of "arousal" or activation of the individual.

While, as we have emphasized, our proposed "linkage to memory" conception of brain stem function has many precedents as an explanation for intelligence and emotional restraint, its use as an explanation for a high level of activity and achievement is somewhat novel and considerably more tenuous. We earlier referred to the significant accomplishment which might be expected of persons having the non-frivolous, goal-oriented, objective type of personality conferred by a neural mechanism especially adapted for evaluating stimuli. Achievement might also be enhanced in a more positive way by the neural mechanism under discussion if one thinks of the motivating effects of having the rewards and consequences of behavior ever-present before consciousness. Teachers, preachers, coaches, and advertising copywriters are expected to enhance this function—"dangling the carrot"—even more than they are expected to impart information.

To take an obverse view of the problem, lassitude and indolence, the enemies of achievement, often seem to involve the glossing over, blocking, or ignoring of their consequences, even when the individual "knows" at the verbal level the consequences of failure to act. Inactivity, in the face of a need for action, may thus be partially the result of an inhibition or suspension in imagining the results of such inactivity. Many forms of sacrifice of long-term welfare for immediate gain are difficult to explain in any other way. Such a maladaptive repression may be more likely to occur in a neural structure already marginal with respect to the function of bringing the content of memory into useful conjunction with the present content of attention.[4] When we say someone "closes his eyes to" or "is deaf to" something, we refer to centrally mediated selective inattention closely related to the processes under discussion, but seemingly at a less consistent or habitual level.

The apathy and loss of motivation one experiences on first awakening, when fatigued or ill, or, as Hebb (1958b) has emphasized, as part of the sensory deprivation syndrome, may represent normal physiological variations in the neural mechanism proposed.

A malfunction very similar to the one proposed here could, if genetically based, provide an explanation for the highly consistent finding, which has baffled many investigators, of a much higher concordance rate for criminality in monozygotic than dizygotic twins. That there could be an inherited tendency to break laws which are socially defined is regarded as incredible, even though the results of a number of studies have confirmed a significant difference in concordance rates (Cattell, 1950; Dobzhansky, 1962). That certain persons may have inherited a weakness in the neural structure which performs the function, so important in humans, of keeping the consequences of one's actions in the foreground of consciousness is by no means incredible, however. A pathological tendency to repress, or to fail to imagine, the consequences to oneself and to others of an antisocial act could well account for a good deal of criminal and psychopathic behavior. On a shorter time scale, the defect to which we refer is thought of as impulsiveness. The tendency for normal persons to become accident prone—to act without due heed to consequences—when angry or tired may possibly have a related neural basis.

In view of our previous discussion of the importance of this mechanism to the strongly motivated individual, it is interesting that Levine (1955a) finds somewhat similar symptoms in psychopaths, lobotomized persons, and in normal persons characterized as low perseverators. High perseveration is associated with obsessive and depressive syndromes (Levine, 1955b), an important and interesting finding in view of our next topic.

---

4   We refer, of course, to but one way in which initiative or ambition may be neurally modulated. That such experiential factors as prior successes and failures, imitation of parents, nearness and value of incentive, etc. are important determinants of behavior is not at issue here. We seek instead to explain that variation in drive not adequately explained by the more easily, frequently, and uncritically invoked experiential explanations.

C. CYCLOTHYMIA, SCHIZOTHYMIA, AND
THE PARENTAL PERSONALITIES

One might say that an individual having the type of neural structure we have envisioned is very tightly bound to reality as he knows it. Taken to an extreme, he may be incapable of repressing its demands upon himself. Such close ties to reality may explain not only the high achievement but also the very low rate of mental illness in the families of autistic children. On the other hand, it is easy to see that if it occurred to excess, the condition we describe could be pathological. The person afflicted, too persistently aware of problems and consequences, and unable to release himself from concern, might be driven to activity by uncontrolled internal pressures. Alternatively, he might become depressed by the unrelenting weight of cares which more typical individuals are able to disregard, at least temporarily.

The discussion which ensues is a further attempt to relate Kanner's findings regarding the parental personalities to the mainstream of thought in the domain of personality theory. The steps we can make in this direction are admittedly halting, but they lead along an intriguing path.

Perhaps the most valuable clue to the problems at hand relates to the nature and incidence of mental illness in the parents and relatives of autistic children. Kanner and others have commented upon the quite unexpected fact that the parents and near-relatives of autistic children are "remarkably" free of mental illness. Only one of the first 200 of Kanner's group of parents had ever experienced a psychotic episode, and of the group of 793 grandparents, aunts, and uncles, only 12 had experienced mental illness (Eisenberg & Kanner, 1956). This incidence is far too low to be shrugged off as a chance fluctuation. Especially when this fact is considered in conjunction with the highly consistent and unique intellectual-emotional configuration of the parents of autistic children does it appear that the parents represent an unusual and homogeneous group, linked by their sharing of a specific genetic background.

Not only is the incidence of mental illness unusually low, but the nature of the disorder when it does occur is unexpected. The present writer's study of the problem shows that in those few cases where mental illness has been reported in a relative, the classification was in the manic-depressive category and never schizophrenia, even though schizophrenia is considerably the more prevalent of the two conditions in the general population. In beginning this section we offered an implied explanation of why this might be so.

That manic-depressive psychosis and schizophrenia form the two main classes of mental illness is well known. The presently available evidence suggests that these two conditions are to a large extent mutually exclusive. Families in which one form of abnormality occurs very rarely have members afflicted with the other (Kallman, 1953). Between schizophrenia and manic-depressive disorder, the latter has the higher hereditary loading, as shown in a number of ways. For instance, where schizophrenics and manic-depressives have married, the children have far more frequently been manic-depressives (Cattell, 1950). Kraines (1957) has reviewed the evidence and emphasized the very strong physiological basis for manic-depressive illness.

Kretschmer, following Kraepelin's original delineation of the manic-depressive–schizophrenic classes of psychosis, developed a general theory of personality in which manic-depressive psychosis and schizophrenia represent the extremes of a continuum along which the mass of humanity is distributed.[5] Those near the schizophrenia extreme of the distribution were "schizoids," exhibiting the "schizothymic" temperament, while those near the manic-depressive extreme possessed the "cyclothymic" temperament. Later research has for the most part supported Kretschmer, although the phenomena in question are more complex than the original theory would indicate. Cattell (1957), for instance, found from factor analysis that several "cooperative factors," especially his Factor H (Parasympathetic Immunity), tend consistently to obscure the interpretation that can be given to research findings involving the cyclothymic dimension.

It should be emphasized at this point that the personality characteristics to which Kretschmer referred are not necessarily accurately described by their titles. As he later pointed out (in the preface to his second edition) "cyclothymic" or "cycloidal" personalities need *not* show periodic variations in emotion. As another cautionary note, it may be well to point out that much of the criticism directed at Kretschmer's theory has been based on a misconception of Kretschmer's use of the "typology" concept. To Kretschmer a type was merely a conceptual tool, and not a rigid mold into which the infinitely variable products of nature were assumed to fit.

Kretschmer believed the vast majority of both cyclothymes and schizothymes to be normal people. When a cyclothyme became psychotic however, it was manic-depressive psychosis, and when a schizothyme

---

5   The present account of Kretschmer's theory is necessarily very sketchy. Only enough information can be given in this section to permit the interested reader to pursue the relationships further if he wishes. The reviews by Eysenck (1950) and Rees (1961) are especially recommended. Even Eysenck's extensive review does not cover Bleuler's closely related theory in which a "schizoid-syntonic" dimension was postulated. Bleuler's textbook (1924) carries only a brief outline of this concept. The original exposition of "schizoidie und syntonie" (1922) appears to have been overlooked and still remains to be translated into English.

became psychotic, it was schizophrenia. In view of the occurrence, albeit rare, of the depressive disorder and not schizophrenia among the relatives of autistic children, the relevance of Kretschmer's theory to Kanner's group must be considered.

Difficulty is immediately met, however, because most cyclothymes tend to be outgoing, warm, and friendly people, quite unlike those Kanner described. But hidden among Kretschmer's cyclothymes is a smaller subgroup of quiet and serious persons whose description is familiar. These Kretschmer describes as "'Cats that walk by themselves,' people who take things rather to heart, who like to live their lives quietly and in contemplation" (1936, p. 129). This subgroup of cyclothymes would presumably tend to be free of mental illness partly by virtue of being undisposed toward the highly prevalent schizophrenic disorders. They may constitute the group from which autistic children spring.

While neither Kretschmer's theory itself nor the evidence on the specific relevance of the theory to the present problem may be considered to be established, there are nonetheless some interesting corroborative points. In view of previous discussion implicating the cerebral vasculature in autism, it is of interest that several investigators report cyclothymia to be associated with cerebrovascular disease. Ciocco (1936, cited by Rees, 1961), after reviewing the literature, concluded that the pyknic body type (Kretschmer's somatic correlate of cyclothymia) is associated with a high incidence of several types of vascular disorder, including cerebral hemorrhage. Cady, Gertler, Gottsch, and Woodbury (1961) have shown in their investigation of the relationship of personality factors to coronary artery disease that the cyclothymic personality complex is linked to the susceptibility of the blood vessels to certain pathological conditions. Whether this susceptibility is related to the capillary damage the present writer has suggested earlier in this paper to be a possible cause of autism can only be speculated upon.

It is perhaps also of interest to our discussion that the manic-depressive condition has been reported by several investigators to be associated with above-average intelligence (e.g., Slater, 1936; Mason, 1956); while schizophrenics tend to be below average in intelligence (e.g., Reuter, Albee, & Lane, 1962). Slater also reported a higher than average level of *drive* to be related to depressiveness.

Sir Russell Brain (1948, 1960) has called attention to the many men of genius who have either been cyclothymic or have been cycloids with a family history of cyclothymia. He includes in his list such men as Goethe, Cowper, Johnson, and Newton. (Kretschmer [1936], however, regarded Newton as a schizothyme.)

Kretschmer, in his *The Psychology of Men of Genius* (1931), provides many examples of high achievement having been the product of an extraordinary amount of attention being turned upon a problem by an individual. In certain cases the person's entire life has been altered by his unceasing focus of thought and effort upon a topic. Kretschmer's description of Robert Mayer, the physician who discovered the law of conservation of energy and spent his life trying to convince the scientific world of its validity, is a classic case in point. It is easy to see how a very tight linkage between present attention and memory can be simultaneously productive and pathological. "Absent-mindedness is a proverbial characteristic of learned men. Perhaps one ought to say: 'Overconcentration of attention,' which leaves the individual blind and deaf to all else" (Kretschmer, 1931, p. 140). The possible relevance of these concepts to the unusual parental personalities described by Kanner, and to the "recirculating" brain structure described in the beginning of this section should be obvious.

As we have noted, Kretschmer believed these mental traits to be strongly hereditary. His theory will be seen to have an interesting relationship to our next topic.

D. THE RELATIONSHIP BETWEEN AUTISM AND SCHIZOPHRENIA: A HYPOTHESIS

Whether or not one subscribes to the hypothesis that the genetic background for early infantile autism relates to Kretschmer's cyclothymic-depressive complex, the fact remains that in autism the family incidence of mental illness—particularly of schizophrenic mental illness—is extremely low. As has been pointed out in Chapter 4, this is in sharp contrast to the findings in childhood schizophrenia.

Despite the many behavioral, somatic, and demographic differences between autism and schizophrenia, we would be doing injustice to the data to ignore the similarities. Turning to our description of autism in terms of perceptual and conceptual failure, due perhaps to impairment of the reticular formation, we find childhood schizophrenia to have been similarly considered. Eickhoff (1952), for instance, has postulated that childhood schizophrenia involves "an arrest in the development of abstract thought" and "a defect in the acquisition of general sensation" (p. 234). Koegler and Colbert (1959) and Bender (1961) are among those who mention the reticular formation as a possible site of impairment in childhood schizophrenia, and Fish (1961) has provided a theory linking reticular dysfunction to adult schizophrenia.

Singer (1960) has shown the similarity between the views of Rashkis (1958) and Rosenzweig (1955) concerning the nature of schizophrenia. After citing Magoun's work on the reticular system to show the basis of Rosenzweig's thinking, Singer writes:

> From this neurophysiological viewpoint Rosenzweig comes, remarkably enough, to almost exactly the same conclusions that Rashkis did from the psychological point of view. Rosenzweig ascribes two functions to this nonspecific system: (1) selective conation, the responsibility for focusing of attention on a single thought or idea at a time (Rashkis' notion of attention); (2) relating idea and affect in a harmonious manner (Rashkis' coordination of information from various systems). Again, in striking similarity with Rashkis' notion…Rosenzweig holds that the brain functions…as a mechanism which analyzes and interprets incoming stimuli in terms of past experience and inherent neural patterns… (p. 68)

If, as Singer says, the foregoing presents a remarkable confluence of thought from two directions on the nature of schizophrenia, no less remarkable is its resemblance to the independently formulated theory of autism provided in Part II of this paper. It will be profitable to consider these concepts more closely.

It was pointed out in Chapter 4 (especially on pages 97 and 98) that despite certain superficial similarities in the behavior manifested in the two classes of behavior disturbance, there are nevertheless distinct, though difficult to define, differences. Cappon (1953) has emphasized this with both case histories and by attempting to characterize the two disorders separately. Benda (1960) and Despert and Sherwin (1958) also provide case histories designed to illustrate behavioral differences in schizophrenia and autism.

Close consideration of the behavioral symptomatology, taken in conjunction with certain relevant research findings, leads to a hypothesis concerning the nature of both the schizophrenic and autistic disorders: Differences in the symptomatology of early infantile autism and schizophrenia appear to reflect differences in the manner in which stimuli are associated with memory. Our hypothesis is that in autism necessary neural associations are made with extreme difficulty and only the strongest and most relevant impulses traverse the pathways, while in schizophrenia associations are made *too* freely, sometimes perhaps almost randomly. Stated differently, in autism it seems that the mental associations made by the afflicted child are exceedingly limited, that he has access to only highly specific fragments of memory. The schizophrenic child, in contrast, appears to be pathologically *unrestrained by relevance* in making associations. In terms of our hypothesis that it is the reticular formation which is of central importance in performing this role, one might say that in the autistic child the reticular formation is essentially *nonfunctioning*, while in the schizophrenic child the reticular formation is *malfunctioning*.

Some support is afforded our hypothesis that autism and schizophrenia reflect differences in the facility with which associations are made by the previously noted finding that schizophrenics condition readily in the experimental laboratory (Mednick, 1958, cites several studies in support of this point) while Anthony (1958) found autistic children unusually difficult to condition.[6]

As opposites it would seem that there would be little occasion to confuse autism and schizophrenia. Yet confusion of autism with schizophrenia is (in the United States at least) more common than differentiation. This apparent paradox is readily resolved by relating the problem to one of the major controversies regarding the nature of the schizophrenic thought disturbance.

Goldstein regards schizophrenics as excessively concrete in their thought (as a reaction to anxiety), and describes them as typically unable to generalize or think abstractly. A group typified by Cameron (1947), on the other hand, regards schizophrenic thought as characterized by *excessive* generalization. The latter group believes thought to be impaired by "over-inclusion"—the disruptive incorporation into a concept of non-essential elements which merely happen to be associated with it in some manner.

Payne, Mattussek, and George (1959) have reviewed this controversy and have pointed out that these apparently opposing views are by no means incompatible. Over-inclusiveness may lead to the appearance of excessive concreteness. And to the extent that this can be so, the overassociating schizophrenic may manifest behavior which is also typical of the under-associating, literal, and concrete autistic child.

The process whereby these diametrically different mechanisms yield similar-appearing behavior had been described earlier, in a different context, by Norman (1954) in terms of undue perceptual perseveration. She noted that non-fading of the accidental and non-repeating aspects of images interferes with learning and understanding because fading of what is irrelevant is necessary to make the figure contrast with the background. A too-vivid memory, in this context, could become pathological.

---

6   Conditioning requires certain aspects of reticular function (Gastaut 1958a, 1958b; Samuels 1959) but can be accomplished even without the cortex (e.g., Bromiley, 1948). This implies sensation-to-motor linkages need be intact but not necessarily be subject to higher cognitive influences. See discussion of motor abilities, next chapter.

Payne et al. discussed the problem in terms of acquired inhibitions:

> "Over-inclusive thinking" may be the result of a disorder of the process whereby inhibition is built up to "circumscribe" and "define" the learned response (the word or "concept"). In short, it could be an extreme degree of "stimulus generalization." (p. 631)

These writers go on to develop this idea in terms of a defect in a "filtering" process, a process of sorting out irrelevant stimuli scheduled for inhibition or extinction. (The filtering process will be taken up again, in a different context, in the next chapter.) A related explanation, i.e., failure to inhibit sensation selectively, was used earlier (page 131–132) to help explain hyper-reactivity in autism.

Thus, the schizophrenic's preoccupation with concrete details and literal meanings may be derived from his failure to inhibit non-essential associations. His expression of these non-essential associations as they impinge upon his consciousness is what is regarded as a manifestation of over-inclusive thinking.

As has been indicated earlier, the autistic person's predicament is to a great extent similar. He too cannot develop the concepts which he needs to cope with reality. In his case, we suggest that this is because relevant associations are not made, rather than that they are overwhelmed by competing ones. It was demonstrated earlier that the autistic child is limited to the associations gained in the original context of the stimulus. One might say that the autistic child is as lost in his forest of unmarked trees as is the schizophrenic child in his forest where *every tree* is blazed. A similar metaphor might describe our hypothesis of nerve impulse behavior in their respective brain stems.

The syndromes of autism and schizophrenia, though they do share the above described superficial similarities in the realm of conceptual thought, are not identical in their manifestations of the conceptual disability. And the differences appear, in the opinion of the present writer, to be in accord with the hypothesis advanced here. As was noted earlier in discussing the differentiation of autism from schizophrenia, the schizophrenic child seems *dis*oriented and confused, while the autistic child is *un*oriented and aloof. As van Krevelen (1952) has observed, autism lacks the element of dementia which is so characteristic of schizophrenia. Behavior is less bizarre. The differences in age of onset of autism and schizophrenia, and the occurrence of remissions (at least in adult schizophrenia), are also consistent with the concepts proposed here.

Consideration of the perceptual element in autism and schizophrenia, like consideration of their conceptual aspects, would appear to lend support to the idea that these two disorders represent problems of underassociative and overassociative brain stem function.

Hallucinations and delusions are largely the rule in schizophrenia, while they are very nearly absent in autism. Eisenberg and Kanner (1956) have stated that of some 50 children followed for an average of eight years, none is reliably known to have hallucinated.[7]

A hallucination may be regarded as a perceptual over-response to some external or internal stimulus. Harris (1959) reports that schizophrenics experienced pleasure and a reduction in symptoms, including hallucinations, under conditions of sensory deprivation. A triggering of *too many* associations by the ordinary sensory environment is consonant with the concept of schizophrenia being developed here.

Schizophrenic hallucinations are most often auditory, less often visual, and least often olfactory, gustatory, tactual, and visceral (Cameron, 1947). We suggest that the order of these senses is about what one would place them in if asked to rank them in terms of their abstractness, or of the extent to which they require mediation—relating to past experience—in order to be meaningful. If the reticular formation had the function hypothesized for it here—that of tying sensation to memory—the degree of involvement of the senses in the reticular formation would be expected to be in the above order, and dysfunction of the reticular formation might be expected to affect them differentially in somewhat that same order. (Since the foregoing paragraphs were written a symposium on hallucinations has appeared in which several contributors have also related hallucinations to reticular dysfunction. See especially Scheibel & Scheibel, 1962.)

Under the same assumptions, one would expect the *impairment* of the senses to fall in the same order if the reticular formation were the site of damage in autism, and the impairment in autism consisted of a partial blockage of the nerve impulses in the reticular formation. In this case, one would expect persons afflicted with autism to tend to use the senses in the *reverse* order. That they do has been indicated earlier in reference to the studies of Ritvo and Provence (1953) and several other writers.

Evidence drawn from psychopharmacology lends support to the notion that schizophrenia is an excessive disinhibition of the reticular formation, and suggests an approach to drug therapy for early infantile

---

7   The case reported by C. Bradley (1943) appears to be a classic one of autism, with the exception that the afflicted girl may have had hallucinations. Whether she actually had hallucinations (i.e., apparently experienced what was to her real sensory stimulation), or whether she was merely reporting fantasies is not clear. At any rate, whether she hallucinated or not, hers is one of the few cases in the literature where there is even a suggestion of hallucinating in autism.

autism. P. B. Bradley (1957), using microelectrode techniques, found that chlorpromazine, which is very effective in reducing the symptoms of schizophrenia, *depresses* the activity of the reticular formation. Further, LSD-25, which produces schizophrenia-like symptoms in normal persons, exerts an *excitant* effect on the reticular formation and a heightened awareness of sensory stimuli (Elkes, 1958; Kaneko et al., 1960). These findings are supportive of the theory presented here that schizophrenia is a result of an excessively disinhibited or overassociating reticular formation. Fish (1961) has also presented psychopharmacological data in support of his related theory of reticular overactivity in schizophrenia.

As a corollary, if it were true that early infantile autism is a resultant of a *blocked* or *overinhibited* reticular formation, LSD may prove useful in facilitating reticular function. In other words, LSD or a similar drug may have a normalizing effect on autistic children. Several recent studies have described the use of LSD with "autistic" children, but correspondence with their authors has established that the term "autistic" was not used to designate children having Kanner's syndrome (Bender, Goldschmidt, & Sankar, 1962; Freedman, Ebin, & Wilson, 1962). Research is needed on the use of LSD with accurately diagnosed cases of infantile autism.

Elkes (1958) has provided evidence supportive of our hypothesis by showing that animals given high dosages of chlorpromazine simulate autism by becoming markedly indifferent to the environment, show resistance to behavioral or electrical arousal, and become somewhat aggressive when disturbed. This is true even of formerly affectionate animals. Elkes' animals appear to bear certain similarities in behavior to the brain-stem-operated cats of Sprague, Chambers, and Stellar (1961) described earlier.

That deanol, a precursor of acetylcholine and therefore presumably a facilitator of transynaptic impulses, appears to be helpful in autism is also in accord with the hypothesis. The finding that deanol is sometimes helpful in schizophrenia runs counter to the theory, however (e.g., Barsa & Saunders, 1959). The latter finding may possibly be explained by suggesting that by facilitating controllable transynaptic firing, deanol may preclude disruptive transneuronal discharge, or otherwise permit more orderly neural transmission.

Carbon dioxide inhalation, like the use of chlorpromazine, has proven useful in the treatment of schizophrenia. This treatment may bring startlingly lucid communication from even deeply withdrawn cases of long-standing affliction. The increased accessibility induced by carbon dioxide often includes spontaneous comment from the patients as well as responsive replies to questions. Unfortunately, the improvement is of a very transitory nature and disappears soon after the treatment is stopped (Lorenz, 1952).

The mechanism of carbon dioxide action upon the brain is unknown, but Meduna (1952) has expressed his belief that "...a salient point in the carbon dioxide treatment is an increase in the threshold of stimulation of those synapses of the nervous system that were pathologically irritable. The increase of threshold of stimulation in these structures amounts to a decrease of irritability of the affected systems" (p. 581). French (1959) indicates that the reticular formation is a site of carbon dioxide action.

Thus, the hypothesis of overassociation would seem to gain support from a variety of sources. The basis of the weakness for pathological overassociation is unknown, outside of Kallman's very frequently cited demonstrations that the tendency is to a large extent genetically determined. It would, however, seem very likely that environmental stress or anxiety create the biochemical conditions leading to excessive disinhibition in individuals genetically vulnerable to schizophrenia. Mednick (1958) has proposed a learning theory model which suggests that the irrelevant thought reinforces itself by providing an increasingly welcome divorcement of the patient from what he perceives as punishing reality. The utility of schizophrenia is doubtful. An explanation preferred by the present writer is that normally adaptive endocrine responses to psycho-social environmental stress may trigger the neural dysfunction postulated here and initiate, in persons vulnerable to schizophrenia, a self-sustaining "vicious circle" of schizophrenic mental illness.

It was earlier mentioned that the reticular formation has sometimes been referred to as a likely site for the schizophrenic disorder (e.g., Fish, 1961). Kraines (1957) has shown that it is probable that the reticular formation is intimately involved also in the depressive disorder. It is interesting, in view of the interpretation of manic-depressive psychosis as partly an excessive tendency to dwell on limited aspects of experience, that it has sometimes been suggested that electroshock therapy, which tends to be effective only in depression, functions by "blasting open" neural circuits in the brain. (See Gerard, 1953). Electroshock has not been effective in autism, however, according to Kanner.

To relate the immediately foregoing discussions more closely to the preceding parts of our theory, we should indicate that in Kretschmer's theory an intrinsic aspect of cyclothymic thought is *integration*, while *dissociation* characterizes schizothymic thought. Eysenck (1952 and elsewhere) has presented some of the related empirical research. While the work of Eysenck and his co-workers has not been corroborative of Kretschmer on this point, the picture is far from clear. Juda, for instance (cited by Cowie and Slater, 1959), found some tendency for artists to have a schizophrenic familial background, with no cases of manic-depressive illness; while the *opposite* was found to be true for the sample of scientists. (Juda's investigation of German genius, incidentally, showed the same overrepresentation of the first-born found in other studies of great men.)

To summarize the major concept of this chapter, there appear to be a number of lines of evidence for considering the schizophrenically disposed individual to have a loosely associating brain stem while depressively inclined persons have a brain stem which functions in a tightly knit, possibly reverberating and self-feeding manner which involves characteristic changes in the content and mood of mentation. In a certain subgroup of persons, genetically disposed to be of the latter type, there is a tendency for the brain configuration to result in an unusual, introverted personality and in high intelligence, with an accompanying tendency for their children to be vulnerable to early infantile autism.

INTRODUCTION TO CHAPTER 10
Stephen M. Edelson

In Chapter 10, Rimland discussed several topics pertaining to perception and cognition. He was very interested in savant abilities, and he felt that if the mechanisms underlying such abilities were revealed, the findings would have a huge impact on the understanding of cognition in the general population.

In 1978, Rimland wrote an influential article in *Psychology Today* in which he described savant abilities. Rather than using the then-accepted term "idiot savants" to refer to individuals with such innate abilities, he coined the term "autistic savants" (Rimland, 1978). He also was the head consultant on the movie *Rain Man*, and suggested that Raymond play a savant with autism rather than someone who was intellectually challenged. Darold Treffert, a long-time friend and colleague and an expert on savant abilities, contributed an update on this topic.

Rimland also commented on the distractibility and concentration of those with autism. Over the years, research has shown a comorbidity of autism with ADHD, estimated to be as high as 30 percent (Rao & Landa, 2014). With respect to concentration, as discussed in the update for Chapter 5, research has shown that many children on the autism spectrum have "tunnel vision," or overly focused attention.

Delayed audition, sometimes referred to as delayed echolalia, involves a person repeating words and phrases from the past. Although this phenomenon is not well understood, there is much research on the impairments in hearing exhibited by many individuals with autism. Findings include abnormal brainstem recordings (Maziade et al., 2000) and lower cerebral blood flow when presented with an auditory stimulus (Bruneau et al., 1992). Researchers often speculate that impairment in the auditory system may impact language acquisition in autism.

REFERENCES

Bruneau, N., Dourneau, M.C., Garreau, B., Pourcelot, L., & Lelord, G. (1992). Blood flow response to auditory stimulations in normal, mentally retarded, and autistic children: A preliminary transcranial Doppler ultrasonographic study of the middle cerebral arteries. *Biological Psychiatry*, 32(8), 691–699.

Maziade, M., Merette, C., Cayer, M., Roy, M.A., et al. (2000). Prolongation of brainstem auditory-evoked responses in autistic probands and their unaffected relatives. *Archives of General Psychiatry*, 57(11), 1077–1083.

Rao, P.A., & Landa, R.J. (2014). Association between severity of behavioral phenotype and comorbid attention deficit hyperactivity disorder symptoms in children with autism spectrum disorders. *Autism*, 18(3), 272–280.

Rimland, B. (1978). Inside the mind of the autistic savant. *Psychology Today*, 12(3), 68–80.

CHAPTER 10

Further Implications of the Study of Autism

Being an effort to tie up loose ends, this chapter includes varied topics that defy categorization in any brief descriptive title. Some of the sections which follow attempt to suggest answers to several of the questions about early infantile autism which still are unanswered. Included also are points which emphasize certain deficiencies of the theory. But perhaps overshadowing these functions is the presentation of a still more basic element—a consideration of some of the hypotheses the study of early infantile autism has suggested which underlie the science of psychology.

A. THE ABILITIES OF AUTISTIC CHILDREN

The tenability of the hypothesis of reticular impairment in autism rests not only upon the consistency of the hypothesis with the *disability* pattern of the children, discussed in Part II, but also upon its agreement with what is known of their *unimpaired* and *superior* performances. The issue is raised for heuristic purposes, since the information presently available does not appear to be sufficient to change the weight of evidence significantly either for or against the hypothesis. It is hoped that the present explicit focus of attention will encourage the more detailed attention by others which is necessary to the evaluation, revision, or, possibly, rejection of the hypothesis.

The *motor abilities* of autistic children have been consistently remarked upon as being outstanding. With few exceptions, the children are described as displaying highly unusual grace and agility. In some cases walking has been delayed, but even in these cases the child will often suddenly begin walking quite well for his age. Oppenheim (1961) gives a recent example of this. Fine finger movements as well as gross coordination often prove to be superior, and the finger dexterity of autistic children has been described with adjectives like "uncanny," "fascinating," and "amazing."

Is this consistent with the hypothesis of reticular impairment? According to studies cited by Samuels (1959), proprioceptive stimuli have a particularly strong effect upon the cortex through the reticular formation. But it has been known for many years that posture and locomotion may be carried on fairly effectively even in decorticate animals.

Penfield (in Penfield & Roberts, 1959) has emphasized the importance of the centrencephalic system by pointing out that voluntary speech movements "arise in the circuits of integration in the brain stem." French (1959) discusses the importance of the reticular formation in motor behavior, and Jasper (in Ciba Symposium 1958, p. 291) has emphasized the importance of the reticular formation over the cortex in motor response (see also Gastaut's reply to Jasper). It is difficult to reconcile our hypothesis of reticular impairment in infantile autism with the excellence of the motor performance autistic children display.

One possible solution to this dilemma might be that reticular interchange with the cortex is primarily for the facilitation of cognitive aspects of behavior, and relates more to the *purpose* than to the *motor quality* of the activity. Autistic children are notoriously purposeless even in their most skilled activities. Creak (1951, 1952) and Loomis (1960), who have emphasized both the agility and dexterity of autistic children, have also remarked on how utterly devoid of any visible purpose the behavior is. Benda (1960) has made a related point:

> The observer is always surprised at how these children are able to run away, climb, handle mechanical problems, avoid being hurt, and achieve their own purposes though these may be different from the demands made on them by the environment. (p. 472)

Could interference with reticular interchange with the cortex somehow *facilitate* motor performance (there being little doubt from the consistency of the reports that *something* facilitates performance)? To this question we may say, "Yes," providing that the reticular formation functions as we have surmised. It has long been believed that higher centers "looking over one's shoulder" may have *disruptive effects* on his motor ability. Smooth and errorless performance in a typist, radio operator, or key-punch operator is achieved only when finger movements become automatic and the content of the material being coded is not considered.

The role of practice in sports, as well as in skills involving coordinated finger movements, seems to consist, in part, in crowding out the disturbing effects of awareness (the cortex?) and letting lower centers take over. Gilbreth's findings in his classic studies of bricklaying, in which the cognitively oriented set for accuracy rather than speed was determined to be "most pernicious," may rest upon this principle. Stephen Potter, in his learned treatise on "Gamesmanship," has suggested one pernicious use to which (presumably) cortical intervention may be put. The "gamesman" may effectively disable his golf opponent, Potter suggests, by admiring his opponent's form, then innocently posing a disarming inquiry such as "Just where does your sequence of muscular response begin?" There is, of course, the legendary centipede who was rendered immobile by a similar question.

Whether or not it is an *incapacity* for self-awareness which accounts for the autistic child's motor excellence can only be a matter for surmise at the present time. One possibility suggested by consideration of the above matters is that the impairment in autism may be in tracts to and from the cortex rather than in the reticular formation itself.

With regard to *sensory abilities*, we have already referred to the preferences autistic children show for their proximal senses, with the implication that their ability to make use of the information derived is greater for this class of receptors. Reference was made above to research showing that proximal stimuli have a relatively great general effect through the reticular formation. It was also reported that such stimuli could be differentiated from auditory and visual stimuli in terms of specificity of cortical area aroused (Samuels, 1959). The former class of stimuli tended to activate the hypothalamic portion of the reticular system while auditory and visual stimulation did not. This may provide a clue to the specific locus of the lesion in autism, if a lesion there be.

At least one proximal sense, smell, does appear to have a mechanism for linking stimuli to memory which is different from that used by the other senses. It is well known that the sense of smell tends to evoke an unusually rich stream of memories in most persons—markedly more than the other senses. Olfactory input does take a different route than the other senses (Magoun, 1958b; Arnold, 1960, Vol. 1).

Consideration of *musical performance and interest*, almost universal in autistic children, casts little light on the nervous mechanisms involved. Samuels (1959) cites several studies of the reticular formation relating to perception and habituation of auditory stimuli varying in tonal pattern, but their relevance to the present problem is not clear. Musical appreciation does not seem to require the *inter-connecting* of separately learned sensations and ideas, which is the function the present theory regards as being impaired. Autistic children seem to enjoy music and are able to duplicate what they hear, but there is no evidence of creativity. If the theory is correct that reticular "arousal," brought about by anticipation of subsequent parts of incoming music, is the source of musical pleasure (Royer, 1961) at least a partially functioning reticular formation is implied. If it is not reticular arousal but some other aspect of the anticipation theory which applies, the autistic child's excellent memory for sounds could provide an abundance of anticipatory potential.

The higher functions manifest in autistic children are virtually limited to *memory and number manipulation* (including calendar operations). These abilities, which have given rise to the occasional identification of autistic children as *idiot savants*, could be explained in terms of impairment of the arousal function.[1] Once the child's attention had become fixed on a task, extraneous distracting stimuli might have little effect. This point will be discussed in the section immediately following.

All in all, the attempt to derive meaning from consideration of the positive capabilities of autistic children is not highly rewarding in terms of present knowledge. It is to be hoped that similar consideration ten years hence will present a more favorable picture.

B. DISTRACTIBILITY, CONCENTRATION, AND INTELLIGENCE

The brain has been likened to an electronic computer by innumerable writers. But despite the unquestionably greater theoretical capacity of the brain, even the simplest of computers can outperform the brain on practically all those tasks for which computer programs have been devised. Part of this discrepancy may be attributed to the adaptive aspect of the brain's alerting mechanism. Survival demands that, first and foremost, the organism be distractible.

It does not seem entirely unlikely that the extraordinary mental performances of otherwise severely retarded autistic children may result from a reduction in their distractibility conferred by reticular damage. Feats of memory, "calendar manipulation," and simple (though extended) arithmetic computations are frequent manifestations of *idiot savant* performance, and are as well typical of the kinds of operations for which electronic computers may most readily be programed.

Another way of accounting for *idiot savant* performance in autistic children might be in terms of impaired generalization ability. The fading of images, as Norman (1954) has earlier been cited as emphasizing, is requisite to the process of developing abstractions. Just as the non-fading of the irrelevant parts of images may interfere with the development of abstractions, an inability to generalize may conversely result in the non-fading of images, and thus account for *idiot savant* memory. That is, abnormally vivid imagery may be either the cause or the effect of a failure

---

1   Familial studies of *idiot savants* would be of interest. One would predict a greater incidence of depressives than schizophrenics among the relatives and in the ancestry.

in conceptual thinking. Selective inhibition is a *sine qua non* for effective mental performance. This may account for Galton's (1907) "astonishing" finding that eminent scientists and mathematicians reported vivid imagery far less frequently than his less distinguished respondents. Galton had elsewhere observed (as cited by Brain, 1948) that "an over-ready perception of sharp mental images is antagonistic to the acquisition of habits of highly generalized and abstract thought."

To return to the concepts of alertness and distractibility, it is of more than passing interest that both ends of the intelligence continuum tend to be characterized by differences in the quality of attentional ability. The term "mental alertness" is often used synonymously with "intelligence," and words like "dull" and "bright" carry a similar connotation. Anyone dealing at all frequently with persons below average in mentality is reminded again and again of how intrinsically important it is to intelligence to have a flexible and readily adaptable capacity for attending and for changing the focus of attention.

Somewhat paradoxically, despite the obvious importance of alertness to intelligent behavior, there must go with alertness a certain indistractibility, an ability to concentrate and ignore irrelevant stimuli in order to proceed with thought on the problem at hand. Keynes has commented on this point in his interesting analysis of Sir Isaac Newton (in Newman, 1956, Vol. I):

> ... (Newton) was a wrapt, consecrated solitary, pursuing his studies by intense introspection with a mental endurance perhaps never equalled.
>
> I believe that the clue to his mind is to be found in his unusual powers of continuous concentrated introspection... His peculiar gift was the power of holding continuously in his mind a purely mental problem until he had seen straight through it... Anyone who has attempted pure scientific or philosophical thought knows how one can hold a problem momentarily in one's mind and apply all one's powers of concentration to piercing through it, and how it will dissolve and escape and you find that what you are surveying is a blank. I believe that Newton could hold a problem in his mind for hours and days and weeks until it surrendered to him its secret. (p. 278)

Roe (1952) reported that the one common element in her sample of eminent scientists was a "driving absorption in their work." Inasmuch as the reticular formation is well established as being of prime importance in maintaining alertness, it does not seem amiss to urge that for this reason, if no other, the quality of reticular function may be an important prerequisite to intelligence. It is of some interest that perseveration, which may be viewed as a form of indistractibility, appears to be associated with Kretschmer's cyclothymic dimension (Levine, 1955a, 1955b).

In view of our earlier discussion concerning inheritance of a sensitive and perhaps vulnerable reticular formation by autistic children, it is also of interest that Kanner has emphasized the indistractibility of the fathers of his group of autistic children. He has often commented on their "preoccupation with scientific and literary abstractions" (e.g., 1958, with Lesser) and had earlier remarked:

> Many of the fathers remind one of the popular conception of the absent-minded professor who is so engrossed in lofty abstractions that little room is left for the trifling details of everyday living. (1949, p. 422)[2]

In view of the obvious importance of control over one's distractibility to the accomplishment of certain tasks (e.g., the study of mathematics), it would seem that exploration of individual differences in such traits as habituation, duration of arousal, etc. might hold considerable promise as an approach to the measurement of differential aptitudes.

C. DELAYED MENTAL AUDITION

As Maslow (1961) has recently emphasized, psychology makes little provision for utilizing personal experiences. Yet, after recently experiencing a certain moderately common auditory phenomenon and realizing how closely related the event was to the problem of early infantile autism and to the theory of brain function discussed in this paper, the writer has decided that the incident warrants exemption from the convention of impersonality.

The incident occurred while I was deeply engrossed in reading. Some time had passed before I became aware that someone had asked me a question and was awaiting a response. My mind was quite blank. I had no idea what I had been asked. I was about to ask that the question be repeated when this suddenly became unnecessary. I could hear the query, phrased in two short but complete sentences, being repeated word for word, the "sound" coming from within my head. The effect was that of an echo, except that several seconds, perhaps as many as ten, had passed.

The experience was not unfamiliar, though never before had it been so vivid. This experience of what I shall call "delayed mental audition" was striking in two respects which pertain to the topic of this monograph. First, the question had been *sensed and recorded without interpretation*. I had no idea of what had been said to me until the *second* (internalized) hearing. The usual step whereby incoming stimuli are integrated with the prior content

---

2   With permission of *Amer. J. Orthopsychiat.* and the author.

of the brain—are given meaning—was bypassed. This is exactly what I had much earlier postulated for stimuli entering the brain of the autistic child.

The second striking aspect of the event was the nature of the echo-like voice repeating the question. I could identify it as the voice of the person who asked the question, but the sound of the voice was different, in an extremely unique and peculiar way. The voice had a high-pitched, hollow, wooden sound. The inflections were somehow preserved, despite the parrot-like meaninglessness of the vocalization. In short, *the internally experienced voice duplicated precisely and unmistakably the classical manner of speech of the child with early infantile autism.* This was the high-pitched, wooden monotone the autistic child characteristically uses to indicate "Yes"; the mechanical verbatim repetition of the question—including its inflection—which Kanner has named "affirmation by repetition." This was the voice one hears when the child repeats later exactly what he has heard some time before—Kanner's "delayed echolalia." This was the "closed-loop" phenomenon described in Chapter 5—the stimuli had entered memory and later emerged unchanged.

The auditory experience described above is not unusual. Informal inquiry has disclosed that many persons have similar experiences, although most persons who are asked about delayed mental audition and who assert that they have experienced it are initially unable to describe the voice quality. If they are asked to remember their next experience of it, the "hollow, wooden, echo-like" description will usually be forthcoming. Of course, it is necessary not to reveal what description is expected.

The recent literature on perception contains several references to apparently similar phenomena. Hebb (1949, p. 152) refers to becoming aware of and responding to a question or remark after a delay of 30 seconds or a minute. Broadbent (1958, p. 211) mentions previously ignored sounds later "striking home to consciousness" in subjects who were attending to other stimuli.

There are numerous instances of affirmation by repetition and delayed echolalia in the literature on autism, in the work of other writers as well as Kanner. Popella (1955), for example, described a girl who gave no indication of having heard a nursery rhyme, but later spontaneously reproduced it. Van Krevelen's first case (1952, 1962a) showed a great deal of this kind of behavior:

> ...the child often seems secluded from her environment, but then she gives proof after days or even weeks that she has taken in much of what has been said...

At the age of 1½ years, when the child had barely begun to speak, she sang several melodies. (van Krevelen, 1962a, p. 136)

The often noted excellent memory for music and the occurrence of perfect pitch in autistic children are probably examples of very closely related auditory phenomena. There is also some reason to believe that related phenomena may occur in other than the auditory modality. The accurate visual memory of autistic children (e.g., for a jumbled mass of blocks) has already been referred to, as have Kanner's (1952) and Benda's (1960) cases of autistic children who could read fluently with no understanding of what they were reading. Morgan (1961, p. 328) has cited what appears to be a visual analogue to delayed audition.

An attempt to find published qualitative descriptions of the phenomenon has met little success.[3] Most of Galton's work on imagery relates to visual phenomena (e.g., 1907) although he did refer briefly to a "parrot-like" auditory image which acted "in a meaningless way, just as a machine might act" (1879–1880). Little of Galton's earlier work is readily available to the present writer, and it may be that Galton did write more extensively on the topic.

William James' chapter on *Memory* cites an example of auditory memory given by Exner, where one can count the strokes of a clock shortly after the hour, even if attention had been directed elsewhere during the actual striking of the clock.

The topic would seem to be of considerable theoretical interest not only in the study of attention (e.g., Hebb and Broadbent) but also in studying the temporal characteristics of the distortion (or "editing") produced by memory (e.g., Oldfield, 1954; Sperling, 1960). The major relevance of delayed audition to the present discussion is that (a) stimuli *can* be sensed and remembered without being integrated in any conscious way with what is already known; and (b) if one were to imitate the sound of speech so remembered, he would be imitating exactly in content and manner the speech of the autistic child.

Whether or not it is the reticular formation which is bypassed in delayed audition is of course not known. If one were to hazard a guess as to what is taking place in delayed mental audition, it might be well to consider the possibility that the "message" has entered the brain only by the

---

3   Professor E. G. Boring has advised the writer that the phenomenon is related to the "memory after image" or "Erinnerungnachbild," which was studied by a number of early psychologists. Most of this work involved considerably briefer time lags and smaller units of auditory content than those of present interest. Some related work is in the early German psychological literature, dating back to Fechner, and is not available to the present writer.

specific sensory pathways. EEG studies show "the arrival of specific sensory impulses in the cortex is not, in the absence of nonspecific reticular activity, a sufficient condition for the conscious perception of these impulses" (Samuels, 1959, p. 2; see also Lindsley, 1958). The message might later reach the reticular formation through the *descending* tracts in order to imbue itself with meaning (in terms of the present hypothesis of reticular function). As we noted earlier, the biochemistry of the ascending and descending tracts of the reticular formation differ, as, for example, in their reactivity to reserpine (Bein, 1957). Studies of the possibly differential effects of various narcoleptic drugs on learning and conditioning during induced sleep might be of interest in testing hypotheses related to this problem. It is conceivable that the phenomenon of delayed audition may provide clues to the site of the autistic impairment.

D. THE PROBLEM OF INNATENESS OF THE SPECIFIC AFFECTIVE DISTURBANCE

As given in Part II, the present theory of autism holds that the affective disturbance in autism is a consequence of failure in association, a failure to associate biological rewards (food, warmth, etc.) with social (mainly maternal) relationships. Russell (1959) reflects the common view in saying, "...it will be generally agreed that the earliest reactions of the infant to his mother can be explained as an elaboration of simple neuronal networks" (p. 126). This seems reasonable, and failure to associate stimulus and reward appears to be a more parsimonious explanation of autism, in general, than Kanner's concept of *inborn* affective disturbance.

Some writers have in fact pointed out that lack of affect is rarely the presenting symptom, so far as the parents are concerned, and that it is generally the psychiatrist who identifies (or should we say designates?) the basic problem as affective.

Kanner's description of the early life of the autistic infant permits both an associational and a specific affective disturbance to be inferred. Note that the child ignores *anything* that comes to him from the outside, and that his reaction to his mother is of indifference:

> The case histories indicate invariably the presence from the start of *extreme autistic aloneness* which, wherever possible, disregards, ignores, shuts out anything that comes to the child from the outside. Almost every mother recalled her astonishment at the child's failure to assume at any time the usual anticipatory posture preparatory to being picked

up. According to Gessell this kind of adjustment occurs universally at 4 months of age. (1944, p. 211)

That the so-called affective disturbance in autism is basically a defect in associative processes is a belief that has been expressed by a number of writers on the topic. The present writer feels it is the most appropriate explanation in most cases of autism. There are some cases, however, which do not permit this interpretation, and indicate instead a specific inborn disturbance such as Kanner has suggested.

The writer must admit to an initial reluctance to consider as such the possibility of an *inborn* affective disturbance. His training (and this may be true also of the reader's) occurred while it was modish to consider as impossible that behavior tendencies of any degree of complexity could be innate.[4] (Previous discussions relating to "heredity versus environment" were concerned only with biological differences in the *capacity* for learning and making use of learning.) Preconceptions notwithstanding, recent evidence demands consideration of the possibility of an instinctual deficit in autism.

Cattell (1950) has noted that the concept of instinct was at last being rescued after being buried alive for a generation. Sperry (1956) has made a similar point in stating that:

> The whole idea of instincts and the inheritance of behavior traits is becoming much more palatable than it was 15 years ago, when we lacked a satisfactory basis for explaining the organization of inborn behavior. Today we can give more weight to heredity than we did then. Every animal comes into the world with inherited behavior patterns of its species. (p. 52)

Thorpe, in a recent review (1961), has said that if instinct were ever dead there has been a "remarkable resurrection."

Without attempting to review any of the surprising and unprecedented work to which the above writers refer, we may say that the possibility must be now considered that at least some cases of autism suffer a specific affective disturbance *in addition* to the basic associational disturbance which we feel is the basic characteristic of early infantile autism.

The case histories which cause the writer to entertain the possibility of a specific inborn affective disturbance most strongly are those reported by Plenter (1955) and Lewis and Van Ferney (1960), in which *human contact was*

---

4   Breland and Breland (1961), Hunt (1961), and Hunt and Quay (1961) have recently made very similar reluctant repudiations of their earlier training on this matter, in favor of a wave of undeniable new evidence. Hunt says he has been "jolted" by recent findings (p. 65).

actively avoided from birth. Most autistic children are described as *indifferent* to others, not hostile or aversive.

The revulsion against being touched or caressed remained very strong in Plenter's case through childhood. Plenter was explicit in pointing out that the child was not fearful or shy. She did not mind being in strange surroundings, even among strangers, so long as no attempt was made to hold or touch her. It is possible that the girl described by Benda (1960) whose vigorous resistance defeated attempts to examine her may also have been exhibiting this active resistance against physical contact.

Plenter's paper is especially valuable in making it clear that it was only humans (or, at any rate, animate beings) that the girl avoided. One cannot simply postulate a general apathy, because there was considerable affect shown toward toys and other inanimate parts of the environment. Such specifically directed affect is not inconsistent with recent findings on lower animals. Thorpe cites animal studies in which brain stem stimulation resulted in highly specific behavior, dependent partly on the object in the visual field at the time of stimulation. Penfield (1959, 1960, and elsewhere) has reported very specific affective feelings (loneliness, aloofness, fear) to result from temporal lobe stimulation in humans.

In describing the girl with secondary autism we have discussed earlier, Ross (1959) pointed out that prior to her infection the child had been normally responsive. But kissing her after her illness, according to Ross, was like kissing a rag doll. This *indifference* to affection is the usual case in autism. However, Ross calls attention to the lesions found post-mortem in the girl's fornix, mammilothalamic pathways, and anterior nucleus of the thalamus. Ross points out that these lesions occur in areas identified by Olds (1956) as being concerned with apparent pleasure, and they may thus help account for the girl's affective disturbance. Daly and Love (1958) have suggested that the lack of affect in their case of akinetic mutism might be the result of his impairment of the reticular formation.

It is of considerable interest that the Ross patient suffered from a markedly deficient appetite, which Ross suggested might be explained by a congenital hypothalamic lesion. Gross deviations from the mean in both directions is commonly reported in the food intake of autistic children. The Lewis and Van Ferney case, for example, had a voracious appetite from birth. Brobeck (cited by Brady and Bunnell, 1960) has reported that lesions in the ventromedial nucleus of the hypothalamus and nearby centers may markedly increase or depress appetite.

It is perhaps also worthy of mention that in the cases of Plenter, Ross, and Benda, which could be singled out as being particularly suggestive of brain lesions involving affective centers, there also occur what is a rarity in autism—skin disorder. Kanner (1949 and elsewhere) has observed that autistic children are singularly free of skin disorders. The present writer's work tends to bear out that skin trouble does not occur in autism—outside of these three cases. Ross comments that part of his patient's skin problem (*café au lait* spots) is seen frequently in children with neuro-degenerative disease, particularly neurofibromatosis.

The nature of relationship between early skin disorder and inherent affective disturbance is unclear, but interesting to consider. The nervous system is formed ontogenetically of the same ectodermal material from which the skin develops, so joint vulnerability of the two systems is enhanced in probability. Several types of mental deficiency are characterized by unique skin disorders. Further, it is well known that certain kinds of stimulation of the skin produce affective and erotic responses. Harlow's previously discussed experiments (Chapter 3) show the significance played by tactile stimulation in the emotional development of young monkeys. Terrycloth-covered mother surrogates were far more effective than the equally biologically adequate wire-mesh-covered "mothers." At any rate, the possibility seems worth considering that there may be a skin-defect linkage in those cases of autism characterized by antipathy rather than apathy toward humans.

It may be that the present context is the best one in which to refer to the lack of empathy that Kanner says characterizes even the recovered cases of autism. "This amazing lack of awareness of the feelings of others, who seem not to be conceived of as persons like the self, runs like a red thread through our case histories" (Eisenberg & Kanner, 1956, p. 559). One of Kanner's few recovered patients had this experience:

> Attending a football rally of his junior college and called upon to speak, he shocked the assembly by stating that he thought the team was likely to lose—a prediction that was correct but unthinkable in the setting. The ensuing round of booing dismayed this young man who was totally unable to comprehend why the truth should be unwelcome. (Eisenberg & Kanner, 1956, p. 559)[5]

The cases reported by Darr and Worden (1951) and Anastasi and Levee (1960) also showed the lack of empathy very clearly.

As an alternative to an explanation in terms of an innate nerve center which subtends empathy, one might refer to Kuttner's previously described theory which holds that the nervous system becomes less plastic as it matures. Kuttner points out that certain behavior patterns (e.g., language) must be

---

5   Reprinted with permission of the *Amer. J. Orthopsychiat.* and the authors.

learned before the nervous system fully matures if the individual is to make most efficient use of the ability (see also Penfield & Roberts, 1959). It may be that the time for the development of empathy was reached and passed during the time of affliction, in the cases of recovered autistic children. While the current concepts of innately predisposed behavior tendencies in animals assume that relevant stimulation must be received early in life for proper development of relevant behavior, only the grossest kinds of stimulus deprivation seem successful in interfering with such development (Waters, Rethlingshafer, & Caldwell, 1960). Alternatively, such deprivation could, in effect, result from impairment of a stimulus processing center, such as the reticular formation, even though the requisite stimulation was present. The relevance to this discussion of the previously mentioned high incidence of affectionate mongoloid children (page 70) should not be overlooked.

The research on specific affective brain centers has been mainly the product of the animal laboratory, and the applicability of the above concepts to humans is not known.

SPECIAL ABILITIES AND SAVANT SYNDROME

An Update on Dr. Rimland's Observations

Darold A. Treffert

I happened to have the good fortune of meeting and learning from both Dr. Leo Kanner and Dr. Bernard Rimland. While Dr. Kanner ignited my interest in autism, it was Dr. Rimland who taught me much of what I know about autism. In 1962 I was assigned the responsibility of starting a Children's Unit at Winnebago Mental Health Institute in Wisconsin. There was very little written about autism at that time, but fortunately Dr. Rimland's book *Infantile Autism* came out in 1964. It became my compass and guide. It is remarkable how well researched, comprehensive, and insightful that book was, and still is. I am so pleased it is being re-issued.

Because of our mutual interest in autism, Dr. Rimland and I corresponded regularly and met occasionally. It was his conviction that the "refrigerator mother" psychological theory of causation of autism was a cruel error that especially caught my interest because it appeared to me that the mothers of the autistic children on my unit were as caring, loving, and warm as any other mothers. So I set about doing a state-wide Wisconsin study named the "Epidemiology of Infantile Autism." It reviewed 270 cases in Wisconsin of what at that time was called "childhood schizophrenia." It examined a wide variety of variables in that population and demonstrated that the mothers of autistic children were no different from the mothers of children with other developmental or other disabilities. It found the prevalence of autism to be 2.5/10,000 children which was a nearly identical figure to that found in the UK at that same time. Of course, that is a very different figure than present-day estimates. Dr. Rimland was the discussant when my paper was presented at the 1971 American Psychiatric Association meeting.

It was on that unit at Winnebago that I met my first savant. Three such cases ignited my interest in savant syndrome, an interest I have pursued actively since that time. In 2010 my most recent book on the topic was published by Jessica Kingsley, titled *Islands of Genius: The Bountiful Mind of the Autistic, Acquired, and Sudden Savant*. The book quotes extensively from Dr. Rimland's important work through the years, including his 1964 classic text.

On the early pages of *Infantile Autism*, Dr. Rimland mentions "the special abilities in autism" in what at that time was still called "idiot savant." In Chapter 10 he explores those special abilities in some depth, noting especially those unique skills in music including perfect pitch, art, spatial abilities including jig-saw puzzle tasks, heightened sensory sensitivity, calendar calculating, and extraordinary memory to mention only some.

When Dr. Rimland wrote these chapters in 1964 the regrettable term "idiot savant" was still applied to what is now called savant syndrome. It was in 1887 that Dr. J. Langdon Down used that term, already in existence, to apply to ten children he had seen in his long career at Earlswood Asylum caring for children and adults where extraordinary ability in some in some areas stood in stark contrast to permeating disability withn the same individual. At that time "idiot" was an accepted scientific term for IQ below 25, and "savant" was derived from a French word meaning "learned person." So the designation "idiot savant" did not have the negative connotation that term carried in subsequent years. In a 1988 paper in the *American Journal of Psychiatry* I suggested the term "savant syndrome" be substituted for "idiot savant" and that has largely been the case since that time.

Rimland's description of those "special abilities" coupled with massive memory is as pertinent now as it was in 1964. It remains remarkable, considering all the skills in the human repertoire, that savant syndrome abilities generally narrow to five areas of expertise—music, art, calendar calculating, lightning calculating, and spatial skills such as map reading or estimating height or distance. Those always are linked with extraordinary memory which is very, very deep but also very narrow within the confines of the special skill.

In Chapter 10 Dr. Rimland noted that those "special abilities" were particularly conspicuous in frequency in autistic children especially, and he explained the origin of those unique skills within his theory of dysfunction in the retricular activating system being central to the cause of infantile autism. His interest in savant syndrome continued and in 1978 he reported that in his survey of 5400 children with autism, 531, based on parental reports, had savant skills in the five general areas of expertise above. To this day, that one in ten (10%) figure is most often cited as the prevalence of savant syndrome in persons with autism. Subsequent reports, based on much smaller samples, however, put that prevalence figure from 13 percent to as high as 26 percent. In my experience, based on reports to me about savants from various sources worldwide, I find Rimland's 10 percent figure still to be the most accurate assessment of the link between savant syndrome and autism.

The question as to why savant syndrome occurs so much more commonly in autism than in other developmental or central nervous system disabilities is still an unanswered one but is under active investigation.

AUTISM, SAVANT SYNDROME, AND INTELLIGENCE

Throughout his book, Rimland refers to the relationship between autism and intelligence, seeking, appropriately, to point out that autism is separate from "mental deficiency" and IQ levels can vary widely in autistic disorder. He was correct in making that observation in autism specifically and the same is true in savant syndrome generally. While some persons with savant syndrome do have IQ levels below 70, in about 30 percent of cases IQ levels can be as high as 141 or more. Yet the myth seems to persist that all persons with savant syndrome have mental deficiency. Not so.

SAVANT SYNDROME 1945 TO PRESENT

In updating savant syndrome to the present time some facts are of interest:

1. About 1 in 10 persons with autism have savant syndrome. That is in contrast to 1 in 1400 in other developmental disabilities or other brain disorders. And it is important to note that approximately 50 percent of savants have autism as the underlying disability while the other 50 percent have some other developmental or brain disorder as the underlying disability. *Therefore not all savants are autistic, and not all persons with autism are savants.*

2. The special skills and abilities in autism are generally in music, art, calendar calculating, lightning calculating, and mechanical/spatial areas. Occasionally one sees other abilities such as special sensory capacity; exceptional knowledge and expertise in certain intellectual areas such as geography, philosophy, or history, for example; hyperlexia; athletic ability; or paranormal abilities. *Whatever the special skill, it is always linked to massive memory within the area of that skill.*

3. Prevalence ranges from 4:1 to 6:1 male: female ratios.

4. Measured IQ in savants can range to sub-normal to exceptional. *Therefore, low IQ is not a prerequisite for being classified as a savant.*

5. *Savant syndrome skills are on a spectrum.* Some are classified as "splinter skills" such as memorizing birthdays, sports trivia, license plate numbers, or other trivia. A second level is classified as Talented which includes a more highly honed skill typically in music, art, or math. The third level is classified as Prodigious which is a high threshold level reserved for those persons who, absent the disability, would otherwise be considered to be a "genius."

6. *The special savant skill is most often in a single area, but multiple skills can exist in some savants.*

7. *Savant skills typically persist and improve and rarely disappear.*

8. *Savant skills are not frivolous. Rather, by "training the talent" there is an accompanying increase in language, social, and daily living skills as a conduit toward independence.*

9. *With most savant skills there is a transition from recollection, to improvisation, to creation.* These skills typically surface as extraordinary memory or recollection of vast inventories of facts, musical pieces, or the capacity of drawing or painting a scene or animal in spectacular detail after only a single viewing, for example. Over time that remarkable recollection morphs into improvisation with variations on a musical tune after dutifully playing it back exactly as heard, or adding a tree or other item into a landscape scene. Finally, over time, an ability to create something entirely new emerges. In that sense the savant is not a mere tape recorder or digital camera, and even though vivid recall can be sensational, the *savant can be creative.*

10. While most often savant syndrome is evident from birth or early childhood (congenital), in some cases savant abilities suddenly and unexpectedly surface in some adolescents or adults following head injury, stroke, or other central nervous system disorder (acquired). This hints at dormant potential—a little *Rain Man* perhaps—within us all.

11. Whether congenital or acquired, the mechanism of savant syndrome is the same. There is dysfunction or damage in one area of the brain, most often left hemisphere. Following that there is *recruitment* of still intact undamaged brain capacity in other areas (most often right hemisphere) with *rewiring* to that still intact brain area and *release* of stored, dormant capacity within that area.

12. Savants, whether autistic or not, clearly demonstrate that they "know things they never learned." The knowledge and "rules" of music, art, and mathematics are innate and come "factory installed." These skills and funds of knowledge are inherited (nature) through what is called "genetic memory," but repetition, training, and practice (nurture) can increase repertoire and ability to even more extraordinary levels.

So many of Dr. Rimland's observations and theories on special abilities in persons with autism have been supported through the years. And savant syndrome continues to provide a unique window into the brain, memory, and creativity. Now new imaging and other techniques allow study of the brain "at work," providing much clearer identification of brain areas and pathways as the savant carries out his or her particular tasks and expertise. These newer findings will propel us along further than we have ever been in better understanding both the brain and human potential.

REFERENCES

Rimland, B. (1978). Savant characteristics of autistic children and their cognitive implications. In G. Serban (ed.) *Cognitive Deficits in the Development of Mental Illness*. New York: Brunner/Mazel.

Treffert, D.A. (1970). The epidemiology of infantile autism. *Archives of General Psychiatry*, 22, 431–438.

Treffert, D.A. (1988). The "idiot savant": A review of the syndrome. *American Journal of Psychiatry*, 145, 563–572.

Treffert, D.A. (2010). *Islands of Genius: The Bountiful Mind of the Autistic, Acquired, and Sudden Savant*. London: Jessica Kingsley Publishers.

INTRODUCTION TO CHAPTER 11
Stephen M. Edelson

In his final chapter, Rimland summarized the key points of the previous ten chapters. Expanding his insights beyond the scope of autism, he also shared his thoughts on topics including arousal, habituation, perceptual and neural coding, information processing, and memory. Further, he described how these may influence reasoning, phobias, creativity, personal interests, and much more.

Because the central thesis of *Infantile Autism* was that autism is an organic condition, Martha Herbert's contribution to this chapter summarizes research on the reticular formation and describes findings from current neurological research on autism.

CHAPTER 11

Some Implications of Early Infantile Autism for a Theory of Behavior

"...we have no choice, really, but to physiologize if we are to have any hope of solving our problems..." (Hebb, 1958a, p. 462)

This chapter is concerned with a question which is pivotal for much of the theory and discussion which have preceded it: How can a single specific brain area (presumably the brain stem reticular formation)[1] influence so profoundly the various apparently diverse cognitive phenomena which have been attributed to the site of the organic impairment in early infantile autism? The first part of this chapter proposes an answer to this question. The concluding pages of this chapter consist of a discussion of several supplementary ideas which, if considered in conjunction with the brain mechanism discussed below, appear to have merit in helping fill certain long-existing gaps in psychological theory.

---

1 The reader is again reminded that the theorizing which has preceded and which follows is not contingent upon the reticular formation's being the actual locus of the postulated brain mechanism. Several neurophysiologists who kindly consented to review an earlier draft of this chapter (R. W. Gerard, H. H. Jasper, H. J. Waller) have been frankly skeptical that the reticular formation could function as I have suggested. Attneave (in *Sensory Communication*, edited by W. A. Rosenblith, 1961) has provided a brief formulation similar to mine in many ways (pp. 777–782); and, referring to Hernández-Peón's chapter in the same volume, also posits a reticular locus. After puzzling over this problem for several years, I am pleased to join Attneave in his apt remark, "...the system blocked out above is not one I propose to defend for the rest of my life" (p. 781). So far as I am concerned, the question is still very much open.

A. A HYPOTHESIS CONCERNING RETICULAR FUNCTION

Throughout this monograph we have suggested that the puzzling phenomena associated with early infantile autism—the peculiar pattern of ability and disability in the children as well as the unusual but highly consistent pattern of intelligence and personality in their parents—result from the mode of operation of the brain mechanism which links sensation to memory. Although the validity of our speculation does not hinge upon the reticular formation's being the actual site of the mechanism in question, a good deal of evidence has been cited in support of the suggestion that it may be the reticular formation which is impaired in autism and which plays an important role in the function indicated. Let us examine the question more carefully.

Our hypothesis implies that the reticular formation does not, as is commonly believed, supply undifferentiated stimulation to higher brain centers. If one is willing to postulate that the impulses which traverse the paths to and from the reticular formation may not merely convey diffuse energy, but instead transmit a certain type of highly specific information, the phenomena discussed throughout this monograph become entirely plausible as qualities which may be mediated in reticular function. As we shall see, such an assumption has considerable support. If one is willing to make a few not untenable further assumptions, a surprisingly large array of additional psychological phenomena find ready explanations.

Coding of sensory input. Let us start with the impulses which enter the reticular formation from virtually all the internal and external sensory modalities. These carry an enormous amount of information (Barlow, 1959). Recent research provides some ideas on how this information may be conveyed (e.g., Amassian, Macy, & Waller, 1961).

Scott and Williams (1959) have suggested several mechanisms by which temporal coding of visual input may be achieved. They report that the transmission rate for light appears to be dependent upon its wave length—red and green light striking the retina simultaneously do not arrive in the brain simultaneously. Further possibilities for temporal coding of stimulation are opened by the tremor of the eyeball at a relatively constant rate of 10 cps. As Pritchard, Heron, and Hebb (1960) have shown, vision cannot take place if the effects of this tremor are negated. Scott and Williams have reported similar tremor in the fingers, and suggest that tremor may be fundamental to sensory coding (but see Gibbs, 1961). Tremor may be a primary function of the alpha rhythm, the utility of which remains unknown.

The intensity of the stimulus (i.e., the brightness of the light) is encoded in terms of frequency of neuronal firing. Estimates of the firing rates of individual neurons range from about 300 to 700 per second (Barlow, 1959; Russell, 1959; Scott & Williams, 1959). The shape of the retinal area stimulated by the light, as well as the context of retinal stimulation by light from adjoining space or objects, also helps provide uniqueness to the stimulating situation.

Thus, the pattern of stimulation from a simple visual object may be translated into a highly unique pattern of neural response. At least four factors appear to be operative: (1) differential transmission rate; (2) neural impulse frequency; (3) number and distribution of neurons receiving stimulation (a function of stimulus object size, shape, and placement compounded with tremor displacement); and (4) time sequence imposed by periodicity of the tremor. Amassian and his coworkers (e.g., Amassian, Macy & Waller, 1961) have shown that input from several sensory pathways may converge to a single reticular neuron, and that the discharge pattern of the neuron is a reflection of this complex input.

Memory. Let us for the moment leave the highly complex streams of coded transmission converging on the reticular formation from the various receptors and turn our attention briefly to the problem of memory. At the present time the manner in which experience is recorded in the brain is unknown (Galambos & Morgan, 1960; Halstead, 1960). There are, however, two prevailing theories, not necessarily mutually exclusive (Gerard, 1953). The more popular view has been that memory traces are recorded in terms of synaptic modifications which facilitate certain connections and inhibit competing ones (e.g., von Neumann, in Jeffress, 1951). The "cell assemblies" of Hebb (1949) and Milner (1957) are by and large of this type. Since it is generally considered that millions of neurons would be required for storing even simple memories, the adequacy of this concept is frequently questioned (e.g., Jeffress, 1951; Delafresnaye, 1954; Ciba Symposium, 1958; National Physical Laboratory Symposium, 1959).

The alternate view is that the traces are intracellular. This view has in recent years received considerable support from the finding of geneticists that the arrangements of components in certain giant protein molecules (especially deoxyribonucleic acid, DNA; and ribonucleic acid, RNA) provide the capability for encoding vast quantities of information. Crick (cited by Gaito, 1961) asserts that there are enough DNA molecules in a single cell of the human body to encode some 1000 large textbooks. When one considers that a single germ cell can and does somehow contain the information which determines whether its development will produce a red-haired man, a black widow spider with an affinity for dark corners, or a stately poplar tree, it does not seem unlikely that neurons can and do store significant increments of data. (See Elsasser, 1958, for a further discussion of this point.) Gaito has reviewed some of the developments which lead to the consideration of DNA and RNA as intraneuronal storage units. A growing body of evidence indicates that RNA does indeed appear to play a part in memory storage (e.g., Dingman & Sporn, 1961).

There is at present no known mechanism by which memory traces may become intracellular. The process would presumably be somewhat analogous to recording on magnetic tape, where the variations in an electrical signal bring about rearrangements in the molecular structure of the tape; or the process might be compared with the chemical changes which take place in color photography, where stimulation of molecules differentially sensitive to various wave lengths may permanently record an accurate and life-like representation of a complex scene. (For an interesting mechanical analogy to neuron memory, see Lichtmann, 1960.)

There are many advantages to assuming that memory traces are at least in part intracellular. The above analogies help conceptualize this process, even though they are obviously only grossly analogous at best. Even if one favors the concept of cell-group memory traces, the problem of which cells will enter a cell assembly or which synapse an impulse will cross is instantly simplified by accepting the notion of stimulus-relevant intra-neuronal differences.

Specificity. Even though there is evidence to suggest that the impulses which enter the reticular formation carry information in the form of highly complex patterns, the impulses which leave the reticular formation toward the cortex are described by most workers as "diffuse," "non-specific," or "undifferentiated," capable only of "arousing," "alerting," or "toning up" the cortex (e.g., Ivanitskiy, 1960). This is true even of many who attribute high functions to the reticular formation. Berlyne (1960), for example, attributes such things as curiosity and the appreciation of art and humor to the "reticular arousal system." Royer (1961) suggests that enjoyment of music is a consequence of cycles of tension and release operating through the reticular arousal system. However, most investigators do not ascribe high functions to the reticular formation (e.g., Anokhin & Agafonov, 1961).

Hebb expresses the prevailing view of reticular function clearly in describing the two routes of sensory input:

> In the classical conception of sensory function, input to the cortex was via the great projection systems only: from sensory nerve to sensory tract, thence to the corresponding sensory nucleus of the thalamus, and

thence directly to one of the sensory projection areas of the cortex. These are still the direct sensory routes, the quick efficient transmitters of information. The second pathway is slow and inefficient; the excitation, as it were, trickles through a tangled thicket of fibers and synapses, there is a mixing up of messages, and the scrambled messages are delivered indiscriminately to wide cortical areas. In short, they are messages no longer. They serve, instead, to tone up the cortex, with a background supporting action that is completely necessary if the messages proper are to have their effect. Without the arousal system the sensory impulses by the direct route reach the sensory cortex, but go no farther; the rest of the cortex is unaffected, and thus learned stimulus-response relations are lost. (1955, pp. 248–249)

We offer the alternative hypothesis that the two routes serve functions quite different than those described by Hebb.[2] The direct route seems well suited to maintain the *physical* integrity of the sensation (as was suggested in the preceding chapter, in discussing the phenomenon of delayed mental audition). The "slow and inefficient" reticular route, rather than "mixing up" the messages so they are "messages no longer," instead, we suggest, unscrambles the sensations so that they can be imbued with meaning. Specifically, we suggest that it is the function of the reticular formation to help decode or translate the otherwise unmanageably complex sensory input. The slowness, we suggest, is brought about by both the demands of the decoding operation itself (to be discussed below) and the time needed to permit descending cortical influences to help determine which aspects of the stimulus situation will be decoded (i.e., where attention is to be directed, or to which incoming patterns the reticular neurons are to be tuned).

The idea that the reticular formation may serve as a decoder is not new (although, so far as the writer has been able to determine, the idea has not been given detailed attention as such). Jasper (1952), for example, refers to the participation of the reticular formation in "correlative" circuits. Jasper (1958b) also discusses the reticular formation in terms of "central integrative functions." Fessard (1954), who was cited at some length in Chapter 5, refers to "integration of experience" as a function of the reticular formation and discusses certain properties of the reticular formation which

---

2   Scheibel and Scheibel (1961) agree with Hebb in saying that the reticular formation is constructed so "qualitative specificity must be lost," but say that the reticular core is concerned with "the investment of a neural event with significance, without which...the event is apparently neither experienced nor remembered" (p. 864). We have suggested in Chapter 10 that the event may not be immediately experienced but may sometimes be remembered. (See also John, cited by French, 1960, p. 1285; and by Rosenblatt, 1962, pp. 47, 65.)

support integrative functions. "Integration" seems to imply a process akin to "coding" in that both terms entail the making of necessary adjustments so that previously incompatible units may be combined. The reticular formation is said by Fessard to be part of a system seemingly fitted to "transform and reshape incoming messages" (p. 209). Clark (1958) similarly writes of reticular function in terms of "sorting" and "unshuffling" of impulses.

Coding seems implicit in Lindsley's very important observation (1958) that when only the classical sensory pathways to the cortex were open the stimulation was received in the cortex, "but whatever is required for their integration is absent since the animal or human does not respond to these messages in any meaningful way. Hence without the reticular activating system it appears that discrimination is not possible" (p. 55). He refers to recent research (by Jasper and others) which suggests that the reticular formation may act differentially as well as diffusely and refers to the possibility that psychological phenomena may thereby be explained.

The possibility must be considered that what appears to be "diffuse" energy may appear so only because of our present inability to analyze it (see Gerstein, 1960). The immense complexity which characterizes neural impulses is obvious when one considers how responsive the transmission must be to even minute variations in the stimulus. Peimer (1959) discusses "non-specificity" in terms of the apparent similarity of cerebral response to stimuli in different modalities, but observes that non-specificity is relative. Television transmission might look "diffuse" to an observer having equipment not compatible with the signal.

The "jumbledness" of the neurons constituting the reticular formation may be another reason for regarding it as capable of only non-specific transmission (e.g., Scheibel & Scheibel, 1958). However, as Hughlings Jackson observed long ago, there is no necessary inconsistency in a system being simultaneously highly complex yet highly disorganized (cited by Strauss & Kephart, 1955, p. 199).

At any rate, *our hypothesis is that the reticular formation is the site at which sensory input (and perhaps also imaginal input), represented as highly complex electrical patterns, is integrated and converted to a code which makes it compatible with the retrieval system used in making available a wide range of the content of memory.*[3] It is assumed that information carried by the direct route is also necessary, so that the appropriateness of the total code is the resultant of a sort of "triangulation" process. The role of direct route information would

---

3   To better understand this conception of the role of the reticular formation, consider the cognitive processes of autistic children (Chapter 5), in whom it was assumed this function was absent or severely impaired.

seem to be analogous to the pure reference tests which are included in factor analyses to enhance the interpretation of variance which would otherwise be unclear.

Arousal. The finding that reticular arousal of the cortex will take place only on initial stimulus presentation and not after the animal has become habituated (Sharpless & Jasper, 1956) implies that reticular output is in terms specific enough to interact uniquely with memory, although there are alternative explanations (e.g., Sharpless, 1958). Similarly, Sokolov (1960) reports habituation in humans to words of similar meaning, but not to words semantically different.

What are the arousal and habituation phenomena which are perhaps the most conspicuous element of reticular function? These are considered to be highly puzzling. Ashby (1959) concurs with Sharpless and Jasper in observing that there is no known physiological principle which accounts for habituation. Jasper, Ricci, and Doane (1958) note that the evidence that the blocking of brain waves is due to "arousal" is indirect and not entirely consistent. Brown (1960), in discussing theories of attention, writes, "What is difficult is to suggest how and why attention is directed to any one particular stimulus" (p. 108). Whether or not it is at all accurate, our foregoing formulation will be seen to provide us with at least the beginnings of an explanation for the heretofore unexplained phenomena of arousal, attention, and habituation.

Let us assume that over a given interval of time a certain variety of stimuli (represented by unique signal patterns) have been sensed by the animal and that the neurons or neuron assemblies responsive to the given pattern of frequencies have been stimulated and remain so. Additional sensings of these stimuli do not result in cortical excitement or "arousal." Presumably the neurons or circuits involved are already in a functioning state.

When a new or different stimulus is presented however, arousal occurs, *but only if the reticular formation is functioning.*[4] Could the so-called "diffuse" flow of energy from the reticular formation really represent scanning of the cortex with a signal pattern reflective of the environment to activate those neurons most responsive to that particular signal? Let us assume that once stimulated by the appropriate new code, the previously dormant neurons respond (resonate) and continue to remain excited, lowering for a time the thresholds between themselves and the reticular formation so that subsequent presentations of that stimulus (subsequent impulses with

---

4   Certain evidence makes this statement less clearly defensible than before. See, for example, Antonelli and Rudiger (1960), Feldman and Waller (1962), and Sprague, Chambers, and Stellar (1961).

that signal) are no longer out of synchrony with what might be called the "current content of the mind." The organism would thus be habituated to that stimulus. Arousal reactions as seen by EEG methods would thus represent a disruption of the patterns currently dominant in the cortex by new (or at least unanticipated) stimulus patterns. The concept is analogous to the clashing of unsynchronized gears prior to their meshing into a smoothly functioning unit. Upon the onset of a new stimulus, the organism would become "aroused" and attend to the change with an adaptive "reduction of disruption" reflex (the orienting reflex).

In delayed mental audition, it is suggested that the coding capacity has been pre-empted by earlier stimuli, and decoding will ordinarily not take place until the channel is cleared, unless the secondary stimuli are unusual enough to create arousal and lead to their being decoded. (See Sutherland, 1959, for a discussion of conscious perception being sidetracked while the coding channel is being cleared. Broadbent, cited earlier in connection with delayed audition, provides experimental data on this phenomenon.)

It is clear from studies of direct stimulation of the temporal lobes (Penfield, 1950, 1960) and of hypnotically induced recall (Gerard, 1953, 1960) that enormous amounts of sensory input are recorded in the human brain. Much of the detail does not appear to have been specifically attended to. Gerard (1953), for example, cites a bricklayer who under hypnosis described minute details of a single brick in a wall he had built 20 years earlier. It is interesting to consider that this input may have been sensed and stored without coding, via (according to our hypothesis) the direct sensory route. Clark (1958) discusses such accretion of unconscious percepts in an interesting mating of neurophysiology with Bergson's concept of creative evolution.

The coding process. We have surmised, then, that the reticular formation accepts the infinitely varied patterns of stimulation streaming in from the receptors and somehow integrates and reconstitutes the impulses so that, in conjunction with the information carried by the primary route, they may serve to discharge those memory neurons responsive to the particular signal complex. Thus would a representation of external reality be recreated within the brain. In this sense the reticular formation is analogous to a human translator, who receives what is a clearly sensed but meaningless message to the unskilled listener, and transforms the previously incomprehensible material he has sensed into a form designed to trigger relevant memories in the mind of the listener. To carry the metaphor further, in selective attention the listener instructs the translator to translate only one of several possible messages from which the translator may choose.

How might the reticular formation perform this function? Clues are scant, but do exist. Impulses which enter the reticular formation at several hundred per second emerge in some cases at a mere two or three per second (French, 1960). Oldfield (1954) has shown the role time lags may play in setting up unique codes for storage in memory.

There are similarities between the model for the reticular formation we propose and the "comparators" used by Barlow (1959) in his electronic model of a highly simplified brain. Barlow describes his comparators as "leaky condensers," and uses them to summate the repeating (redundant) aspects of input so that random noise may be dissipated. We suggest an analogy between Barlow's comparators and the unmyelinated multisynaptic reticular neurons. In the face of a great many redundant aspects of the stimulus, we suggest that what becomes random, in effect, is in part determined by input to the reticular neurons from the cortex. Each reticular neuron receives input from the cortex (Gastaut, 1958a; Samuels, 1959). Stimulus patterns irrelevant to cortical attention are filtered out and tend either to be dissipated or stored without coding, unless they are strong enough or unusual enough to "clash" with active brain patterns and create an arousal reaction. Relevant stimulus patterns, once sorted and molded jointly by the characteristics of the reticular formation and the content of the cortex, could course to the cortex and other parts of the brain translated into a form compatible with that in which memories are stored and await retrieval.

The consequences of variations in reticular function. If the reticular formation serves the function we attribute to it, it is clear that the many diverse phenomena which we and other writers have hypothetically traced to it might indeed be brought about by interindividual variation in reticular function. The process of relating sensation to memory is a critical one.

The effectiveness with which the reticular formation could code its input would determine in part how appropriate and adequate the cortical response would be. In an intelligent human, one might guess that a sufficient number of harmonics and variations would ascend to activate a sizable number of responsive neurons and thus, in effect, recreate and make accessible many memories relevant to that stimulus pattern. A stimulus evoking a very rich memory supply may be termed a concept. Slower and less accurate coding would result in inadequate evocation of some relevant memories (experience) and the making of faulty interpretations of the meaning of events. This would correspond to dullness, and, in the extreme, to feeble-mindedness.

In an autistic child, whose reticular formation were impaired so that it coded in a very literal way, only an exceedingly small range of memory neurons would be activated, and only a very limited variety of responses would be evoked. He could respond to only the letter and not the "spirit" of his sensory input. Phenomena we have referred to as "closed-loop" processes could be expected—a virtual identity between input and response. Generalization and abstract thought could not take place. In terms of our concept of autism, then, the child would be grossly impaired in the ability to link sensation with all but a highly delimited fraction of memory. To take a specific example, the child might be able to read aloud, as could the cases reported by Kanner (1952), and Benda (1960), since this requires learning only the simple association between sounds and letters, but the child could have no conception of the *meaning* of what he read, since reading with meaning requires connotative association rather than mere stimulus-response *denotation*.

The above is of course merely speculation. It is interesting, however, to compare these views with Cappon's (1953) strikingly similar hunch about the nature of autism. Cappon makes no reference to the reticular formation but suggests, "The writer would place the pathological locus of this manifestation at the level of the mysterious translation of 'organic' perceptions (the result of 'mechanical' stimuli from the inner and outer physical worlds) into meaningful and integrated psychic experiences" (p. 3).

Cognition in autism and schizophrenia. Cappon, one of the few non-European writers who differentiates autism from schizophrenia, had preceded the above observation with, "This writer would like to postulate that, as we move in our spectrum of schizoid phenomena towards the more virulent and morbid extreme, autism increases and that at one point of loading it becomes the primary defect" (p. 2). It should be evident that the present writer would place schizophrenia at the other extreme from autism and on quite a different continuum. *In our interpretation of schizophrenia, coding would be so loose, the emissions from the reticular formation would cover so broad a spectrum, that various remotely relevant neurons (or neuron assemblies) might become activated and lead to the initiation of only remotely relevant, sometimes bizarre, perceptions and responses.*

Could this type of associational disorder be what Bleuler (1950) had in mind when he wrote in description of schizophrenia, "It appears as if those pathways of association and inhibition…had lost meaning and their significance. Associations seem to take new pathways more easily, and thus no longer follow the old preferred ways, that is the logical pathways indicated by past experience" (pp. 349–350).

Disorder brought about by excessively loose coding would account for what Cameron and Magaret described when they wrote:

> Contradictory, competing and more or less irrelevant responses can no longer be excluded... Schizophrenic patients themselves often complain...everything seems mixed up...thoughts rush in and are jumbled... Another patient...complained that thoughts had been rushing through her mind so that she could say nothing. (1951, p. 511)

Payne, Mattussek, and George discuss the schizophrenic thought disorder in terms of a defect in the "filter mechanism," which again is quite consistent with the concept we propose to account for schizophrenic thought:

> ...normal people are quite unaware of most stimuli irrelevant to the task. It is as if some "filter mechanism" cuts out or inhibits the stimuli, both internal and external, which are irrelevant to the task in hand, to allow the most efficient "processing" of incoming information. Over-inclusive thinking might be only one aspect of a general breakdown of this "filter mechanism." (p. 631)

Scheibel and Scheibel (1960) describe the reticular formation as perhaps being the locus for such a stimulus "filter." (See also Bruner's [1957] filtering or "gating" process.)

A number of writers have noted that it is very often the socially relevant aspects of thought which are most disturbed in schizophrenia (e.g., Bernstein, 1960). This is often construed as indicating psychogenic etiology in schizophrenia. In terms of the present hypothesis, a special decrement in ability to deal with social phenomenon would be anticipated, because socially oriented behavior would seem to demand very many more associations to be made than are required by object-oriented behavior. That is, the use of a great deal of prior relational learning is required in social situations, and such learning would therefore seem to be especially vulnerable to a defect in the associational or retrieval apparatus.

The above descriptions of the schizophrenic thought process are fairly commonplace and easily understood. Our conception of thought in autism, characterized by paucity rather than superfluity of associations, is much less common and considerably more difficult to describe or imagine. Perhaps the best way of simulating the thought disorder we postulate in autism is to speak a word ordinarily rich in associations aloud repeatedly for several minutes (try: monkey monkey monkey...). The physical stimulus remains but all significance soon vanishes. Another example is found when one's attention wanders while reading aloud, as in the case of reading a story to one's children for the seventeenth time. The visual and vocal mechanisms do their work while requiring only the barest participation from the reader's memory bank—participation of a denotative rather than connotative sort. This is of course directly comparable to the reading without understanding found in autistic children.

Affect in autism and schizophrenia. The models of autistic and schizophrenic thought proposed here are entirely cognitive and have not yet explained the disturbances of affect which are found in both autism and schizophrenia. Bleuler regarded a disturbance in affect, along with the disturbance in associations, as being of primary importance in schizophrenia. Kanner has emphasized that autistic children typically fly into a rage when their "insistence on the preservation of sameness in the environment" is not heeded.

The affective response of autistic and of schizophrenic persons may be readily derived from the cognitive aspects of these conditions, as described in the foregoing paragraphs, if one is willing to accept the theoretical formulation of affect derived by Rosenzweig (1958) and a similar one derived independently by Rodgers (1962). Briefly, these theories suggest, in effect, that an organism functions cognitively by creating an internalized model of reality which it responds to and compares with external reality. Negative affect is the result of the experience of discongruence between the model and reality. Rashkis and Singer make a related point in saying, "If externally or internally arising stimuli can, when received by a central integrating mechanism, be so thoroughly distorted or misdirected that the response is no longer referable to the stimulus...no further explanation for schizophrenia is required" (1959, p. 412).

Obviously, from the foregoing descriptions of the cognitive process in autism and schizophrenia, discrepancies between reality and expectancy, and therefore much affect, will be the rule. In schizophrenia the discrepancy which gives rise to anxiety stems from faulty perception, and in autism it arises because the environment, which the child "imperiously posits as static" (Kanner) does in fact change.

Diamond, Balvin, and Diamond (1963) give a good example of discrepancy between expectation and actuality giving rise to emotion in an autistic child:

> Lily, a beautiful girl of five, with autism, finally made contact with her nursery school teacher. Each morning she had to be greeted with the set phrase, "Good morning, Lily. I am very, very glad to see you." If

even one of the very's was omitted or another added, she would start to scream wildly. As soon as the expected salutation was given, she became calm. (p. 334)

The theory of cognition in the context of information theory. In the preceding paragraphs, as elsewhere in this monograph, autism and schizophrenia have been described as being directly antithetical concepts. We have earlier referred to the apparently non-overlapping hereditary backgrounds of children suffering from autism and childhood schizophrenia. The relevance of the problem to Kretschmer's cyclothymic and schizothymic bipolar types was noted. Autistic children were described as "underassociating" and schizophrenic children as "overassociating" in their mental functioning, as apparent in their verbal behavior, and this was found to fall in line with Kretschmer's characterization of cyclothymic thought as "integrative" and schizothymic thought as "disassociative."

In the preceding section an explanation was given for the difference in autistic and schizophrenic thought in terms of the range of relevant memories elicited by external or internal input to the brains of persons afflicted with these mental conditions. Autism was said to be characterized by elicitation of a pathologically narrow range of memories, and schizophrenia was hypothesized as eliciting a pathologically wide range. It was suggested that malfunction of the reticular formation in its specificity of coding might be the source of both difficulties.

Having articulated our conceptions of reticular function and of the antithetical relationship between mental function in autism and schizophrenia, it becomes possible to relate the present theory to Shannon's "Mathematical theory of communication" (Shannon & Weaver, 1949). As we have described it, the reticular formation acts as a communication transmitter, relaying messages to various parts of the brain in a form which permits the elicitation of memory. The messages may be so tightly knit that they elicit only literal, specific responses (autism); or so loosely knit that all manner of extraneous memories are aroused (schizophrenia). The extremes of loose and tight transmission correspond closely to the two counterposed qualities of information transmission: *fidelity* and *band-width*. According to the theory, information can be transmitted with high fidelity at the expense of band-width, or with reduced fidelity and enlarged band-width. Most of the symptoms of autistic children could be explained by very high fidelity transmission from the reticular formation to their brain storage areas, resulting in elicitation of highly stimulus-specific responses, but with very few less specific but meaningful memory traces being aroused. The broad band-width of intracerebral transmission aroused by stimulation of a schizophrenic person would elicit so many responses that disorganization would result.[5, 6]

The phenomena of early infantile autism, described in Part I, present many clear examples of what might be considered high-fidelity, low-band-width retrieval of what has been previously sensed. The girl with extraordinary imagery who remembered the exact state of a jumble of toy blocks and screamed when one had been turned in her absence is an example. The child who repeated an aria with musical perfection in a foreign language is another, as are the children who can read aloud very well (even in German; Kanner, 1952) but do not know what they are saying. Note the high-fidelity reproduction of the environment implied in Arnold's description of his four-year-old Negro boy with autism who could not speak and showed little comprehension; "he had spontaneously acquired an exceptional ability to read, write, spell correctly, and to make paper cuts of letters and numbers with extraordinary manual dexterity" (1960, p. 161).

Note also the fidelity showed by the boy Bruch saw some 13 years after first seeing him as a four-and-a-half-year-old patient with infantile autism: "It was amazing, he even remembered the words I had used and I am pretty sure they were correct, including certain Germanisms" (1959, p. 14). This phenomenon seems related to what was referred to earlier as "delayed audition," which too appears potentially ascribable to high fidelity and attenuated band-width, albeit in normal persons.

It may be mere coincidence that the present independently derived theory counterposing the autistic and schizophrenic thought disorders should correspond closely in concept with the counterposing of fidelity and band-width in information theory. However, the thesis finds support from other sources as well.

A colleague of the writer's, upon reading an earlier draft of this chapter, observed that if the information theory approach were valid, one should find a negative relationship between accuracy of imagery and "associative and abstractive potential." Had he been provided the entire manuscript, he would have noted that Sir Francis Galton (p. 176) had indeed remarked on the "astonishing" finding that scientists in general have poor imagery, and had specifically commented on the antagonism between sharp mental imagery and abstract thought. Betts (1909) confirmed Galton's findings in his study in which the imagery of a group of psychologists was found to be distinctly poorer than the imagery of the other less selected groups

---

5   For a different but related application of information theory to schizophrenia, see Miller (1960).
6   Faibish's (1961) finding that schizophrenics are especially impaired in dealing with words of multiple meaning is of relevance here.

Betts tested. Betts also confirmed an earlier study by Armstrong by finding a negative correlation between quality of imagery and college grades in his group of college students. Galton was concerned with men of genius and Betts also studied especially intelligent subjects. Fidelity has also been found to counterbalance band-width at the other end of the scale. Langdon Down had noted in 1887 (p. 99) that extraordinary memory is often found in conjunction with a great defect in reasoning power, and Nietzsche (cited by Leddy, 1960) has remarked that "many a man fails to become a thinker for the sole reason that his memory is too good." More recently, Gerard (1959) also observed that "people with phenomenal memories are rarely very imaginative or creative" (p. 19). (Of special interest are those persons of great genius who are also endowed with extremely retentive memories. Macauley, Coleridge, and von Neumann are notable cases in point. There may, however, be important distinctions to be made between memory and imagery.)

The well-established finding that young children exhibit eidetic imagery which fades away as the reasoning process develops is consistent with the opposed concepts of fidelity and band-width as described here. Leddy (1960) shows that the especially retentive memory of children has been recognized since the time of Plato.

The foregoing discussion has suggested that it is variation in reticular function which determines the balance of band-width and fidelity in the ascending neural paths. Autistic, normal, and schizophrenic persons would differ in the manner but not necessarily the degree of function of the reticular formation. An alternate formulation having certain advantages is that it is the direct sensory pathways which transmit high fidelity representation of the environment, and it is the job of the reticular formation to broaden the band-width of the input (under the supervision of the cortex) so that a wider range of relevant memory neurons can be evoked. This is the complementary "triangulation" role of the two pathways suggested earlier.[7]

One final point which relates to the fidelity of sensory information in the autistic child: Judging from his excellent ability to reproduce nursery rhymes and melodies, his memory for spatial relations, and his motor

---

7   The writer's attempt to investigate these suggested roles of the two pathways has foundered on a mass of neurophysiological evidence which is highly complex and apparently quite contradictory. Relevant references to the relationship between the direct and reticular pathways by Antonelli and Rudiger; Feldman and Waller; Sprague, Chambers, and Stellar, and Sharpless were mentioned earlier. The discussions by Pribram, Galambos, Magoun, Anokhin, and Kupalov in the Pavlovian Conference (1961, pp. 890–897) are particularly relevant to the points at issue and should not be missed by those interested in this problem.

performance and finger dexterity, the child with infantile autism has a clear and precise focus on the physical, if not the psychological, aspects of reality. (This is not true of the schizophrenic child.) These facts suggest adequacy of transmission along the direct route in autism whether or not one subscribes to the remainder of the theory.

The foregoing exposition has rounded out our theory of what early infantile autism is and what it may mean. Although the monograph could logically stop at this point, the writer has yielded to the temptation to complete the theory of mental function which has evolved from his study of autism. The hypothesized brain mechanism which developed from and helps explain our theory of early infantile autism needs but one additional concept to become a framework for a broader theory possessing considerable explanatory power for mental function in general. The closing pages of this monograph will be devoted to a brief discussion of this concept.

B. TOWARD A NEURON ENTELECHY THEORY OF COGNITION[8]

Perhaps the best way of introducing this topic is to cite the comments made by Gerard in discussing the paper given by Warren McCulloch at the Hixon Symposium on Cerebral Mechanisms in Behavior:

> Dr. McCulloch just stated that he is interested in devising a theory that would account for the brain as a calculating machine... What about the non-rational side? What about the urge of the machine to calculate? What about the drive, so striking in some of the men in this symposium, which, perhaps even more than the elegance of the calculating machine, determines whether or not something worthwhile comes out of the system in the course of its lifetime? (in Jeffress, 1951, p. 107)

Professor Gerard's questions, as well as a surprisingly diverse range of other problems which confront students of behavior, become considerably less puzzling if one will but tentatively add two simple related assumptions to the brain mechanism described in the first half of this chapter.

---

8   The concept proposed on the following pages was originally titled "neuron resonance." After this chapter was first written the writer discovered that Paul Weiss had employed the term neuron resonance nearly four decades ago in describing certain phenomena relating to neuron growth and development, as well as to certain motor aspects of neuron function. Some of Weiss' views will be cited a few pages hence. Although there is an overlap in the thinking of Weiss and the present writer, the present writer's concepts apply to hypotheses in the realm of mental function rather than neurology and the term "neuron entelechy" has been adopted to permit distinction from the work of Weiss.

Perhaps it is necessary at this point to caution again, explicitly, that the ideas developed below are merely schematic oversimplifications of enormously complicated reality. We will try to avoid crossing the line beyond which simplification transforms into distortion or error, but the boundary is not well marked, and the path, so far as the writer is able to tell, is largely new.

It has already been suggested that the paths upward from the brain stem carry coded transmission from the sensory organs. The sensory input has been shaped by the character and organization of the reticular neurons so that minute fractions of the environment are represented by momentary but highly complex patterns of stimulation.[9]

The major assumption. Let us now assume that the brain contains neurons which are particularly responsive to certain specific patterns of stimulation, and that an experience of "pleasure," "reward," "satisfaction," or "realization" for the organism occurs when a neuron is stimulated by an appropriately patterned pulse of coded sensory input. The degree of "satisfaction" would be in part a function of the number of neurons responding. *For lack of better terminology* we may say the neurons "want" to discharge, and that they "resonate" (cf., Weiss, 1950) when stimulated by their appropriate pattern, or by patterns similar to it. The neuron would have previously been conditioned or tuned to respond to its critical stimulus pattern by genetic and/or experiential factors, usually acting jointly. The threshold of response would be, in part, a function of the similarity between the neuron's prior setting and the pattern of the new stimulus input to the neuron. Even an inappropriate stimulus pattern might cause discharge if sufficiently intense (as may be the case in certain laboratory studies of nerve conduction).

The objections. The above approach will immediately be challenged on the grounds that it is imparsimonious and animistic to attribute "wants" or "motives" to a cell. The writer must insist that these ideas are neither animistic nor metaphysical.[10] It is regrettable that the concept we invoke requires the use of expressions which mankind rather jealously resents being applied to individuals of lower than human status (an extremely large category which includes even the cells of our own central nervous systems). Custom enjoins us from assuming that the parts can share the properties of the whole. But

9   See Greene (1961) for an interesting account of *A search for the fundamental units of perception.*

10 Since writing this section, I have come across a closely related supporting essay, *The Biology of Purpose,* by the noted biologist, E. W. Sinnot (1952).

the fact is that bodily cells do exhibit just such highly specific "wants" or "appetites." Red blood cells have an "affinity" for oxygen, thyroid gland cells "seek" iodine, etc. The list is probably very nearly endless. We suggest that the list should include neuron cells which "await" certain patterns of stimulation. The tropisms evinced in one-celled organisms would appear to offer evidence that individual cells can exhibit such properties. That we do not know why this is so should not deter us from recognizing that it is so.

So basic is the affinity of a cell for its adequate stimulus, so universal is the striving of each cell for interaction with a specific electrochemical aspect of its surroundings that the life process and what is called the "life instinct" appears to rest upon it. Behavior might very well be defined in terms of an organism's efforts toward attempting to maximize this intra-neuronal reward. In a sense, our thesis is the application at the neuron level of the view Goldstein expounds so ably in his book *The Organism* (1939). Briefly stated, Goldstein asserts that the goal of the organism is self-actualization, and that all "drives" are but manifestations of this single purpose. Our view is that the same principle accounts for neuron function; and that it is the summation of this tendency in neurons which accounts for the behavior of the total organism.

In addition to the objection of "animistic," the present thesis might also be objected to because it does not accord very well with the simple "on–off" behavior that classical neurons are believed to exhibit. But note the words of Weiss (1950) on the adequacy of neuron theory. Weiss was referring to his experiments involving the study of coordination of central and peripheral functions by such means as limb and eye transplants. He had cited evidence in support of "neuron resonance"—the idea that neurons operate by a "peculiar mechanism perhaps best described in figurative terms as 'tuning in'" (p. 3).

> That existing theories of conduction and synaptic transmission contain no clue to the described phenomena is amply proven by the fact that they could not have predicted them. Since the reality of the phenomena is undeniable, they will have to find a place in our neurological thinking. Whether they can be accommodated by mere additions to current physiological concepts without resorting to major revisions, is an open question... (p. 19)

> ...I have mentioned above the fanciful idea that these may be engendered by chains of complex chemical reactions whose constituent links would "unlock" correspondingly tuned neural elements. Though being sheer speculation, it indicates the direction in which we may have to look.

It may be comforting to keep pretending that the resonance phenomena are matters of development and required no major innovations of physiological theory; but I doubt whether it is realistic… (p. 20)

More recently, Bullock (1959) has noted that "a quiet but sweeping revolution" has taken place in neurophysiology, and that the old "doctrine" of neuron behavior may not be valid.[11] Bullock notes, in fact, that the problem now seems to be to find the restrictions on neuron behavior, "…perhaps much of the normal functioning is carried out *without nerve impulses*…" More recently (1961) Bullock reported that, "even patterned clusters of nerve impulses, like the more complex patterns of a snare drum, can arise within a single neuron" (p. 56). Samuels also cites research providing similar conclusions: "…individual cells respond with different patterns and latencies of firing, depending upon the source of stimulation" (1959, p. 15).

Suppose, then, that neurons are not merely simple "on–off" switches. What evidence is there for believing that their simple exercise of function is experienced as reward, and what would it mean if this were true?

Antecedents. The beginnings of the concept have a long history. Nearly a century ago Bain wrote of the craving of the senses for stimulation, and almost a half-century ago Thomas listed a desire for new experience and stimulation as one of the instincts (see Fiske & Maddi, 1961). In 1947 Woodworth wrote of "the will to perceive"; and in 1938 Lashley referred to what appeared to be sensory deficit behavior in the mother rat deprived of her young, and in the web-building of spiders and nest-building of birds. Leuba (1955) cited evidence for a somewhat related viewpoint in his discussion of "optimum stimulation."

The disastrous effects which quickly follow extended sensory deprivation (Hebb, 1958b) are in particular consistent with our thesis that neurons seek stimulation. Many studies show that these effects can include cell degeneration as well as the experience of extreme discomfort (e.g., Gyllensten, 1959). Again, boredom, as Berlyne (1960) emphasizes, seems to involve an increase in drive (Berlyne attributes it to an increase in arousal) which again implies that sensory stimulation may have an incentive value. The often-cited inseparability of affect and perception, even in an infant too

---

11 Estable too feels that neurophysiology has been excessively doctrinaire: "The rigidity of our conceptions concerning inter-neuronal relationships contrasts with the functional plasticity of the nervous system…" (1961, p. 331). "But there is at least serious question whether any digital activity takes place at the level of single nerve fibers…and it is certainly true that the great bulk of the activity that is cited by the neurophysiologist as digital is not so in fact" (Elias, in *Sensory Communication*, 1961, p. 795).

young to have learned such an association, also lends support. Curiosity, playfulness, even card and chess playing and working crossword puzzles suggest a positive search for mental stimulation, and the very existence of art and music offer abundant evidence that sensory stimulation itself can yield pleasure.

In view of Bullock's report on the disintegration of "neuron doctrine" at the physiological level, a recent statement by Hunt and Quay (1961), which indicates parallel disintegration of doctrine at the psychological level, is of special interest:

> We come somewhat reluctantly to an espousal of this hypothesis of innate reinforcement values for receptor inputs. The concept is dissonant with our past theoretical prejudices. Nevertheless...the evidence available is sufficiently supportive to indicate that the hypothesis of innate reinforcement values deserves serious investigative consideration. (pp. 154–155)

The utility of the concept

Let us now outline briefly some of the many psychological phenomena which can be better understood through the concept that the "striving" of neurons forms the basis for behavior. The discussions below are obviously gross oversimplifications, for the purposes of illustration.

1. *Learning.* Under the stated assumptions, learning would consist of modifying neurons so that they respond to new patterns of stimulation. As learning progresses, successively larger numbers of neurons become increasingly adapted to the stimulus patterns, and are brought into closer and more stable resonance with the recurring (and often relevant) stimulus cues.

(a) A *learning set* is a condition which results in the neurons molding more quickly to the stimulus—possibly through the use of feedback circuits which purify the impulses by selective coding of sensory input.[12] Learning is easiest when the new data can be fit into an existing framework (Miller, 1956) (i.e., when neurons having closely relevant code patterns are available in good supply) but can be made more difficult if new and old patterns are so similar that interference or "jamming" occurs (negative transfer).

(b) *Distraction* occurs when two or more stimulus configurations are emitted alternately by the encoding mechanism, thus preventing an orderly consummation of the cognitive process initiated by either of the stimuli.

---

12 There is at present no theory for accounting for the role of attention in the fixation of learning (cf., Hebb, 1949, pp. 173–174; discussion by Adrian & Olds, Ciba Symposium, 1958, pp. 380–382; Galambos & Morgan, 1960, p. 1495).

(c) *Conditioning* would result from the gradual harmonizing of neurons activated by stimulus and reward, each retaining a pattern which overlaps or mediates other activated patterns as the discrepancy between the UR and CR patterns is bridged.

(d) The role of *reward or incentive* in learning would also entail the coactivation of neurons representative of both cue and goal, so that intermediary neurons capable of bridging or overlapping the discrepancy in the stimulus patterns can be recruited.

(e) *Insightful learning* would entail the availability of already coded intermediary neurons which readily provide solidly overlapping patterns between cue and goal.

(f) *Practice* serves to solidify the neural modifications and, by gradually bringing the originally responding neurons into closer resonance with the sensory signal, strengthens and purifies it. Marginally relevant neurons are either adapted and recruited or tend to drop out. As practice continues, shorter paths of overlapping neurons are developed. (This may be the "crowding out of cortical influences" referred to earlier.)

(g) *Phobias.* In line with the idea that the strength of the ascending signal (attention) helps configure the neurons to respond to the given stimulus is the concept that an extreme of attention, such as great fright, can cause overlearning of the bond between the stimulus and the bodily response, as may be the case in the establishment of phobias. In support of the idea that the reticular formation is important in determining the specific signal is Hunt's documented "suspicion" that response patterns "show resistance to change which is proportional to the degree of arousal at the time these habits were acquired" (1961, p. 70). Imprinting, preventable by chlorpromazine, may be analogous.

Most other learning phenomena also fit readily into the neural-entelechy conceptual framework. Learning consists of an environmentally induced binding together of sensitive and responsive elements within an organism. The stimulus, in this context, serves as a switch to activate selected neurons and/or as an agent for shaping or adapting neurons so they will later respond to stimuli perceived as (encoded as) similar.

2. *Specific likes, appetites, motives, and interests* may easily be derived by assuming that certain neuronal tendencies may be expressed both genotypically and phenotypically, or may be induced by repeatedly attended-to experience. As noted earlier, the giant molecules associated with somatic inheritance seem more adapted than most for the retention of memory traces.

(a) *Specific aptitudes* in which individual differences are prominent, such as for music or art, would be differentially inherited as neurons responsive to sound patterning (for music) or visual patterning (to color and shape) for art. (See Royer [1961] for a discussion of possibly innate aesthetic values. Also, compare this concept with Brain's [1948] discussion of inherited "schemata." Hayes' [1962] interpretation of intelligence in terms of specific motivations is highly compatible with the present concept.)

(b) *General tendencies*, common to most persons, such as a liking for sweets, music, certain colors, etc.; or behavior tendencies, such as the nursing instinct, could be similarly understood.

(c) The phenomena wherein repeated stimulation or behavior acquires an apparently motivating function of its own (e.g., Allport's functional autonomy and Fechner's and Maslow's findings showing that repeated stimulation can yield pleasure) would be explained by the proposed mechanism.[13] Once neurons have been trained (altered by experience) to respond to certain stimulus configurations, they strive for and yield pleasure upon subsequent response to these stimuli. A similar interpretation can be used to explain the manner in which interest appears to "feed on itself," becoming more intense with additional exposure to a class of stimuli, such as in stamp collecting.[14]

(d) In animal behavior, the concept of inherited neural resonance tendencies would help explain *imprinting,*[15] *hoarding, homing instincts,* and much else.

(e) The puzzling *regrowth of severed nerves* through scar tissue to make specific connections, as well as related phenomena (e.g., Clark, 1958; Sperry, 1956; Weiss, 1950) becomes less difficult to understand in terms of the present concept, which, as was noted earlier, was anticipated by Weiss in his concept of "neuron resonance."

3. *Affect.* The theories of affect of Rosenzweig and of Rodgers described earlier in this chapter which regard emotion as the resultant of a discrepancy between expectation and actuality are readily compatible with the present concept of neuron function. The varieties of displeasure would result from a deficit in the fulfillment of neurons aroused but not enabled to respond to the anticipated configuration of the stimulus. Pleasure or joy would result from an excess of neuronal reward when the environment exceeded immediate expectation in a manner consistent with dormant tendencies (Rodgers, 1962). In the case of the autistic child, only identity between occurrence and expectation would ordinarily bring this about.

---

13 There are at present no completely satisfactory theories to account for these phenomena (Braun, 1962; Prentice, 1961).

14 There are no adequate theories of interest (Smith, 1958).

15 There is at present no theory which accounts for both reinforcement learning and imprinting (Maier, 1960).

4. *Higher mental processes.* Characteristics such as reasoning, the desire to know and understand, and the thrill of discovery are readily compatible with the view proposed. These conditions and behaviors might result from assemblies of neurons nearly but not quite resonant. When these nearly resonant assemblies are aroused, the organism would be motivated to try to resolve the discrepancies or incongruities in his overall cerebral activity pattern. He might, in other words, try to achieve what the Gestalt psychologists would call "closure."

(a) *Reasoning.* The present hypotheses of brain function lead to the suggestion that the brain operates on the basis of analogies, rather than in terms of a more rigorously analytical process (analogically rather than logically). Objects, situations, and problems would be responded to as being similar to previously experienced objects, situations, and problems as a function of the overlap in the neurons they discharge when their sensory representations are coded and transmitted through the brain's memory bank. Partial evidence that this is so—that an object is responded to on the basis of analogical similarities—is found in the ready perception of a spoken word irrespective of loudness, pitch, and the many physical variations brought on by such factors as the age, sex, mood, and geographic origin of the speaker. Written words provide an even more striking example, since a word is easily recognized on a printed page, in handscript, presented vertically on a neon sign, or by means of white ink on black paper. A sufficiency of microelements, rather than any more formal "blueprint" would seem to be necessary to account for these phenomena.

Von Neumann, who spent much of his life trying to explain the brain in terms of a digital computer, wrote in his last published work (*The Computer and the Brain*, 1958) that the brain did *not* appear to follow computer-like processes in solving problems. He found the number of steps required in deductive logic to be surprisingly small, compared with a computer. If the brain operated as we here surmise, by finding similar models or fractions of models from earlier experience and using these to arrive at the sought-for solutions, von Neumann's finding could be accounted for.

The "intuitive" speed and skill of the expert chess player or mathematician, whose experience has provided him with a rich store of relevant memories, would seem to depend on perception of new problems in terms of remembered experience, rather than on any strictly deductive process. Most chess experts deny that they attempt any verbal evaluation of each possible move.

Such phenomena as the "atmosphere effect" in logical problem solving, and the pervasiveness of individual views, biases, and beliefs which color nearly every human thought and deed suggest that people systematically code into their perceptions analogical memories in excess of those which would be required by an objective and analytical view of the situation. For some persons each situation is seen to have elements of threat; for others, traces leading to the possibility of gain appear to be "read into" or projected into almost every perceived situation. Historically, man has been believed to be substantially a rational being, with frequent and visible aberrations from rationality. If the brain operates as we here propose, in terms of analogies and perceived similarities rather than analytically, as has heretofore been believed, it would be instances of rational behavior which could be called aberrant. This is perhaps the more realistic view. Consideration of possible conflict between the pressures exerted by unfulfilled neurons striving against the limits imposed by reality carries us into the realm of Freud.

(b) *Creativity.* A great deal of research has shown that intelligence is a necessary but not a sufficient prerequisite to creativity. We have earlier suggested that reticular function is intimately tied up with intelligence. In terms of the hypotheses we have proposed, intelligence would reside in large part in the effectiveness of coding applied to the focus of attention. Memory is utilizable only to the extent to which relevant memories are accessible: [Intelligence is] "...the ability to see relationships and meanings by having access to as many alternatives as possible at approximately the same instant of time" (Travis & Hunter, 1928, cited by Goddard, 1946).

Reference was made earlier to the evidence which suggests that the amount of data stored in the human brain is enormously greater than normal remembering processes would indicate (e.g., Gerard, 1953, 1960; Penfield, 1959, 1960). It would seem that access to the stored memory—coding and decoding capability—is of extreme importance not only in providing a basis for intelligent actions, but also for the seeing of new relationships which creativity requires.

If there be the force we referred to as "affinity" causing neurons to seek to discharge when stimulus patterns approximating theirs are experienced, there are likely to be important differences between people in the intensity of such affinity. We suggest that the driving force which causes intelligence to fill the gaps in knowledge, to bring order to the content of mind, to *create* new coherences, may be that same force.

In terms of the present theory, then, the mysterious missing link in present theories of creativity would be related to the intensity with which neurons "strive" to cohere in relevant groupings. This concept is analogous to the idea of chemical valence. William James observed that "The philosophic brain responds to an inconsistency or gap in its knowledge, just as the musical brain responds to a discord in what it hears" (cited by Berlyne, 1960, p. v).

The common element in creativity in both the arts and sciences is that the creative person is able to see similarities and relationships that are new and unique. As we have suggested, this requires both intelligence and the tendency to bind ideas into cohesive larger assemblies. It is very commonly reported (e.g., Cattell, 1957; Roe, 1961; Carnegie Corp., 1961) that creative persons tend to be strong individualists. In terms of the present discussion it might seem that the individualism which accompanies creativity is simply another aspect of the cohesiveness of ideas—not only do ideas tend to combine, they also resist efforts to reshape them. Hence, the creative person tends to see things as "right" only one way—and acts accordingly.

The almost mystical thrill reported by even a "dispassionate" scientist upon learning or discovering what to him is importantly true would, in terms of the present theory, represent the simultaneous satisfaction of an especially large number of heretofore unsynchronized neurons. Maslow has recently written on this experience (1961).[16] (See also the comment by Sir Charles Snow [Life, April 7, 1961, p. 136].) Bruner has reported that he became "overjoyed" (1957) on learning of a brain mechanism (the reticular formation!) which corresponded to his earlier speculations on a "gating" process in the brain. Kepler's works show he experienced extremes of ecstasy on discovering the links between mathematics and astronomy.

Readers interested in possible neural bases for creativity will be interested in Eccles' (1958), Clark's (1958), and Lehrmann's (1960) discussions. The latter two writers have also related reticular function to the creative process, but in ways quite different from that presented here. Campbell's paper on creative thought as scanning (1960) will also be of interest, particularly in view of our own previously expressed hypothesis of reticular function.

In concluding this chapter in which were suggested some possible implications of early infantile autism for the science of behavior, it is interesting to recall the prediction made by Sarason and Gladwin to the effect that the importance of the cases of early infantile autism "to the development of a science of psychology would seem to be vastly beyond what their relatively rare occurrence in the general population would suggest" (1958, p. 345). Whether or not his own speculations and hypotheses are

---

16 It is interesting that the key thought which led to the present theory occurred to the writer immediately after hearing Maslow speak on the topic of such "peak experiences." The idea that the "flash" might be a result of a sudden insight which fuses or makes compatible several large and heretofore independent concepts, and that nerve cells might yield pleasure as a consequence of such optimum exercise of their function, was conceived as a direct result of the writer's wondering how his developing concept of brain function could account for such semi-mystical experiences as Maslow described. Coincidentally, its conception was accompanied by just such a "flash" or "peak experience."

considered as corroborating Sarason and Gladwin, the writer is convinced of the accuracy of their prediction. Similarly, irrespective of the validity of what has been presented on the foregoing pages, the writer agrees with Gerard (1953), French (1957), and Lindsley (1958) that continued study of the reticular formation will provide major advances in our understanding of the mechanisms which underlie behavior. Whether the present writer is correct in proposing that these two prophecies really converge to one is a question which only time can answer.

RIMLAND'S RETICULAR FORMATION THEORY OF AUTISM IN LIGHT OF 50 YEARS OF BRAIN RESEARCH

Martha R. Herbert

Bernie Rimland's pioneering opus *Infantile Autism* broke ground in linking careful observations of behavioral complexity with informed speculation on possible underlying brain mechanisms. He argued that individuals with autism "had an impairment in the ability to relate the current objects of sensation with what had previously been stored in memory." He suggested that the "resulting behavioral pathology" was divisible into two major components, the conceptual and the perceptual. In Chapter 5 he then hypothesized a relationship between the cognitive dysfunction in autism and the reticular formation of the brainstem, with this part of the brain being "a possible site of the organic impairment which resulted in these cognitive problems" (page 124). One reason for his choice of this area was generic—given what he described as the "remarkable specificity" of features of autism, he felt that it must derive from a specific and localized brain abnormality. Even so, he stated clearly and repeatedly that his theory did not depend on the ultimate validation of the reticular formation as the brain origin of autism.

What attracted Rimland to the "reticular formation" was both its anatomical features and the functions with which it is associated. Anatomically it is a complex "thicket" of interconnected fibers, connecting a huge number of functional regions with each other. It is located in the deep central core of the brain, the brainstem, which houses ancient regulatory centers governing core functions keeping us alive, such as sleep–wake cycles, heartbeat, and breathing. But in addition to regulating these core physiological functions, it was also felt to be what he described as "the 'communications center,' 'central relay station,' or 'master switchboard' of the brain" (page 115).

Rimland was careful to note that his emphasis on the "linkage" functions of the reticular formation was at odds with, or at least different in emphasis from, the more commonly held theory of its function as centered in the regulation of "arousal" and of the "tone of the cortex and other parts of the brain..." (page 115). With reference to autism, Rimland argued that an impairment of the arousal function of the reticular formation could not explain autism, "because autistic children learn very well, at least insofar as purely rote memory is concerned" (page 116).

After extensive review of various biological and behavioral considerations, Rimland returns to his hypothesis concerning reticular function in Chapter 11, and states again that his hypothesis implies that the reticular formation does not simply supply undifferentiated stimulus to higher brain centers— that is, cannot be described purely in terms of conveying diffuse energy—but rather more likely conveys "a certain type of highly specific information" (page 247). He proceeds to anticipate in some detail the domains that neurobiology and cognitive neuroscience have fleshed out in massive detail over subsequent decades – all the more amazing at a time when, as he describes, the very act of considering brain foundations of behavior was condemned by some as "neurologizing," to the point where he had to say that we "must cease regarding the brain as 'just so much porridge' and instead focus attention upon the brain's mechanisms for employing the informational input available to it" (page 183). We have come a long way in 50 years!

Rimland finally returns to a clear and concise summary statement of his reticular formation theory:

> ...our hypothesis is that the reticular formation is the site at which sensory input (and perhaps also imaginal input), represented as highly complex electrical patterns, is integrated and converted into a code which makes it compatible with the retrieval system used in making available a wide range of the content of memory. (page 251; italics in original)

THEN AND NOW

How does Rimland's formulation compare with present formulations of the brain basis of autism spectrum disorders, and with our understanding more broadly of the functions of the reticular formation and of integration of information in the brain?

INTEGRATION AND CONNECTIVITY

First, Rimland was remarkably prescient in focusing on the information integration functions in the brain and their compromise in ASDs. In the first years of the 21st century—40 years after the publication of *Infantile Autism*—a body of work related to brain connectivity and coherence began to emerge, first based upon functional MRI measurements of "brain connectivity" and subsequently also in EEG (electroencephalographic) and MEG (magnetoencephalographic) measures of "brain coherence" (Wass, 2011; Muller et al., 2011; Billeci et al., 2013). These measures indicate the extent of correlation of brain activity between one place and another place, and this can be mapped between many combinations of places across the whole cerebral cortex.

This body of research into widely distributed connectivity differences emerged at a time when most brain researchers were still looking for the specific regions of the brain that might be driving the autism; it was initially resisted but has now become dominant in the field. The dominance of connectivity approaches exists side by side with documentation of abnormalities in size and function that have been measured in many areas of the brain, ranging from cortical regions such as prefrontal cortex and temporal cortex, to subcortical regions such as the amygdala, and even also including white matter (consisting of the nerve fibers with their white myelin sheaths linking neurons across longer distances), which would not have been a candidate for regional dysfunction prior to our understanding that connectivity is compromised, or different, in autism.

Connectivity is now studied structurally (in terms of differences in the size, density, and mapping of fiber tracts), functionally (in terms of electrical brain activity—oscillations or "brain waves"), and with regard to activation (increased activity of various regions either at rest or while the person performs particular tasks). Current network theory suggests that there are differences both in network connections (structural and functional connectivity) and in network hubs (particular regions of the brain with relative specializations in different functions) (e.g., language, emotion processing, sensory processing, motor function, coordination).

RETICULAR FORMATION

Second, a search of the titles and abstracts of the scientific literature indexed in PubMed for "autism and reticular formation" comes up with only 12 articles, of which only one relates to a theory of the relationship between the reticular formation and autism. Does this mean that Rimland's theory was wrong? No—incomplete perhaps, but not wrong. One reason for the minimal follow-up to Rimland's theory is the difficulties in studying the reticular formation, or reticular activating system, in living human beings. With its circuitry being deep in the brain, with this part of the brain pulsating in rhythm with the heartbeat, and with the "tangled thicket" of its circuitry, the reticular formation is hard to study with contemporary brain imaging techniques, although some of the problems are being conquered. It can be studied in post-mortem tissue, but that will not help so much in teasing out the *functional* contribution of this part of the brain. It might be fair to say that Rimland captured the *spirit* of connectivity but was overly specific and localized with regard to the site (or, we would now say, sites) of the brain associated with these types of brain coordination challenges.

Looking at the neuroscience literature about the reticular formation more broadly than in autism alone, there is much on its association with phenomena such as pain, respiratory dysfunction, and sudden infant death syndrome, as well as with consciousness, but not so much pertinent to integration of information at higher levels. Even so, we are appreciating, even with little reference to the reticular formation, that some of the core functions related to the brainstem—such as sleep, emotional and hormonal regulation, and stress management—are significantly disrupted in ASDs.

AROUSAL

Third, the arousal function of the reticular formation that Rimland thought was too diffuse and general brings to mind the growth in studies about the autonomic nervous system and the imbalances in people with ASDs between the sympathetic and parasympathetic nervous systems (fight/flight vs. recovery/regeneration) and the highly prevalent tendency toward a highly stressed state.

EVOLUTION AND COMPLEXITY

Rimland's emphasis on the reticular formation was also prescient regarding the brilliant synthetic neuroanatomical work of the comparative neuroanatomist Frederic Sanides, who traced the evolution of brain functions associated with information integration (Sanides, 1970). Whereas contemporary research on brain connectivity focuses on the cerebral cortex, Sanides turned things on their head, arguing that the functional specificity of cortical mapping was a late evolutionary outcome laid atop of, and differentiated out of, a much more densely interconnected and evolutionary older set of brain areas including not only the reticular formation but also the limbic system. That is, simple organisms were already complex, networked, integrated systems, whereas the ability to cognitively differentiate fine distinctions was late development in the evolution of life on earth. This suggests that the thicket of complex interconnected circuitry in these more ancient parts of the brain may yet turn out to be an important part of the brain basis of autism not only at the brain region level but also at the level of complex information processing, as Rimland posited.

PATHOPHYSIOLOGY

Finally, this consideration of the prescience and brilliance of Rimland's synthesis would not be complete without a consideration of several classes of brain abnormalities that could not have been on Rimland's radar screen when he wrote this book, as well as Rimland's very strong belief that was the core of his program, especially in the last years of his life, namely that "Autism is treatable."

The brain abnormalities that came onto the radar screen well after *Infantile Autism* was published have to do with cellular and physiological problems in the brain such as glial and immune activation, oxidative stress, and mitochondrial dysfunction. Rimland certainly lived long enough to appreciate the importance of these in autism, which could finally be discerned as the science around these phenomena became sufficiently developed. In the latter phase of his life Rimland was greatly involved in the role of healthy vs noxious environmental exposures (e.g., health vs. processed food and safe vs. toxic substances) and even lived to see the emergence of literature linking environmental exposures such as toxicant-laden air pollution to the development of neuroinflammation. These phenomena are known to respond to treatments including nutritional intervention, and this no doubt was an important contributor to Rimland's strong statement that "Autism is treatable."

FRONTIERS REMAINING: NUTRITION, ENVIRONMENT, AND THE BRAIN

Neuroscience to date has almost entirely failed to scratch the surface of the relationships between nutrition, environment, and the brain, though this will probably change soon. The possibility that healthy inputs might support optimum brain coordination—while noxious exposures might interfere with it—is a hypothesis that Rimland would have wanted to test, but to date in the autism research community—and even in brain research more broadly— there are only a few traces of awareness that the health status of the cells in the brain might impact the brain's ability to send and coordinate signals; this limitation probably mainly derives from research on brain coordination being mostly carried on separately from research on brain tissue and pathophysiology problems (Herbert, 2005, 2012, 2014).

Some scientists have suggested that the brainstem might be particularly vulnerable to noxious environmental exposures (McGinnis, Audhya, & Edelson, 2013) due to gaps or windows in the blood–brain barrier there, which that part of the brain utilizes to monitor the status of the blood in order to inform how it regulates the body; these researchers have suggested that autism might on this account arise in the brainstem, but they have not integrated these informed speculations and neuropathological investigations with an appreciation of the information-processing functions that were so central to Rimland's theory. A full account of environmental contributors to autism will need to include not only the nature of the cellular injury but the nature of alterations of brain function, particularly the brain's electrical activity. Conversely, a full account of the efficacy of treatment will need to include not only the reversal of physiological abnormalities but also the recovery of more coordinated and integrated electrophysiological activity of the brain.

Rimland's book and lifework are still a beacon

As we work to understand, honor, and be informed by Rimland's brilliant and multifaceted legacy, we would do well to integrate in scientific research, and in brain research in particular, the many facets Rimland integrated in his brain theory and in his life's work (Herbert, in preparation).

REFERENCES

Billeci, L., Sicca, F., Maharatna, K., Apicella F., et al. (2013). On the application of quantitative EEG for characterizing autistic brain: A systematic review. *Frontiers in Human Neuroscience*, 7, 442.

Herbert, M.R. (2005). Large brains in autism: The challenge of pervasive abnormality. *Neuroscientist*, 11(5), 417–440.

Herbert, M.R. (2012). Why aren't we there yet? Valuable but incomplete measures of brain changes in babies with autism. Available at www.autismwhyandhow.org/why-arent-we-there-yet-valuable-but-incomplete-measures-of-brain-changes-in-babies-with-autism, accessed on September 9, 2014.

Herbert, M.R. (2014). Translational implications of a whole-body approach to brain health in autism: How transduction between metabolism and electrophysiology points to mechanisms for neuroplasticity. In V.W. Hu & N.J. Hackensack (eds) *Frontiers in Autism Research: New Horizons for Diagnosis and Treatment*. Singapore: World Scientific.

Herbert, M.R. (in preparation). *Rimland after 50 Years: Still a Beacon for Effective Understanding of Autism*.

McGinnis, W.R., Audhya, T., & Edelson S.M. (2013). Proposed toxic and hypoxic impairment of a brainstem locus in autism. *International Journal of Environmental Research and Public Health*, 10(12), 6955–7000.

Muller, R.A., Shih, P., Keehn, B., Deyoe, J.R., Leyden, K.M., & Shukla, D.K. (2011). Underconnected, but how? A survey of functional connectivity MRI studies in autism spectrum disorders. *Cerebral Cortex*, 21(10), 2233–2243.

Sanides, F. (1970). Functional architecture of motor and sensory cortices in primates in the light of a new concept of neocortex evolution. In C.R. Noback & W. Montagna (eds) *The Primate Brain: Advances in Primatology*. New York: Meredith Corp. Available at www.marthaherbert.org/wp-content/uploads/2011/10/Sanides1970FunctnlArchitecture MotorSensoryCorticesPrmiateNewConceptNeocortexEvolution.pdf, accessed on October 20, 2014.

Wass, S. (2011). Distortions and disconnections: Disrupted brain connectivity in autism. *Brain and Cognition*, 75(1), 18–28.

Suggested Diagnostic Check List (Experimental Form 2)

The accompanying experimental check list is intended to facilitate accurate differentiation of individual cases of infantile autism from cases of childhood schizophrenia and other conditions which sometimes obscure the diagnosis of autism. As has been emphasized in the relevant chapters, such an instrument is an essential tool in the ultimate development of methods of treating or preventing infantile autism. The form is designed for completion by the child's parents. An age range of about three to five years is assumed. The instructions tell the parent to respond as of age five for an older child.

The present list, Form 2, is a revision of Form 1 which appeared in the first printing of this book. In the year that has passed since publication of the book, enough experience was had with Form 1 to point the way clearly to the improvements which are incorporated into the present form. Appleton-Century-Crofts, publishers of the volume, realizing that the check list has already found essential use, have very generously agreed to incorporate the revision in the second printing of this book.

Form 1 was found to work surprisingly well for an "armchair" instrument. It has been changed by eliminating or rewording a number of non-differentiating items, adding items designed to bolster weak points in the list (some of the new items having been suggested by parents who completed Form 1), and, perhaps most important, clarifying the instructions with regard to responses for children over five years of age. Between ages five and six, autistic children lose many of the traits that characterized them, and begin to adjust to their disability in various highly individual ways. It is believed that making each item age-specific will overcome the problem these changes pose to diagnosis.

Most of the items have been carried over from Form 1 because they were found empirically to differentiate children with infantile autism from children having other, usually undiagnosed, disorders. These items, plus some of the new ones which are found to be discriminating, will form the scoring key. Certain items have been included only because they may shed light on the etiology of autism (e.g., sex of child, use of oxygen in infancy) or because they are of interest for other reasons (e.g., educational level of parents).

The revision of the Check List has been completed too recently to permit evaluation of the tentative scoring key nor the establishment of cutting scores. Publication of the keys and cutting scores must therefore await the collection and analysis of additional data. The author invites correspondence from persons having one or more Check Lists completed for children affected with infantile autism, or whose diagnosis might possibly be autism. The Check List may be reproduced for research or diagnostic purposes without requesting specific permission from the author or publisher. (Researchers should note that the format is designed for direct copying of virtually all responses to a single IBM card, with column 80 left bank for group coding.)

Analysis of Form 1 and the development of Form 2 are being carried out in 1964–65 during the author's residency at the Center for Advanced Study in the Behavioral Sciences. Dr. Isabelle Liberman has contributed greatly to this project. The author wishes to express his appreciation to the Center for providing the necessary professional, clerical, and statistical support.

DIAGNOSTIC CHECK LIST FOR BEHAVIOR-DISTURBED CHILDREN (FORM E-2)

Name of Child:_____ Birth Date: _____

Name of Person Completing this form: _____

Street Address: _____

_____

City: _____

Relationship to Child:

Mother:_____

Father:_____ Other: _____

Father's Occupation: _____

Mother's Occupation (Present): _____

(Before Marriage): _____

Has this child been diagnosed before?

If so, what was diagnosis? _____

Diagnosed by:_____

Where? _____

Instructions: You are being asked to fill out this questionnaire concerning your child in order to provide research information which will be helpful in learning more about the causes and types of behavior disturbances in children. Please pick the one answer you think is most accurate for each question. If you want to comment or add something about a question, add it right next to the question, if there is room. Or circle the number of the question, copy the number on the back of the questionnaire and write your comment there. Your additional comments are welcome, but even if you do add comments, please mark the printed question as well as you can. Remember, pick just one answer, and mark it with an "X," for each question.

It would be helpful if, on a separate sheet, you would write in any information about the child and his sisters or brothers which you think may be significant. (For example: Twins, living or dead; Behavior problems; IQ scores, if known.)

Use an "X" to mark one answer for each question. Do not skip main questions. Sub-questions (not along left margin) may be skipped.[1]

1. Present age of child:

    _____ 1   Under 3 years old

    _____ 2   Between 3 and 4 years old

    _____ 3   Between 4 and 5 years old

    _____ 4   Between 5 and 6 years old

    _____ 5   Over 6 years old (Age: ___ years)

2. Indicate child's sex:

    _____ 1   Boy

    _____ 2   Girl

3. Child's birth order and number of mother's other children:

    _____ 1   Child is an only child

    _____ 2   Child is first born of ___ children

    _____ 3   Child is last born of ___ children

    _____ 4   Child is middle born; ___ children are older and ___ are younger than this child

    _____ 5   Foster child, or don't know

4. Were pregnancy and delivery normal?

    _____ 1   Pregnancy and delivery both normal

    _____ 2   Problems during both pregnancy and delivery

    _____ 3   Pregnancy troubled, routine delivery

    _____ 4   Pregnancy untroubled; problems during delivery

    _____ 5   Don't know

5. Was the birth premature (birth weight under 5 lbs)?

    _____ 1   Yes (about ___ weeks early; ___ lbs)

    _____ 2   No

    _____ 3   Don't know

---

*   Note: This Check List is designed primarily for children three to five years old. If the child is over five, answer as well as you can by recall of the child's behavior.

6. Was the child given oxygen *in the first week?*

_____ 1 Yes

_____ 2 No

_____ 3 Don't know

7. Appearance of child during first few weeks after birth:

_____ 1 Pale, delicate-looking

_____ 2 Unusually healthy-looking

_____ 3 Average, don't know, or other

8. Unusual conditions of birth and infancy (check only one number in left-hand column):

_____ 1 Unusual conditions (Indicate which: blindness ___, cerebral palsy ___, birth injury ___, seizures ___, blue baby ___, very high fever ___, jaundice ___, other _____

_____ 2 Twin birth (identical ___, fraternal ___)

_____ 3 Both 1 and 2

_____ 4 Normal, or don't know

9. Concerning baby's health in first 3 months:

_____ 1 Excellent health, no problems

_____ 2 Respiration (frequent infections ___, other ___

_____ 3 Skin (rashes, infection ___, allergy ___, other ___

_____ 4 Feeding (learning to suck ___, colic ___, vomiting ___, other _____)

_____ 5 Elimination (diarrhea ___, constipation ___, other _____)

_____ 6 Several of above (indicate which: 2 ___, 3 ___, 4 ___, 5 ___, 6 ___)

10. Has the child been given an electroencephalogram (EEG)?

_____ 1 Yes, it was considered normal

_____ 2 Yes, it was considered borderline

_____ 3 Yes, it was considered abnormal

_____ 4 No, or don't know, or don't know results

11. In the first year, did the child react to bright lights, bright colors, unusual sounds, etc.?

_____ 1 Unusually strong reaction (pleasure ___, dislike ___)

_____ 2 Unusually unresponsive

_____ 3 Average, or don't know

12. Did the child behave normally for a time before his abnormal behavior began?

_____ 1 Never was a period of normal behavior

_____ 2 Normal during first 6 months

_____ 3 Normal during first year

_____ 4 Normal during first 1–2 years

_____ 5 Normal during first 2 years

_____ 6 Normal during first 3 years

_____ 7 Normal during first 4–5 years

13. (Age 4–8 months) Did the child reach out or prepare himself to be picked up when mother approached him?

_____ 1 Yes, or I believe so

_____ 2 No, I don't think he did

_____ 3 No, definitely not

_____ 4 Don't know

14. Did the child rock in his crib as a baby?

_____ 1 Yes, quite a lot

_____ 2 Yes, sometimes

_____ 3 No, or very little

_____ 4 Don't know

15. At what age did the child learn to walk alone?

_____ 1 8–12 months

_____ 2 13–15 months

_____ 3 16–18 months

_____ 4 19–24 months

_____ 5 25–36 months

_____ 6 37 months or later, or does not walk alone

16. Which describes the change from crawling to walking?

_____ 1 Normal change from crawling to walking

_____ 2 Little or no crawling, gradual start of walking

_____ 3 Little or no crawling, sudden start of walking

_____ 4 Prolonged crawling, sudden start of walking

_____ 5 Prolonged crawling, gradual start of walking

_____ 6 Other, or don't know

17. During the child's first year, did he seem to be unusually intelligent?

_____ 1 Suspected high intelligence

_____ 2 Suspected average intelligence

_____ 3 Child looked somewhat dull

18. During the child's first 2 years, did he like to be held?

_____ 1 Liked being picked up; enjoyed being held

_____ 2 Limp and passive on being held

_____ 3 You could pick child up and hold it only when and how it preferred

_____ 4 Notably stiff and awkward to hold

_____ 5 Don't know

19. Before age 3, did the child ever imitate another person?

_____ 1 Yes, waved bye-bye

_____ 2 Yes, played pat-a-cake

_____ 3 Yes, other _____

_____ 4 Two or more of above (which? 1 ___, 2 ___, 3 ___)

_____ 5 No, or not sure

20. Before age 3, did the child have an unusually good memory?

_____ 1 Remarkable memory for songs, rhymes, TV commercials, etc., in words

_____ 2 Remarkable memory for songs, music (humming only)

_____ 3 Remarkable memory for names, places, routes, etc.

_____ 4 No evidence for remarkable memory

_____ 5 Apparently rather poor memory

_____ 6 Both 1 and 3

_____ 7 Both 2 and 3

21. Did you ever suspect the child was very nearly deaf?

_____ 1 Yes

_____ 2 No

22. (Age 2–4) Is child "deaf" to some sounds but hears others?

_____ 1 Yes, can be "deaf" to loud sounds, but hear low ones

_____ 2 No, this is not true of him

23. (Age 2–4) Does child hold his hands in strange postures?

_____ 1 Yes, sometimes or often

_____ 2 No

24. (Age 2–4) Does child engage in rhythmic or rocking activity for very long periods of time (like on rocking-horse or chair, jumpchair, swing, etc.)?

_____ 1 Yes, this is typical

_____ 2 Seldom does this

_____ 3 Not true of him

25. (Age 2–4) Does the child ever "look through" or "walk through" people, as though they weren't there?

_____ 1 Yes, often

_____ 2 Yes, I think so

_____ 3 No, doesn't do this

26. (Age 2–5) Does child have any unusual cravings for things to eat or chew on?

_____ 1 Yes, salt or salty foods

_____ 2 Yes, often chews metal objects

_____ 3 Yes, other _____

_____ 4 Yes, more than 2 above (which? _____)

_____ 5 No, or not sure

27. (Age 2–4) Does the child have certain eating oddities such as refusing to drink from a transparent container, eating only hot (or cold) food, eating only one or two foods, etc.?

_____ 1 Yes, definitely

_____ 2 No, or not to any marked degree

_____ 3 Don't know

28. Would you describe your child around age 3 or 4 as often seeming "in a shell," or so distant and "lost in thought" that you couldn't reach him?

_____ 1 Yes, this is a very accurate description

_____ 2 Once in a while he might possibly be like that

_____ 3 Not an accurate description

29. (Age 2–5) Is he cuddly?

  _____ 1 Definitely, likes to cling to adults

  _____ 2 Above average (likes to be held)

  _____ 3 No, rather stiff and awkward to hold

  _____ 4 Don't know

30. (Age 3–5) Does the child deliberately hit his own head?

  _____ 1 Never, or rarely

  _____ 2 Yes, usually by slapping it with his hand

  _____ 3 Yes, usually by banging it against someone else's legs or head

  _____ 4 Yes, usually by hitting walls, floor, furniture, etc.

  _____ 5 Several of above (which? 2 ___, 3 ___, 4 ___)

31. (Age 3–5) How well physically coordinated is the child (running, walking, balancing, climbing)?

  _____ 1 Unusually graceful

  _____ 2 About average

  _____ 3 Somewhat below average, or poor

32. (Age 3–5) Does the child sometimes whirl himself like a top?

  _____ 1 Yes, does this often

  _____ 2 Yes, sometimes

  _____ 3 Yes, if you start him out

  _____ 4 No, he shows no tendency to whirl

33. (Age 3–5) How skillful is the child in doing fine work with his fingers or playing with small objects?

  _____ 1 Exceptionally skillful

  _____ 2 Average for age

  _____ 3 A little awkward, or very awkward

  _____ 4 Don't know

34. (Age 3–5) Does the child like to spin things like jar lids, coins, or coasters?

  _____ 1 Yes, often and for rather long periods

  _____ 2 Very seldom, or never

35. (Age 3–5) Does child show an unusual degree of skill (much better than normal child his age) at any of following:

_____ 1 Assembling jig-saw or similar puzzles

_____ 2 Arithmetic computation

_____ 3 Can tell day of week a certain date will fall on

_____ 4 Perfect musical pitch

_____ 5 Throwing and/or catching a ball

_____ 6 Other (_____)

_____ 7 More than one of the above (which? _____)

_____ 8 No unusual skill, or not sure

36. (Age 3–5) Does the child sometimes jump up and down gleefully when pleased?

_____ 1 Yes, this is typical

_____ 2 No, or rarely

37. (Age 3–5) Does child sometimes line things up in precise, evenly spaced rows and insist they not be disturbed?

_____ 1 No

_____ 2 Yes

_____ 3 Not sure

38. (Age 3–5) Does the child refuse to use his hands for an extended period of time?

_____ 1 Yes

_____ 2 No

39. Was there a time before age 5 when the child strongly insisted on listening to music on records?

_____ 1 Yes, insisted on only certain records

_____ 2 Yes, but almost any record would do

_____ 3 Liked to listen, but didn't demand to

_____ 4 No special interest in records

40. (Age 3–5) How interested is the child in mechanical objects such as the stove or vacuum cleaner?

_____ 1 Little or no interest

_____ 2 Average interest

_____ 3 Fascinated by certain mechanical things

41. (Age 3–5) How does child usually react to being interrupted at what he is doing?

_____ 1   Rarely or never gets upset

_____ 2   Sometimes gets mildly upset; rarely very upset

_____ 3   Typically gets very upset

42. (Age 3–5) Will the child readily accept new articles of clothing (shoes, coats, etc.)?

_____ 1   Usually resists new clothes

_____ 2   Doesn't seem to mind, or enjoys them

43. (Age 3–5) Is child upset by certain things that are not "right" (like crack in wall, spot on rug, books leaning in bookcase, broken rung on chair, pipe held and not smoked)?

_____ 1   Not especially

_____ 2   Yes, such things often upset him greatly

_____ 3   Not sure

44. (Age 3–5) Does child adopt complicated "rituals" which make him very upset if not followed (like putting many dolls to bed in a certain order, taking exactly the same route between two places, dressing according to a precise pattern, or insisting that only certain words be used in a given situation)?

_____ 1   Yes, definitely

_____ 2   Not sure

_____ 3   No

45. (Age 3–5) Does child get very upset if certain things he is used to are changed (like furniture or toy arrangement, or certain doors which must be left open or shut)?

_____ 1   No

_____ 2   Yes, definitely

_____ 3   Slightly true

46. (Age 3–5) Is the child destructive?

_____ 1   Yes, this is definitely a problem

_____ 2   Not deliberately or severely destructive

_____ 3   Not especially destructive

47. (Age 3–5) Is the child unusually physically pliable (can be led easily; melts into your arms)?

_____ 1 Yes

_____ 2 Seems normal in this way

_____ 3 Definitely not pliable

48. (Age 3–5) Which single description, or combination of two descriptions, best characterizes the child?

_____ 1 Hyperactive, constantly moving, changes quickly from one thing to another

_____ 2 Watches television quietly for long periods

_____ 3 Sits for long periods, staring into space or playing repetitively with objects, without apparent purpose

_____ 4 Combination of 1 and 2

_____ 5 Combination of 2 and 3

_____ 6 Combination of 1 and 3

49. (Age 3–5) Does the child seem to want to be liked?

_____ 1 Yes, unusually so

_____ 2 Just normally so

_____ 3 Indifferent to being liked; happiest when left alone

50. (Age 3–5) Is child sensitive and/or affectionate?

_____ 1 Is sensitive to criticism and affectionate

_____ 2 Is sensitive to criticism, not affectionate

_____ 3 Not sensitive to criticism, is affectionate

_____ 4 Not sensitive to criticism nor affectionate

51. (Age 3–5) Is it possible to direct child's attention to an object some distance away or out a window?

_____ 1 Yes, no special problem

_____ 2 He rarely sees things very far out of reach

_____ 3 He examines things with fingers and mouth only

52. (Age 3–5) Do people consider the child especially attractive?

_____ 1 Yes, very good-looking child

_____ 2 No, just average

_____ 3 Faulty in physical appearance

53. (Age 3–5) Does the child look up at people (meet their eyes) when they are talking to him?

_____ 1 Never, or rarely

_____ 2 Only with parents

_____ 3 Usually does

54. (Age 3–5) Does the child take an adult by the wrist to use adult's hand (to open door, get cookies, turn on TV, etc.)?

_____ 1 Yes, this is typical

_____ 2 Perhaps, or rarely

_____ 3 No

55. (Age 3–5) Which set of terms best describes the child?

_____ 1 Confused, self-concerned, perplexed, dependent, worried

_____ 2 Aloof, indifferent, self-contented, remote

56. (Age 3 and 5) Is the child extremely fearful?

_____ 1 Yes, of strangers or certain people

_____ 2 Yes, of certain animals, noises, or objects

_____ 3 Yes, of 1 and 2 above

_____ 4 Only normal fearfulness

_____ 5 Seems unusually bold and free of fear

_____ 6 Child ignores or is unaware of fearsome objects

57. (Age 3–5) Does he fall or get hurt in running or climbing?

_____ 1 Tends toward falling or injury

_____ 2 Average in this way

_____ 3 Never, or almost never, exposes self to falling

_____ 4 Surprisingly safe despite active climbing, swimming, etc.

58. (Age 3–5) Is there a problem in that the child hits, pinches, bites, or otherwise injures himself or others?

_____ 1 Yes, self only

_____ 2 Yes, others only

_____ 3 Yes, self and others

_____ 4 No (not a problem)

59. At what age did the child say his first words (even if later stopped talking)?

_____ 1 Has never used words

_____ 2 8–12 months

_____ 3 13–15 months

_____ 4 16–24 months

_____ 5 2 years–3 years

_____ 6 3 years–4 years

_____ 7 After 4 years old

_____ 8 Don't know

59a. On lines below list child's first six words (as well as you can remember them):

_____　　_____

_____　　_____

_____　　_____

60. (Before age 5) Did the child start to talk, then become silent again for a week or more?

_____ 1 Yes, but later talked again (age stopped ___, duration _____)

_____ 2 Yes, but never started again (age stopped ___)

_____ 3 No, continued to talk, or never began talking

61. (Before age 5) Did the child start to talk, then stop, and begin to whisper instead, for a week or more?

_____ 1 Yes, but later talked again (age stopped ___, duration _____)

_____ 2 Yes, still only whispers (age stopped talking ___)

_____ 3 Now doesn't even whisper (stopped talk ___; stopped whisp. ___)

_____ 4 No, continued to talk, or never began talking

62. (Age 1–5) How well could the child *pronounce* his first words when learning. to speak, and how well could he pronounce difficult words between 3 and 5?

_____ 1 Too little speech to tell, or other answer

_____ 2 Average or below average pronunciation of first words ("wabbit," etc.), and also poor at 3–5

_____ 3 Average or below on first words, unusually good at 3–5

_____ 4 Unusually good on first words, average or below at 3–5

_____ 5 Unusually good on first words, and also at 3–5

63. (Age 3–5) Is the child's vocabulary (the number of things he can name or point to accurately) greatly out of proportion to his ability to "communicate" (to answer questions or tell you something)?

_____ 1 He can point to many objects I name, but doesn't speak or "communicate"

_____ 2 He can correctly name many objects, but not "communicate"

_____ 3 Ability to "communicate" is pretty good—about what you would expect from the number of words he knows

_____ 4 Doesn't use or understand words

64. When the child spoke his first sentences, did he surprise you by using words he had not used individually before?

_____ 1 Yes (Any examples? _____)

_____ 2 No

_____ 3 Not sure

_____ 4 Too little speech to tell

65. How did child refer to himself on first learning to talk?

_____ 1 "(*John*) fall down," or "*Baby (or Boy)* fall down"

_____ 2 "*Me* fall down," or "*I* fall down"

_____ 3 "(*He, Him, She, or Her*) fall down"

_____ 4 "*You* fall down"

_____ 5 Any combination of 1, 2, and/or 3

_____ 6 Combination of 1 and 4

_____ 7 No speech or too little speech as yet

66. (Age 3–5) Does child repeat phrases or sentences that he has heard in the past (maybe using a hollow, parrot-like voice), what is said having little or no relation to the situation?

_____ 1 Yes, definitely, except voice not hollow or parrot-like

_____ 2 Yes, definitely, including peculiar voice tone

_____ 3 Not sure

_____ 4 No

_____ 5 Too little speech to tell

67. (Before age 5) Can the child answer a simple question like "What is *your* first name?" "Why did *Mommy* spank Billy?"

　　_____ 1　Yes, can answer such questions adequately

　　_____ 2　No, uses speech, but can't answer questions

　　_____ 3　Too little speech to tell

68. (Before age 5) Can the child understand what you say to him, judging from his ability to follow instructions or answer you?

　　_____ 1　Yes, understands very well

　　_____ 2　Yes, understands fairly well

　　_____ 3　Understands a little, if you repeat and repeat

　　_____ 4　Very little or no understanding

69. (Before age 5) If the child talks, do you feel he understands what he is saying?

　　_____ 1　Doesn't talk enough to tell

　　_____ 2　No, he is just repeating what he has heard with hardly any understanding

　　_____ 3　Not just repeating—he understands what he is saying, but not well

　　_____ 4　No doubt that he understands what he is saying

70. (Before age 5) Has the child used the word "Yes"?

　　_____ 1　Has used "Yes" fairly often and correctly

　　_____ 2　Seldom has used "Yes," but has used it

　　_____ 3　Has used sentences, but hasn't used word "Yes"

　　_____ 4　Has used a number of other words or phrases, but hasn't used word "Yes"

　　_____ 5　Has no speech, or too little speech to tell

71. (Age 3–5) Does the child typically say "Yes" by repeating the same question he has been asked? (Example: You ask "Shall we go for a walk, Honey?" and he indicates he does want to by saying "Shall we go for a walk, Honey?" or "Shall we go for a walk?")

　　_____ 1　Yes, definitely, does not say "Yes" directly

　　_____ 2　No, would say "Yes" or "OK" or similar answer

　　_____ 3　Not sure

　　_____ 4　Too little speech to say

72. (Before age 5) Has the child asked for something by using the same sentence you would use when you offer it to him? (Example: The child wants milk, so he says: "Do you want some milk?" or "You want some milk")

    _____ 1 Yes, definitely (uses "You" instead of "I")

    _____ 2 No, would ask differently

    _____ 3 Not sure

    _____ 4 Not enough speech to tell

73. (Before age 5) Has the child used the word "I"?

    _____ 1 Has used "I" fairly often and correctly

    _____ 2 Seldom has used "I," but has used it correctly

    _____ 3 Has used sentences, but hasn't used the word "I"

    _____ 4 Has used a number of words or phrases, but hasn't used the word "I"

    _____ 5 Has used "I," but only where word "you" belonged

    _____ 6 Has no speech, or too little speech to tell

74. (Before age 5) How does the child usually say "No" or refuse something?

    _____ 1 He would just say "No"

    _____ 2 He would ignore you

    _____ 3 He would grunt and wave his arms

    _____ 4 He would use some rigid meaningful phrase (like "Don't want it!" or "No milk!", "No walk!")

    _____ 5 Would use phrase having only private meaning like "Daddy go in car"

    _____ 6 Other, or too little speech to tell

75. (Before age 5) Has the child used one word or idea as a substitute for another, for a prolonged time? (Example: always says "catsup" to mean "red," or uses "penny" for "drawer" after seeing pennies in a desk drawer)

    _____ 1 Yes, definitely

    _____ 2 No

    _____ 3 Not sure

    _____ 4 Too little speech to tell

76. Knowing what you do now, at what age do you think you could have first detected the child's abnormal behavior? That is, when did detectable abnormal behavior actually begin? (Under "A," indicate when you *might* have; under "B" when you *did*)

A   B

_____ 1 In first 3 months   _____

_____ 2 4–6 months   _____

_____ 3 7–12 months   _____

_____ 4 13–24 months   _____

_____ 5 2 years–3 years   _____

_____ 6 3 years–4 years   _____

_____ 7 After 4th year   _____

Parents' highest educational level (77 for father, 78 for mother)

77.   78.

		1	Did not graduate high school
		2	High school graduate
		3	Post high school tech. training
		4	Some college
		5	College graduate
		6	Some graduate work
		7	Graduate degree (_____)

79. Indicate the child's nearest blood relatives, including parents, who have been in a mental hospital or who were known to have been seriously mentally ill or retarded. Consider *parents, siblings, grandparents, uncles,* and *aunts.*
If none, check here ☐

Relationship   *Diagnosis (if known)*

_____ 1 _____   Schizophrenia __ Depressive __ Other __

_____ 2 _____   Schizophrenia __ Depressive __ Other __

_____ 3 _____   Schizophrenia __ Depressive __ Other __

_____ 4 _____   Schizophrenia __ Depressive __ Other __

_____ 5 _____   Schizophrenia __ Depressive __ Other __

80. Go back and star(*) the 10 answers that best describe the child. Note request for special information at bottom of cover sheet.

THE INVISIBLE WALL

Stephen M. Edelson

The film documentary titled *The Invisible Wall* was released in 1968. After receiving much international attention for his book, *Infantile Autism*, Rimland felt that he had to continue his mission to change the mindset in which parents were blamed for causing their children's autism. In the film, the viewer listens to parents telling their personal stories and sees photographs and film footage of the children.

The documentary film is more than 26 minutes in length, and is available online at www.AutismTheInvisibleWall.com. Although the black-and-white film appears dated, with the women wearing Sixties hairstyles and one parent commenting that an expensive, "posh" hamburger costs 40 cents, it still provides an accurate description of autism and what parents often face while raising a child on the spectrum. Note: If you are familiar with Rimland's iconic bearded image, you will be treated to the sight of a clean-shaven, mid-30s Rimland in the film.

The documentary was partially financed by a training grant from the National Institutes of Mental Health, and Rimland invited several families to participate in the filming. In addition, he invited two of his colleagues, Drs. Polv W. Toussieng and Richard Sternlof from the University of Oklahoma Medical Center, to interview him about his theories and thoughts on autism.

Much of the film focuses on the symptoms of autism as well as the parents' amusing personal stories, such as tales of their children making handprints on the ceiling and noticing that the title page of a book chapter does not include page numbers. Rimland's interview, which was interpersed throughout the film, touched on many different topics. He discussed the evidence clearly pointing to an organic rather than a psychological cause of autism. In addition, he mentioned his theory regarding the core attribute of autism. He stated: "I regard autism as being, to an extreme degree, the inability to relate incoming sensation to the existing content of the child's mind, to his existing memories." As mentioned in my update to his Chapter 5, Rimland's theory is consistent with the findings that episodic or autographical memory (memory for personal information unique to the individual) is impaired in many individuals on the autism spectrum.

Rimland also discussed the importance of subtyping autism. He stated:

I, myself, am working on an objective diagnostic checklist approach to this problem. This checklist is capable of picking out cases of infantile autism, and we're doing factor analytical studies on this checklist now so as to section the whole area off into smaller, more manageable groups. Once these smaller groups are identified and children who cluster together in terms of their symptomatology are identifed, then electroencephalographic, biochemical, chromosomal, and other work can proceed toward the goal of finding the drugs or the diets which will, in my opinion, be the ultimate answer to severe behavior disorders.

Beginning in the mid-1960s, Rimland distributed his Diagnostic Check List Form E-2 to parents and professionals. (This form is included in Appendix I.) For many years, he had planned to analyze the data to see if there were subtypes; however, he could never find the time because of his hectic schedule. In the early 1990s, he assigned me to analyze the E-2 data. I was midway through the analyses when he redirected the Institute's efforts, including mine, to focus on understanding and treating medical and biomedical problems often associated with autism.

A few years ago, a graduate student in computer science, Curtis Jensen, approached me and asked if he could analyze ARI's huge E-2 database, now with more than 40,000 cases worldwide. After applying several high-powered statistical tools, he found approximately 10 to 12 subtypes. In November of 2013, ARI began an online survey to obtain additional cases to determine if the subtype findings can be replicated. We hope to have initial results in 2015.

One more comment regarding Rimland's quote from above: He mentioned "drugs or diet" as a viable treatment. Over the years, Rimland became very suspicious of drugs, since most drugs prescribed for autism had terrible side effects and did not treat the core problems. In addition, Rimland became more and more convinced over the years that restricted diets were very important as an effective treatment for autism.

Rimland also suggested that the underlying cause of autism would likely involve an interaction between genetics and the environment. At that time, he hypothesized that the parents' "extreme ability to concentrate" (genetics) combined with exposure to excessive oxygen soon after birth (environment) might be the cause for many cases of autism. However, we have learned quite a bit since the premier of The Invisible Wall. Although Rimland was correct in suggesting a genetic–environmental interaction (i.e., epigenetics), much has changed. Martha Herbert writes about epigenetics in Appendix III.

One parent who was interviewed throughout the film was Ruth Sullivan, Ph.D. Together, Rimland and Sullivan formed the Autism Society of America (formerly the National Society for Autistic Children). In the documentary, Sullivan describes her son in great detail, and also comments on the parent-blaming position taken by the majority of mental health professionals at that time. One of her quotes, which I remember very clearly from when I first saw the film as a sophomore at UCLA, is:

> Joseph [her son] is in the middle of a large, articulate, normal, outgoing family. I know that I didn't treat him so badly that he is going to be maimed for the rest of his life.

The Invisible Wall was widely distributed to universities and colleges and was often shown in psychology courses. It greatly advanced two of Rimland's goals: to inform the public about autism, and to encourage academic researchers to consider studying this elusive disorder.

ENVIRONMENTAL VULNERABILITY AND EVERYDAY EPIGENETICS

Empowering Treatment and Recovery

Martha R. Herbert

In Chapter 3 of *Infantile Autism,* Rimland disagreed with the way that Kanner and Eisenberg framed the idea of the interpenetration of heredity and environment. Here is what he said:

> That heredity and environment are "interpenetrating" cannot be denied. But the conclusion that their interpenetration precludes analysis does not follow. Complex problems require that we *increase,* not decrease, our analytic efforts... (page 64)

Subsequent to this assertion, to Rimland's careful review in *Infantile Autism* of many possible scenarios from case reports where environmental factors might have contributed to autism, and to his statement in the film *The Invisible Wall* that autism may be a function of the environmental, we entered the "age of the gene" where genetics almost entirely eclipsed environment.

Now, like a phoenix, environmental considerations have arisen again. This is in part because of evidence that various environmental factors may contribute to autism, partly because it is becoming harder to deny that at least some portion of increasing numbers of people with autism represent true increases, and partly because several large studies have now suggested that the contribution of genetics may be as low as or even lower than 50 percent, with the contribution of environment to autism being much higher than previously thought.

The rise of epigenetics also plays an important role. Epigenetics refers to "gene expression"—the mechanism by which genes may be turned on—expressed, or turned off—not expressed. This, alongside of other means by which gene expression and splicing and protein function may be regulated, have changed the playing field. The "central dogma" that there was a one-way path of influence going from DNA to RNA to proteins no longer holds, because we now know about numerous ways in which the direction of influence can go in the reverse direction. That is, environment and physiology can influence what goes on in the organism, and they can also influence gene expression.

Moreover, the idea that DNA's only role was to code for proteins, and that the large swaths of DNA that did not do that were therefore "junk DNA," is also out the window, as we now recognize that non-coding DNA can regulate genes and can also influence diseases sometimes even more than protein-coding genes.

Although pharmaceutical companies are focusing on targeting epigenetic mechanisms with drugs, it is well known that everyday lifestyle choices have big impacts on epigenetics. While epigenetic pharmaceuticals will hit single targets hard and risk side effects that it may take years to detect, safe "everyday epigenetics" (Herbert, 2013)—changes in diet, exercise, sleep and stress reduction, as well as reduction of noxious exposures— are available to everyone and could improve the health level of the entire population, including people with autism.

One particularly important way to influence epigenetics is through nutrition. Even in *Infantile Autism* 50 years ago Rimland made references to the possible impact of some vitamins and minerals on the functioning of people with ASDs. As time went on he became intensively interested in this topic, but for a long time it was hard to get scientific support. Clinical trials yielded equivocal or negative results. There were strong attacks on the idea of orthomolecular medicine, pioneered by the two-time Nobel Prize winner chemist Linus Pauling (Pauling, 1968), that nutrients can compensate for genetic variants that may increase a person's need for vitamins and minerals that are critical cofactors for enzymes/catalysts for which genes can code (Ames, Elson-Schwab, & Silver, 2002). In spite of the attacks, orthomolecular medicine built up a considerable body of clinical experience and literature supporting their idea that although such gene variants may create vulnerabilities to physical and mental illness, appropriately chosen nutrients could compensate for these vulnerabilities. But in the face of heavy pressure to focus on pharmaceuticals and behavioral therapy and the promises made for gene-based solutions, these approaches were marginalized.

Advances in genomics contributed to the emergence of nutrigenomics, the study and measurement of individual differences in genetically based nutritional needs (Zeisel, 2007). This helped give a scientific rationale for a more individualized approach to nutrition. Each person has a unique set of genes, and genes can be altered in many ways, introducing great variability between individuals regarding how much nutrients they need. Even though we still have not arrived at a thoroughly precise way of predicting nutrient needs based upon laboratory tests, the rapid advances in testing technologies are allowing some clinically useful approximations and raising hopes that more precision may be on the way.

Epigenetics may also be negatively influenced by the environment (Kim et al., 2012), with toxicants and other environmental stressors changing gene expression, as well as interfering with metabolism, leading to increased nutritional needs that normal dietary sources might not meet, and creating damage to our genes (Su et al., 2011).

In *Infantile Autism* Rimland made mention of a number of inborn errors of metabolism that seemed to be associated with autism. Since then, awareness of how toxicants and other exposures exert their destructive impacts has led some clinicians and investigators to describe a "secondary metabolic dysfunction," arising not from primary inherited genetic alterations, but downstream of the injuries to physiology caused by environmental exposures and stressors. The parts of our physiology that can be hurt in this way, and there are many, can be called "environmentally vulnerable physiology" (Herbert, 2010).

Identification and treatment of secondary metabolic dysfunction have not yet become fully mainstreamed, in part because so many people in the population suffer from these kinds of problems that they are not confined to rare cases at the extremes of the population bell curve, but rather can be identified in millions or even billions of people with chronic illnesses such as diabetes, obesity, heart disease, hormonal dysfunction, and cancer. If our laboratory references are determined by statistical calculations that consider the "typical" to be "normal"—and lose sight of what is optimal—we will miss huge amounts of subclinical ill health.

Over the past ten years research has increasingly supported clinical observations that gene variants in pathways associated with methylation and transsulfuration are present in many people with ASDs. Methylation in particular is one of the main mechanisms associated with epigenetic alteration of gene expression. It also plays vital roles in many other biological processes that influence how well or how poorly we function. As it turns out, various toxicants and heavy metals can interfere with these metabolic pathways, and various nutrients, including B-vitamins and a number of minerals, can help these pathways' resiliency in the face of exposures and other stressors.

Published studies have now shown that mothers with metabolic and inflammatory problems that can be influenced by these pathways and by noxious environmental exposures have a higher risk of giving birth to a child with autism. One study showed that this risk could be increased in the setting of mutations in the methylation and transsulfuration pathways, and could be reduced even in the setting of these mutations by taking prenatal vitamins containing folate. This supports concern for our future generations—and also gives us things we can do to lower these risks.

Epigenetics and nutrigenomics are providing support for social movements seeking to improve the quality of the food that is grown and the food that people eat. These growing scientific domains support the idea that in a toxic world nutrients can provide some protection, shoring up the body's protective and detoxification mechanisms (Aggarwal & Shishodia, 2006; Aggarwal et al., 2009). But it is important to remember that from a practical point of view, while we know that epigenetics is impacted by such approaches, actual clinical decisions are still guided more by biochemistry, since metabolic pathways have been mapped out in far greater detail than epigenetic changes.

Rimland's advocacy of the idea that "Autism is treatable" can be traced back at least as far as *Infantile Autism* where he described cases of people with autism who achieved high levels of function, as well as treatments that markedly improved symptoms. As reports of recoveries from autism began to circulate more widely, the "Autism is treatable" theme became a centerpiece of his approach, with metabolic and nutritional approaches being central to what he and his colleagues taught and advocated.

Yet although the number of papers documenting potentially treatable physiological mechanisms implicated in autism is now in the thousands, there are still hardly any studies presenting rigorous prospective documentation of the metabolic, immune, brain—and epigenetic, gene expression—changes that would most likely be associated with this improvement and recovery process. Research based on clinical trials can demonstrate that individual components of this overall approach may create significant changes, but they are unlikely to lead to the more dramatic transformations that led Rimland to say not only that "Autism is treatable" but also that "Recovery is possible." A number of clinicians practicing these approaches report close to no autism in over 1500 children born into their practices, defying statistical odds when the population prevalence is 1 in 68 (Mumper, 2013). But appropriately scaled, carefully designed prospective studies of these approaches, including rigorous documentation of their outcomes, have not yet been implemented and published. This approach can be attacked because optimizing health at multiple levels does not let you sort out "which one" of the interventions is responsible. But from a multi-targeting point of view, the interventions are aimed at addressing interconnected pathways in a synergistic fashion, with the whole being far greater than the sum of its parts. Making progress in this issue will require a firm elucidation and defense of multi-targeting methodologies (Hopkins, 2008; Russo et al., 2013; Sucher, 2006).

Rimland's vision of transforming autism may be fulfilled by social movements of people maximizing the pro-health aspects of the nutrition and environment of their families—that is, engaging in "everyday epigenetics" —and may be supported by rigorous prospective data documenting how people get better from autism (and from other chronic conditions). This data may allow us to "reverse-engineer" autism (Herbert & Weintraub, 2012), guided by data from measurement technologies more sophisticated than ever before in history. Once it is clearly established that these transformations are possible, public policy and medical standards of care may be impacted more than they have been to date.

Much more can be said to honor and contextualize Rimland's brilliant contributions, and I am preparing such a more detailed discussion (Herbert, in preparation).

REFERENCES

Aggarwal, B.B., & Shishodia, S. (2006). Molecular targets of dietary agents for prevention and therapy of cancer. *Biochemical Pharmacology*, 71(10), 1397–1421.

Aggarwal, B.B., Van Kuiken, M.E., Iyer L.H., Harikumar, K.B., & Sung, B. (2009). Molecular targets of nutraceuticals derived from dietary spices: Potential role in suppression of inflammation and tumorigenesis. *Experimental Biology and Medicine (Maywood)*, 234(8), 825–849.

Ames, B.N., Elson-Schwab, I., & Silver, E.A. (2002). High-dose vitamin therapy stimulates variant enzymes with decreased coenzyme binding affinity (increased K(m)): Relevance to genetic disease and polymorphisms. *American Journal of Clinical Nutrition*, 75(4), 616–658.

Herbert, M.R. (2010). Contributions of the environment and environmentally vulnerable physiology to autism spectrum disorders. *Current Opinion in Neurology*, 23(2), 103–110.

Herbert, M.R. (2013). Everyday epigenetics: From molecular intervention to public health and lifestyle medicine. *North American Journal of Medicine and Science*, 6(3), 167–170.

Herbert, M.R. (in preparation). *Rimland after 50 Years: Still a Beacon for Effective Understanding of Autism*.

Herbert, M.R., & Weintraub, K. (2012). *The Autism Revolution: Whole-Body Strategies for Making Life All It Can Be*. New York: Random House with Harvard Health Publications.

Hopkins, A.L. (2008). Network pharmacology: the next paradigm in drug discovery. *Nature Chemical Biology*, 4(11), 682–690.

Kim, M., Bae, M., Na, H., & Yang, M. (2012). Environmental toxicants—induced epigenetic alterations and their reversers. *Journal of Environmental Science and Health Part C, Environmental Carcinogenesis & Ecotoxicology Reviews*, 30(4), 323–367.

Mumper, E. (2013). Can awareness of medical pathophysiology in autism lead to primary care prevention strategies? *North American Journal of Medicine and Science*, 6(3), 134–144.

Pauling, L. (1968). Orthomolecular psychiatry: Varying the concentrations of substances normally present in the human body may control mental disease. *Science*, 160(3825), 265–271.

Russo, P., Frustaci, A., Del Bufalo, A., Fini, M., & Cesario, A. (2013). Multitarget drugs of plants origin acting on Alzheimer's disease. *Current Medicinal Chemistry*, 20(13), 1686–1693.

Su, L.J., Mahabir, S., Ellison, G.L., McGuinn, L.A., & Reid, B.C. (2011). Epigenetic contributions to the relationship between cancer and dietary intake of nutrients, bioactive food components, and environmental toxicants. *Frontiers in Genetics*, 2, 91.

Sucher, N.J, (2006). Insights from molecular investigations of traditional Chinese herbal stroke medicines: Implications for neuroprotective epilepsy therapy. *Epilepsy & Behavior,* 8(2), 350–362.

Zeisel, S.H. (2007). Nutrigenomics and metabolomics will change clinical nutrition and public health practice: Insights from studies on dietary requirements for choline. *American Journal of Clinical Nutrition*, 86(3), 542–548.

MARK RIMLAND
An Inspiration to Us All
Stephen M. Edelson

The year 2014 marks the 50th anniversary of Dr. Bernard Rimland's book, *Infantile Autism: The Syndrome and Its Implications for a Neural Theory of Behavior.* With the publication of this revolutionary book, Dr. Rimland single-handedly transformed the field of autism research and treatment.

Soon after he realized that his son, Mark, had autism, Dr. Rimland began scouring the research literature to figure out how best to help him. Dr. Rimland reviewed the literature in great detail, and he soon realized that the entire professional community supported a psychodynamic cause of autism, without any scientific evidence. In his book, Dr. Rimland convincingly demonstrated that the published evidence was consistent with an organic, physiological cause.

When I travel around the country to attend conferences and meetings, many parents and professionals ask me about Dr. Rimland's son, Mark. How old is he? What does he do? Where does he live?—and so on. I feel fortunate to know Mark very well. I met him when I was 19 years of age, and he was 21. Over the years, we have developed a very close friendship. We usually go out for breakfast on Sunday mornings, and we try to get together at least one or two more times during the week.

Mark is now 58 years old, and lives with his mother and brother in Kensington, a small district in San Diego. Similar to his father, Mark loves to converse with people, has a great sense of humor, and has many friends in the neighborhood. People in the community often comment that Mark is the unofficial "Mayor of Kensington."

One of Mark's closest friends is Gregory Page, a popular singer-songwriter in San Diego who also has a strong following in countries including Australia and Holland. Internationally acclaimed singer and songwriter Jason Mraz and Jim Croce's son, A.J., have produced many of Gregory's albums. Gregory has used Mark's artwork on two of his album covers, and wrote the cover track about Mark for one of his albums titled "All Make Believe."

Mark does not drive a car, but he can take the city bus. He often strolls around his neighborhood to greet people and to get a little sunshine. He likes to visit a local coffee shop in the evenings and spends time visiting with friends and drinking herbal tea.

Mark has a calendar memory, and he sometimes entertains people by telling them what day of the week they were born when given their birth date. He also has an incredible memory for events in his life, often describing minute details and the exact date. He loves listening to music, including songs by the Beatles and the Doors, and enjoys reading books.

Mark is an established artist, and his works sell for hundreds or sometimes even thousands of dollars. He started painting at the age of 21. Mark even remembers the date when he started painting—September 15, 1977—since this was a memorable moment in his life.

In 1998, Mark teamed up with his sister, Helen Landalf—who is a professional writer and editor and has published several fiction books for teenagers—to create a very special book titled *The Secret Night World of Cats*. Mark painted the images, mostly of cats, and Helen wrote the story. The Autism Research Institute sells copies of the book as well as many of Mark's images as prints and note cards. Visit www.MarkRimland.com to view/print an order form and to watch a video of Mark describing many of his paintings for the book.

During the week, Mark attends the St. Madeleine Sophie Center, a training center for adults with developmental disabilities. The center is located in El Cajon, California, about 15 miles east of San Diego. In 1977, Dr. Rimland and his wife were among the founding families of the center. The center began with 22 students and now serves more than 400 adults with developmental disabilities. Mark often comments that he probably has the best eye contact at the center.

St. Madeleine Sophie Center also runs an off-site art gallery for adults with developmental disabilities. Mark spends three to four days a week working on various art projects including mosaics, watercolors, acrylic paintings, and much more. The gallery, named Sophie's Gallery, uses one of Mark's images as their logo. The public is welcome to visit the gallery to purchase many of the students' artworks and crafts (109 Rea Ave., El Cajon).

Besides working at Sophie's Gallery on weekdays, Mark is the resident artist of Kensington Gallery. Kensington Gallery is associated with ARI, and a portion of the sales are earmarked for autism research. The gallery is located next to ARI, and shows include artists with and without disabilities. Mark usually spends a few hours on Saturday afternoons at the gallery, where he enjoys visiting with people as well as painting. To learn more about the gallery, visit www.KensingtonGallery.org.

Dr. Rimland often attributed Mark's good nature and general happiness to three factors: supplementation with vitamin B_6 along with other vitamins and minerals; behavior modification techniques; and a supportive community.

Mark was an inspiration to his father, who dedicated nearly 50 years of his life to autism research. And today he is an inspiration to us all: his family, the ARI staff, his teachers and peers at St. Madeleine Sophie Center, the people of Kensington, and the autism family worldwide.

MY BROTHER, MARK RIMLAND

Helen Landalf

A handsome middle-aged man with graying temples strolls the sidewalks of Kensington, a newly upscale neighborhood of San Diego. He stops by the outdoor tables at Starbucks to greet friends, then heads to his favorite hangout, the Kensington Coffee Company, for an iced cappuccino. After a quick glance at one wall of the café (graced by some of his own wonderfully colorful paintings), he settles down at a window table to read the newspaper.

If you were to sit down with this man, you might at first think that he's just a regular guy enjoying his afternoon coffee. But if you stayed, you'd realize he doesn't quite understand the give and take of a real conversation. He talks a little too loudly about things, and too much about people you don't know. He tells you all about himself, but he doesn't seem that interested in you.

That's because he has autism.

Almost everyone in Kensington knows this man. They might know him as Mark Rimland, the late Dr. Bernard Rimland's son. They might know him as the partially recovered autistic man who was one of Dustin Hoffman's models for his role in the film *Rain Man*. Or perhaps they know him as the talented artist whose work has appeared in galleries and books, and even on CD covers.

To me, he's just Mark, my big brother.

When I was born, Mark was already two years old. Infant that I was, it was impossible for me to appreciate how challenging it was for my parents to deal with an autistic toddler and a newborn baby at the same time. I don't remember much about our early days, but some stories have become family legend: the way Mark would scream when our mother changed her dress; his fascination with the vacuum cleaner, and a complete lack of interest in people; the fact that one physician who examined him told my parents they should put my brother in an institution and forget they ever had him.

I was too young when these things happened to remember them, but as I got older, I became aware that Mark was somehow different. Several mornings a week, he threw screaming fits because he hadn't had time to dress his dolls, which had to be meticulously taken care of in a particular order each day. He had inappropriate fits of giggling at the dinner table and often had to be sent into another room. But even more fascinating to me was Mark's uncanny ability to remember the exact date and time that something happened. If you asked him, "When did we get our cat, Mark?" he'd answer, "At 10:35 on June 21st, 1961. It was a Thursday." And he might even add, "It was cloudy."

The birth of my younger brother, Paul, made Mark's deviations from normal even clearer to me. Although Paul was quite a few years younger than I was, we were able to interact and play with each other in a way Mark and I never could.

When I started school, I was aware that Mark was receiving an education too. I remember coming into the house one afternoon to see Mark working with a tutor who was teaching him to read by giving him M&Ms as a reward. With the self-interest of a seven-year-old, I was struck by the unfairness of the situation: I was learning to read at school; why weren't my teachers giving me M&Ms?

During our teenaged years, my awareness of Mark's differences increased. While I was involved with music, drama, and dance and had an active social life, my older brother spent much of his time when he wasn't in school sitting in a rocking chair, rocking back and forth while he listened to the same phonograph records over and over.

I was aware that other people noticed Mark's differences, too. On Friday nights, Mark liked to play pool at the neighborhood church Youth Hall. Apparently the other teenagers teased Mark, because he came home one night and asked me, "Am I retarded?" I didn't know what to say. I knew my brother was autistic, not retarded, but wasn't he really asking, "Am I normal?" There was no good response to that.

At 16, I got my driver's license. This was a real turning point for me, of course, but it was for Mark, as well. I remember him asking, "How come Helen is younger than me, and she can drive and I can't?" His question haunted me and injected a dash of guilt into my newfound freedom.

There were definitely times when I felt guilty for being able to live a normal life when my brother could not, through no fault of his own. I'm sure there were times I was jealous because Mark needed more of our parents' attention, and I probably felt guilty about that, too. But mostly I felt protective of my older brother who functioned more like a younger sibling, even though he was two years older.

Although Mark's childhood was difficult, in a way he was extremely lucky. He had the advantage of having a father who was at the forefront of autism research, so he was always the first beneficiary of my father's discoveries. I grew up watching him swallow a multitude of pills each day, little knowing that he was participating in my father's now-famous studies on the effect of mega-doses of vitamins on autistic children.

My father's scientific research was beyond me; what I did understand were his attempts to encourage Mark to look and act as normal as possible.

Like many autistic children, Mark had an unusual posture and gait. My father encouraged him to stand up straight and, when introduced to someone, to offer a firm handshake. To this day, Mark has better posture than most people I know.

It was more difficult getting Mark to stop giggling at inappropriate times. Many family meals were interrupted by my father shouting, "Stop giggling!" It frightened me to hear Daddy yell at my brother like that, but I could see the results: Mark's giggling fits gradually lessened, and now they are nonexistent.

One of the behaviors that my father was not able to change was Mark's habit of speaking too loudly. Whether it's because Mark can't hear himself talk or because he gets so excited about what he's saying that he forgets to modulate his volume, it irritated my father to no end to hear Mark's voice booming from down the street. Even in the last months of his life, he was working with Mark to lower the volume of his voice.

My father's dedication to Mark was well known, but he's not the only one; my mother has always been willing to drive Mark to the school that's best for him, no matter how far away. Currently, she drives from San Diego to El Cajon in rush-hour traffic so that he can attend Saint Madeleine Sophie's, a wonderful center for developmentally disabled adults. She also keeps him involved in extracurricular activities, including swim practice and Special Olympics.

Special Olympics has been an important part of Mark's life since he was 15. He competes in sports including floor hockey, swimming, skiing, and volleyball. In addition to the fun and physical conditioning these sports provide (and the many blue ribbons Mark has brought home over the years!), Special Olympics has broadened his world by giving him an opportunity to make friends with other athletes and with coaches, and he's also gained a degree of independence through going on overnight trips to compete in other cities.

But perhaps the most important thing our mother does is nurture Mark's artistic talent. His aptitude for visual art wasn't discovered until he was 21, when his teacher asked him to draw an eagle at school. Although Mark had never drawn anything (in fact had never even produced a scribble) he amazed his teacher with a wonderful picture of an eagle.

After that, he began doing artwork at school on a regular basis and also began taking private art lessons. As he learned to work in different media, including watercolor, acrylics, and computer-generated art, his natural ability developed by leaps and bounds. At first he was most interested in painting animals and landscapes, but now his paintings often feature people—a fact that may be indicative of his blossoming social skills and his widening awareness of others.

Mark's paintings, with their vivid colors and unique, sometimes quirky take on their subjects, have brought him a great deal of attention and praise. He's shown his work in galleries across the country, and his paintings have been featured on posters, greeting cards, and, most recently, the cover of a CD called *Daydreaming at Night* by musician Gregory Page, who Mark met on one of his daily rounds of Kensington. Several television stations have done documentaries on Mark's art, and he now regularly displays his work at Sophie's, a gallery connected to St. Madeleine Sophie's Center that features art by developmentally disabled adults.

By 1997 I'd published several books, and when I decided to write a children's book, I knew that I wanted Mark to be my illustrator. We both love cats, and after seeing one of his paintings titled *Kitten in a Basket*, I wrote *The Secret Night World of Cats*. With his art teacher Kathy Blavatt's help, Mark painstakingly created illustrations to go along with my text, using both traditional painting and computer-generated art.

Mark had no trouble painting the cats in my story. His illustrations feature cats so vivid and lifelike they practically leap from the page, but painting the main character, a little girl named Amanda, proved to be problematic. His illustrations of her are flat and almost cartoon-like. At first, my publishers were unhappy about the discrepancy between the way that Amanda and the cats were depicted. But when I explained to them that this probably represented how Mark sees the world as a person with autism—animals and inanimate objects in the foreground, people in the background— they agreed that this actually added to the interest of the book, and they published his illustrations as he created them.

The Secret Night World of Cats was published in 1998. *CBS This Morning* did a spot about our collaboration. We did a number of signings at bookstores; all my life I'd wanted to create something with my older brother, and I was filled with pride as we stood side-by-side, pens in hand, signing the book we'd created together. *The Secret Night World of Cats* received a National Parent Publishing Association Honor Award in 1998, and is still in print after almost ten years.

Although we have yet to do another book together, Mark and I continue to have a close relationship, even though we live in different states. We have occasional phone conversations in which Mark updates me on his most current art project. He looks forward to my visits to San Diego, telling everyone he comes in contact with that his sister Helen is coming. In classic autistic fashion, though, no matter how excited he is to see me, he declines to vary his routine while I'm visiting. If I want to spend time with Mark, I accompany him on his daily rounds of Kensington.

Every time I see Mark now, I'm amazed by how much he's changed. He's gone from the child who wouldn't look you in the eye and was unable to speak in a full sentence, to a gregarious adult who knows how to make and keep friends and can even appreciate a good joke, a skill that isn't possible for most people with autism. He's gone from the boy who struggled to learn his letters in order to earn a handful of M&Ms, to a man who enjoys reading. He reads his favorite books over and over again, and is taking a class to improve his reading comprehension.

Along with Mark's improved social and cognitive abilities has come a decrease in his special, or "savant," calendar abilities. A number of years ago, if you told Mark the date and year of your birthday, he could tell you which day of the week you were born. I used to have him demonstrate this ability for my friends as a kind of parlor trick. Once, when I asked him how he did it, he replied by reciting a long, complicated mathematical formula that I couldn't begin to understand—a formula that he'd figured out on his own.

If you ask Mark to do the same trick today, he can still produce the correct answer, but it takes him longer than it used to. I like to think this is because, as he becomes more normal, he can no longer work on the problem with the intense focus so characteristic of people with autism. He's having a more difficult time shutting the world out, and that's a good thing.

As Mark leaves his calendar-calculation abilities behind, I see him taking more pride in himself as a human being. He sees himself—as he should—as an artist, an athlete, and a man who knows how to make friends. He's beginning to identify less with people with developmental disabilities, and more with normal folks.

One of the most striking changes in Mark is his new ability to tolerate change. People with autism cling to routine, and through much of his life Mark has been no different. He had routines for dressing, for eating—he even had to water the lawn in a certain way. But recently there have been monumental changes in Mark's life, and he's coping surprisingly well.

When we knew that my father was dying, a major concern was how Mark would cope. During my father's illness, my mother was careful to keep Mark's daily life as normal as possible. He went to school, to Special Olympics and art lessons, and he did his daily round of the Kensington coffee shops. We weren't sure what grasp Mark had of the concept of death, and we were worried he might become unhinged by such a huge change in the family.

When I came home for my father's funeral, I was still unsure how Mark was dealing with the situation. But when I walked into the room, he looked at me calmly and said, "Did you hear that Daddy passed away?" There was no huge display of emotion, but looking into my brother's eyes, I could tell that he had grasped the finality of our father's death. Although his capacity for the expression of feelings differs from mine, I have to believe that, in his own way, he feels the same deep sense of loss that I do.

Although I've seen huge improvements in Mark over the years, many challenges still remain. He is comfortable in the places he knows—his neighborhood, his school—but he has little experience of independent living in the larger world. On the rare occasions that he travels, my mother packs Mark's suitcase, labeling each article of clothing with the day of the week he is to wear it. She alerts the airline personnel, who assist Mark on the plane, and he must have someone meet him at his destination. He has only a rudimentary understanding of money—he knows how much a cappuccino costs—and he depends on my mother to feed him, transport him, and keep track of his weekly schedule.

Yet, in spite of the challenges, Mark has a good life. He is comfortable in himself and enjoys everything he does. That's more than I can say about a lot of "normal" people I know.

People sometimes ask me what it was like to grow up with a brother with autism. "That must have been tough," they say. "Weren't you jealous of how much attention he got?"

Some things about growing up with Mark were tough, but, in retrospect, I feel my experience of having a sibling with autism has made me a stronger person. Through Mark, I learned compassion at a young age. I was never tempted to join in the usual schoolyard occupation of relentlessly teasing anyone different.

I believe that growing up with Mark has given me the capacity to see beyond a person's disability, and to appreciate him or her for who they are. In fact, I'm now happily married to a man who has cognitive disabilities due to the removal of a brain tumor. His level of disability is nowhere near Mark's, of course, but I know that having an autistic brother enabled me to see beyond Steven's cognitive challenges, and to embrace the wonderful human being that he is.

Most important, I think having Mark as a brother has taught me never to give up on someone. Just as the boy who doctors told my parents was hopeless and belonged in an institution is now a happy, well-adjusted adult, I believe that given enough love, attention, and advantages, anyone can overcome the challenges life hands them. In my roles as teacher and stepparent to two teenaged boys, I am given opportunities to put this belief into practice every day.

No one is sure what Mark's future holds. Will he continue to improve, so that one day he can live in the community as a fully independent adult? Or is he now functioning at the highest level possible for him? And what will happen when my mother can no longer care for him? Will my brother Paul and I become his caretakers, or will he live in a group home with other developmentally disabled adults?

I push these questions away when they begin to plague me. I will deal with them when the time comes. For now, I celebrate my brother the artist, the Special Olympics athlete, the caring human being and am grateful for how far he has come.

AFTERWORD

The author of this award-winning book was embraced by the majority of the academic and professional community touched and persuaded by *Infantile Autism*'s systematic review of the medical and scientific literature. Within a decade Dr. Rimland's assessment ended a wide professional adherence to the "cold mothering" theory of causality of the rare and unique condition first described in 11 children by Kanner in 1943.

Bernard Rimland PhD had been a fledgling research psychologist outside the academic settings of medicine and psychiatry and a parent of an autistic child when he began his five-year study of the published literature and opened a correspondence with many of its authors. In the second decade following this book's publication four strong tides pulled him away from the affection and respect of the scientific community from which he had drawn the evidence, with 481 supportive references. The forces of these separating tides came from the voice of parents, the ascendency of genetics research, psychopharmacology's rising influence over medical thinking, and the psychologist's peril found when steering into medical waters.

Bernie, as parents and colleagues knew him, heard the voice of a flood of correspondence initiated by parents and then supported by his keen interest in letting those data talk. Responses to his open-minded questionnaires to parents gave forceful backing for treatment options that would become known as biomedical. This bottom-up flow of information about positive, negative, or neutral responses embodied medicine's high and humble maxim: "Listen to the patient." Year after year, statistically robust and consistent parental ratings showed an antifungal medication, nystatin, with ratings that were ten-fold higher than psychopharmaceutical drugs, the ratings of which hovered at equal scores for negative versus positive effects. Non-drug nutritional supplements and dietary interventions showed equally extraordinary benefits. Listening to parents well after the publication of this book by these and less formal means including the observations of medical colleagues, but particularly with the superb help of Stephen M. Edelson PhD, his long-standing tech-savvy protégé and successor to the leadership of Autism Research Institute, led to findings very different from the top-down flow of genetic theories and psychopharmacologic practices filling a vacuum left by Dr. Rimland's 1964 book.

The message that runs—with subtlety—between the lines of *Infantile Autism* was simple: common sense. Think Emperor's New Clothes. Children raised by parents of above-average intelligence among normally developing siblings, without traces of cruelty or neglect, and who are not infrequently physically fine-looking, remarkably dexterous, sensitive, musically gifted, capable of mind-boggling feats of memory, numerosity, and calendar operations are massively damaged and it's all because their mothers are "cold"? Really? That doctors could in the past—and still now in some parts of the world—collectively hold such a view of human development was simply preposterous.

Dr. Rimland's approach to the subject was, however, to bring to bear on his medical and scientific audience an epitome of his readers' taste for exhaustive, detailed, thoroughly documented, and clearly presented argument complete with a names index showing the pages where each of 551 quoted authors could find his or her mention. Overkill? Yes. Necessary? I believe so. Enormously tasteful, respectful, clever, and convincing? Yes, and the proof lies largely in the acceptance of Dr. Rimland's thesis, but also, to some extent, in the understandable rejection he later experienced personally in the medical world into which his book thrust him. The word "medical" does not appear in the index. Dr. Rimland took care to respect the boundaries that we medical doctors place around our turf.

I belief, however, that the frosty reception I witnessed Dr. Rimland receive in the mid-1970s at the Yale Child Study Center was not just about grazing rights. It was about foundational principles of medicine. Dr. Rimland's thesis carried an implicit challenge that is still being worked out in the language of medicine with respect to chronic illness. It has to do with whether the target of treatment is the individual patient or the disease entity of which the name —autistic, schizophrenic, diabetic, asthmatic—becomes part of the patient's identity. When I rose to agree with Dr. Rimland's presentation in that noon conference at Yale I was already inured to the chilly and dismissive reception that his remarks had received. As a recent academic and then fledgling family practitioner and pediatrician I had learned from my patients a core medical truth. Treatment involving *avoiding* or being rid of some allergen or toxin or *getting* some nutrient or filling some other unmet *special* need would hasten Nature's buoyant impulse toward healing the individual.

When I described to my academic colleagues a dramatic response of a patient with a "particular disease" to supplementation with, say, magnesium and vitamin B_6, or a prescription of an antifungal medication and change in diet, I would engender an incensed response beginning with, "Are you trying to tell me that magnesium- and B_6-deficiency is the cause of migraine? Or that yeasts cause autism? That's ridiculous!" I would say, "No, I am talking about particular patients, not particular diseases." Were the conversation to continue it would be across an abyss. On one side is the notion that the individual is the target of treatment and on the other side is the conventional medical principle that diagnosis is the prerequisite, basis, and source of prescriptive consensus. Nowhere in this book was such a schism described. Instead, that fundamental and enduring and often hidden quarrel emerged to bedevil Dr. Rimland's relationship with the academic and medical world in the decades of his tireless advocacy of common sense before the orthodoxy of name-it, blame-it, tame-it prescription-pad medicine and the magnification of the small truth that everything is genetic.

The disfavor shown to Dr. Rimland's work starting a decade after the publication of this book was not because he was a non-physician. It was not only because listening to patients inspired his medical advocacy. His medical thinking was simply a radically modern mismatch to contemporary medicine's fallacy that the patient must be labeled and that treatment be aimed not at the individual but to the disease, or even separate diseases, of the patient. Note that the notion of comorbidity is not raised in this book. Instead Dr. Rimland places late in this book the presentation of its opposite; the co-occurrence of multiple aptitudes to serve as a final round-up of common sense.

The words "life-long" and "incurable" are found in nearly all lay and scientific writing about autism over the past five decades. In the pages of this book, however, the word "recovery" describes several children's responses to treatment. And Dr. Rimland, along with those medical practitioners who joined his movement to promote a deeper understanding of the immunology, biochemistry, and toxicology of individuals on the autism spectrum, came under fire for documenting hundreds of cases of recovery based on *different* kinds of biomedical intervention.

This book represented a revolution in thinking about one chronic illness. It was part of a larger story that is still unfolding in medicine as research reveals the roots of all chronic illnesses to be not separating but unifying. Autism, once seen as a unique and rare "disease entity"—something simply very separate—is turning out to be just the opposite. It is the worse manifestation, in children, of the modern world's chronic illnesses in which oxidative stress, problems in detoxification, and inflammation are expressed in different ways in different people. Research supported by the Autism Research Institute has revealed these core issues in common with autism and all chronic illness within the embracing framework of loss of immune tolerance combined with damage to the microbiome by sugar and antibiotics as well as perinatal events with lasting effects. Five decades from now this prophetic book's story will have been concluded. Its underlying message regarding the relative value of consistency over plausibility will have emerged to illuminate the still dark picture of autism's controversies.

At the heart of those controversies as this 50-year memorial publication of *Infantile Autism* goes to press are two overarching issues. One concerns the persistence of medicine's traditional linear thinking about disease causation in the face of the progress of systems thinking in mainstream science. The other is the growing recognition of systemic but individually controllable etiological factors. These factors will place blame on the variable interaction of individuals with private and public health policies, toxins and triggers of immune dysfunction, and the adverse effects of medical and dietary exposures as well the vast array of industrial sources. By the centennial observation of this book's initial publication we will know how that blame fell, not on mothers as it once so tragically and unjustifiably had, but on others with more elaborate capacities for eluding shame.

Sidney M. Baker, M.D., Founder, Autism360.org and
Co-Founder, Defeat Autism Now!
Sag Harbor, New York, May 2014

Bibliography

Note: This Bibliography lists a number of items which purport to deal with infantile autism but which were not available to the writer. These are Bosch (1962), Drenth (1955), Grewel (1954), Hirai et al. (1961), Lehembre (1962), Saito (1960), Spiel (1961a, 1961b), Takahashi (1960), Tokutaro (1961), and Veiga (1961). The Bosch monograph, which the writer was able to inspect briefly, lists in its bibliography several German papers previously unknown to the present writer. These references, plus several of a biochemical or psychopharmacological nature listed in the chapter by Rimland (in press), make up what is believed to be an essentially comprehensive Bibliography of substantial contributions to the literature on early infantile autism through 1962.

Ader, R., & Belfer, M. L. Prenatal maternal anxiety and offspring emotionality in the rat. *Psychol. Rep.*, 1962, *10*, 711–718.

Allen, G., & Kallman, F. J. Frequency and type of mental retardation in twins. *Amer. J. Hum. Genet.*, 1955, *7*, 15–20.

Amassian, V. E., Macy, J. Jr., & Waller, H. J. Patterns of activity of simultaneously recorded neurons in midbrain reticular formation. *Ann. N.Y. Acad. Sci.*, 1961, *89*, 883–895.

Anastasi, Anne, & Levee, R. F. Intellectual defect and musical talent: A case report. *Amer. J. Ment. Defic.*, 1960, *64*, 695–703.

Anokhin, P. K., & Agafanov, V. G. *Current problems of the physiology, morphology, pharmacology and clinical picture of reticular formation of the brain.* (Transl. from the Russian) Office of Technical Services, U.S. Dept. of Commerce: JPRS Report 4559, 24 April 1961.

Anthony, J. An experimental approach to the psychopathology of childhood: Autism. *Brit. J. Med. Psychol.*, 1958, *31*, 211–225.

Antonelli, A. R., & Rüdiger, W. On the role of the extralemniscal pathways in the EEG arousal reaction elicited by reticular stimulation. *Arch. Ital. Biol.*, 1960, *98*, 423–429.

Arnold, G. E. Writing instead of speaking. *Curr. Probl. Phoniat. Logoped.*, 1960, *1*, 155–162.

Arnold, Magda B. *Emotion and personality: Vol. 1, Psychological aspects; Vol. 2, Neurological and physiological aspects.* New York: Columbia University Press, 1960.

Ashby, W. R. The mechanism of habituation. In *Mechanisation of thought processes*. National Physical Laboratory Symposium No. 10. London: Her Majesty's Stationery Office, 1959, Vol. 1, pp. 95–113.

Ashton, N. Retinal vascularization in health and disease. *Amer. J. Ophthal.*, 1957, *44* (Part II), 7–17.

Astin, A. W. The functional autonomy of psychotherapy. *Amer. Psychologist*, 1961, *16*, 75–78.

Axelrod, S. Effects of early blindness. *Amer. Found. for the Blind, Res. Series Publ. No. 7*, 1959.

Bakwin, H. Early infantile autism. *J. Pediat.*, 1954, *45*, 492–497.

Barlow, H. B. Sensory mechanisms, the reduction of redundancy, and intelligence. In *Mechanisation of thought processes*. National Physical Laboratory Symposium No. 10. London: Her Majesty's Stationery Office, 1959, Vol. 2, pp. 537–559.

Barsa, J. A., & Saunders, J. C. Deanol (Deaner) in the treatment of schizophrenia. *Amer. J. Psychiat.*, 1959, *116*, 255–256.

Beaujard, M. La schizophrenia infantile: Expose de quelques travaux américains contemporains. *Ann. Medico-Psychol.*, 1958, *116*, 785–804.

Bello, F. The young scientists. *Fortune*, June 1954, 142–148, 172–182.

Bein, H. J. Effects of reserpine on the functional strata of the nervous system. In S. Garattini & V. Ghetti (Eds), *Psychotropic drugs*. Amsterdam: Elsevier Publ. Co., 1957, pp. 325–331.

Benda, C. E. *Developmental disorders of mentation and cerebral palsies*. New York: Grune & Stratton, Inc., 1952.

Benda, C. E. The differentiation between mental deficiency and emotional disorders, and some therapeutic experiments with rauwolfia serpentina (Koglucoid). *Archivos de Pediatria del Uruguay*, 1955, *26*, 32–46.

Benda, C. E. Childhood schizophrenia, autism and Heller's disease. In P. W. Bowman & H. V. Mautner (Eds), *Mental retardation: Proceedings of the first international conference on mental retardation*. New York: Grune & Stratton, Inc., 1960, pp. 469–492.

Benda, C. E., & Melchior, J. C. Childhood schizophrenia, childhood autism, and Heller's disease. *Internat. Rec. Med.*, 1959, *172*, 137–154.

Bender, Lauretta. Childhood schizophrenia. *Psychiat. Quart.*, 1953, *27*, 663–681.

Bender, Lauretta. Twenty years of clinical research on schizophrenic children, with special reference to those under six years of age. In G. Caplan (Ed.), *Emotional problems of early childhood*. New York: Basic Books, 1955, pp. 503–515.

Bender, Lauretta. Schizophrenia in childhood: Its recognition, description and treatment. *Amer. J. Orthopsychiat.*, 1956, *26*, 499–506.

Bender, Lauretta. Autism in children with mental deficiency. *Amer. J. Ment. Defic.*, 1959, *63*, 81–86.

Bender, Lauretta. The brain and child behavior. *AMA Arch. Gen. Psychiat.*, 1961, *4*, 531–547.

Bender, Lauretta, Goldschmidt, L., & Sankar, D. V. Siva. Treatment of autistic schizophrenic children with LSD-25 and UML-491. In J. Wortis (Ed.), *Recent advances in biological psychiatry.* New York: Grune & Stratton, 1962, *4,* pp. 170–177.

Bender, Lauretta, & Grugett, A. E. Jr. A study of certain epidemiological factors in a group of children with childhood schizophrenia. *Amer. J. Orthopsychiat.,* 1956, *26,* 131–145.

Bender, Lauretta, & Helme, W. H. A quantitative test of theory and diagnostic indicators of childhood schizophrenia. *AMA Arch. Neurol. Psychiat.,* 1953, *70,* 413–427.

Bergman, P., & Escalona, Sibylle K. Unusual sensitivities in very young children. *Psychoanal. Stud. Child.* New York: Internat. Univ. Press, 1949, *3–4,* pp. 333–352.

Berlyne, D. E. *Conflict, arousal and curiosity.* New York: McGraw Hill, 1960.

Bernstein, L. The interaction of process and content on thought disorders of schizophrenic and brain-damaged patients. *J. Gen. Psychol.,* 1960, *62,* 53–68.

Bettelheim, B. Schizophrenia as a reaction to extreme situations. *Amer. J. Orthopsychiat.,* 1956, *26,* 507–518.

Bettelheim, B. Joey: A "mechanical boy." *Scient. American,* 1959, *200* (Mar.), 116–217. (a) (See also exchange with J. M. May in Letters to Editor, May, pp. 12–18.)

Bettelheim, B. Feral children and autistic children. *Amer. J. Social.,* 1959, *64,* 455–467. (b)

Betts, G. H. *The distribution and functions of mental imagery.* New York: Teachers College Columbia University, 1909.

Bharucha-Reid, Rodabé, P. Disorganization-organization and the reticular formation. *Nature,* 1960, *188,* 123–124.

Bharucha-Reid, Rodabé, P. Disorganization-organization and cognitive motivation. *Brit. J. Psychol.,* 1961, *52,* 349–360.

Bharucha-Reid, Rodabé, P. The internal modulating system and stress: A physiological model. *J. Gen. Psychol.,* 1962, *66,* 147–158.

Blank, H. R. Psychiatric problems associated with congenital blindness due to retrolental fibroplasia. *New Outlook for the Blind,* 1959, *53,* 237–244.

Bleuler, E. Die Probleme der Schizoidie und der Syntonie. *Zeitschr. f. d. gesam. Neurol. u. Psychiat.,* 1922, *68,* 373–399.

Bleuler, E. *Textbook of psychiatry.* (Transl. by A. A. Brill.) New York: Macmillan, 1924.

Bleuler, E. *Dementia praecox or the group of schizophrenias.* (Transl. by J. Zinkin.) New York: Internat. Univer. Press, 1950.

Boatman, Maleta J., & Szurek, S. A. A clinical study of childhood schizophrenia. In D. D. Jackson (Ed.), *The etiology of schizophrenia.* New York: Basic Books, 1960, pp. 389–440.

Bosch, G. *Der frühkindliche autismus.* Berlin: Springer-Verlag, 1962.

Bovet, D., Longo, V. G., & Silvestrini, B. Les méthodes d'investigatans electrophysiologiques dans l'étude des médicaments tranquillisants. In S. Garattini & V. Ghetti (Eds), *Psychotropic drugs.* Amsterdam: Elsevier Publ. Co., 1957, pp. 193–206.

Bowlby, J. *Maternal care and mental health.* Geneva: World Health Organization, 1951.

Bowlby, J., Ainsworth, Mary, Boston, Mary, & Rosenbluth, Dina. The effects of mother-child separation: A follow-up study. *Brit. J. Med. Psychol.*, 1956, *29*, 211–247.

Bradley, C. Biography of a schizophrenic child. *Nerv. Child*, 1942–43, *1*, 141–171.

Bradley, P. B. Microelectrode approach to the neuropharmacology of the reticular formation. In S. Garattini & V. Ghetti (Eds), *Psychotropic drugs*. Amsterdam: Elsevier Publ. Co., 1957, pp. 207–216.

Brady, J. V., & Bunnell, B. N. Behavior and the nervous system. In R. H. Waters et al. (Eds), *Principles of comparative psychology*. New York: McGraw Hill, 1960, pp. 355–377.

Brain, W. R. Some reflections on genius. *Lancet*, 1948, *1*, 661–665.

Brain, W. R. The physiological basis of consciousness. *Brain*, 1958, *81*, 426–455.

Brain, W. R. *Some reflections on genius and other essays*. London: Pitman, 1960.

Braun, J. R. Three tests of the McClelland Discrepancy Hypothesis. *Psychol. Rep.*, 1962, *10*, 271–274.

Breland, K., & Breland, Marian. The misbehavior of organisms. *Amer. Psychologist*, 1961, *16*, 681–684.

Bridger, W. H. Sensory habituation and discrimination in the human neonate. *Amer. J. Psychiat.*, 1961, *117*, 991–996.

Broadbent, D. E. *Perception and communication*. New York: Pergamon, 1958.

Brobeck, J. R. Mechanism of the development of obesity in animals with hypothalamic lesions. *Physiol. Rev.*, 1946, *26*, 541–559.

Bromiley, R. B. Conditioned responses in a dog after removal of neocortex. *J. Comp. Physiol. Psychol.*, 1948, *41*, 102–110.

Brown, N. Attention: A theoretical note. *J. gen. Psychol.*, 1960, *62*, 103–111.

Bruch, Hilde. Studies in schizophrenia: The various developments in the approach to childhood schizophrenia. Psychotherapy with schizophrenics. *Acta Psychiat. Neurol. Scand., Kbh.*, 1959, *34* (Suppl. 130).

Bruner, J. S. Neural mechanisms in perception. *Psychol. Rev.*, 1957, *64*, 340–358.

Bruner, J. S. The cognitive consequences of early sensory deprivation. *Psychosom. Med.*, 1959, *21*, 89–95.

Bullock, T. H. Neuron doctrine and electrophysiology. *Science*, 1959, *129*, 997–1002.

Bullock, T. H. The origins of patterned nervous discharge. *Behaviour*, 1961, *17*, 48–59.

Burt, C. The inheritance of mental ability. *Amer. Psychologist*, 1958, *13*, 1–15.

Burt, C. The gifted child. *Brit. J. Statist. Psychol.*, 1961, *14*, 123–139.

Cady, L. D. Jr., Gertler, M. M., Gottsch, L. G., & Woodbury, M. A. The factor structure of variables concerned with coronary artery disease. *Behav. Sci.*, 1961, *6*, 37–41.

Cameron, N. *The psychology of the behavior disorders*. Boston: Houghton-Mifflin, 1947.

Cameron, N., & Magaret, Ann. *Behavior pathology*. Boston: Houghton-Mifflin, 1951.

Campbell, A. C. P. In discussion of Michaelson, I. C. and Campbell, A. C. P. The anatomy of the finer retinal vessels and some observations on their significance in certain retinal diseases. *Trans. Opthalm. Soc. Un. K.*, 1940, *60*, 71–112.

Campbell, D. T. Blind variation and selective retention in creative thought as in other knowledge processes. *Psychol. Rev.*, 1960, *67*, 380–400.

Cappon, D. Clinical manifestations of autism and schizophrenia in childhood. *Canad. Med. Ass. J.*, 1953, *69*, 44–49.

Cappon, D., & Andrews, E. Autism and schizophrenia in a child guidance clinic. *Canad. Psychiat. Ass. J.*, 1957, *2*, 1–25.

Carnegie Corporation. Creativity. *Carnegie Corp. of New York Quarterly*, 1961, *9*, No. 3.

Carrigan, Patricia M. Extraversion–introversion as a dimension of personality: A reappraisal. *Psychol. Bull.*, 1960, *57*, 329–360.

Cattell, R. B. *Personality.* New York: McGraw-Hill, 1950.

Cattell, R. B. *Personality and motivation structure and measurement.* New York: World Book, 1957.

Cattell, R. B. The multiple abstract variance analysis equations and solutions: For nature–nurture research on continuous variables. *Psychol. Rev.*, 1960, *67*, 353–372.

Cattell, R. B., Stice, G. F., & Kristy, N. F. A first approximation to nature–nurture ratios for eleven primary personality factors in objective tests. *J. Abnorm. Soc. Psychol.*, 1957, *54*, 143–159.

Chapman, A. H. Early infantile autism in identical twins: Report of a case. *AMA Arch. Neurol. Psychiat.*, 1957, *78*, 621–623.

Chapman, A. H. Early infantile autism: A review. *AMA J. Dis. Child*, 1960, *99*, 783–786.

Chisholm, J. F. The progressive changes in the pathology of early retrolental fibroplasia. *Amer. J. Ophthal.*, 1960, *49*, 1155–1162.

Ciba Foundation. *Symposium on the neurological basis of behavior.* G. E. W. Wolstenholme & Cecelia M. O'Connor (Eds). Boston: Little, Brown, 1958.

Clark, W. LeGros. Sensory experience and brain structure. *J. Ment. Sci.*, 1958, *104*, 1–13.

Cohen, J. A natural experiment in visual deprivation. *Amer. Psychologist*, 1960, *15*, 395. (Abstract)

Colver, T., & Kerridge, D. F. Birth order in epileptic children. *J. Neurol. Neurosurg. Psychiat.*, 1962, *25*, 59–62.

Courville, C. B. Vascular patterns of the encephalic gray matter in man. *Bull. Los Angeles Neurol. Soc.*, 1958, *28*, 30–43.

Cowie, Valerie, & Slater, E. Psychiatric genetics. In G. W. T. H. Fleming & A. Walk (Eds), *Recent progress in psychiatry*, Vol. 3. New York: Grove Press, 1959, pp. 2–53.

Creak, Mildred. Psychoses in childhood. *J. Ment. Sci.*, 1951, *97*, 545–554.

Creak, Mildred. Discussion: Psychoses in childhood. *Proc. Roy. Soc. Med.*, 1952, *45*, 797–800.

Creak, Mildred, & Ini, Sylvia. Families of psychotic children. *J. Child Psychol. Psychiat.*, 1960, *1*, 156–175.

Cunningham, M. A., & Dixon, Cynthia. A study of the language of an autistic child. *J. Child Psychol. Psychiat.*, 1961, *2*, 193–202.

Daly, D. D., & Love, J. G. Akinetic mutism. *Neurology*, 1958, *8*, 238–242.

Darr, G. C., & Worden, F. G. Case report twenty-eight years after an infantile autistic disorder. *Amer. J. Orthopsychiat.*, 1951, *21*, 559–570.

Davenport, C. B. Human variability and mate selection. In C. B. Davenport et al., *Medical genetics and eugenics.* Philadelphia: Women's Med. College of Pennsylvania, 1940, pp. 9–39.

Delafresnaye, J. F. (Ed.) *Brain mechanisms and consciousness.* Springfield, Ill.: C. C. Thomas, 1954.

Dennis, W. Infant development under conditions of restricted practice and of minimum social stimulation. *Genet. Psychol. Monogr.,* 1941, *23,* 143–191.

Despert, J. Louise. Schizophrenia in children. *Psychiat. Quart.,* 1938, 12, 366–371.

Despert, J. Louise. Prophylactic aspects of schizophrenia in childhood. *Nerv. Child,* 1941–42, *1,* 199–231.

Despert, J. Louise. Psychotherapy in child schizophrenia. *Amer. J. Psychiat.,* 1947, *104,* 36–43.

Despert, J. Louise. Some considerations relating to the genesis of autistic behavior in children. *Amer. J. Orthopsychiat.,* 1951, *21,* 335–350.

Despert, J. Louise, & Sherwin, A. C. Further examination of diagnostic criteria in schizophrenic illness and psychoses of infancy and early childhood. *Amer. J. Psychiat.,* 1958, *114,* 784–790.

Diamond, S., Balvin, R. S., & Diamond, Florence R. *Inhibition and choice.* New York & Evanston: Harper & Row, 1963.

Dingman, W., & Sporn, M. B. The incorporation of 8-azaguanine into rat brain RNA and its effects on maze learning by the rat: An inquiry into the biochemical basis of memory. *J. Psychiat. Res.,* 1961, *1,* 1–11.

Dobzhansky, T. *Mankind evolving.* New Haven: Yale Univ. Press, 1962.

Donaldson, H. H. The brain problem—in relation to weight and form. *Amer. J. Psychiat.,* 1932, *12* (Vol. 89 new series), 197–214.

Down, J. L. *On some of the mental affections of childhood and youth.* London: J. & A. Churchill, 1887.

Drenth, F. Een bidjdrage tot bestudering en behandeling van het autistiche kind. *Vlaam. Opvoedk. Tijdschr.,* 1955, *35,* 279–305, 332–336. (*Psychol. Abstr.,* 31:3339).

Duffy, Elizabeth. The psychological significance of the concept of "arousal" or "activation." *Psychol. Rev.,* 1957, *64,* 265–275.

Easton, K. Considerations on autism in infancy and childhood. *N. Y. State J. Med.,* 1962, *62,* 3628–3633.

Eccles, J. C. The physiology of imagination. *Scient. American,* 1958, *199* (Sept.), 135–146.

Eickhoff, Louise F. W. The aetiology of schizophrenia in childhood. *J. Ment. Sci.,* 1952, *98,* 229–234.

Eisenberg, L. The autistic child in adolescence. *Amer. J. Psychiat.,* 1956, *112,* 607–612.

Eisenberg, L. The fathers of autistic children. *Amer. J. Orthopsychiat.,* 1957, *27,* 715–724.

Eisenberg, L. Emotional determinants of mental deficiency. *AMA Arch. Neurol. Psychiat.,* 1958, *80,* 114–121.

Eisenberg, L., & Kanner, L. Early infantile autism, 1943–1955. *Amer. J. Orthopsychiat.,* 1956, *26,* 556–566.

Ekstein, R. The space child's time machine: On "reconstruction" in the psychotherapeutic treatment of a schizophrenoid child. *Amer. J. Orthopsychiat.*, 1954, *24*, 492–506.

Ekstein, R. Special training problems in psychotherapeutic work with psychotic and borderline children. *Amer. J. Orthopsychiat.*, 1962, *32*, 569–581.

Ekstein, R., Bryant, K., & Friedman, S. W. Childhood schizophrenia and allied conditions. In L. Bellak & P. K. Benedict (Eds), *Schizophrenia.* New York: Logos Press, 1958, pp. 555–693.

Elkes, J. Drug effects in relation to receptor specificity within the brain: Some evidence and provisional formulation. In G. E. W. Wolstenholme & Cecelia M. O'Connor (Eds), *The neurological basis of behavior.* (Ciba Foundation Symposium.) Boston: Little, Brown, 1958, pp. 303–332.

Ellingson, R. J. Brain waves and problems of psychology. *Psychol. Bull.*, 1956, *58*, 1–34.

Elsasser, W. M. *The physical foundations of biology.* New York: Pergamon Press, 1958.

Estable, C. Considerations on the histological bases of neurophysiology. In J. F. Delafresnaye (Ed.), *Brain mechanisms and learning.* Oxford: Blackwell, 1961, pp. 309–334.

Eveloff, H. H. The autistic child. *AMA Arch. Gen. Psychiat.*, 1960, *3*, 66–81.

Eysenck, H. J. Cyclothymia and schizothymia as a dimension of personality: I. Historical review. *J. Pers.*, 1950, *19*, 123–152. II. Experimental. *J. Pers.*, 1952, *20*, 345–384.

Eysenck, H. J. *The scientific study of personality.* London: Routledge & Kegan Paul, 1952.

Eysenck, H. J. The inheritance of extraversion–introversion. *Acta Psychol., Amst.*, 1956, *12*, 95–110.

Eysenck, H. J. The effects of psychotherapy. In H. J. Eysenck (Ed.), *Handbook of abnormal psychology.* New York: Basic Books, 1961, pp. 697–725.

Faibish, G. Schizophrenic response to words of multiple meaning. *J. Pers.*, 1961, *29*, 414–427.

Feldman, S. M., & Waller, H. J. Dissociation of electrocortical activation and behavioural arousal. *Nature*, 1962, *196*, 1320–1322.

Ferster, C. B. Positive reinforcement and behavioral deficits of autistic children, *Child Develpm.*, 1961, *32*, 437–456.

Ferster, C. B., & DeMyer, Marian K. The development of performances in autistic children in an automatically controlled environment. *J. Chron. Dis.*, 1961, *13*, 312–345.

Ferster, C. B., & DeMyer, Marian K. A method for the experimental analysis of the behavior of autistic children. *Amer. J. Orthopsychiat.*, 1962, *32*, 89–98.

Fessard, A. E. Mechanisms of nervous integration and conscious experience. In J. F. Delafresnaye (Ed.), *Brain mechanisms and consciousness.* Springfield, Ill.: C. C. Thomas, 1954, pp. 200–236.

Fish, Barbara. The detection of schizophrenia in infancy: A preliminary report. *J. Nerv. Ment. Dis.*, 1957, *125*, 1–24.

Fish, Barbara. Longitudinal observations of biological deviations in a schizophrenic infant. *Amer. J. Psychiat.*, 1959, *116*, 25–31.

Fish, F. A neurophysiological theory of schizophrenia. *J. Ment. Sci.*, 1961, *109*, 828–838.

Fishberg, M. *The Jews: A study of race and environment.* London: Walter Scott, 1911.

Fiske, D. W., & Maddi, S. R. *Functions of varied experience.* Homewood, Ill.: Dorsey Press, 1961.

Fontes, V., & Schneeberger-Ataíde, J. Schizophrénie infantile (contribution portugaise). *Ztschr. f. Kinderpsychiat.*, 1958, *25*, 183–190.

Frankl, G. Language and affective contact. *Nerv. Child*, 1943, *2*, 251–262.

Freedman, A. M. Treatment of autistic schizophrenic children with marsilid. *J. Clin. Exp. Psychopath.*, 1958, (Suppl. 1) *19*, 138–145. (a)

Freedman, A. M. Drug therapy in behavior disorders. *Pediat. Clin. N. Amer.*, 1958, *5*, 573–594. (b)

Freedman, A. M., Ebin, Eva V., & Wilson, Ethel A. Autistic schizophrenic children: An experiment in the use of d-Lysergic Acid Diethylamide (LSD-25). *AMA Arch. Gen. Psychiat.*, 1962, *6*, 203–213.

French, J. D. Brain lesions associated with prolonged unconsciousness. *AMA Arch. Neurol. Psychiat.*, 1952, *68*, 727–740.

French, J. D. The reticular formation. *Scient. American*, 1957, *196* (May), 54–60.

French, J. D. The reticular formation. In H. W. Magoun (Ed.), *Handbook of physiology* (Sect. 1: Neurophysiology). Washington, D.C.: Amer. Physiol. Soc., 1960, Vol. 2, pp. 1281–1305.

Fuller, J. L., & Thompson, W. R. *Behavior genetics.* New York: Wiley, 1960.

Fuster, J. M. Effects of stimulation of brain stem on tachistoscopic perception. *Science*, 1958, *127*, 150.

Gaito, J. A biochemical approach to learning and memory. *Psychol. Rev.*, 1961, *68*, 288–292.

Galambos, R., & Morgan, C. T. The neural basis of learning. In H. W. Magoun (Ed.), *Handbook of physiology* (Sect. 1: Neurophysiology). Washington, D.C.: Amer. Physiol. Soc., 1960, Vol. 3, pp. 1471–1499.

Galvin, J. Mothers of schizophrenics. *J. Nerv. Ment. Dis.*, 1956, *123*, 568–570.

Galton, F. Psychometric experiments. *Brain*, 1879–1880, *2*, 149–162.

Galton, F. *Inquiries into human faculty.* London: Macmillan, 1907.

Gangloff, H., & Brown, B. *Effect of deanol on rhinencephalo-di-encephalic and reticular pathways in unanesthetized, curarized cats.* Northridge, California: Riker Laboratories, 1959. (Mimeo.)

Gastaut, H. Some aspects of the neurophysiological basis of conditioned reflexes and behaviour. In G. E. W. Wolstenholme & Cecelia M. O'Connor (Eds), *The neurological basis of behavior.* (Ciba Foundation Symposium.) Boston: Little, Brown, 1958, pp. 255–276. (a)

Gastaut, H. The role of the reticular formation in establishing conditioned reactions. In H. H. Jasper et al. (Eds), *Reticular formation of the brain.* Boston: Little, Brown, 1958, pp. 561–579. (b)

Geller, S. J. Comparison of a tranquilizer and a psychic energizer used in treatment of children with behavioral disorders. *J. Amer. Med. Ass.*, 1960, *174*, 481–484.

Gellner, Lise. *A neurophysiological concept of mental retardation and its educational implications.* Chicago: Dr. Julian D. Levinson Research Foundation for Mentally Retarded Children (Cook County Hospital), 1959.

Gerard, R. W. What is memory? *Scient. American,* 1953, *189* (Sept.), 118–126.

Gerard, R. W. Brains and behavior. *Human Biology,* 1959, *81,* 14–20.

Gerard, R. W. Neurophysiology: An integration (molecules, neurons and behavior). In H. W. Magoun (Ed.), *Handbook of physiology* (Sect. 1: Neurophysiology). Washington, D.C.: Amer. Physiol. Soc., 1960, Vol. 3, pp. 1919–1965.

Gerstein, G. L. Analysis of firing patterns in single neurons. *Science,* 1960, *181,* 1811–1812.

Gibbs, C. B. Function of limb tremor. *Nature,* 1961, *190,* 540.

Goddard, H. H. What is intelligence? *J. Soc. Psychol.,* 1946, *24,* 51–69.

Goldfarb, W. Receptor preferences in schizophrenic children. *AMA Arch. Neural. Psychiat.,* 1956, *76,* 643–652.

Goldfarb, W. Pain reactions in a group of institutionalized schizophrenic children. *Amer. J. Orthopsychiat.,* 1958, *28,* 777–785.

Goldfarb, W. *Childhood schizophrenia.* Cambridge, Mass.: Harvard Univer. Press, 1961.

Goldstein, K. *The organism.* New York: American Book, 1939.

Goldstein, K. Abnormal mental conditions in infancy. *J. Nerv. Ment. Dis.,* 1959, *128,* 538–557.

Gottesman, I. I. The psychogenetics of personality. *Dissert. Abstr.,* 1960, *21,* 957–958.

Graham, Frances K., Caldwell, Bettye M., Ernhart, Claire B., Pennoyer, Miriam M., & Hartmann, A. F., Sr. Anoxia as a significant perinatal experience: A critique. *J. Pediat.,* 1957, *50,* 556–569.

Graham, Frances K., & Ernhart, Claire B. Comments on "What price intelligence?" *Amer. Psychologist,* 1961, *16,* 38–40.

Green, M. R., & Schecter, D. E. Autistic and symbiotic disorders in three blind children. *Psychiat. Quart.,* 1957, *81,* 628–646.

Greene, P. H. *In search of the fundamental units of perception: An outline.* Air Force Office of Scientific Research Report TN60–622 (AF 49 (638)-414, Project 9777C) Washington, D.C., June 1, 1961.

Grewel, F. (Ed.). *Infantiel autisme.* (Symposium of the Dutch Society for Child Psychiatry.) Amsterdam: Musses te Purmerend, 1954. (*Psychol. Abstr.,* 29:7528)

Grossman, H. J., & Greenberg, N. H. Psychosomatic differentiation in infancy: I. Autonomic activity in the newborn. *Psychosom. Med.,* 1957, *19,* 293–306.

Gyllensten, L. Oxygen exposure and brain damage. *Nature,* 1959, *183,* 1068–1069. (a)

Gyllensten, L. Influence of oxygen exposure on the postnatal vascularization of the cerebral cortex in mice. *Acta morph. neerl. scand.,* 1959, *2,* 289–310. (b)

Gyllensten, L. Influence of age on the oxygen-induced swelling of the cerebral cortex in mice. *Acta morph. neerl. scand.,* 1960, *3,* 103–106.

Halstead, W. C. Thinking, imagery, and memory. In H. W. Magoun (Ed.), *Handbook of physiology* (Sect. 1: Neurophysiology). Washington, D.C.: Amer. Physiol. Soc., 1960, Vol. 3, pp. 1669–1678.

Harlow, H. F. The nature of love. *Amer. Psychologist,* 1958, *13,* 673–685.

Harlow, H. F., & Harlow, Margaret K. The effect of rearing conditions on behavior. *Bull. Menninger Clin.,* 1962, *26,* 213–224. (a)

Harlow, H. F., & Harlow, Margaret K. Social deprivation in monkeys. *Scient. American,* 1962, *207* (Nov.), 137–146. (b)

Harlow, H. F., & Woolsey, C. N. (Eds). *Biological and biochemical bases of behavior.* Madison, Wis.: University of Wisconsin Press, 1958.

Harris, A. Sensory deprivation and schizophrenia. *J. Ment. Sci.,* 1959, *105,* 235–237.

Hayes, K. J. Genes, drives, and intellect. *Psychol. Rep.,* 1962, *10,* 299–342.

Hebb, D. O. *The organization of behavior: A neuropsychological theory.* New York: Wiley, 1949.

Hebb, D. O. Drives and the C.N.S. (conceptual nervous system). *Psychol. Rev.,* 1955, *62,* 243–254.

Hebb, D. O. Alice in wonderland or psychology among the biological sciences. In H. F. Harlow & C. N. Woolsey (Eds), *Biological and biochemical bases of behavior.* Madison, Wis.: University of Wisconsin Press, 1958, pp. 451–467. (a)

Hebb, D. O. The motivating effects of exteroceptive stimulation. *Amer. Psychologist,* 1958, *13,* 109–113. (b)

Hebb, D. O. Intelligence, brain function and the theory of mind. *Brain,* 1959, *82,* 260–275.

Heron, W. The pathology of boredom. *Scient. American,* 1957, *196* (Jan.), 52–56.

Heyns, O. S., Samson, J. M., & Graham, J. A. C. Abdominal decompression and foetal oxygenation. *Lancet I,* 1962, 289–292.

Hill, L. B. *Psychotherapeutic intervention in schizophrenia.* Chicago: University of Chicago Press, 1955.

Himwich, H. E. Stimulants. *Proc. Ass. Res. Nerv. & Ment. Dis.,* 1959, *37,* 356–383.

Hirai, N., Saito, K., Koisumi, E., Kawai, N., & Fujisima, T. Case study on five children tentatively diagnosed as early infantile autism. *Jap. J. Child. Psychiat.,* 1961, *2,* 337–342. (*Amer. J. Ment. Defic. Abstr.,* 66:2890).

Hollingworth, Leta S. *Children above 180 IQ.* New York: World Book, 1942.

Hood-Williams, J. The results of psychotherapy with children: A revaluation. *J. consult. Psychol.,* 1960, *24,* 84–88.

Hunt, J. McV. In discussion of Goodrich, D. W., Recent research in early family development and child personality. In R. H. Ojemann (Ed.), *Recent research looking toward preventative intervention.* Proceedings of the Third Institute on Preventative Psychiatry. Ames, Iowa: State University of Iowa Press, 1961, pp. 62–72.

Hunt, J. McV., & Quay, H. C. Early vibratory experience and the question of innate reinforcement value of vibration and other stimuli: A limitation on the discrepancy (Burnt Soup) principle in motivation. *Psychol., Rev.,* 1961, *68,* 149–156.

Ilg, Frances L., & Ames, Louise B. *Child behavior.* New York: Dell, 1955.

Ivanitskiy, A. M. *The functions of the reticular formation of the brain stem.* (Transl. from the Russian). Office of Technical Services, U.S. Dept. of Commerce: JPRS Report 2935, 15 Aug. 1960.

James, G. The epidemiology of mental disorder associated with damage to the brain after birth. In *Causes of mental disorder*. New York: Milbank Mem. Fund, 1961, pp. 121–152.

Jasper, H. H. Electrical activity and mechanisms of cerebral integration. In *Biology of mental health and disease*. New York: Hoeber, 1952, pp. 226–243.

Jasper, H. H. (Ed.) *Reticular formation of the brain*. Boston: Little, Brown, 1958. (a)

Jasper, H. H. Reticular–cortical systems and theories of the integrative action of the brain. In H. F. Harlow & C. N. Woolsey (Eds), *Biological and biochemical bases of behavior*. Madison, Wis.: University of Wisconsin Press, 1958, pp. 37–61. (b)

Jasper, H. H., Ricci, G. F., & Doane, B. K. Patterns of cortical neuronal discharge during conditioned responses in monkeys. In G. E. W. Wolstenholme & Cecelia M. O'Connor (Eds), *The neurological basis of behavior*. (Ciba Foundation Symposium.) Boston: Little, Brown, 1958, pp. 277–294.

Jeffress, L. A. (Ed.) *Cerebral mechanisms in behavior: The Hixon Symposium*. New York: Wiley, 1951.

Kahn, E., & Cohen, L. H. Organic drivenness: A brain stem syndrome and an experience. *New Engl. J. Med.*, 1934, *210*, 748–756.

Kallman, F. J., Barrera, S. E., & Metzger, H. Association of hereditary microphthalmia with mental deficiency. *Amer. J. Ment. Defic.*, 1940, *45*, 25–36.

Kallman, F. J. *Heredity in health and mental disorder*. New York: W. W. Norton, 1953.

Kallman, F. J., & Roth, B. Genetic aspects of preadolescent schizophrenia. *Amer. J. Psychiat.*, 1956, *112*, 599–606.

Kaneko, Z., Hishikawa, Y., Shimizu, A., Yasuhiko, H., Kageyama, N., & Fukui, S. Effects of psychotropic drugs on the electrical activity of the brain and behavior of the cat. *Folia psychiat. neurol. Jap.*, 1960 (Suppl. *6*), 73–88.

Kanner, L. Autistic disturbances of affective contact. *Nerv. Child*, 1943, *2*, 217–250.

Kanner, L. Early infantile autism. *J. Pediat.*, 1944, *25*, 211–217.

Kanner, L. Irrelevant and metaphorical language in early infantile autism. *Amer. J. Psychiat.*, 1946, *103*, 242–246.

Kanner, L. *Child psychiatry*. (2nd ed.) Springfield, Ill.: C. C. Thomas, 1948. (a)

Kanner, L. Feeblemindedness: Absolute, relative and apparent. *Nerv. Child*, 1948, *7*, 365–397. (b)

Kanner, L. Problems of nosology and psychodynamics of early infantile autism. *Amer. J. Orthopsychiat.*, 1949, *19*, 416–426.

Kanner, L. The conception of wholes and parts in early infantile autism. *Amer. J. Psychiat.*, 1951, *108*, 23–26.

Kanner, L. Emotional interference with intellectual functioning. *Amer. J. Ment. Defic.*, 1952, *56*, 701–707.

Kanner, L. To what extent is early infantile autism determined by constitutional inadequacies? *Proc. Ass. Res. Nerv. & Ment. Dis.*, 1954, 83, pp. 378–385. (a)

Kanner, L. General concept of schizophrenia at different ages. *Proc. Ass. Res. Nerv. & Ment. Dis.*, 1954, *33*, pp. 451–453. (b)

Kanner, L. Causes and results of parental perfectionism. *J. So. Carolina Med. Ass.*, 1957, *53*, 379–383.

Kanner, L. The specificity of early infantile autism. *Ztschr. f. Kinderpsychiat.*, 1958, *25*, 108–113. (a)

Kanner, L. History and present status of childhood schizophrenia in the USA. *Ztschr. f. Kinderpsychiat.*, 1958, *25*, 138–149. (b)

Kanner, L. Early infantile autism. *Feelings and their medical significance.* Columbus, Ohio: Ross Laboratories, 1961, 3 (No. 3), 1–3.

Kanner, L., & Eisenberg, L. Notes on the follow-up studies of autistic children. In P. Hoch & J. Zubin (Eds), *Psychopathology of childhood.* New York: Grune & Stratton, 1955, pp. 227–239.

Kanner, L., & Lesser, L. I. Early infantile autism. *Pediat. Clinics N. Amer.*, 1958, *5*, 711–730.

Keeler, C. E. The value of animal experiments to the understanding of human genetics. In C. B. Davenport et al. (Eds), *Medical genetics and eugenics.* Philadelphia: Women's Med. College of Penn., 1940, pp. 87–108.

Keeler, W. R. In discussion. In *Psychiat. Reports of Amer. Psychiat. Ass.*, 1957, No. 7, pp. 66–88.

Keeler, W R. Autistic patterns and defective communication in blind children with retrolental fibroplasia. In P. Hoch & J. Zubin (Eds), *Psychopathology of communication.* New York: Grune & Stratton, Inc., 1958, pp. 64–83.

Kennard, Margaret A. Inheritance of electroencephalogram patterns in children with behavior disorders. *Psychosom. Med.*, 1949, *11*, 151–157.

Kennard, Margaret A. The electroencephalogram in psychological disorders: A review. *Psychosom. Med.*, 1953, *15*, 95–115.

Kety, S. S. Biochemical theories of schizophrenia. *Science*, 1959, *129*, 1528–1532, 1590–1596.

Killam, K. F. Pharmacological influences upon evoked electrical activity in the brain. In S. Garattini & V. Ghetti (Eds), *Psychotropic drugs.* Amsterdam: Elsevier, 1957, pp. 244–251.

Killam, Eva K., Gangloff, H., Konigsmark, B., & Killam, K. F. The action of pharmacologic agents on evoked cortical activity. In J. H. Masserman (Ed.), *Biological psychiatry.* New York: Grune & Stratton, 1959, pp. 53–74.

Kinsey, V. E., Jacobus, June T., & Hemphill, F. M. Retrolental fibroplasia. Cooperative study of retrolental fibroplasia and the use of oxygen. *AMA Arch. Ophthal.*, 1956, *56*, 481–543.

Knobloch, Hilda, & Grant, D. K. Etiologic factors in "early infantile autism" and "childhood schizophrenia." *Amer. J. Dis. Child*, 1961, *102*, 535–536.

Knobloch, Hilda, & Pasamanick, B. Some thoughts on the inheritance of intelligence. *Amer. J. Orthopsychiat.*, 1961, *31*, 454–473. (a)

Knobloch, Hilda, & Pasamanick, B. Reply to report by G. Allen: Intellectual potential and heredity. *Science*, 1961, *133*, 379–380. (b)

Koegler, R. R., & Colbert, E. G. Childhood schizophrenia: Role of the family physician. *J. Amer. Med. Ass.*, 1959, *171*, 1045–1050.

Koegler, R. R., Colbert, E. G., & Eiduson, S. Wanted: A biochemical test for schizophrenia. *Calif. Med.*, 1961, *94*, 26–29.

Kraines, S. H. The physiologic basis of the manic-depressive illness: A theory. *Amer. J. Psychiat.*, 1957, *114*, 206–211.

Kramer, Y., Rabkin, R., & Spitzer, R. L. Whirling as a clinical test in childhood schizophrenia. *J. Pediat.*, 1958, *52*, 295–303.

Krause, A. C. Effect of retrolental fibroplasia in children. *Arch. Ophthal.*, 1955, *53*, 522–529.

Kretschmer, E. *The psychology of men of genius.* New York: Harcourt-Brace, 1931.

Kretschmer, E. *Physique and character.* London: Kegan Paul, 1936.

Kubala, A. L., & Katz, M. M. Nutritional factors in psychological test behavior. *J. genet. Psychol.*, 1960, *96*, 343–352.

Kugelmass, I. N. Chemical therapy of mentally retarded children. *Int. Rec. Med.*, 1959, *172*, 119–136.

Kuten, J., & Kuten, Sandra, L. Childhood schizophrenia: A review. *Dis. nerv. Syst.*, 1958, *19*, 253–260.

Kuttner, R. An hypothesis on the evolution of intelligence. *Psychol. Rep.*, 1960, *6*, 283–289.

Lashley, K. S. Experimental analysis of instinctive behavior. *Psychol. Rev.*, 1938, *45*, 445–471. Also in: F. A. Beach, D. O. Hebb, C. T. Morgan, & H. W. Nissen (Eds), *The neuropsychology of Lashley.* New York: McGraw-Hill, 1960, pp. 372–392.

Lashley, K. S. Structural variation in the central nervous system in relation to behavior. *Psychol. Rev.*, 1947, *54*, 325–334.

Lasko, Joan K. Parent behavior toward first and second children. *Genet. Psychol. Monogr.*, 1954, *49*, 97–137.

Lassek, A. M. *The human brain.* Springfield, Ill.: C. C. Thomas, 1957.

Lazure, D. Un cas de réaction psychotique chez un enfant d'age prescholaire. (A case of psychotic reaction in a child of pre-school age.) *Canad. Psychiat. Ass. J.*, 1959, *4*, 19–22.

Lebowitz, M. A., Colbert, E. G., & Palmer, J. O. Schizophrenia in children. *Amer. J. Dis. Child*, 1961, *102*, 25–27.

Leddy, J. F. An historical introduction. In W. Feindel (Ed.), *Memory learning and language.* Toronto: University of Toronto Press, 1960, pp. 3–10.

Lehembre, J. Psychopharmakologische behandeling van autisme. *Acta Neurol. Belg.*, 1962, *62*, 611–618.

Lehman, E., Haber, J., & Lesser, S. R. The use of reserpine in autistic children. *J. Nerv. Ment. Dis.*, 1957, *125*, 351–356.

Lehrmann, N. S. Creativity, consciousness and revelation. *Dis. nerv. Syst.*, 1960, *21*, 431–439, 499–504.

Leuba, C. Toward some integration of learning theories: The concept of optimal stimulation. *Psychol. Rep.*, 1955, *1*, 27–33.

Levine, A. S. "Perseveration" or "the central factor." *Psychol. Rep.*, 1955, *1*, 247–265. (a)

Levine, A. S. Perseveration, rigidity, and persistence. *Psychol. Rep.*, 1955, *1*, 107–125. (b)

Levine, A. S. Psychometric considerations in selecting personnel for unusual environments. *Personnel Psychol.*, 1960, *13*, 233–243.

Levitt, E. E. The results of psychotherapy with children: An evaluation. *J. Consult. Psychol.*, 1957, *21*, 189–196.

Levitt, E. E. Reply to Hood-Williams. *J. consult. Psychol.*, 1960, *24*, 89–91.

Lewis, N. D. C. In discussion. *Proc. Ass. Res. Nerv. Ment. Dis.* Baltimore: Williams & Wilkins, *33*, 1954, p. 364.

Lewis, R. S., Strauss, A. A., & Lehtinen, Laura E. *The other child.* New York: Grune & Stratton, 1951.

Lewis, S. R., & Van Ferney, Shirley. Early recognition of infantile autism. *J. Pediat.*, 1960, *56*, 510–512.

Lichtmann, I. E. The substratum of memory. *Dis. nerv. Syst.*, 1960, *21*, 350–351.

Lindsley, D. B. Emotion. In S. S. Stevens (Ed.), *Handbook of experimental psychology.* New York: Wiley, 1951, pp. 473–516.

Lindsley, D. B. Psychophysiology and perception. In *Current trends in the description and analysis of behavior.* Pittsburgh: University of Pittsburgh Press, 1958, pp. 48–91.

Lindsley, D. B. Attention, consciousness, sleep and wakefulness. In H. W. Magoun (Ed.), *Handbook of physiology* (Sect. 1: Neurophysiology). Amer. Physiol. Soc., Washington, D.C., 1960, Vol. 3, pp. 1553–1593.

Loeb, L. *The biological basis of individuality.* Springfield, Ill.: C. C. Thomas, 1945.

Loomis, E. A., Jr. Autistic and symbiotic syndromes in children. *Monogr. Soc. Res. Child Develpm.*, 1960, *25*, 39–48.

Lorenz, W. F. Use of carbon dioxide in dementia praecox. In *Biology of mental health and disease.* New York: Hoeber, 1952, pp. 568–572.

Lovatt, Margaret. Autistic children in a day nursery. *Children*, May–June, 1962, 103–108.

Luborsky, L. In discussion of Ekstein, R. Special training problems in psychotherapeutic work with psychotic and borderline children. *Amer. J. Orthopsychiat.*, 1962, *32*, 569–581.

McClelland, D. C., Baldwin, A. L., Bronfenbrenner, U., & Strodtbeck, F. L. *Talent and society.* New York: Van Nostrand, 1958.

MacLean, P. D. The limbic system ("Visceral Brain") in relation to central gray and reticulum of the brainstem. *Psychosom. Med.*, 1955, *17*, 355–366.

MacLean, P. D. Contrasting functions of limbic and neocortical systems of the brain and their relevance to psychophysiological aspects of medicine. *Amer. J. Med.*, 1958, *25*, 611–626.

MacMahon, B., & Sowa, J. M. Physical damage to the fetus. In *Causes of mental disorder.* New York: Milbank Memorial Fund, 1961, pp. 51–120.

Magoun, H. W. *The waking brain.* Springfield, Ill.: C. C. Thomas, 1958. (a)

Magoun, H. W. Non-specific brain mechanisms. In H. F. Harlow & C. N. Woolsey (Eds), *Biological and biochemical bases of behavior.* Madison, Wisconsin: University of Wisconsin Press, 1958, pp. 25–36. (b)

Magoun, H. W. Recent contributions to the electrophysiology of learning. In N. S. Kline (Ed.), Pavlovian conference on higher nervous activity. *Ann. N.Y. Acad. Sci.*, 1961, *92* (Art. 3), pp. 818–829.

Mahler, Margaret S. On child psychosis and schizophrenia: Autistic and symbiotic infantile psychoses. *Psychoanal. Stud. Child.* New York: Internat. Univ. Press, 1952, *7*, pp. 286–305.

Maier, N. R. F. Maier's law. *Amer. Psychologist*, 1960, *15*, 208–212.

Malzberg, B. Statistical aspects of mental deficiency due to birth traumas. *Amer. J. Ment. Defic.*, 1950, *54*, 427–433.

Malzberg, B. Sex differences in the prevalence of mental deficiency. *Amer. J. Ment. Defic.*, 1953, *58*, 301–305.

Masland, R. L. Researches into the prenatal factors that lead to neuropsychiatric sequelae in childhood. In G. Caplan (Ed.), *Prevention of mental disorders in childhood.* New York: Basic Books, 1961, pp. 52–73.

Masland, R. L., Sarason, S. B., & Gladwin, T. *Mental subnormality.* New York: Basic Books, 1958. (See also Sarason and Gladwin, 1958.)

Maslow, A. H. Are our publications and conventions suitable for the personal sciences? *Amer. Psychologist*, 1961, *16*, 318–319.

Mason, C. F. Pre-illness intelligence of mental hospital patients. *J. Consult. Psychol.*, 1956, *20*, 297–300.

May, J. M. *A physician looks at psychiatry.* New York: John Day, 1958.

May, J. M., & May, Marie Anne. The treatment and education of the atypical, autistic child in a residential school situation. *Amer. J. Ment. Defic.*, 1959, *64*, 435–443.

Mednick, S. A. A learning theory approach to research in schizophrenia. *Psychol. Bull.*, 1958, *55*, 316–327.

Meduna, L. J. The carbon dioxide treatment. In *Biology of mental health and disease.* New York: Hoeber, 1952, pp. 572–577.

Meehl, P. Schizotaxia, schizotypy, schizophrenia. *Amer. Psychologist*, 1962, *17*, 827–838.

Melzack, R. The perception of pain. *Scient. American*, 1961, *204* (Feb.), 41–49.

Michaelson, I. C. Retinal circulation in man and animals. Springfield, Ill.: C. C. Thomas, 1954.

Michaux, L., Duché, D., Stein, C., & Mlle Lepage. Dispositions musicales precoces chez une fille de cinq ans grande arrieree de l'intelligence et de la parole. (Avec presentation de malade.) *Rev. Neuropsychiat. Infant*, 1957, *5:5–6*, 284–291.

Milbank Memorial Fund. *The causes of mental disorder.* New York: Milbank Memorial Fund, 1961.

Miller, G. A. Information and memory. *Scient. American*, 1956, *195* (Aug.), 42–46.

Miller, J. G. Information input overload and psychopathology. *Amer. J. Psychiat.*, 1960, *116*, 695–704.

Milner, P. M. The cell assembly: Mark II. *Psychol. Rev.*, 1957, *64*, 242–252.

Moorhead, P. S., Mellman, W. J., & Wenar, C. A familial chromosome translocation associated with speech and mental retardation. *Amer. J. Hum. Genet.*, 1961, *13*, 32–46.

Morgan, C. T. *Introduction to psychology.* (2nd ed.) New York: McGraw-Hill, 1961.

Morgan, C. T., & Stellar, E. *Physiological psychology.* (2nd ed.) New York: McGraw-Hill, 1950.

Mosse, Hilde, L. The misuse of the diagnosis childhood schizophrenia. *Amer. J. Psychiat.,* 1958, *114,* 791–794.

Murphree, H. B., Jenney, Elizabeth H., & Pfeiffer, C. C. 2-Dimethylaminoethanol as a central nervous system stimulant—one aspect of the pharmacology of reserpine. *Proc. Assoc. Res. Nerv. Ment. Dis.* Baltimore: Williams & Wilkins, 1959, *37,* 204–217.

Murphy, R. C., & Preston, C. E. *Three autistic brothers.* Paper presented at the 1954 Annual Meeting of the American Orthopsychiatric Association.

Nagle, J. M. Emotional content, extroversion, and aptitude, in man. *Dis. Nerv. Syst.,* 1960, *21,* 335–339.

National Physical Laboratory Symposium No. 10. *Mechanisation of thought processes.* London: Her Majesty's Stationery Office, 1959. 2 vols.

Nesnidalova, R., & Fiala,V. K. Otázce Kannerova časného détského autismu. (On the question of Kanner's early infantile autism.) *Ceskoslov. Psychiat.,* 1961, *57,* 76–84.

Newman, J. R. *The world of mathematics.* New York: Simon and Schuster, 1956, Vol. 1.

Nielsen, J. M. In discussion. In L. A. Jeffress (Ed.), *Cerebral mechanisms in behavior. The Hixon Symposium.* New York: Wiley, 1951, pp. 183–193.

Norman, Elizabeth. Reality relationships of schizophrenic children. *Brit. J. Med. Psychol.,* 1954, *27,* 126–141.

O'Connor, N., & Franks, C. M. Childhood upbringing and other environmental factors. In H. J. Eysenck (Ed.), *Handbook of abnormal psychology.* New York: Basic Books, 1961, pp. 393–416.

Oldfield, R. C. Memory mechanisms and the theory of schemata. *Brit. J. Psychol.,* 1954, *45,* 14–23.

Olds, J. Pleasure centers in the brain. *Scient. American,* 1956, *195* (Oct.), 105–116.

Oppenheim, Rosalind C. They said our child was hopeless. *Sat. Eve. Post,* June 17, 1961, 23, 56–58.

Orlansky, H. Infant care and personality. *Psychol. Bull.,* 1949, *46,* 1–48.

Osterkamp, Annemargret, & Sands, D. J. Early feeding and birth difficulties in childhood schizophrenia: A brief study. *J. Genet. Psychol.,* 1962, *101,* 363–366.

Pasamanick, B., & Knobloch, Hilda. Epidemiologic studies on the complications of pregnancy and the birth process. In G. Caplan (Ed.), *Prevention of mental disorders in childhood.* New York: Basic Books, 1961, pp. 74–94.

Pasamanick, B., Rogers, Martha E., & Lilienfeld, A. M. Pregnancy experience and the development of behavior disorder in children. *Amer. J. Psychiat.,* 1956, *112,* 613–618.

Patz A. The role of oxygen in retrolental fibroplasia. *Pediatrics,* 1957, *19,* 504–524.

Patz, A., Eastham, Anne, Higginbotham, D. H., & Kleh, T. Oxygen studies in retrolental fibroplasia. II. The production of the microscopic changes of retrolental fibroplasia in experimental animals. *Amer. J. Ophthal.,* 1953, *36,* 1511–1522.

Pavlovian conference on higher nervous activity. N. S. Kline (Ed.) *Ann. N.Y. Acad. Sci.*, 1961, *92* (Art. 3), pp. 813–1198.

Payne, R. W., Mattussek, P., & George, E. I. An experimental study of schizophrenic thought disorder. *J. Ment. Sci.*, 1959, *105*, 627–652.

Pearson, K. *The handicapping of the first born.* London: Galton Laboratory Publications, 1914. (Cited by Rosanoff et al., 1937.)

Peck, H. B., Rabinovitch, R. D., & Cramer, J. B. A treatment program for parents of schizophrenic children. *Amer. J. Orthopsychiat.*, 1949, *19*, 592–598.

Peimer, I. A. Local electrical responses in the cerebral cortex of man and their relationship to generalized reactions in the process of conditioned reflex activity. In *The central nervous system and behavior: Selected translations from the Russian medical literature*, U. S. Dept. of Health Educ. and Welfare, Public Health Service, 1 Dec. 1959, pp. 771–784.

Penfield, W. The interpretive cortex. *Science*, 1959, *129*, 1719–1725.

Penfield, W. A surgeon's chance encounters with mechanisms related to consciousness. *J. Roy. Coll. of Surgeons of Edinburgh*, 1960, *5*, 173–190.

Penfield, W., & Roberts, L. *Speech and brain mechanisms.* Princeton: Princeton University Press, 1959.

Pennoyer, Miriam M., Graham, Frances K., & Hartmann, A. F., Sr. The relationship of paranatal experience to oxygen saturation in newborn infants. *J. Pediat.*, 1956, *49*, 685–698.

Penrose, L. S. *Biology of mental defect.* New York: Grune & Stratton, 1949.

Pfeiffer, C. C., Jenney, Elizabeth H., Gallagher, W., Smith, R. P., Bevan, W. Jr., Killam, K. F., Killam, Eva K., & Blackmore, W. Stimulant effect of 2-dimethylaminoethanol, possible precursor of brain acetylcholine. *Science*, 1957, *126*, 610–611.

Pfeiffer, C. C., Goldstein, Leonide, Munoz, C., Murphree, H. B., & Jenney, Elizabeth H. Quantitative comparisons of the EEG stimulant effects of deanol, choline, and amphetamine. *Clin. Pharmacal. Therapeut.*, 1963, *4*, 461–466.

Phillips, E. L. Contributions to a learning theory account of childhood autism. *J. Psychol.*, 1957, *43*, 117–124.

Plenter, A. M. De ziekte van Kanner. *Ned. Tijdschr. Geneesk*, 1955, *99*, 428–434.

Pinneau, S. R. The infantile disorders of hospitalism and anaclitic depression. *Psychol. Bull.*, 1955, *52*, 429–452. (See also pp. 453–462 for Spitz–Pinneau exchange.)

Podolsky, E. The genius and his brain. *Med. Rec.*, 1946, *179*, 162–163.

Polan, C. G., & Spencer, Betty L. A check list of symptoms of autism of early life. *W. Virg. Med. J.*, 1959, 55, 198–204.

Popella, E. Zum Krankheitsbild des frühkindlichen Autismus (On the syndrome of early infantile autism). *Nervenarzt*, 1955, *26*, 268–271.

Prentice, W. C. H. Some cognitive aspects of motivation. *Amer. Psychologist*, 1961, *16*, 503–511.

Pritchard, R. M., Heron, W., & Hebb, D. O. Visual perception approached by the method of stabilized images. *Canad. J. Psychol.*, 1960, 14, 67–77.

Pronovost, W. The speech behavior and language comprehension of autistic children. *J. Chron. Dis.*, 1961, *13*, 228–233.

Putnam, Marian C. Case study of an atypical two-and-a-half-year-old. *Amer. J. Orthopsychiat.*, 1948, *18*, 1–30.

Pytel, Laura. Influence of delivery and pregnancy on mental development of child. *Gynaecologia (Basel)*, 1960, *149*, 131–142.

Rank, Beata. Adaptation of the psychoanalytic technique for the treatment of young children with atypical development. *Amer. J. Orthopsychiat.*, 1949, *19*, 130–139.

Rank, Beata, & MacNaughton, Dorothy. A clinical contribution to early ego development. *Psychoanal. Stud. Child.* New York: Internat. Univ. Press, 1950, *5*, pp. 53–65.

Rashkis, H. A. The organization factor as an explanatory principle in functional psychosis. *AMA Arch. Neurol. Psychiat.*, 1958, 80, 513–519.

Rashkis, H. A., & Singer, R. D. The psychology of schizophrenia. *AMA Arch. Gen. Psychiat.*, 1959, *1*, 406–416.

Rattner, L. J., & Chapman, A. H. Dangers of indiscriminate hospitalization of the preschool child. *J. Dentistry Child.*, 1959, *26*, 55–62.

Rees, Elizabeth L. Metabolism of the schizophrenic child; Etiologic hypotheses. *J. Amer. Med. Wom. Ass.*, 1956, *11*, 11–16.

Rees, L. Constitutional factors and abnormal behavior. In H. J. Eysenck (Ed.), *Handbook of abnormal psychology.* New York: Basic Books, 1961, pp. 344–392.

Renaud, H., & Estess, F. Life history interviews with one hundred normal American males. *Amer. J. Orthopsychiat.*, 1961, *81*, 786–802.

Reuter, Jeanette, Albee, G. W., & Lane, Ellen A. The early childhood intelligence of adult schizophrenics. *Amer. Psychologist, 1962, 17,* 296. (Abstract)

Ribble, Margaret. In discussion of Despert, J. Louise. Some considerations relating to the genesis of autistic behavior in children. *Amer. J. Orthopsychiat.*, 1951, *21*, 347–350.

Richmond, J. B., & Lustman, S. L. Autonomic function in the neonate: I. Implication for psychosomatic theory. *Psychosom. Med.*, 1955, *17*, 269–275.

Rimland, B. The psychopharmacology of infantile autism: A jeremiad. In E. Harms and N. S. Kline (Eds.), *Drug therapy in youth.* New York: Pergamon Press (in press).

Ritvo, S., & Provence, Sally. Form perception and imitation in some autistic children: Diagnostic findings and their contextual interpretation. *Psychoanal. Stud. Child.* New York: Internat. Univ. Press, 1953, *8*, pp. 155–161.

Roberts, J. A. F. *An introduction to medical genetics.* London: Oxford Univ. Press (2nd ed.), 1959.

Rodgers, D. A. *A theory of cognition.* Scripps Clinic and Research Foundation: La Jolla, Calif. 1962. (Mimeo.)

Roe, Anne. A psychologist examines 64 eminent scientists. *Scient. Amer.*, 1952, *187* (Nov.), 21–25.

Roe, Anne. The psychology of the scientist. *Science*, 1961, 184, 456–459.

Rosanoff, A. J., Handy, Leva M., & Plesset, Isabel R. The etiology of mental deficiency with special reference to its occurrence in twins. *Psychol. Monogr.*, 1937, *48* (Whole No. 216).

Rosen, V. H. On mathematical "Illumination" and the mathematical thought process. *Psychoanal. Stud. Child.* New York: Internat. Univ. Press, 1953, *8*, pp. 127–154.

Rosenblatt, F. *Principles of neurodynamics.* Washington, D.C.: Spartan Books, 1962.

Rosenthal, D. Problems of sampling and diagnosis in the major twin studies of schizophrenia. *J. Psychiat. Res.*, 1961, *1*, 116–134. (a)

Rosenthal, D. Sex distribution and the severity of illness among samples of schizophrenic twins. *J. Psychiat. Res.*, 1961, *1*, 26–36. (b)

Rosenzweig, N. A mechanism in schizophrenia. *AMA Arch. Neurol. Psychiat.*, 1955, *74*, 554–555.

Rosenzweig, N. The affect system: Foresight and fantasy. *J. Nerv. Ment. Dis.*, 1958, *127*, 113–118.

Ross, I. S. An autistic child. *Pediatric Conferences.* Babies Hosp. Unit, United Hospitals of Newark, N. J., 1959, 2, No. 2, 1–13.

Ross, S., & Denenberg, V. H. Innate behavior. In R. H. Waters et al. (Eds), *Principles of comparative psychology.* New York: McGrawHill, 1960, pp. 43–73.

Rothballer, A. B. Studies on the adrenaline-sensitive component of the reticular activating system. *E.E.G. Clin. Neurophysiol.*, 1956, *8*, 603–621.

Rothenberg, Mira. The rebirth of Jonny. *Harper's Magazine*, 1960, *220* (Feb.), 57–66.

Royer, F. L. Esthetics and the orienting response. *Amer. Psychologist*, 1961, *15*, 431. (Abstract)

Rowe, R. P. A pharmacologic summary of nialamide. *Dis. Nerv. Syst.*, 1959, *20* (No. 8 Suppl.), 5–9.

Russell, W. R. *Brain, memory, learning.* London: Oxford Univ. Press, 1959.

Sackler, M. D., Sackler, R. R., LaBurt, H. A., Co, T., & Sackler, A. M. A psychobiologic viewpoint on schizophrenias of childhood. *Nerv. Child*, 1952, *10*, 43–59.

St. Onge, K. R., & Calvert, J. J. The brain stem damage syndrome: Speech and psychological factors. *J. Speech and Hearing Disord.*, 1959, *24*, 43–50.

Saito, Y. A psychopathological study of daydreaming in early childhood schizophrenia. *Jap. J. child Psychiat.*, 1960, *1*, 13–31. (*Psychol. Abstr.*, 35:5260)

Samuels, Ina. Reticular mechanisms and behavior. *Psychol. Bull.*, 1959, *56*, 1–25.

Sankar, D. V. Siva, & Sankar, Barbara D. Biochemical studies on childhood schizophrenia and autism. *Federat. Proceed.*, 1962, *21*, 348. (Abstract)

Sarason, S. B., & Gladwin, T. Psychological and cultural problems in mental subnormality: A review of research. *Genet. Psychol. Monogr.*, 1958, *57*, 3–289. (See also Masland, Sarason, & Gladwin, 1958.)

Sarvis, Mary A., & Garcia, Blanche. Etiological variables in autism. *Psychiatry*, 1961, *24*, 307–317.

Schachter, M. Contribution a l'étude de l'autisme infantile précoce de Kanner. *Pediatre.*, 1958, *13*, 175–191.

Schain, R. J., & Yannet, H. Infantile autism: An analysis of 50 cases and a consideration of certain neurophysiologic concepts. *J. Pediat.*, 1960, *57*, 560–567.

Schallek, W. Neurophysiological studies with monoamine oxidase inhibitors. *Dis. nerv. Syst.*, 1960, *21* (No. 3 Suppl.), 64–66.

Scheerer, M., Rothmann, Eva, & Goldstein, K. A case of "Idiot Savant": An experimental study of personality organization. *Psychol. Monogr.*, 1945, *58* (Whole No. 269).

Scheibel, Madge E., & Scheibel, A. B. Structural substrates for integrative patterns in the brain stem reticular core. In H. H. Jasper (Ed.), *Reticular formation of the brain*. Boston: Little, Brown, 1958, pp. 31–55.

Scheibel, Madge E., & Scheibel, A. B. The physiology of consciousness. *Amer. J. Orthopsychiat.*, 1960, *30*, 10–14.

Scheibel, Madge E., & Scheibel, A. B. On circuit patterns of the brain stem reticular core. *Ann. N.Y. Acad. Sci.*, 1961, *89*, 857–865.

Scheibel, Madge E., & Scheibel, A. B. Hallucinations and the brain stem reticular core. In L. J. West (Ed.), *Hallucinations*. New York: Grune & Stratton, 1962, pp. 15–35.

Schooler, Carmi. Birth order and schizophrenia. *AMA Arch. Gen. Psychiat.*, 1961, *4*, 91–97.

Schoonover, Sarah M. The relationship of intelligence and achievement to birth order, sex of sibling and age interval. *J. Educ. Psychol.*, 1959, *50*, 143–146.

Schopler, E. The development of body image and symbol formation through bodily contact with an autistic child. *J. Child Psychol. Psychiat.*, 1962, *3*, 191–202.

Scott, P., & Williams, K. G. A note on temporal coding as a mechanism in sensory perception. *Inform. and Control*, 1959, *2*, 380–385.

Scott, W. A. Social psychological correlates of mental illness and mental health. *Psychol. Bull.*, 1958, *55*, 65–87.

Scott, T. H. Literature review of the intellectual effects of perceptual isolation. *Dept. Nat. Def. Res. Rep.*, 1957, No. HR 66. (Canada.)

Shannon, C. E., & Weaver, W. *The mathematical theory of communication*. Urbana, Ill.: University of Illinois Press, 1949.

Sharpless, S. The role of the reticular formation of the brain stem in influencing sense perception. Proceedings of the XVth Internat. Congress of Zoology, July, 1958, 1–4.

Sharpless, S., & Jasper, H. Habituation of the arousal reaction. *Brain*, 1956, *79*, 655–681.

Sherwin, A. C. Reactions to music of autistic (schizophrenic) children. *Amer. J. Psychiat.*, 1953, *109*, 823–831.

Sherwin, A. C., Flach, F. F., & Stokes, P. E. Treatment of psychoses in early childhood with triiodothyronine. *Amer. J. Psychiat.*, 1958, *115*, 166–167.

Shore, P. A. Possible mechanism of antidepressant action of marsilid. *J. Clin. Exper. sychopath.*, 1958, *19* (No. 2, Suppl. 1.), 56–60.

Singer, R. D. Organization as a unifying concept in schizophrenia. *AMA Arch. Gen. Psychiat.*, 1960, *2*, 61–74.

Sinnot, E. W. The biology of purpose. *Amer. J. Orthopsychiat.*, 1952, *22*, 451–468.

Slater, E. The inheritance of manic depressive insanity and its relation to mental defect. *J. Ment. Sci.*, 1936, *82*, 626–633. (*Psychol. Abstr.*, 11:1345)

Smith, D. D. Abilities and interests: I. A factorial study. *Canad. J. Psychol.*, 1958, *12*, 191–201.

Sokolov, E. N. Neuronal models and the orienting reflex. In Mary A. B. Brazier (Ed.), *The central nervous system and behavior.* New York: Josiah Macy Jr. Found., 1960, pp. 187–276.

Solomon, P., Leiderman, P. H., Mendelson, J., & Wexler, D. Sensory deprivation. *Amer. J. Psychiat.*, 1957, *114*, 357–363.

Sperling, G. The information available in brief visual presentations. *Psychol. Monogr.*, 1960, *74*, 11 (Whole No. 498).

Sperry, R. W. Neurology of the mind-brain problem. *Amer. Scientist*, 1952, *40*, 291–312.

Sperry, R. W. The eye and the brain. *Scient. American*, 1956, *194* (May), 48–52.

Spiel, W. *Die endogenen Psychosen des Kindes- und Jugendalters.* Basel: Karger, 1961. (a)

Spiel, W. Oligophrenia as a sequel to infantile psychoses. (*Excerpta Med. Sect. VIII*, 1961, No. 5975.) (b)

Sprague, J. M., Chambers, W. W., & Stellar, E. Attentive, affective and adaptive behavior in the cat. *Science*, 1961, *133*, 165–173.

Stellar, E. Drive and motivation. In H. W. Magoun (Ed.), *Handbook of physiology* (Sect. 1: Neurophysiology). Washington, D.C.: Amer. Physiol. Soc., 1960, Vol. 3, pp. 1501–1527.

Stern, E. A propos d'un cas d'autisme chez un jeune enfant. *Arch. Franc. Pédiat.*, 1952, *9*, 157–164.

Stern, E., & Schachter, M. Zum Problem des frühkindlichen Autismus. *Prax. Kinderpsychol. Kinderpsychiat.*, 1953, *2*, 113–119.

Stevenson, I. Is the human personality more plastic in infancy and childhood? *Amer. J. Psychiat.*, 1957, *114*, 152–161.

Stockard, C. R. The physical basis of personality. New York: W. W. Norton, 1931.

Stott, D. H. Evidence for pre-natal impairment of temperament in mentally retarded children. *Vita Hum.*, 1959, *2*, 125–148.

Stott, D. H. Interaction of heredity and environment in regard to "measured intelligence." *Brit. J. Educat. Psychol.*, 1960, *30*, 95–102. (See also exchange with Burt, pp. 273–276.)

Stott, D. H. Evidence for a congenital factor in maladjustment and delinquency. *Amer. J. Psychiat.*, 1962, *118*, 781–794.

Strauss, A. A., & Kephart, N. C. Psychopathology and education of the brain-injured child: Vol. II. Progress in theory and clinic. New York: Grune & Stratton, 1955.

Stuart, N. G. Scream in the night. *Ladies' Homes Journal*, Sept. 1960, 163–172.

Sutherland, N. S. Stimulus analysing mechanisms. In *Mechanisation of thought processes.* National Physical Laboratory Symposium No. 10. London: Her Majesty's Stationery Office, 1959, Vol. 2, pp. 575–601.

Sutton, H. E., & Read, J. H. Abnormal amino acid metabolism in a case suggesting autism. *AMA J. Dis. Child.*, 1958, *96*, 23–28.

Takahashi, A. On psychotic symptoms (especially the autistic tendency) of mentally retarded children. *Jap. J. Child. Psychiat.*, 1960, *1*, 50–57. (*Psychol. Abstr.*, 35:5188)

Taterka, J. H., & Katz, J. Study of correlations between electroencephalographic and psychological patterns in emotionally disturbed children. *Psychosom. Med.*, 1955, *17*, 62–72.

Taylor, D. W. Toward an information processing theory of motivation. In M. R. Jones (Ed.), *Nebraska Symposium on Motivation*. Lincoln: Univ. of Nebr. Press, 1960, pp. 51–79.

Terman, L. M. *Genetic studies of genius, Vol. I.* Stanford University, Calif.: Stanford Univ. Press, 1925.

Terman, L. M., & Merrill, Maud A. *Measuring intelligence.* Boston: Houghton Mifflin, 1937.

Terman, L. M., & Oden, Melita H. *Genetic studies of genius, Vol. IV.* Stanford University, Calif.: Stanford Univ. Press, 1947.

Terman, L. M., & Oden, Melita H. *Genetic studies of genius, Vol. V.* Stanford University, Calif.: Stanford Univ. Press, 1959.

Thompson, W. R. Influence of prenatal maternal anxiety on emotionality in young rats. *Science*, 1957, *125*, 698–699.

Thorpe, W. H. Comparative psychology. *Annu. Rev. Psychol.*, 1961, *12*, 27–50.

Tobias, M. The disturbed child—a concept: Usefulness of deanol in management. *Amer. Practit. Dig. Treat.*, 1959, *10*, 1759–1766.

Tokutaro, I. The low-grade idiot and so called early infantile autism. *Jap. J. Child. Psychiat.*, 1961, *2*, 226–231. (*Amer. J. ment. Defic. Abstr.*, 66:2951)

Tredgold, R. F., & Soddy, K. *A textbook of mental deficiency.* (9th ed.) Baltimore: Williams & Wilkins, 1956.

Vaillant, G. E. John Haslam on early infantile autism. *Amer. J. Psychiat.*, 1962, *119*, 316.

Van Krevelen, D. A. Early infantile autism. *Z. f. Kinderpsychiat.*, 1952, *19*, 91–97. (a)

Van Krevelen, D. A. Een geval van "early infantile autism." *Ned. Tijdschr. Geneesk.*, 1952, *96*, 202–205. (b)

Van Krevelen, D. A. Quelques remarques sur l'usage abusif du diagnostic d'autisme. *Acta neural. Belg.*, 1954, 207–212. (Also in *Ann. Neurol.*, 1953, *59*, 191–197.)

Van Krevelen, D. A. Zur Problematik des Autismus. *Prax. Kinderpsychiat.*, 1958, *7*, 87–93.

Van Krevelen, D. A. Autismus infantum. *Ned. Tijdschr. Geneesk.*, 1959, *103*, 2194–2198. (Cited by van Krevelen, 1960.)

Van Krevelen, D. A. Autismus infantum. *Acta Paedopsychiat.*, 1960, *27*, 3, 97–107.

Van Krevelen, D. A. Critica sobre el diagnostica del autismo infantil precoz. *Rev. Psiquiat. Psicol. méd.*, 1955, *2*, 316–325. (Cited by van Krevelen, 1960.)

Van Krevelen, D. A. Autismus infantum and autistic personality: Two clinical syndromes. *Jap. J. Child Psychiat.*, 1962, *3*, 135–146.

Van Krevelen, D. A. Personal Communication, Jan. 7, 1963.

Van Krevelen, D. A., & Kuipers, Christine. The psychopathology of autistic psychopathy. *Acta Paedopsychiat.*, 1962, *29*, 22–31.

Veiga, M. Some aspects of differential diagnosis in borderline cases of infantile autism and mental retardation. (*Excerpta Med. Sect. VIII*, 1961, No. 5925.)

Voronin, L. G. [Comparative physiological data on the function of the reticular formation.] *Zh. vyssh. nervn. Deiatel.*, 1961, *11*, 179–805. (*Psychol. Abstr.*, 36: 5DB95V)

Waal, N. A special technique of psychotherapy with an autistic child. In G. Caplan (Ed.), *Emotional problems of early childhood*. New York: Basic Books, 1955, pp. 431–449.

Ward, A. A. Efferent functions of the reticular formation. In H. H. Jasper (Ed.), *Reticular formation of the brain*. Boston: Little, Brown, 1958, pp. 263–273.

Ward, T. F., & Hoddinott, B. A. Early infantile autism in fraternal twins: A case report. *Canad. Psychiat. Ass. J.*, 1962, 7, 191–195.

Waters, R. H., Rethlingshafer, Dorothy, & Caldwell, D. F. *Principles of comparative psychology*. New York: McGraw-Hill, 1960.

Wechsler, D. *The range of human capacities*. (2nd ed.) Baltimore: Williams and Wilkins, 1952.

Weidenreich, F. The human brain in the light of its phylogenetic development. *Sci. Month.*, 1948, *67*, 103–109.

Weiland, I. H., & Legg, D. R. The use of formal speech characteristics as a diagnostic aid in childhood psychosis. *Amer. J. Orthopsychiat.*, 1962, *82*, 260. (Abstract)

Weiland, I. H., & Rudnik, R. Considerations of the development and treatment of autistic childhood psychosis. *Psychoanal. Stud. Child.* New York: Internat. Univ. Press, 1961, 16, pp. 549–563.

Weiss, P. Central versus peripheral factors in the development of coordination. *Proc. Ass. Res. Nerv. Ment. Dis.*, 1950, *80*, 3–23.

West, S. S. Sibling configurations of scientists. *Amer. J. Sociol.*, 1960, *66*, 268–274.

Williams, C. E. Retrolental fibroplasia as associated with mental defect. *Brit. J. Ophthal.*, 1958, *42*, 549–557.

Williams, R. J. *Biochemical individuality*. New York: Wiley, 1956.

Witmer, L. Orthogenic cases, XIV-Don: A curable case of arrested development due to a fear psychoses the result of shock in a three-year-old infant. *Psychol. Clinic*, 1920, *18*, 97–111.

Wolman, B. B. Explorations in latent schizophrenia. *Amer. J. Psychother.*, 1957, *11*, 560–588.

Woodworth, R. S. Reenforcement of perception. *Amer. J. Psychol.*, 1947, *60*, 119–124.

Yacorzynski, G. K., & Tucker, Beatrice E. What price intelligence? *Amer. Psychologist*, 1960, *15*, 201–203.

Zubek, J. P., Pushkar, Dolores, Sansom, Wilma, & Gowing, J. Perceptual changes after prolonged sensory isolation (darkness and silence). *Canad. J. Psychol.*, 1961, *15*, 83–100.

Subject Index

Author Index